# TECHNODEMOCRATIC ECONOMIC THEORY

From Capitalism and Socialism
to Democracy

**Reza Rezazadeh**

*To those aspiring to a just society; to those exploited, alienated, made homeless and victims of poverty and injustice; and to those looking for a concept of a just society; to all those, this book is dedicated as a guide hoping that one day it will be understood by the common people and the idea will become materialized.*

## FIRST EDITION

Copyright 1991 by Reza Rezazadeh

Published by Eternalist Foundation
1080 Eastman Street, Platteville,
Wisconsin 53818 (608)348-7064

Manufactured in the United States of America
ISBN: 0-9629032-0-5

Library of Congress Catalog Card No.: 91-070823

# Contents

# PREFACE

The essence of the economic theory presented in this writing was published as part of a societal democratic concept in *Technological Democracy: A Humanistic Philosophy of the future Society.* The first four chapters and the last are new materials. The rest are extractions from and expansion of the theory of the technodemocratic economy from the above publication.

This writing is concerned primarily with the economic concepts and principles of the technodemocratic society. For other aspects of such a future society the reader is advised to refer to the above mentioned publication.

The present conditions of the industrialized world call for attention to their destructive consequences. The greatest threat to our future comes from our own ignorance of the real threat, apathy, and lack of care. Nineteen of twenty-one civilizations have died from within and not by foreign conquest. Each decayed slowly from within until it fell apart. Our society shows many symptoms of such decay. But, as in those fallen societies, we do not see and feel the threat. We need understanding and action before it is too late. And the time is running short. This book is a desperate effort to awaken our people and those of other nations, to illustrate the dangerous situation, and hopefully, present the way to save our society and of course the humanity.

I am a United States citizen by choice. I did not make this choice on the grounds of the availability of better economic opportunities in the United States and the expectation of making lots of money, although I knew, based upon my educational background, that I would make a comfortable living here. Such a standard of living was not to be very different from the socio-economic status I enjoyed in my native country, Iran. At the time of my immigration I was a high-ranking officer within the privileged class of the armed forces, and among the intelligentsia as well, since I was a graduate of military technical college, held a law degree, and spoke four languages. I chose the United States as my country because I found here a fertile ground for democracy with deeply rooted values relating to liberty, justice and equality. I found Americans endowed with some of the greatest human values: honesty, integrity, and individualism. I am referring to American people rather than American government. They are miles apart. The government represents a small economic elite with interests, aspirations, and characteristics quite different from those of the people.

I had one main objective in my new life in my new country: to seek knowledge leading toward the understanding of an advanced society from the social, economic, cultural, and political viewpoints, and toward acquiring competence, first, in understanding its present values and organizations, and second, in making rationally sustainable projections about its future.

I chose the study of law as the most appropriate field to help me toward my aim. When I received my first law degree from the Indiana University Law School, I was not satisfied and continued my education in the areas of international law, economics, political science and finally, comparative law. Altogether, I spent 18 years as a college student, attempting to gain a comprehensive knowledge of an advanced society like the United States as well as the Third World.

Sitting back then and evaluating myself, one thing stood out in my mind: the more I sought knowledge, the more I found how little I knew. Consequently, striving for more knowledge, I concluded that the best place to satisfy my aim would be to sustain my attachment to the academic community. Thus I accepted a teaching position in a small but good university and rejected offers extended to me from some big universities, law firms, and industries. I did not accept offers from big universities because I did not want to subject myself to the rule of "publish or perish". I needed to be left alone for quite a few years to be able to think and do research in my own pace. I had lots of creative thinking to do in order to develop my theory of the future society. After 18 years as a university student, I changed my official status to university professor, but in fact I remained, as always, a student.

I have devoted most of my adult life to development of a concept which would provide ground for better living conditions, opportunities and freedom not only to my fellow countrymen but to all human beings regardless of place, race, sex, or origin. Toward this end I have tried to present a socio-economic way of life which is the foundation for a truly democratic society. Political democracy, which has been erroneously presented as the main requirement for a democratic society, in my analysis, takes the backseat. Not that it is not important, but it is the least important. Economic democracy is the backbone of democratic society. With this understanding I have devoted much of my thinking and efforts toward realization of such a system. The heart of my theory is its economic system. With reference to human nature and individual expectations from life, I think I have arrived to an appropriate economic system, which is not utopian like that of Marx, but practical, rational, and reasonable. It appears to be the unavoidable course of society beyond the era of socialism if democracy, I mean a true democracy, succeeds to replace the present authoritarian systems, whether capitalist or Marxist, of the developed world.

As a strong devotee of peace, for nearly five decades I have had great attention, not to the causes of conflict alone, but to the grounds for peace. Presently, an approach toward achieving peace has been, first, a piecemeal type, and second, through force and strength which has been an utterly erroneous approach. Being obliged to keep peace through the presence of force means that there is a disequilibrium among the nations and, thus, force is necessary to sustain that disequilibrium. This is not actually a peaceful condition. Nations are being forced to accept the existing conditions regardless of injustices and suppressions these create. For a true and permanent peace, there will be no need for any force to sustain it. It is automatically sustained when nations of the world enjoy equality of opportunity in existence along with one another. Peace, on a prolonged and permanent basis, can be possible only when the grounds for conflict have been removed. Toward this phenomenal task, I hope I have taken an appropriate step. Under my theory, not only will we provide ground for prosperity and well being of all human race with equal opportunity, but also, for the first time in human history, we will provide conditions for permanent peace, without requirement of international agreements or treaties, by the very nature of a technological democratic society and respect for the principle of equality of opportunity applied to the relations of the nations with one another.

Toward understanding this grand purpose in human history, I beg your indulgence, patience, seriousness, and impartiality in reading, analyzing, and attempting to comprehend not only the content but the essence of materials presented here. It is our life, our happiness, and our future which is at stake. Please join me and others who believe in true democracy, first, toward its understanding and then toward its realization. Let us explore the way and work and proceed together hand-in-hand toward a permanent peace and prosperity.

# INTRODUCTION

Human civilization has gone from barbarianism through many stages of development to its present status in which, despite some democratic and humanistic tendencies and pretensions, the character of bestiality and barbarianism still prevails.

First, and perhaps the most important, is the nature of ownership and desire for possession. The scarcity in early stages of human life created the concept of property and ownership. If a man killed an animal for food, he was considered to have a right over his kill. But other hungry humans could not see him having all to eat and yet preserve the rest while others were badly in need of food. Thus the food, whoever had produced it, was forcefully and frequently brutally shared and consumed. Then came the muscle man who intended to keep his prey, and whatever he had taken from others. Those who dared to force him to share his fortune with the others were brutally banished in individual battles. The others submitted to his power. Later, he extended his right of possession to other human beings and subjugated them to his command by force. This was the beginning of the era of slavery which has continued since in different forms. Until the wake of capitalism, kings and nobles ruled with absolute power over property rights, and the rest were either subjects or held property rights at the mercy and pleasure of the ruler. The ruler could confiscate property of one and banish him from the society.

Capitalism tended to eliminate this absolute power of the ruler by recognizing inalienability of property rights of every individual. The

1

concept of life, liberty, and property was advocated and advanced. Of course the main purpose was to guard the possessions and persons of the capitalist from being at the mercy of the ruler. Consequently, the absolute monarch systems were abolished and the representative system was established over which the capitalist expected to have controlling influence. This property right and individual freedom became absolute rights and their protection was made the prime obligation of the state. These rights were made to appear universal, covering every citizen, but the main purpose was to protect the capitalist class, and in actual operation it achieved this goal.

Thus, the capitalist was allowed to accumulate wealth under protection of the state, without infringement on his right to life, liberty, and property. Initially, the free enterprise system or laissez-faire economic concept was favored and sustained. The state was denied power to interfere in the operation of the economy and was given the obligation of protecting this absolute private property right.

Capitalism created a dynamic society by giving each individual the right to his creation and the absolute right for its possession and ownership. It also allowed unrestricted exploitation of workers. This dynamism during the last two centuries did cause an unprecedented industrial and economic development. But, as capital tended to accumulate in the hands of a few, the societal system tended to become more and more stratified and undemocratic. The primary factor causing capital accumulation was exploitation of labor, which was the essential principle of the capitalistic system. Exploitation caused a drastic class stratification topped with a small class of economic elite and bottomed with a large class of people plunged in poverty and despair. Capitalism also created a large middle class which was and is being used by the elite as its main source of capital, management, technology, and maintenance of the state. To expand legal control beyond one's own possession, and in order to create an open ended access to the capital for production purposes, the capitalist invented an economic institution, the corporation, which has served very well its purpose up to the present. Most of the capital comes from the middle class and goes directly under the control of the capitalist elite, by different means under its control. In its face, like the state, a corporation appears to be a democratic business organization. It consists of the shareholders which could number in millions, a board of directors elected each year by the shareholders in their annual convention, a president, and other chief officers selected by the board of directors.

In reality the incorporating directors, who belong to the elite class, perpetuate themselves as board members through an electoral process over which they have full control.

Most of the corporation shares are purchased in small numbers by the middle class. First, the value of shares is made affordable even for the upper lower class. In general, the value of a share of giant corporations is under 100 dollars. This allows even the low income class to purchase a few shares a year.

All this capital goes under the control of the board of directors of the corporation. Each year all the shareholders receive a notice of the annual shareholder convention and an invitation to participate in the annual electoral and policy-making process. Along with this notice the shareholder also receives a copy of the balance sheet of the corporation showing the operational account of the corporation including a favorable return for the investment.

The notice asks the shareholder that if he or she is not able to attend the convention, after investigating the balance sheet of the corporation, he or she may like to sign and return the enclosed proxy card bestowing upon the board of directors the right to represent the shareholder at the convention meetings and vote on his behalf.

Those who hold a small amount of shares, say 2,000 out of 20 million, who also do not find it economically or financially feasible to afford the expenditures of attending the convention, and who are satisfied with the financial report relating to the past year's operation as presented in the attached balance sheet, sign and return the proxy card allowing the board to vote on their behalf.

Statistics show that only a small percentage of shareholders actually attend the annual conventions. By the time of the convention the board of directors has collected enough shares by proxy to command a safe majority.

They reelect themselves and vote for their own policies. The convention becomes nothing more than a ceremonial gathering and serves no shareholder, but only serves the directors.

By this process the elite members perpetuate their hold on immense capital of the shareholders and on its full control. For example , the family wealth of the Rockefellers is estimated around four billion, but the family has full control over the corporate assets far in excess of

$300 billion, including many giant banks and corporations. This is the way this very small economic elite sustains its monopoly over major lines of production and distribution of goods and services.

Through this economic power, the elite controls the media of information, controls and manipulates both major political parties, and determines the selection of the majority of candidates to Congress as well as to the presidential office. It also substantially influences the social processes such as the educational systems, even their contents, always preparing ground for better maximization of profit and further accumulation of wealth and power. Laissez-faire capitalism has now transformed itself into monopoly capitalism, a true menace to democratic norms and processes, to human well being and preservation of natural resources, and environmental quality.

Multinational or global corporations are the result of such concentration of immense capital, resources, and power in the hands of the elite in a global scale. A multinational corporation is a new monster with hundred arms. It is responsible to no state yet has provided circumstances which make it protected by every government in any country where it has expanded its operation.

This stage of capitalism, particularly during the last three decades, has caused by necessity an increasing number of workers to become better educated, an increasing number of citizens to become conscious of its deteriorating effect on the environment and quality of life; of its increasing hold, through the control and use of technology, on workers as well as consumers; and of its utter disregard for human dignity, well being, and life as a whole. Since its entity expands beyond national boundaries, the existing systems of government not only have not been able to control it but have become enslaved by it and turned into its protectors.

Democracy in its proper essence has disappeared, leaving behind only a deceitful facade, causing many to believe in its true existence. The global corporation has made all capitalistic democracies essentially outmoded, powerless, and obsolete. There is an urgent need for a new theory of modern state which will liberate the societies from the yoke of these giants and establish a truly democratic system that will return power to the individuals, restore and foster human honesty, dignity, integrity, and happiness.

The problem is much simpler in Marxist systems. There a small political elite controls the means of production and distribution and through it dominates the society as a whole. Since this is a political power, it can be overthrown by social consciousness and through general strike. The question here is what to put in the place of the toppled system? As it will be demonstrated, the new theory presented here is more suitable and easier for adoption by these socialist systems than by those of the capitalist.

All present deficiencies in our modern societal systems are the result of our inherited barbarian characteristics. After several thousand years of organized societal life we humans have not yet been able to rid ourselves from the barbarian and bestial nature of our early ancestors. Possessiveness is a barbarian characteristic. We aspire to own things, earlier we aspired to own even humans, not mainly as a means to satisfy our needs but mainly for selfish ends. As our barbarian ancestors, we pride ourselves in having big muscles and punch someone in the nose whom we don't like. As barbarians we pay and enjoy watching two boxers demolish one another, we admire bull fights and cock fights where one side has to face torturous attacks and ultimately be defeated and often perish. With advanced technology in our possession we have even become a thousand times more barbarian. We have fought several bloody war during this century, killed over 50 million people, destroyed thousands of cities, nature, and environment for no sustainable humanistic cause but for property, power, and domination over more humans and resources.

We are still quite far from a truly civilized society when wisdom and fairness take place of force and power; where simplicity of life overshadows its complexities; where we as humans look beyond our own interest to those of others around us, even far away from us; and where we are fair and affectionate toward the natural environment, plants and animals, and ultimately toward our fragile planet.

None of the existing societal systems has moved us toward this end. We need a theory of society which will open the road toward achieving these humanistic aims, and lead us toward a gentle, clean, simple, and affectionate societal environment.

Let us now first look into the reality of the situation facing technological societies and then present a theory of a true democratic economy and its corresponding society.

For over thirty years, I have looked upon the United States through the eye of an outsider, devoid of prejudices imposed upon native-born Americans by their historical, socio-economic, and cultural values and their lack of intellectual contact with and understanding of other concepts and cultures.

The more one looks into the history of the American Revolution and the formation of its constitutional government, the more one becomes astonished about the depth of knowledge, dedication, and sincerity of a few men who led this nation from colonialism to independence and beyond. The Federalist Papers alone are indicative of the tremendous wealth of knowledge, wisdom, and intelligence of those who laid down, so carefully and so wisely, such a radically liberal foundation for the political system of this country. It is further astonishing how, after nearly 200 years of advancement, leaders with the caliber and philosophical influence of the founding fathers have disappeared from our society and narrow-minded specialists and uncivilized, sociopolitically ignorant business executives have taken their place. Those individual rights and liberties for which the Founders so persistently preached and violently fought have been overshadowed today by economic values and capitalistic monopolies or oligopolies. However, there is a consolation. What the revolutionaries did fight for has not been banished, only suppressed. It is at the foundation of American society, at the grass roots, that one finds honesty and integrity still strong. It has been molested, but not destroyed. Erosion and corruption have moved in and firmly established themselves primarily in the upper echelon of our society, fostered by unethical norms established by what is variously known as the "corporate state," "military-industrial complex." Our representatives and leading bureaucrats are mostly a part of, or heavily influenced by, this cooperative power of industry and the military. None of these dominating factors existed in the early years of our independence, nor were they imaginable to this extraordinarily dominant extent until after World War II.

President Eisenhower was the first president to warn the American people in his farewell address of the dangers of a military-industrial complex to our democracy.

The result has been the suppression of individual rights and freedoms and, particularly since 1960s, extraordinary privileges to big business and effective control of our socio-economic and political system by a privileged group consisting of only four-tenths of one percent of American households.[1] From all the investment assets, one percent are owned by the $5,000 to $9,999 income group, 7 percent by the $10,000 to $24,000 group, 11 percent by the $25,000 to $49,000 group and 15 percent by the $50,000 to $99,999, or 34 percent in all. A small elite controls the rest.[2]

With the exception of this very small number of beneficiaries of American wealth, and those who are ignorant of the facts, probably no one needs to be told today that there is much that is wrong in America. The events of the past three decades have demonstrated to every American the enormity and variety of the problems that plague this society and its economy. These problems take different forms for different people, and some people suffer much more than others. However, no one remains unaffected, since a society is an organic whole that is shaped by all its component parts, including every individual.

Corruption, hypocrisy, suppression, poverty, alienation, racism, crime, destruction of the environment, waste, and exploitation of our natural resources are just a few of our major problems. They are the result of our neglect and lack of interest in developing our social and political system, in contrast to our zeal and drive in developing our economic system. Thus, we have created an imbalanced society-- highly developed scientifically and economically; quite backward and outmoded socially and politically.[3] The combined effect has been not only to oppress a great many people at home and abroad, but to generate a widespread sense of anxiety among those who do not perceive themselves to be oppressed.

America outside of its borders is perceived to be a democratic society, and for this perception is admired and desired by many foreigner who get its image from television programs or movies or read about it in our publications. American citizens, a majority of them, also think of the system as being democratic.

But what both foreigners and Americans see is a facade of democracy. The foreigners have no opportunity to understand the real autocratic operation of the system behind this facade, and what the citizens see, they are conditioned to think so by continuous propaganda supported by the elite and being conditioned and indoctrinated from the childhood.

American "democracy" has been carefully designed, in an evolutionary process of some two hundred years, by the economic elite, to satisfy, provide for, maintain, and protect the capitalist needs for our stable, delicately but firmly controlled, and economically productive society. The American society has three basic complex and perplexing components which are quite difficult to be understood by ordinary citizens or outsiders except for some experts in the fields of social sciences.

The three components are individuals, private organizations, and public institutions within a highly materialistic society. As an individual, an American has two standards: one ideal and the other real. He believes in equality of opportunity for everyone but he always desires to be considered more equal than others. It appears that this reality is the result of keen competition for materialistic success which is the basic ingredient of the American daily life. Practically everything is evaluated in terms of dollars and cents. The other important non-material aspects of life become marginal in this process of evaluation. For this reason it becomes difficult of an American to stop and relax and enjoy the life. An American works very hard not only to achieve economic security but to accumulate wealth. As a result of strained lifestyle he encounters all kinds of dangerous ailments; ulcers and heart problems plus mental pressures being just a few. In the drive for accumulation an American never stops. He always thinks of enjoying life one day but that one day never arrives. Then one day he has a heart attack and dies. The strange thing with American psychology is that those who take over the accumulated wealth don't relax and try to enjoy life, but follow exactly the same course of action of the deceased from whom they inherited the wealth. This is the main characteristic of the lower middle class, middle, and upper middle class American which constitute some seventy percent of the population.

The bottom thirty percent who suffer at the expense of the rest sincerely believe in equality of opportunity but find nearly all the doors shut on their faces. The elite considers them as a societal garbage yet among these one may find the best "human Americans". But since they are not and cannot be economically productive they don't sustain value in they eye of the capitalist elite.

There is always a growing discontent among this group combined with the lower middle class work force. The worsening situation is carefully watched by the elite. When it approaches the point of uprising and violence then certain welfare legislation is passed to stabilize the situation.

Individualism is another ideal belief of ordinary Americans yet every day, more and more, he wants the government to take care of the socioeconomic ills and discomforts. As a result of this demand the United States has, gradually, become an expanded welfare state spending hundreds of billions of dollars in an array of welfare programs. The money for these exuberant expenditures does not come out of the pocket of the elite. This is paid through revenues received by heavily taxing the middle class. So, in America, the middle class, constituting the majority, supplies expert knowledge and technology to the elite through the production process and pays to quiet the lower class in order to stabilize the environment for steady production and maximization of profits.

Consequently, American capitalism has persisted in its dynamic operation because of special arrangements through the passage of special welfare laws tending to stabilize the American society.

Another peculiar characteristic of Americans is their ideal thoughts about democracy on the one hand and their lack of interest in democratic process on the other. It might be quite surprising to outsiders, who have a rosy picture of the American democracy, and great many Americans themselves, that only little over 50 percent of Americans participate in presidential elections. Thirty to 40 percent participate in congressional elections which is the major policy-making body of the nation, and more surprisingly, only 10 to 15 percent vote in local elections where most of the regulation of their daily life rests. Yet, from an idealistic viewpoint, Americans strongly favor political equality in voting and political expression, yet overall, the majority of them do not bother to vote. They believe in free market economy and yet strongly resent the concentration of power in the hands of a few corporations and the huge amounts of profit made by them. While over 90 percent believe in equality of opportunity they also know that the rich get richer while the poor get poorer. The following table is an evidence of such contrasting attitudes.

Americans want both equality of opportunity and capitalistic prosperity, yet tensions and incompatibilities exist between these values. Capitalistic opportunities lead to unequal economic rewards causing ever expanding class stratification. Economic rewards and resources accumulated by the wealthy are then converted into political resources creating political disparities. The resulting political influence

TABLE 0-1: AMERICAN ATTITUDES ON BUSINESS AND FAIRNESS

|  | AGREE | DISAGREE | DON'T KNOW |
|---|---|---|---|
| Today it's really true that the rich get richer while the poor get poorer. | 67% | 31% | 2% |
| There is too much power concentrated in the hands of a few big companies. | 67% | 20% | 3% |
| Business corporations make too much profit | 61% | 33% | 7% |
| Business corporations generally strike a fair balance between making profits and serving the public interest. | 42% | 53% | 5% |
| Our Society should do what is necessary to make sure that everyone has an equal opportunity to succeed. | 94% | 7% | 1% |
| The government should guarantee every citizen enough to eat and a place to sleep. | 66% | 31% | 3% |

Source: Surveys of thousands of adults conducted for the Times Mirror Corporation by the Gallup Organization, October 1988; James Burnes, J.W. Peltason, and T.E. Cronin, *Government by the People*, 14th ed., p. 181.

of the small rich elite, thus constituted, allows it unrivaled opportunity to shape public policies.

However, one strong positive factor is that American basic ideals of equality of opportunity carries comparatively heavier weight in contrast to economic and resulting political inequalities, in proportion to the level of individuals' social consciousness. But capitalistic indoctrination through childhood education and continuing blitz of propaganda has left very few unaffected and with such social consciousness. There are, however, indications of slow but steady increases in their numbers.

The second component of the American society is that of private organizations, mainly economic institutions. This is where the heart of the problem rests as far as it relates to democracy and equality of opportunity. Under the domain of monopoly capitalism, which is the main feature of American economy, as concluded by one study, a few thousand super rich (little over seven thousand) control or at least highly influence not only the economy of the country but also its essential political and social institutions such as media, education, and health care.[4]

Control of the information system is vital to the economic elite in order to control public attitude about justification of capitalism and also major domestic and foreign policies. Freedom of thought and speech is essential to a democratic system. There must be a free competition of ideals and symbols. In America this freedom is guaranteed by the First Amendment to the U.S. Constitution.

In modern society the interchange of information and expression of ideas is to be achieved through the mass media. The American mass media includes about 19,000 radio and television stations, 1700 daily newspapers, 7000 other newspapers, 9000 periodicals, over 4300 film producers and distributors, and 1300 publishing companies.[5] Then, business and financial firms control the three major television and radio networks--ABC, NBC, and CBS--34 subsidiary stations, 201 cable television systems, 62 major radio stations, 59 magazines, including Newsweek and Time, 58 newspapers, including The New York Times, The Washington Post, The Wall Street Journal, and The Los Angeles Times, and 41 publishing companies.[6] Seventy-five percent of the major stockholders of the three major television networks, where the American public receives most of its information, are owned by five major banks.[7] The following table shows the effect of this control upon the American public, specifically those under 30 years of age.

According to another study, in the long run, the mass media cater to elite individuals and elite institutions and uphold their actions. [8]

Besides the information system, the elite family, while it consists of only 0.4 of one percent of American households, controls the economy and government. This nuclear family extends to embrace the top one - fifth of the population as its supporters and beneficiaries.

Accordingly, the richest fifth of the population owns about 77 percent of all personally held wealth and 97 percent of the personally owned corporate stock. This means that the richest one-fifth has three times as much wealth as the remaining 80 percent of the population.

Through the control of the governmental process the elite rips off the American taxpayers by the means of government subsidies. Gaylord Shaw of the Associated Press has pointed out that private enterprise in America collects roughly $30 billion a year in government subsidies and subsidy-like aid, much of it hidden or disguised. A government-wide study, undertaken by the Associated Press, disclosed

**TABLE 0-2: THE MEDIA PEOPLE BELIEVE THE MOST**

| 18-29 YEARS | 30-49 YEARS | 50 AND OVER |
|---|---|---|
| 1. Wall Street Journal | 1. MacNeil-Lehrer | 1. MacNeil-Lehrer |
| 2. CBS | 2. Wall Street Journal | 2. Wall Street Journal |
| 3. Time | 3. CNN | 3. Reader's Digest |
| 4. ABC | 4. Time | 4. Local TV |
| 5. CNN  Local TV | 5. CBS  Local TV  Newsweek | 5. CNN |

Source: Michael J. Robinson, "An Absence of Malice: Young People and the Press," *Public Opinion* (Nov.-Dec. 1986), p. 45. J. Burns, J.W. Peltason, T.E. Cornin, *Government by the People*, 14th ed. (Englewood Cliffs, N.J.: Prentice-Hall, 1990), p. 302.

evidence that the total is at least $28 billion a year, and may run as high as $38 billion.[9]

The government's outstanding loans to private business--direct, guaranteed, and insured--came to about $250 billion in 1973, six times the outstanding credit advanced to business by all commercial banks.

The big business gets the big bite. The exploitive benefits appropriated by the economic elite amounts to about $380 billion a year or an annual rip-off of $1700 from every man, woman and child in the United States.

The third component of the American society is its public institutions, namely the government. America is praised and admired by the foreigners as well as most of its people for its political democracy. This is mainly not the result of real representative democracy but the effect of propaganda and conditioning through the mass media and educational systems by the elite family. A few that are expert in American political system and process and have impartially studied the system would find this to be far from the truth. They will attest that there is no democracy in the United States supported by the majority of the voting population. The so called "democracy" is a facade, a pretention created by the elite to sustain its status as well as the stability for its operation and to maximization of its profits.

First, there are only two major political parties which control all the national and state governments. Both of these parties are strong supporters of the concept of capitalism and are controlled by the capitalist elite. Apparent differences are only cosmetic. Through the control of state governments the two parties have been able to establish harsh conditions against the development of any third party and through establishment of single representation district, they have monopolized the electoral system including any hope of success for any minor third party. If these protective devices do not work the parties then use their governmental authority to outlaw the upcoming third party and officially destroy it. This happened in the 1920s when the Socialist Party was able to capture the government of many cities and gain representation in state legislatures. The party was declared illegal, its leaders were arrested, its offices were destroyed and its funds in banks were frozen. It was not until the 1970s that the party had access to government archives and sued the government and was granted damages.

Second, mainly because of the control of the two major parties by the elite, the size of independent voters has doubled during the last 20 years and presently more than one-third of the eligible voters are independent. Identification with one party or another is mostly based on tradition rather than being based on a political philosophy or on the party objectives. In the United States neither of the two parties has a long range objective and philosophically both are strongly capitalistic oriented. For this reason only about 5 percent of the membership take active part in party operation. Members of one party voting for the candidate of another during different elections is not unusual.

Despite their membership in one party or another, very few voters bother to participate in the elections--52 percent in presidential, 30-40 in congressional, and 10-30 in local elections. The result is the takeover of the political system by the elite and major interest groups supporting it. In actual sense, in the United States we do not have majority representation either at the national or state level. Representatives are selected by a small minority of the eligible votes. For example, if a presidential candidate received 54 percent of popular vote, when only 52 percent of the voters actually voted, he is elected by 28.6 percent of the total eligible voters. Thus, he is a minority president. The situation is more tragic in the case of congressmen who are elected by 20 percent or less of the eligible voters.

Third, the machinery of the election, especially in its financing, is established by the two major parties in a way that over 95 percent of the House representatives and 86 percent of senators are continually reelected. Nearly all of these serve the elite family. At the time of any social unrest this Congress passes appropriate welfare legislation by which a few billion is distributed among the poor and lower working class or small farm operators in order to quiet down the situation and maintain stability for the proper operation of the elite institutions. The money for such welfare programs, which presently amounts to hundreds of billions of dollars, does not come from the elite's pocket but mainly from those of the middle class and the working class itself in the form of additional taxation. Many rich people, thanks to legislation passed to protect their income, do not pay a penny of tax or pay a very nominal amount compared to the size of their annual income. For example, according to an Internal Revenue Service report, of 529,460 couples and individuals who reported total income above $200,000 on their tax returns filed in 1987, 595 paid no taxes. These had income averaging $600,000; two out of every three had capital gains averaging $490,000. Another 33,805 having incomes over $200,000 paid only 15 percent tax, typically less than a middle income family. About 3000 paid less than 10 percent.[10]

With all these factual observations it is not difficult to consider that there is no real political democracy in the United States particularly at the national level. The effect of such lack of democracy has put the nation in three trillion dollars debt the major beneficiary of which has been as always the economic elite, and presently over $150 billion of the taxpayers' money is used to pay the interest on the debt.

Not being the representative of the majority of the people, the U.S. Congress and President are both supporters of the economic elite and major interest groups which contribute to their electoral campaigns. For the same reason, the U.S. foreign policy is not based on international law or mutual respect to sovereignty of other nations. The basis for policy is, and has been, to protect U.S. capitalistic interest abroad. Any system not sympathetic to capitalism is not considered democratic. For example, nothing even remotely harmful to capitalism is allowed in the Latin American countries. U.S. seceded Panama from Colombia in 1903 and has controlled the politics and economy of the country since. When General Noreiga disobeyed, Panama was invaded in December 1989 and an "appropriate" obedient government was installed. The head of a foreign country was captured and brought to the United States for trial. Granada was invaded in October 1983 to oust a "Marxist" government. An acceptable government was established under the U.S. occupation. Dominican Republic was invaded in April 1965. It was also occupied from 1916 to 1924. Troops were sent to Mexico in April 1914 to block arms shipments to Mexican revolutionaries. They stayed in Mexico for eight months. Haiti was invaded in 1915 and the country remained under occupation until 1934. U.S. Marines were sent to Nicaragua in 1912 to protect the friendly government. Some Marines stayed for 13 years. Marines were again sent in 1927 and stayed until 1933 when Samosa was established as the ruler. The Samosa family ruled until the Sandinista revolution in 1979. U.S. troops landed in Honduras in three separate occasions, between 1912 and 1926, to protect American business interests. Since 1980 U.S. troops have regularly been stationed there in order to protect Contra rebellion forces and impose pressure on Nicaraguan government. Between 1898 and 1921 Marines were landed in Cuba on four occasions and remained there for a total of 12 years. U.S. established its present naval base at Guantanamo Bay in 1903. In early 1970s Chile democratically elected a Marxist government and chose Dr. Allendo as its president. This tended to destroy the U.S. government's theory of associating Marxism with dictatorship which was the basis for Cold War policies. The Chilean government had to be overthrown. It was done by the CIA and millions of American taxpayers' money.

This is just a regional example. The U.S. policy has followed the same lawless, overt or covert actions in other parts of the world particularly in the Far East and the Middle East when the U.S. elite had substantial economic and ideological interest.

Some half a century ago the great American philosopher John Dewey described the American system as follows:

> The reactionaries are in possession of force,
> in not only the army and police, but in the
> press and the schools. The only reason they do
> not advocate the use of force is the fact that
> they are already in possession of it, so their
> policy is to cover up its insistence with idealistic

phrases--of which their present use of individual
initiative and liberty is a striking example.[11]

In regard he further states, "It is absurd to conceive liberty as that of
the business entrepreneur and ignore the imminent regimentation to
which workers are subjected, intellectual as well as manual workers."[12]
American political democracy is not a true one. It is used carefully
and skillfully as a facade to cover the ills of capitalism and actual
control of the system by a very small elite.

Recent increasing public consciousness shows an increasing distrust
of government by the people since mid 1960s. In 1988, some 65
percent of the people thought that the government was run for the
benefit of a few big interests; some 60 percent believed that
government could not be trusted to do right most of the time; and some
40 percent thought that there were quite a few crooks in government.
Figure 0-1 presents the extent of these feelings since 1964.

However, there is another peculiar picture in American society. The
ideals of democracy, freedom and equality along with honesty and
integrity are quite strong among American people. Outside the domain
of government and big business the operation of the society is based on
these ideals even though sometimes they are not put into real practice.

### FIGURE 0-1: TRUST IN GOVERNMENT, 1964-1980

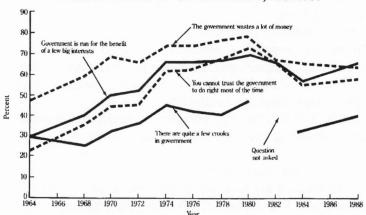

Source: Warren E. Miller, Arthur E. Miller, and Edward J. Schneider, *American Election Studies Data
Sourcebook, 1952-1978* (Cambridge, Mass.: Harvard University Press, 1980). Updated by authors. Paul E.
Johnson and others, *American Government: People, Institutions, and Policies* (Boston: Houghton Mifflin
1990), p. 221.

It is the existence and adherence to these ideals at the grassroot level that makes America greater and dynamic. Since Americans have been systematically deprived from appropriate education inductive to the enhancement of social consciousness, they, though technically and professionally well trained, have remained quite ignorant culturally and intellectually. The system of information and education has been controlled and used in a way that it would not create better thinkers but graduate better producers who would adhere to the rules of production games and cause the maximization of profits for the elite. Knowledge inducing social consciousness is not encouraged since such consciousness is apt to cause instability and initiate and strengthen anticapitalistic sentiments and demand for fundamental changes in socioeconomic system.

Unfortunately, there is no way, despite continuous sharp criticism of it, that the American system of education can be properly reformed short of a revolutionary transformation. Decades of capitalist indoctrination have established deep root in our system of education to the extent that our students in general evaluate each course they intend to take in terms of dollars and cents. One would repeatedly hear: What is the use of taking courses in history, philosophy, and literature? What economic benefits do I get from these? That is why our system of education produces good producers but not conscious thinkers. Perhaps this is one main reason why there is so much political apathy in the United States.

High employment opportunity, even though part-time, is another reason for lack of political concern. As long as people tan make a living they don't care how much and to what extent they are exploited by the elite, particularly, that good part of exploitation is indirect through taxation which a substantial part of it goes to the elite and to maintaining stability through a variety of social and economic aid programs benefiting lower class. Americans are conditioned to think that they are free and they can choose anything they want to do. They miss the point that freedom of choice alone without freedom to act upon the choice is no freedom at all. However, in the realm of unconsciousness it provides for psychological satisfaction. That is exactly what the ruling elite desires, causing us to think that we are free.

Comparatively, there is more social consciousness in Western Europe. There has been substantial conscious move toward democratic socialism since 1940s even though capitalism has remained a dominant factor. The term socialism is not disliked as it has been in the United States. The 1990s will be crucial for Western Europe. One essential question will be the extent of democratic tendencies synonymous to anticapitalistic norms the new system will embody. What kind of structure should and will it take? Will freedom of private exploitive enterprise, an outmoded and disturbing element in democracy,be discouraged in order to open the ground for the enhancement and preservation of democracy? In a mixed economy what will be properly private and what will be properly public? In answering these questions the attention to economic frames of social life must take priority. Presently, among a variety of societal concepts two have been dominant: *democratic capitalism and democratic socialism.*

We have already presented some aspects of democratic capitalism as practiced in the United States and its incompatibility with democratic norms and processes. Simply, democracy and capitalism cannot coexist. What is known as democratic socialism in Western Europe is a mixed system of capitalism--socialism of different varieties. In Western Europe, compared to the United States, there is more social consciousness which I attribute to better cultural education, and there is more interest in political participation as evidenced from Table 0-3. In all of these countries capitalist market economy dominates. This simply means exploitation as well as alienation of labor, sexism, racism, poverty, homelessness, and class stratification. None of these consequences of capitalistic practices is democratic. Therefore, the whole concept of democratic socialism as applied in Western Europe is questionable as far as the essence of democracy is concerned. Is this the kind of societal system that Europe wants to pursue in 1990s and into the 21st century? It would be very sad for the future of Europe if the present leaders are thinking along these lines. The movement toward European federation offers a unique opportunity for new ideas of the future society. Capitalism definitely is not the answer. The presently applied democratic socialism with its heavy capitalistic dose is only marginally better. A true democratic socialism will be still better but will not be the ultimate answer to a true democracy in which the role of government will be nearly nill.

In Eastern Europe there is now in process a tremendous socioeconomic and political transformation. This provides a unique opportunity for thinking about new societal concepts and test them

## TABLE 0-3: VOTER TURNOUT, A COMPARISON

| COUNTRY? | VOTER TURNOUT? | PERSONAL REGISTRATION? | PENALTY FOR NOT VOTING? |
|---|---|---|---|
| Italy | 94.0% | No | Yes |
| Austria | 89.3 | No | No |
| Belgium | 88.7 | No | Yes |
| Sweden | 86.8 | No | No |
| Greece | 84.9 | No | Yes |
| Netherlands | 84.7 | No | Yes |
| Australia | 83.1 | Yes | Yes |
| Denmark | 82.1 | No | No |
| Norway | 81.8 | No | No |
| West Germany | 81.1 | No | No |
| New Zealand | 78.5 | Yes | No |
| France | 78.0 | Yes | No |
| Great Britain | 76.0 | Yes | No |
| Canada | 67.4 | No | No |
| United States | 52.6 | Yes | No |

Source: David Glass, Perverill Squire, and Raymond Wolfinger, "Voter Turnout: An International Comparison," *Public Opinion*, December/January 1984, 50, Thomas E. Patterson, *The American Democracy* (New York: McGraw-Hill, 1990), p. 204.

through implementation. Eastern Europe has a unique experience of some 40 years of socialism under a harsh dictatorship. Eastern Europeans, though technologically not so advanced, comparatively are well educated. There is awareness, high social consciousness, a hunger for democracy but there is no alternative societal concepts to Leninism except those applied in Western Europe and democratic Marxism. To Eastern Europeans to fall back in the pitfalls of capitalism will be regretful. This will be moving many steps backward. It is true that Leninism did not work. It was obvious from the beginning that such system could not mix with Marxism which, even in its process of transition, is applicable only to a highly advanced society.

A true Marxism and its envisioned proletarian revolution has not been experienced yet. Perhaps it requires still many years of technological development and ensuing advancement in education of the labor force which, in Marx view, would create a strong social consciousness and thus unite the labor forces against the capitalist class. Even if we assume that such revolution will occur in the future and a proletarian dictatorship will be formed, its nature will be far different from Lenin's dictatorship of intelligentsia. The former will be a government ruled by an overwhelming majority of intelligentsia (the Communist Party) over the masses. Whether Marx's proletarian revolution will occur in the future is a question mark. In any case, while Leninism is dead, Marxism cannot be considered dead at this time since we may assume that no society has yet reached the stage of development inductive to proletarian revolution. It may be on this ground that the new Soviet leaders want to choose democratic socialism without abandoning the Marx's goal of communism.

The fall of Leninism has created enormous problems for Eastern European countries as well as the Soviet Union. These are political, economic, and social.

Choosing a new political system is the easiest of all since they can copy some of the Western European systems. However, copying will not be enough. Proper knowledge of management, policy-making, and policy implementation are the heart of successful operation of such system. It will also require substantial adjustment to socialistic norms which have been deeply rooted as a result of over seventy years of experimentation with left socialism.

Transformation of economy from centralized planning, production, and distribution system to a decentralized one is perhaps the most burdensome. How is the question of ownership going to be resolved? Who will control natural resources? How is the problem of high unemployment going to be resolved? And most of all how is the economy going to survive during this transition which will be accompanied by higher prices and inflation?

Social problems are also formidable. For forty years in Eastern Europe and over seventy years in the Soviet Union people have been accustomed to receiving free education, nearly free health care, highly subsidized housing, transportation, and recreation along with job security. Many of these services, particularly education and health care, cannot be eliminated. All Western European countries are moving toward providing more and more of these services. Education and health care not only are two most expensive services but also essential for development and progress. It appears that these should be kept as free as they were before.

Housing will be a big problem if government subsidies are eliminated. We must consider that under the centralized economy the government received all the revenues and after paying for all social services distributed the rest as wages among the workers. Therefore, while the wages were low, people received all kinds of public services regardless of how meager these were.

For all these reasons return to capitalism will be highly torturous to the population while after forty years of life under socialism people may have a very hard time making adjustments.

What is the alternative? Our view is that there is no democratic system in its true sense in any place in the world. First, political and social systems in each society are highly influenced by its economic system. The states become supportive and protectors of the existing economic system. Consequently, if the economic system is not democratic the political system, even though intended to be democratic, will follow the suit. Nearly all operational aspects of capitalism--exploitation and alienation of labor, class stratification, racism, and sexism--are undemocratic. Thus, capitalism and democracy are incompatible and cannot coexist. If capitalism is sustained then political democracy will disappear at least in its actual operation. The British economic system has been socialized since World War II. It has affected every Conservative government since then. Even Prime Minister Thatcher, with all her efforts for privatization and reestablishing full capitalism, has not been able to do so and her government had to go along with the socialistic operation of many aspects of the society.

Therefore, it seems that the prime requirement for a true democratic society is a democratic economic system. This is the purpose of this writing. If we could establish a true democratic economic theory which is not utopian but practical as well as applicable to modern society, then we can hope for political and social democracy to accompany it. As it will be demonstrated in the text, technology plays a dominant role in the structure and function of this economic theory.

For this reason it is more appropriate to label it as *technodemocratic economic theory*.

The study of a century of development among advanced societies of Europe and the United States demonstrates a trend toward transformation of economic systems from capitalism to socialism. Today, all Western European countries have adopted, to varying degrees, socialistic elements into their socio-economic systems and the trend continues despite the fact that capitalism is still a dominant factor. In the United States, though the term socialism is not liked, since the 1930s many socialistic programs have been established such as Social Security, Medicaid, Medicare, aid to education, farm subsidies, low and middle income housing, food stamps, unemployment compensation, and scores of others, consuming several hundreds of billions of dollars of the federal and state budgets. It seems also quite certain that the Eastern European countries including the Soviet Union will maintain strong socialistic orientation.

The United States is still the most capitalistic oriented country since the European countries have nationalized, to a varying degree, their basic means of production and distribution. Thus, these nations have moved from an undemocratic state of capitalism toward some extent of democratization of economy. The next step toward which all these countries, with varying speed, are moving is the technodemocratic economic system.

This will be a society quite different from socialism. In this society all means of production and distribution will be owned by the private sector. Therefore, all nationalized production means will be returned to the working class. The theory is scientifically built on the principle of equality of opportunity, technology, and individual. This makes its understanding simple and implementation exact. It shows the way the socialistic societies have to go about transforming themselves to this ultimate democratic state of economy.

As the transition proceeds the role of government diminishes to the extent that in the advanced and mature stage of the theory the functions of government become negligible. The society may not reach the level of total statelessness but will be close to it.

The scientific structure of the theory also gradually eliminates class stratification moving the society toward a single class system. Individual responsibility is gradually multiplied and accepted by the individuals voluntarily as a result of proper democratically oriented education and experimentation. Again, the scientific structure and function of the system prescribes for free, lifelong health care and education for everyone, no individual taxation, no old age or retirement benefits, or any other social welfare program except for those disabled.

Technology and knowledge through continuous education dominates the health and proper operation of the system. Strong individual tendencies, as a matter of duty, are developed to preserve natural resources and eliminate waste and contamination of the nature.

This study first attempts to present the characteristics of capitalism versus democracy in a post-industrialized technological society like the United States. This work is the result of over twenty years of research and study in an attempt to discover the causes of our socio-political backwardness. It presents that for the lack of appropriate education in democratic philosophy, representative democracy, as practiced in America, has become an outdated, undemocratic political system which sustains and protects the existing unjust economic system and its ruling elite; and that the capitalistic economy as practiced in the United States is an antiquated and suppressive system caused and sustained by an utterly defective capitalistic oriented educational system. The results have been social institutions that have remained behind and, thus, incapable of accommodating the demands and needs of a modern technological democratic society.

Secondly, the study examines communism as prescribed by Marx and Marxist-Leninist societies in an attempt to illustrate, first, why Marxism is not applicable in these societies, and then the fallacies of Marxist-Leninist theory which are evident presently by its collapse in many countries of Eastern Europe.

Thirdly, the study attempts to describe the technodemocratic economic theory which the author believes to be the inevitable future course of democratic socialism. The full definition of a true democracy is given for the first time in the field of societal philosophy. Its principles, components, societal structure, operation, and consequences are presented and discussed.

Finally, since all the present advanced societies, Europe less than the United States, are far from being capable of the transformation to a technodemocratic economic system, a stage of gradual transition is presented and discussed. It is argued that though Western Europe has a unique chance to try this new system in its process of integration,

Eastern European countries have a better chance and opportunity to establish and experiment the technodemocratic economic system in their already heavily socialistic societies. The concept should be of great interest to the Soviet Union which has also a better chance to transform its socialistic centralized economy to fully privately owned technodemocratic economy while maintaining most of its social programs.

## NOTES

1 Richard C. Edwards, et al. *The Capitalist System: A Radical Analysis of American Society* (New Jersey: Prentice-Hall, 1972), p. 173.

2 Ibid, p. 174.

3 Erwin Knoll and Judith N. McFadden, *American Militarism 1970* (New York: Viking Press, 1969),
p. 2.

4 Thomas R. Dyue, *Who's Running America?* 4th ed. (Englewood Cliffs, N.J.: Prentice-Hall, 1986),
p. 12.

5 James Burns, J.W. Peltason, and T.E. Cranin, *Government by the People*, 14th ed. (Englewood Cliffs, N.J.: Prentice-Hall, 1990), p. 279.

6 Ibid

7 Ibid

8 Ibid, p. 302.

9 United Press International, "Tax Breaks Cost Treasury $44 Billion," *Wisconsin State Journal*, June 5, 1971, Sec. 1, p. 3.

10 Associated Press, Washington, D.C. "Tax Dodge: Some Still Don't Pay U.S.," *Wisconsin State Journal*, Sunday, October, 1989, p. 6A.

11 Carl Choen, ed. *Communism, Fascism, and Democracy*, 2nd ed. (New York: Random House, 1972), p. 500. The statement is from John Dewey's, "The Future of Liberalism," *The Journal of Philosophy*, Vol. 32, No. 9, April 25, 1935.

12 Ibid.

# PART I.

# THE EXISTING ECONOMIC STRUCTURES

*CHAPTER 1.*

# TECHNOLOGICAL CAPITALISM AND MARKET MONOPOLY

A brief presentation of the present status of capitalism is important for two reasons: First, to demonstrate the lack and impossibility of a true representative democracy under such a system and, second, to prepare ground for later presentation of the new economic theory under which all giant corporations will be automatically transformed into small independent corporations created by their previous subsidiaries and other components. The era of giant corporations will become a history.

Some one hundred forty years ago, Karl Marx stated in the Communist Manifesto as follows:

> The history of all hitherto existing society is the
> history of class struggles. Freemen and slaves,
> patrician and plebeian, lord and serf, guild-master and
> journeyman, in a word, oppressor and oppressed,

stood in constant opposition to one another, carried on
an uninterrupted, now hidden, now open fight, a fight
that each time ended, either in a revolutionary
reconstruction of society at large, or in the common
ruin of the contending class.

The historical background of these class struggles is not our
concern here, and are found in Marx's and other philosophers
writings.   Our concern here is the modern technological society,
capitalistic as well as communistic. This modern society has not done
away with class antagonisms. It has but established new classes, new
conditions of oppression, new forms of struggle in place of the old
ones.

On the capitalistic side, our epoch, which is the epoch of
multinational corporations, unlike those of the past, has complicated
the class antagonisms. Marx simplified the class antagonisms, in his
observations of the mid-nineteenth century, into two classes of
*bourgeoisie* and *proletariat* which directly faced one another.  Unlike
Marx the modern technological capitalism, in order to maintain the
hegemony of the capitalist elite, has interjected into this struggle
complex legal, institutional, economic and technological devices.   It
has been able not only to maintain its power and control over the
means of production and distribution, but to establish a new set of
social relations of production to accommodate its control far beyond
the national boundaries.

For proper analysis of the present status of technological capitalism,
we find it utmost useful to revert to Marx's scientific ideas of historical
materialism and apply them wherever appropriate in analyzing the
present conditions of both capitalistic and communistic societies.

Historical materialism provides a comprehensive and sophisticated
answer to the nature of the system which embodies economic, social
and political evolution in the course of history.  The central point here
is that the analysis of the relations of production in a society is the key
which unlocks the nature of the prevailing societal system.  People
enter into social relations in connection with production, which governs
the general character of a societal system as well as its historical
evolution.

Many of the pervasive societal problems that we face today—inequality, racism, sexism, alienation, militarism, environmental pollution and depletion of natural resources, etc.—are systematically and closely related to our capitalistic economic system.

To understand how to deal with these societal problems and to achieve a better and just society, we must understand the internal structure and the dynamics of modern technological capitalism. To refresh the reader's mind and clarify the specific meaning of the terminology used hereinafter, we make a brief reference to the basic components of capitalism.

*Forces of Production:* A less scientific term often used is the *means of production.* The forces of production in general consist of land, labor, capital and technology. Technology includes any scientific innovation applied to production processes.

Technology which initially related to the machine and physical means of production, by its very rapid and phenomenal advancement since the turn of the century, has expanded its domain to embody also the areas of innovation, management, policy-making, information gathering and its dissemination, counselling, accounting, and banking. In short, it has further enormously expanded from production of goods into vast and rapidly growing areas of services.

During the last four decades, in particular, labor and technology have increasingly been interrelated to the extent that today, under monopoly capitalism, there is hardly a use for labor without certain required know-how. The situation is becoming further complicated by the rapid advancement of computer technology and its infringement in nearly every aspect of economic life of the modern society.

Accordingly, the concept of forces of production envisioned by Marx has gone through substantial modification since his time. The importance of land for production of foodstuff and cash crops has declined while its value as the source of energy and industrial raw materials has increased. The character of labor has substantially changed with the advancement of technological forces, and bearing of technology in the operation of economic life has become enormous. Capital, though multiplied in size, still plays the same important role of bringing the other forces of production together.

*Social Surplus:* A layman's term for this is profit. A social surplus is the part from the total material product which is left to the capitalist after paying the labor and other costs of production. Surplus is understood to be a part of labor used for production which is not paid to the labor but appropriated by the capitalist. Thus, labor produces the surplus and the capitalist appropriates it. Continuous appropriation of surplus causes the accumulation of capital.

*Social Class:* Social class is established through common relationship of those who produce and those who appropriate the surplus. For example, a production firm consists of capitalists, top management, middle management, foremen, skilled workers and unskilled workers. This structure is transferred to the society in the form of upper class, upper middle class, middle class, lower middle class, upper lower class and lower class.

*Social Relation of Production:* These are the relationships between those who produce the social surplus and those who control production and appropriate the social surplus. Each community is divided into sectors based on the structure of the social classes from plush rich neighborhoods to slum areas for poor and unskilled labor. Each person in the production firm tends, and feels comfortable, to interact with members of his or her own class who may live in comparable neighborhoods. This is man's relationship with the material world.

*Mode of Production:* It is the relationship between the existing forces of production and the existing social relations of production. The forces of production are dynamic and progress continually. Social relations of production are somehow static and tend to become traditional and, thus, resist changes. This creates ever increasing contradiction in the society which ultimately forces a new social relation of production compatible with the existing and already advanced forces of production.

Under the capitalist mode of production, the capitalist owns or controls all forces of production—land, capital, and technology—except labor. The capitalist buys labor from the labor market. Thus, in capitalistic societies the social relations of production are characterized by separation of the producers (workers) from other means of production.

As explained before, while the mode of production is crucial in determining the general societal character, the relationship between this economic operation and other aspects of life in a society is not simple or negligible. Marx's famous passage excellently summarizes this concept and deserves careful attention:

> In the social production of their existence, people inevitably enter into definite relations, which are independent of their will, namely relations of production appropriate to a given stage in the development of their material forces of production. The totality of these relations of production constitutes the economic structure of society, the real foundation, on which arises a legal and political superstructure and to which correspond definite forms of social consciousness. The mode of production of material life conditions the general process of social, political and intellectual life. It is not the consciousness of people that determines their existence, but their social existence that determines their consciousness.

Approach to the study of a society from a purely economic viewpoint would be grossly inadequate. Ideology, culture, tradition, religion and other less important non-economic factors each has its own effect, to varying degrees, on the social relations of production. However, the relationship between the economic operation and these other aspects of life is, in general and almost always, asymmetrical. These non-economic factors tend to delay economic progress and corresponding necessary changes. At the same time, forces of production are continually developing and advancing particularly in the area of science and technology. This dynamic process of change tends to lead to a non-correspondence or, scientifically speaking, to contradiction with the prevailing social relations of productions as well as other non-economic factors in the society. Pressure for change as well as resistance for it mounts, leading often, to drastic social action in order to effectuate the required changes.

To consider Marx's concept of historical materialism as a naive economic determinism in which all things depend upon economic forces alone, is an erroneous approach. This is what the capitalist thinkers advocate and maintain. Marx's conception of history was never a simplistic economic determinism. As Marx once wrote "Men make their own history, but they do not make it just as they please. They do not make it under circumstances chosen by themselves."[1]

The fact is that Marx did not try to reduce everything to economic terms. He did rather attempt to uncover the true interrelationships between economic and non-economic forces in the totality of a societal life.[2] Historical materialism is not a set of mechanical formulas but a method of approaching social questions which center on examination of the unfolding contradiction between the forces of production and the relations of production. Thus historical materialism does not deal strictly with the economic aspects of life but gives preference to it as the most important determinant of human behavior.

## Technological Capitalism

If we pay close attention to the process of daily life we will easily go along with Marx's scientific method of approach. First, in a technological capitalistic society, the prime concern of every individual in daily life is to satisfy his or her basic needs such as food, clothing, shelter, transportation, health, education, recreation, employment and old age benefits. Most of these are concerned with the material aspects of life. Second, beyond basic needs, every individual has a desire for the betterment of his or her material life: better food, unnecessary clothing, own a house, own an automobile, personal recreational facilities, art or other collections. Third, beyond the satisfaction of basic needs every individual has a desire to save and accumulate wealth in the form of capital, and invest it for further profits and accumulation.

It is then obvious that the approach to human and societal behavior from an economic viewpoint becomes paramount and essential. However, it must be noticed that this approach does not intend to consider the study of other aspects of life—cultural, political and spiritual—ineffective or unnecessary.

*The Concept of Historical Materialism*: Marx's concept of historical materialism is quite sophisticated and complex. The simplest and briefest way to explain it has been done by Marx himself as presented below.[3]

In the social production which men carry on they enter
into definite relations that are indispensable and
independent of their will; these relations of production
correspond to a definite stage of development of their
material powers of production the sum total of these
relations of production constitutes the economic
structure of society—the real foundation, on which rise
legal and political superstructures and to which
correspond definite forms of social consciousness.
The mode of production in material life determines the
general character of the social, political and spiritual
processes of life. It is not the consciousness of man
that determines their existence, but on the contrary,
their social existence determines their consciousness.
At a certain stage of their development, the material
forces of production in society come in conflict with
the existing relations of production, or—what is but a
legal expression for the same thing—with the property
relations within which they had been at work before.
From forms of development of the forces of
production these relations turn into their fetters. Then
comes the period of social revolution. With the
change of the economic foundation the entire immense
superstructure is more or less rapidly transformed. In
considering such transformations the distinction should
always be made between the material transformation of
the economic conditions of production which can be
determined with the precision of natural science, and
the legal, political, religious, aesthetic or
philosophic—in short, ideological forms in which men
become conscious of this conflict and fight it out. Just
as our opinion of an individual is not based on what he
thinks of himself, so can we not judge of such a
period of transformation by its own consciousness; on
the contrary, this consciousness must rather be
explained from the contradictions of material life,
from the existing conflict between the social forces of
production and the relations of production. No social

> order ever disappears before all the productive forces,
> for which there is room in it, have been developed;
> and new higher relations of their existence have
> matured in the womb of the old society. Therefore,
> mankind always takes up only such problems as it can
> solve; since, looking at the matter more closely, we
> will always find that the problem itself arises only
> when the material conditions necessary for its solution
> already exist or are at least in the process of
> formation. In broad outlines we can designate the
> Asiatic, the ancient, the feudal, and the modern
> bourgeois methods of production as so many epochs in
> the progress of the economic formation of society.
> The bourgeois relations of production are the last
> antagonistic form of the social process of
> production—antagonistic not in the sense of individual
> antagonism, but of one arising from conditions
> surrounding the life of individuals in society; at the
> time the productive forces developing in the womb of
> bourgeois society create the material conditions for the
> solution of that antagonism. This social formation
> constitutes, therefore, the closing chapter of the
> prehistoric stage of human society...[4]

From Marx's viewpoint, historical materialism is an indispensable approach to the understanding of historical constellations by focusing attention on the nature of the principal energies responsible for their emergence, transformation, and disappearance.[5] These energies are traced back to contradictions caused by ever present tension between continually developing forces of production and prevailing social relations of production.

In modern technological society the forces of production encompass in particular, among other things, the existing stage of technology and science which extends to the process of production, mode of organization, innovations, and more importantly, to the development of those who produce.

The social relations of production, on the other hand, relates to the manner of appropriation of the products produced by the labor force, the principles and process of distribution, the social conditions under which goods and services are produced, and finally, the modes of thought and the ideology.

Because of recent rapid technological advancement, the forces of production tend to be highly dynamic gaining continually in scope, strength, and depth.   On the other hand, the established and accustomed social institutions and processes tend to remain somehow static resisting necessary changes to balance or accommodate the advancing forces of production.  This widening contradiction between the two tends to cause increasing class discrimination, oppression, conservatism and cultural lag.  It results in the formation of a dominant class which is not ready to relinquish its gained privileges.

In the early stages of imbalance, the social power of the ruling class is strong enough to maintain the status quo and prevent the emergence of new forms of economic or social institutions.  As the contradictions rise, the ruling elite unwillingly consents to certain relatively peaceful transformations.  If the contradictions strongly persist then the clash becomes violent.

Marx's view is that the developing forces of production have had thus far the commanding role in the historical process.  Despite some temporary setbacks and interruptions, in the long run they have tended to overcome all obstacles, and to conquer and subordinate to their requirements all political, socio-economic and ideological institutions and processes.  However, long periods of siege in which conquests remain elusive, imperfect, and impermanent have been more frequent than dramatic victories.

The course taken by this struggle, its nature and its outcome has varied from period to period depending on the available means, the nature of the class structure, and the multitude and variety of economic, political, ideological, and above all, technological configurations by the confrontation between the forces of production and social relations of production.

## Fallacies of Marx's Projections

While Marx's concept of historical materialism, if properly understood, is a valid one and is applicable, with some modifications, in the study of capitalistic societies of today as it was during his time, his projection of the state of capitalism toward the future is full of fallacies. This by no means affects the enormous value of his scientific and philosophical study of human societies. Frankly speaking, no societal scientist or philosopher has since matched his achievements, all his efforts were sincerely aimed toward the well being of human beings and human societies. But predictions or projections based on scientific findings in a multidisciplinary and extremely broad subject of human society is not a simple thing. It requires taking into consideration enormously large number of variables upon which future changes depend, and many of which are not yet known.

While Marx's study of capitalism is very detailed, exact, sophisticated and complex, his predictions toward the future are relatively simplistic and are based on many uncertain assumptions. There are three major areas of error in Marx's vision of the future post-capitalist society. Here we point out these three areas in brief. Later on we will also be obliged to look critically into his vision of the ultimate state of human society: stateless and classless.

The first, and in our opinion the most important, mistake of Marx was his overestimation of future power and unity of the labor force. He believed that as industrialization progresses and technology advances the labor force will be better and better educated and will increasingly, become conscious of its exploited and deprived status. These common feelings about its status will necessarily unite and unify the labor force in its struggle against the common enemy, the capitalist class. As a result of this unity, as size of the labor force grows so does its power to the extent that ultimately it is capable of rising against and overthrowing the capitalist class. Even though based on the existing facts and circumstances in Marx's time such assumptions may not have been totally out of question, irrational or baseless, the future developments showed that they were substantially erroneous. While the labor force, as predicted by Marx, grew in size and became better educated, it, however, did not become united as one single force against capitalism.

In the first place, labor became fragmented, first into guilds and trade unions and then into diversified industrial unions. Yet with all the efforts of labor leaders to unionize, only a small fragment of labor became unionized, and today, still a majority of the labor force is not unionized. Second, unionization by no means meant unity. Unions often have diverse, conflicting, even rival interests. Thus, contrary to Marx's prediction, the labor did not become unified. In both and most advanced capitalistic societies of his time, England and the United States, where he hoped his predictions would first materialize, they did not. Today, neither in England, nor in the United States, the labor force is unified to the extent of being a real threat to power and status of the capitalist class.

The second mistake of Marx in his predictions toward the future was his underestimation of the power and effect of the middle class in capitalist society. He divided society into two major camps confronting one another: capitalist and proletariat, namely the working class. Whereas, as capitalism along with industrialization and technological developments advanced into the twentieth century the middle class grew in stature and power far beyond that of labor to the extent that today:

1. The middle class supplies most of the capital needed by the monopoly capitalist. They invest in stocks and bonds without having ownership voice in operation of corporations. This embodies a very large well-to-do segment of population.

2. The high technological knowhow, essential to effective operation even to survival of the corporations is supplied by the middle class. Administrators, executives, scientists and experts of all kinds serving the capitalists, nearly all, come from this sector of population.

3. The middle class, the lower middle class in particular, embodies a large sector of the labor force, blue-collar as well as white collar. By this way it provides a link and often a channel of communication between the labor forces and the upper classes.

All these factors put together, make the middle class under monopoly capitalism, and not the proletariat as described by Marx, the main source of potential power. A small group of air-controllers, if they go on strike, can stop air transportation systems. A teamsters union strike can paralyze highway transportation of goods, teachers strike can bring the education process to a brink, doctors strike can paralyze the health care system, fireman's strike can cause irreparable property damage. All these are workers but they are not poor or needy. They belong to different sectors of the middle class in technological capitalistic society.

Marx, practically disregarded this extremely powerful sector of technological society by dividing the society into two opposing camps of capitalist and proletariat with no strong link in between.

The third mistake of Marx was his underestimation of flexibility of capitalists and capitalism. He did not realize the possibility of channels of fruitful communication between capitalists and laborers. He did not visualize that in order to maintain their maximization of profits, capitalists may resort to a variety of peaceful means rather than to force a violent suppression of labor which was practiced in his time. As technology advanced and capitalism expanded production, capitalists and labor forces did learn to live and work together, to discuss grievances, and negotiate wages, fringe benefits and conditions of work.

For these three substantial errors in Marx's projection of his theory toward the future, his predictions did not materialize either in Great Britain or in the United States. Therefore, while we do not deny the enormous value of his theory of historical materialism and empirical study of capitalism, we are obliged to state that the historical events of the last few decades have established substantial and undeniable evidences against his predictions and projections. We will have a further critical look at Marx's theory when we discuss communism and the communist state.

## The Essence of Technological Capitalism

The method of historical materialism can be used not only to illuminate fundamental changes in the mode of production but can also be used to provide a basis for examining revolutionary changes within boundaries of a specific mode of production. The purpose here is to shed light on the changes that have occurred in the nature of capitalism in response to the requirements of the capitalist mode of production in an age of increasing economic and industrial complexity and ever advancing technology.

The variety of changes that have taken place within the modern capitalist system have had a significant impact upon the four major sectors of society: capitalists, labor, the state, and technology. For proper understanding of these changes and their effect, we must take a brief look at the development of each of these four sectors during the last few decades.

## Commercial Concentration

Since the days where small family businesses were the typical unit of enterprise, the increase in size and hierarchical structure have both responded to and tended to produce the development of an increasingly complex technology of production and distribution.

The most important trend in commercial organization in technological capitalism has been the growth of modern multinational corporations and the domination of the means of production and distribution by a small number of huge corporations.

Most major productions have become highly concentrated into the hands of a few large corporations. These corporations as a group have dominated the economy and means of production, and have been increasingly expanding into other societies with an intent to dominate the world capitalist society as a whole.

In the United States, the leading capitalist system in the world, for example, the top 150 corporations, representing 15 out of every half a million individual business units,[6] are so huge and powerful that their removal "would effectively destroy the American economy."[7]

The following three important factors, among others, have helped huge corporations drive out of business those with smaller scale.

1. *Financial economies of scale:* Larger firms are better able to raise money, to take risks, to absorb losses. They often, if not invariably, have access to immense sources of capital through the control of, or influence in, one or more large financial institutions.

2. *Technological economies of scale:* Large scale production is more harmonized, efficient, and less costly than production in smaller institutions. They also have easy access to new technologies either through their own research institutions or by control of others.

3. *Market economies of scale:* With the enormous cost of high technology advertising and marketing, larger corporations are better able to capture markets and promotion of widely known brand names.

All these put together have provided opportunities for the large corporations to translate these advantages into political and economic power and influence, and further enhance their dominant position to the detriment of smaller firms.

A further important fact is that as the large corporations have grown in size, they have, at the same time, expanded their operation beyond the national borders. Thus, it has become less and less meaningful to analyze the modern capitalist system by taking into account only a specific country. It is increasingly important and essential to look upon capitalism as a worldwide system dominated not by a country or set of countries but by a set of multinational corporations.[8]

## The Capitalist Accumulation Process

A small group of large corporations dominate the national economy in the United States, Japan and Western Europe and are rapidly expanding in the worldwide capitalist economy. This increase in size and power and the attachment of multinational characteristics is a systematic consequence of the capitalist accumulation process.

Contrary to individual capitalist tycoons who dominated the nineteenth century capitalist world, the real capitalist of today is not the individual, but the corporation. The giant corporation of today is an instrument for maximizing profits and accumulating capital on a scale not imaginable before. Unlike the individual capitalist, the corporation has a longer time horizon and is a more rational calculator because of its modern technological brain.[9]

Today's most colossal units of capital are the huge financial institutions which have been able to gain control over several of the giant corporations. This has created a few super giant financial industrial groups with an enormous economic and political power.

The giant corporations have been successful in eliminating much of the competition from the smaller firms to the extent that today the predominant market structure has become monopolistic rather than competitive. This situation in the product market has given the large corporations an opportunity to achieve a higher profit margin by raising prices of their commodities. This higher surplus, in turn, has enabled the corporations to accumulate more capital and grow faster leaving the smaller firms far behind.

However, since only a few corporations have co-existed within a specific industry and since they have realized that price competition would likely result in cutting prices and thus lowering profit margin for all involved, they have embarked in advertising in order to increase demand for their product. This has created another kind of competition, competition in advertising toward defending or expanding the volume of sales in relation to other competing corporations.

In this way, monopolistic competition, while it has circumscribed the role of the market in establishing price, and introduced new costs of advertising, it has typically limited each corporation's growth to its share of growth in the industry's total market. This limitation to rapid expansion of the market in its own industry and the high returns from sales has induced the corporation to look for new areas of production for profitable reinvestment. Accordingly, the rim gradually has entered into new areas of production and attempted to enlarge its market by expanding into other countries.

A very important aspect of technological capitalism has been the need of huge corporations for many smaller firms to produce certain items used for completion of the corporation's final products. These are mainly the makers of parts or of specialty tools for the main industry and survive as a result of narrow specialization and production interdependence which are the characteristics of an advanced technological production. Of course, small, competitive firms have retained their importance in wholesale and retail business, in agriculture and all other areas not within the sphere of interest of the large corporations.[10] However, these smaller firms, whether survived by serving the large corporations, or operating independently outside the sphere of activities of the large firms, have, all together, performed a very important role in the economy as employers of the largest sector of the labor force. Table 1-1 illustrates the situation.[11] While monopolistic industries annual income amounted to 40 percent of the national income, that of the competitive industries was 32 percent. On the other hand, the former employed only 33 percent of the labor force against 39 percent for the latter.

Large corporations operate in the context of worldwide economy. Much of the overseas expansion occurred in the post World War II period with speed and without much adverse effect to the home market. In this expansion process, American corporations faced the least threat to their home market from foreign competitors. However, the situation has rapidly been changing in recent years, since the 1970's in particular. Japanese and European corporations have become vigorous competitors to American corporations. In electronics, automobiles, textiles, chemicals, oil, steel and many other important products, foreign firms have significantly increased their share of the U.S. market. This rising international competition has had diminishing effects on the market power of domestic monopolistic corporations. However, the net total market power of the multinational corporations as a whole have substantially increased in the world market.

## The Centralization of Capital

Historically, the firms surviving competition grew larger and advanced from workshop to factory, corporations, and then to national prominence. They expanded to the extent that in each industry only a few survived and produced enough to satisfy nearly the entire national market demand.

**Table 1-1: U.S. Industries,**
**National Income and Employees by Sector, 1974**

| Sector | Value Added During Production (billions) | Percent of National Income | Millions of Workers | Percent of total Workers |
|---|---|---|---|---|
| Monopolistic industries | $453 | 40% | 29 | 33% |
| Competitive industries | 362 | 32 | 34 | 39 |
| Industries not classified | 139 | 12 | 5 | 6 |
| Government | 178 | 16 | 14 | 16 |
| Unemployment | --- | -- | 5 | 6 |
| Total | $1,132 | 100% | 87 | 100% |

Source: Industries classified according to William Sheperd, *Market Power and Economic Welfare* (New York: Random House, 1970), Appendix 14; data calculated from "Statistical Abstract of the United States" (Washington, D.C. Government Printing Office, 1975), pp. 343, 357-58, 387.

However, the internal growth of the corporations was not the only way to advance in size. A substantial factor in this regard has been mergers and combinations.

Before the Civil War of the 1860's the corporate form of business was mainly confined to finance and transportation. The industrial corporations flourished by the merging large scale technology during the second half of the nineteenth century. The Great Depression which lasted from 1873 to about 1895 witnessed pressure on profits rather than unemployment. Pressure emanated from the continuing and dramatic lowering of prices. The situation was due to technological developments causing increase in efficiency and confrontation with domestic as well as foreign competition while the market was relatively competitive.

In an attempt to control price competition, various forms of business reorganization and methods of price agreements were tried. The merger emerged as the most favorable method which became known as the "combination movement," and was well employed by the late 1890's. Under this concept, many firms were combined together under one identity and ownership. Between 1897 and 1905, this merger process reached its peak and some 5300 industrial firms fell under the control of 318 most advanced and economically powerful corporations.

Though, historically, this period witnessed a spectacular and unprecedented wave of merger, the subsequent waves, however, surpassed it. First, a higher peak of merger was attained in the 1920's and then, the largest wave of all began in the 1950's which has been continuous to the present.[12] As evidenced by facts of the last ninety years or so the push for merger has been consistent except for periods of depression. Figure 1-1 illustrates the situation.[13]

In recent decades, since World War II in particular, while as a result of new technological development, production facilities have been geographically decentralized, the control over these facilities has become increasingly centralized expanding over many different industries. Initially, technological development led to merger taking place within one industry. The process toward this concentration which reached its peak in the turn of the century, was brutal and in time merciless on the means employed for control.[14] After the advancement of merger within each specified industry it started to

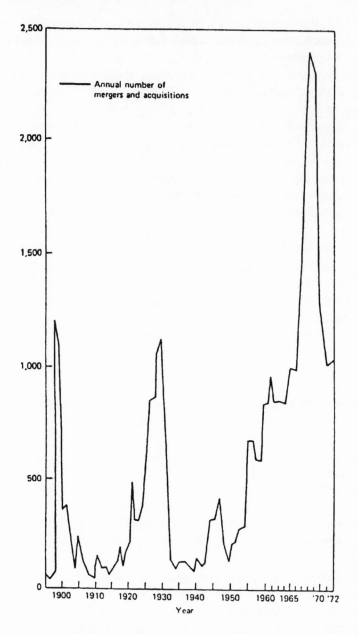

Source: Edwards, Reich and Weisskopf, *The Capitalist System*, 2nd ed. (Englewood Cliffs, N.J.: Prentice-Hall, 1978), p. 127.

expand into other production facilities. The most striking pattern in this regard started during World War II and attained its peak in the late 1960's. Figure 1-2 shows the situation.[15] As evidenced from this figure, such multiple-industry mergers, which have continued to this day, have dominantly concentrated the means of production and distribution of a great variety of important industries in the hands of some 200 top corporations.[16] This is one out of every 25,000 production firms in the United States.

Three main types of merger emerged during this period of drive for concentration: horizontal, vertical, and conglomerate.

Horizontal merger referred to mergers in one industry, where all merging firms produced nearly the same product; competitors in a specific industry came under the ownership and control of one or a few corporations. Therefore, horizontal mergers led to concentration of power within a specific industry and led to the formation of *oligopoly* where a few major corporations dominated the market of that specific industry.

Vertical merger was the next form to develop. Under this kind of merger, the corporation bought out its suppliers and/or its customers. Vertical mergers fortified further the position of large corporations, and made it quite difficult for new firms to enter the market.

The conglomerate was the latest form of merger, where the firms acquired by a corporation were not related, or only distantly related, to its line of production.

In recent decades all of these three forms—horizontal, vertical, and conglomerate—have been used, the latter with increasing importance.[17]

The conglomerate form of merger has enabled the giant corporations to expand control into the area of traditionally fragmented and dispersed small industries such as textile, food processing, etc. Thus, while early horizontal or vertical mergers caused the *concentration* of economic power within each specific industry, the conglomerate mergers led further toward *centralization* of power in one giant corporation relating to a variety of differentiated industries. Table 1-2 illustrates the extent of this concentration. The top 500 controlled 65 percent of sale and 74 percent of the profit, while, the next 500 had 7 percent of sale and 6 percent of profits.

## Competition in a Monopolistic Market

The rise of giant corporations caused significant transformation in competition and market operation. The competition is now among monopolistic firms.[18] It would be more realistic if along with monopolistic corporations we also take into consideration the existence of many smaller firms that enter in many ways into calculations 49 and strategies of giant corporations. However, the dominant factor, the prime mover, real profit maximizer and capital accumulator is a small cluster of giant corporations.

**Table 1-2: The Economic Powers of Giant Industrial Corporations 1973 (in billions of dollars)**

| Corporations | Assets | Sales | Sales | Profits | Industrial Employment |
|---|---|---|---|---|---|
| Top 25 | 238 | 313 | 36% | 41% | 42% |
| Top 500 | 486 | 558 | 65% | 74% | 75% |
| Next 500 | 46 | 59 | 7% | 6% | 9% |
| The rest | --- | --- | 28% | 20% | 16% |

Source: Calculated from *Fortune*, May, 1971, May, 1972, May and June, 1973.

These huge economic institutions embody industrial corporations, utilities, banks, insurance companies, and investment firms. Their decisions affect daily lives of citizens more than any other factor, including decisions made by the government. The extent of their control over economic resources establishes a power base capable of determining the basic social, economic and political norms within a country and even beyond its borders. They determine the nature, quantity and quality of goods and services to be produced, the production process and technologies to be used and developed, the manner of distribution, the extent of costs, wages and profits, availability of loans for capital investment, terms of loans, and interest rates and an array of other important decisions. Yet, the number of institutions that yield such controlling power is unbelievably small in the United States as well as among industrialized countries. According to 1980 statistics 100 out of 197,807 industrial corporations controlled

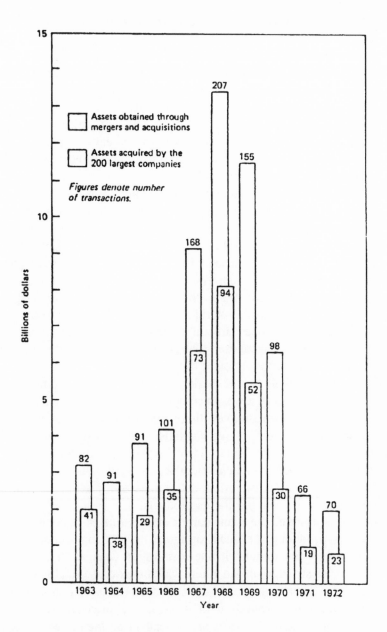

Source: Edwards, Reich and Weisskopf, *The Capitalist System*, 2nd ed. (Englewood Cliffs, N.J.: Prentice-Hall, 1978), p. 129.

55 percent of all industrial assets, with the first fourteen controlling over twenty-five percent of the total. In the fields of transportation, communications, and utilities, only 50 corporations out of 67,000 controlled over two-thirds of the total assets. Among 17,700 commercial banks, 50 institutions controlled 61.3 percent of all banking assets. Three banks alone controlled 19.4 percent of all banking assets, nearly one out of every five dollars. Fifty insurance companies, among 1,890, controlled over 75 percent of all insurance assets. Prudential and Metropolitan alone controlled nearly one quarter of all insurance assets.[19]

The concentration of production and distribution of power in a small group of large institutions is not an exclusively American phenomenon. Developments since World War II have made it global. It includes the industrial nations of Europe, Japan and several oil producing Third World Countries. The result has been the emergence of supernational global corporations with a multinational base of operation. Table 1-3 illustrates the assets of fifty of the largest industrial corporations in the world. Twenty-one of these firms are American, and 12 of those are oil corporations. Seven firms are German and only five Japanese. Oil corporations dominate the list, numbering 22 and occupying eight of the top ten.

In monopoly capitalism, the market is still the controlling factor in relations of production as it was in competitive capitalism preceding it. The essential difference between these two systems relates to price mechanism. Under competitive capitalism each firm relied on the market price. The market determined the price and the corporations took that price and adjusted their prices accordingly. Under monopoly capitalism, the giant corporation determines the price. *It simply chooses prices* to be charged for its products.

Under this system, the giant corporation is one of several major corporations producing products of more or less the same use or substitutable to one another. If one corporation changes its prices, it affects the price structure of the others which may cause retaliation and price rivalry. Therefore, under these circumstances it is practically impossible for one corporation to determine a price which would maximize profits, since its prices are dependent on the prices charged by its rivals. This kind of price competition was a common situation in the earlier phases of monopoly capitalism. It still occurs now and then but it is not typical of monopoly capitalism today. To avoid such situations has become the prime concern in the corporate policy-making process for orderly and profitable operations. This cooperative direction in the policy-making process has gradually established the tendency toward recognizing improperness of price cutting and appropriateness of its elimination. The observance of this policy has gradually removed the dangerous uncertainties from the proper pursuit of profit and its maximization.

However, one essential condition for following this no-price-cut policy has been that the established prices should tend to maximize the profits of the monopoly group as a whole. An agreement in total output has been determinant of the price structure. It has turned the rivalry from price competition to share of the market and profits.

Though the purpose of the pricing process is to maximize group profits, its form differs widely according to circumstances.

Generally, the largest and most powerful corporation within an industry group assuming leadership, determines the price; others adopt it for their products. The tendency to go along with this leadership price rests upon two essential facts: its profitability to each firm within the group, and the capability of the leader to stand pressures better than any other firm in the group in case of a price warfare.[20]

However, this is not the only method of price determination. The pattern may vary. In some cases the giant corporations within an industry may take turns initiating price changes, or different firms may take the lead in different regional markets or at different times. If the pattern of leadership is fairly regular these prices may be considered as modified forms of price leadership.

So long as all firms in a group accept this pattern of practice, maintaining the ban on price competition and the way toward determining the price, which maximizes the group's profits, is clearly established. This is the method of approximation to the theoretical monopoly price. It must be noted that whether the price establishment is through the strict authoritarian way of price leadership or by the tacit consent of group members, the purpose is the same—the maximization of profits for the group as a whole.

### Table 1-3:  The 50 Largest Industrial Corporations in the World

| Rank 1980 | Rank 1981 | Company | Headquarters | Sales ($000) | Net Income ($000) |
|---|---|---|---|---|---|
| 1 | 1 | Exxon | New York | 108,107,688 | 5,567,481 |
| 2 | 2 | Royal Dutch/ Shell Group | The Hague/London | 82,291,728 | 3,567,481 |
| 3 | 3 | Mobil | New York | 64,488,000 | 5,567,481 |
| 4 | 4 | General Motors | Detroit | 62,698,500 | 333,400 |
| 5 | 5 | Texaco | Harrison, N.Y. | 57,628,000 | 2,310,000 |
| 6 | 6 | British Petroleum | London | 52,199,976 | 2,063,272 |
| 7 | 7 | Standard Oil of California | San Francisco | 44,224,000 | 2,380,000 |
| 8 | 8 | Ford Motor | Dearborn, Mich. | 38,247,100 | (1,060,100) |
| 12 | 9 | Standard Oil (Ind.) | Chicago | 29,947,000 | 1,922,000 |
| 9 | 10 | ENI | Rome | 29,444,315 | 383,234 |
| 11 | 11 | International Business Machines | Armonk, N.Y. | 29,070,000 | 3,308,000 |
| 10 | 12 | Gulf Oil | Pittsburgh | 28,252,000 | 1,231,000 |
| 16 | 13 | Atlantic Richfield | Los Angeles | 27,797,436 | 1,671,290 |
| 14 | 14 | General Electric | Fairfield, Conn. | 27,240,000 | 1,652,000 |
| 17 | 15 | Unilever | London/Rotterdam | 24,095,898 | 800,379 |
| 38 | 16 | E.I. du Pont de Memours | Wilmington, Del. | 22,810,000 | 1,401,000 |
| 15 | 17 | Francaise des Petroles | Paris | 22,784,032 | 175,807 |
| 18 | 18 | Shell Oil | Houston | 21,629,000 | 1,701,000 |
|  | 19 | Kuwait Petroleum | Safat (Kuwait) | 20,556,871 | 1,690,312 |
| 22 | 20 | Elf-Aquitaine | Paris | 19,666,141 | 682,316 |
| 20 | 21 | Petroleos de Venezuela | Caracus | 19,659,115 | 3,316,040 |
| 13 | 22 | Fiat | Turin (Italy) | 19,608,480 | NA |
| 33 | 23 | Petrobras (Petroleo Brasileiro) | Rio de Janeiro | 18,946,056 | 831,215 |
| 34 | 24 | Pemex (Petroleos Mexicanos) | Mexico City | 18,804,190 | 40,790 |

| | | | | | |
|---|---|---|---|---|---|
| 21 | 25 | International Telephone & Tel. | New York | 17,306,189 | 676,804 |
| 23 | 26 | Philips' Gloeilampenfabrieken | Eindhoven (Neth.) | 17,069,155 | 143,682 |
| 24 | 27 | Volkswagenwerk | Wolfsburg (Ger.) | 16,822,215 | 99,451 |
| 27 | 28 | Daimler-Benz | Stuttgart | 16,281,398 | 365,212 |
| 37 | 29 | Nissan Motor | Yokohama (Japan) | 16,245,315 | 490,200 |
| 19 | 30 | Renault | Paris | 16,229,762 | (124,916) |
| 26 | 31 | Siemens | Munich | 16,029,835 | 208,157 |
| 39 | 32 | Phillips Petroleum | Bartelsville, OK | 15,966,000 | 879,000 |
| 45 | 33 | Matsushita Electric Industrial | Osaka (Japan) | 15,738,106 | 714,675 |
| 36 | 34 | Toyota Motor | Toyota City (Japan) | 15,712,540 | 619,666 |
| 44 | 35 | Hitachi | Tokyo | 15,519,416 | 596,363 |
| 41 | 36 | Tenneco | Houston | 15,462,000 | 813,000 |
| 29 | 37 | Hoechst | Frankfurt | 15,292,750 | 132,167 |
| 42 | 38 | Nippon Steel | Tokyo | 15,196,945 | 341,196 |
| 43 | 39 | Sun | Randor, Pa. | 15,012,000 | 1,076,000 |
| 30 | 40 | Bayer | Leverkusen (Ger.) | 14,985,272 | 224,639 |
| 47 | 41 | Occidental Petroleum | Los Angeles | 14,707,543 | 722,216 |
| | 42 | BAT Industries | London | 14,301,022 | 370,903 |
| 35 | 43 | Nestle | Vevey (Switz.) | 14,172,074 | 492,604 |
| 46 | 44 | U.S. Steel | Pittsburgh | 13,940,500 | 1,077,200 |
| 31 | 45 | BASF | Ludwigshafen | 13,707,434 | 162,890 |
| 48 | 46 | United Technologies | Hartford | 13,667,758 | 457,686 |
| 50 | 47 | Stadard Oil (Ohio) | Cleveland | 13,457,091 | 1,946,898 |
| 28 | 48 | Peugeot | Paris | 13,396,308 | (368,825) |
| 40 | 49 | Imperial Chemical Industries | London | 13,338,305 | 376,983 |
| 32 | 50 | Thyssen | Duisburg (Ger.) | <u>13,063,961</u> | <u>(32,341)</u> |
| | | Totals | | 1,282,816,420 | 50,937,083 |

Source: "The Largest Industrial Companies in the World" *Fortune*, Aug. 23, 1982, pp. 181-183, 192, and 106.

Competition between giant firms does not end by the ban on price competition. It simply shifts to sales competition which continues with increasing intensity. The purpose here is a non-price competition directed toward increasing the volume of sale and share of the market. The corporation with lower cost and higher profits, enjoys a variety of advantages over the others. The corporation with the lowest cost can afford to be aggressive, spend more on advertising, research and development of new products and the betterment of the old ones. All these tend to provide for a greater share of the market. In such a non-price rivalry, the efforts by all participating firms are aimed toward cutting the costs.

The maximization of profit is the main cause for motivation to reduce the costs. In a monopolistic structure of the market, the motivation to reduce costs tends to maximize profits and enables the giant corporations to appropriate the lion's share of returns, from increasing productivity, in the form of higher profits.

Advertising plays an enormous role in maximizing profits, and expenditures in advertising has increased phenomenally and the growth of the advertising business has been astronomical.[21] The purpose is to penetrate the mind and instill the unquestioned desirability and the imperative necessity of owning the presented product. In order to make the strategy work, producers are obliged to pour on the market a steady flow of so called new products. Much of the newness with which consumers are bombarded is either fraudulent or only trivially related to the function and serviceability of the product. It does not necessarily have a positive or more advanced effect.

Therefore, under the dominance of oligopoly and monopoly, there has emerged a condition in which the production and sales functions interpenetrate and tend to become indistinguishable. This produces a profound change in cost concept. It affects what constitutes sociable necessary costs of production, and the nature of the social product itself.

The ability of the corporations to raise prices depends on the extent of their monopoly power. Furthermore, they can raise their prices as long as such price increases do not become inducive for other large firms to enter the market to capture part from the high profits.

However, the crucial factor for high profits in monopolistic market is not prices, but reduction in the cost of production. The large scale of most monopolistic firms often enables them to reduce per-unit costs far more and more effectively than smaller corporations. Giant corporations are better equipped to cut down costs through long range planning, more rational calculation of profit opportunities, employment of more efficient technologies for large scale production, vertical integration, high volume purchases and manipulation of product market through better coordination of production and demand.

However, it must not remain unnoticed that though in monopolistic competition the cost of production may be reduced, the cost of marketing tends to increase through intensive sales efforts such as advertising, redesigning more visually and physically appealing products, extensive market research, etc. All these efforts are considered necessary and essential, in non-price competitive markets, for maintaining and possibly enlarging the share of the market. The extent of higher profits for each corporation depends on the interplay of all these forces.

If we take into account what has actually happened, and look at the data, we find that, overall, monopolistic firms have earned persistently higher profit rates than other firms.[22] Furthermore, profits tend to be even higher in industries where very few corporations control a big share of the market.[23] Profits are still higher where barriers created by the monopolistic nature of the industry prevents outside corporations from entering the market.[24]

Since monopolistic industries on the average are more profitable than competitive ones they are given the opportunity for better accumulation of capital. Furthermore, while in competitive industries, inequalities in profits will be evened out by the free flow of capital from low-profit to high-profit sectors, in monopolistic systems outside capital is prevented from flowing into monopolistic industries with high profits.

## Reinvestment in a Monopolistic Market

If there is sufficient "aggregate demand" for the output of the economy to employ both the means of production and the labor force, boom conditions will occur as a result of high profits, and accumulation of capital will tend to proceed rapidly. If the level of "aggregate demand" be insufficient, resulting in idle factories and unemployed workers, reduced accumulation of capital will cause stagnation and depression conditions will emerge.

Capitalists produce two major types of output: consumption goods to consumers and capital goods to other capitalist investors. Though consumption goods are by far the largest part of aggregate sales and the level of sales is an important determinant of the level of economic activity nonetheless, consumers by and large spend most of their incomes, which is in turn dependent on the level of economic activity as a whole. Therefore, consumer spending per se is not an important independent cause of depression or prosperity. Simply because if the consumers earn more, they spend more; if they earn less, they spend less.

It is the investment on capital goods and services which is significant and a relatively independent determinant of the level of economic activity. As profits are earned capital is accumulated. The crucial decision is whether or not this accumulated capital should be reinvested. If it is, the demand for investment goods will rise and lead to increased employment and higher wages. The increased "aggregate income" will increase consumer spending, cause full employment and further increase in output. If the accumulated capital is not reinvested, demand for investment goods will fall, employment and wage income will decrease, demand for consumer goods will sink resulting in decreased output and stagnation. Capitalists will tend to reinvest when there is a strong likelihood of large returns. They will be reluctant to do so if future profits appear meager.

Monopolistic competition tends to reduce incentive for each firm to reinvest in its own industry.[25] Competitive firms are continually under pressure by their competitors to invest in new technologies in order to reduce the costs. If they don't, the competitors will invest and ultimately drive out of business the noninvesting firms. Monopolistic firms are not threatened by such competition. They choose when, how and where to invest in new technologies.

Furthermore, in competitive capitalism, new investments are often desirable or profitable if there is an opportunity for the expansion of production. However, in monopolistic capitalism, extra output can be sold when the industry's market can be expanded. Since the market is divided between competing firms within the monopolistic industry, there is little chance of the expansion of markets by one or more of these firms. Consequently, monopolistic firms tend to be less willing to invest in new technologies to expand output within the industry.[26]

If we consider that because of market barriers-to-entry, one monopolistic industry is highly restricted to invest in other monopolistic industries, the only expansion outlet seems to be possible in the market areas of competitive corporations. The enormous changes occur in technologies used in production and marketing, in the kinds of products, and in required skills and relocation of positions. In all these areas, competitive corporations, though striving for technological innovations, tend to be more stagnant because of their limited financial and technological resources. Thus, these firms, being continually under invasion by the monopolistic firms, gradually shrink toward growing stagnation in the areas of monopolized production and are either taken over by a large firm or disappear.

One must be aware of the fact that though incentive to invest is a significant factor in determining economic activity, there are other factors as well, such as technical change and innovation, appearance of new industries and new lines of products, investment in foreign markets, etc. These factors generally tend to offset the impact of monopoly until they themselves become monopolized. Furthermore, one should not disregard the importance of public expenditures. In times of stagnation, appropriate public spending may take up the slack, at least temporarily.

## NOTES

1. Friedrick Engels, "Letter to Block", September 21, 1890; Karl Marx, *The Eighteenth Brumaire of Louis Bonaparte* (New York: International Publishers, 1963).

2. Paul Sweezy, *The Theory of Capitalist Development* (New York: Monthly Review Press, 1942), p. 15.

3. Excerpted from the preface to *A Contribution to the Critique of Political Economy by Karl Marx*, 1859.

4. Marx's theory has served as a guide to the entire discipline of "sociology of knowledge," embracing analytical history of art, literature, religion and science all deriving inspiration and guidance from the same source. His theory of alienation is

a central point in modern study and criticism of culture. His political theory has formed a focal point and provided a conceptual basis that has proved extremely valuable in modern American as well as European scholarship. Among his many excellent scholarly writings *The Eighteenth Brumaire of Louis Bonaparte* is an unsurpassed gem of historical and sociological study which still shines as a model of a comprehensive and penetrating analysis of the significant links between economic and non-economic behavior concerned with one particular historical case.

5. For a short but excellent explanation of the subject see Paul Baran and Eric Hobsbaurn, "The Stages of Economic Growth," *Kyklos*, 14, No. 2, 1961.

6. Richard Caves, *American Industry: Structure, Conduct, Performance* (Englewood Cliffs, NJ: Prentice-Hall, 1967), p. 1.

7. Robert Heilbroner, *The Limits of American Capitalism* (New York: Harper and Row, 1965), p. 13.

8. For brief explanation see Thomas R. Dye, *Who's Running America?* 4th ed. (Englewood Cliffs, NJ: Prentice-Hall, 1983), particularly Chapters 1 and 2; Michael Parenti, *Democracy For the Few*, 4th ed. (New York: St. Martin's Press, 1983), Chapters 2, 5 and 6; for characteristics of these corporations see Morton Mintz and Jerry S. Cohen, *Power, Inc.* (Des Plaines, IL: Bantam Books, 1977), Chapters 3 and 5.

9. Paul Baran and Paul Sweezy, *Monopoly Capital* (New York: Monthly Review Press, 1966), p. 47.

10. In 1972, for example, there were only 13 million U.S. firms of which only 3,000 had assets in excess of 100 million. *Statistical Abstract of the United States*, 1975, pp. 490 and 497.

11. This table is taken from Richard Edwards, M. Reich and T.E. Weisskopf, *The Capitalist System*, 2nd ed. (Englewood Cliffs, NJ: Prentice-Hall, 1978), p. 119.

12. Richard Edwards, *op. cit.*, p. 126.

13. Ibid., p. 127.

14. See Matthew Josephson, *The Robber Barons* (New York: Harcourt Brace Jovanovich, 1934).

15. Richard Edwards, *op. cit.*, p. 129.

16. *Fortune*, April, 1973.

17. In the 1960's, for example, eight major conglomerates were developed: ITT, Gulf and Western, Ling-Temco-Vaught, Occidental Petroleum, Tenneco, White Consolidated, Teledyne, and Litton Industries. See John M. Blair, *Economic Concentration: Structure, Behavior and Public Policy* (New York: Harcourt Brace Jovanovich, 1972), p. 285.

18. Paul Baran and Paul M. Sweezy, *Monopoly Capital* (New York: Monthly Review Press, 1966), Chapters 3 and 5.

19. See Thomas R. Dye, *Who's Running America?*, 3rd. ed. (Englewood Cliffs, NJ: Prentice-Hall, 1983), p. 20.

20. For a detailed explanation of this concept, see Arthur B. Burns, *The Decline of Competition: A Study of the Evolution of American Industry* (New York: Greenwood Hse., 1936).

21. Spending on advertising media amounted to only $360 million in 1890, totaled $10.3 billion in 1957 and reached over $26.5 billion in 1974.

22. William Shepherd, *Market Power and Economic Welfare* (New York: Random House, 1970).

23. See Marshall Hall and Leonard Weiss, "Firm Size and Profitability," *Review of Economics and Statistics*, August, 1967.

24. See Joe S. Bain, *Industrial Organization* (New York: Wiley, 1968). See also Harold Demsetz, *The Market Concentration Doctrine* (Washington, DC: American Enterprise Institute, 1973).

25. Paul Baran, *Political Economy of Growth* (New York: Monthly Review Press, 1957), Chapter 3.

26. Ibid.

*CHAPTER 2.*

# GROWTH OF FINANCE MONOPOLY

From monopolistic control of production industries, we now direct our attention to more important steps toward capital accumulation and monopoly; the growth of finance capital which enables the extension of financial control over corporations large and small and the further emergence of huge financial groups.

## Corporate Control Through Finance Capital

Though there are different kinds of financial institutions, giant banks and insurance companies are the two most important as far as monopoly capital is concerned. Banks take in money from depositors, to hold, invest or transfer. They control great amounts of financial assets, such as cash deposits, stocks, bonds, mortgages, promissory notes, trust funds, etc. The capitalists controlling such giant financial institutions have enormous resources for investment of which they individually own only a small fraction. Table 2-1 illustrates the enormous financial power of the 25 largest commercial banking institutions out of some 15,000 such companies in the United States. The top fifty have control over 64 percent of total commercial banking assets. The top twelve control over 40 percent, and the top three only, control nearly 20 percent of the total assets.

The 50 largest life-insurance companies out of some 1900, have control over nearly 81 percent of the total life insurance assets. The top nine companies control nearly 52 percent of these assets.

These facts represent the extent of capital concentration in the hands of a few firms, resulting in the monopolistic character of control over financial assets as well as their investment. These institutions invest the available resources in non-financial firms and, thus, become industrial capitalists. The fusion of this capital and production capital is termed *finance capital*. When finance capitalists have invested in an industrial corporation to the extent of controlling or influencing its policies, *financial control* over the corporation has taken place. When several financial institutions combine their assets and jointly control production firms, they form what is termed as a *financial group*.

Table 2-2 presents the top 25 financial groups which possess an enormous economic power and a central strategic position in the American economy. As illustrated later on in this chapter, these few financial groups are in a position to determine the terms under which corporations in the need of capital can issue and sell stocks, bonds, and other securities. For operational purpose, these groups, often joining together in a large syndicate, underwrite the sale of such new securities and sell them mainly to their own client investors.

The rise of finance capital has permitted the most important capitalists to diversify their production interests and thus create what is known as a *conglomerate*, which is a profit-making and accumulation device divorced from the constraints of a single industry. Control of finance capital multiplies the power of capitalists and tends to accelerate the identification of leading capitalists with the entire capitalist economy.

Financial control relieves capitalists from the burdens of management and allows the collection of profits without being directly concerned with the extraction of surplus value. Leaving the operation to highly paid managers, corporate owners disappear into the background, and their interests are metamorphosed into corporate imperatives without their intervention. Thus, the need to earn a "sufficient" profit rate appears to outsiders as an unchangeable constraint imposed by impersonal capital market forces.

## Table 2-1: The Top 25 U.S. commercial Banking Companies Ranked by Assets

| RANK | | COMPANY | ASSETS[1] | DEPOSITS | LOANS[2] |
|---|---|---|---|---|---|
| 1 | 1 | Citicorp (New York) | 196,124,000 | 114,689,000 | 129,206,000 |
| 2 | 2 | BankAmerica Corp. (San Franciscon | 104,189,000 | 82,205,000 | 71,783,000 |
| 3 | 3 | Chase Manhattan Corp (New York | 94,765,815 | 66,002,844 | 65,154,782 |
| 4 | 5 | J.P. Morgan & Co. (New York) | 76,039,000 | 42,960,000 | 33,783,000 |
| 5 | 4 | Manufacturers Hanover Corp. (New York) | 74,397,389 | 45,544,277 | 55,264,518 |
| 6 | 7 | Security Pacific Corp. (Los Angeles) | 62,606,000 | 38,408,000 | 43,586,000 |
| 7 | 6 | Chemical New York Corp. | 60,564,123 | 39,054,910 | 38,756,475 |
| 8 | 8 | Bankers Trust New York Corp. | 56,419,945 | 29,535,520 | 28,610,057 |
| 9 | 9 | First Interstate Bancorp (Los Angeles) | 55,421,736 | 39,457,006 | 33,987,675 |
| 10 | 13 | Wells Fargo & Co. (San Francisco) | 44,577,100 | 32,992,800 | 36,037,100 |
| 11 | 10 | First Chicago Corp. | 39,147,996 | 27,024,943 | 24,825,398 |
| 12 | 11 | Melion Bank Corp. (Pittsburg) | 34,499,370 | 21,647,152 | 23,034,755 |
| 13 | 14 | Bank of Boston Corp. | 34,045,409 | 21,724,988 | 23,624,992 |
| 14 | 12 | Continental Illinois Corp. (Chicago) | 32,809,000 | 18,032,000 | 20,207,000 |
| 15 | 15 | First Bank System (Minneapolis) | 28,012,000 | 16,261,000 | 14,640,000 |
| 16 | 23 | NCNB Corp. (Charlotte, N.C.) | 27,472,434 | 18,519,315 | 15,528,982 |
| 17 | 32 | First Union Corp. (Charlotte, N.C.) | 26,820,240 | 17,003,549 | 13,799,947 |
| 18 | 24 | SunTrust Banks (Atlanta) | 26,165,455 | 21,284,007 | 16,642,080 |
| 19 | 16 | Marine Midland Banks (Buffalo and New York) | 24,789,596 | 17,418,418 | 18,420,839 |
| 20 | 20 | Irving Bank Corp. | 24,232,521 | 15,327,955 | 13,793,148 |

| 21 | 28 | Bank of New England Corp. (Boston) | 22,472,935 | 17,676,987 | 15,965,000 |
| 22 | 26 | PNC Financial Corp. (Pittsburgh) | 22,198,930 | 14,315,971 | 12,397,404 |
| 23 | 18 | MCorp (Dallas) | 21,887,000 | 17,492,000 | 14,560,000 |
| 24 | 21 | Norwest Corp. (Minneapolis) | 21,539,400 | 14,099,800 | 13,033,900 |
| 25 | 31 | NBD Bancorp (Detroit) | 21,176,031 | 15,011,323 | 11,151,316 |

Source: *Fortune*, June 8, 1987 p. 200

**Table 2-2: The 25 Largest Diversified U.S. Financial Companies Ranked by Assets**

| RANK | | COMPANY | ASSETS[1] | REVENUES[2] | NET INCOME |
|------|------|---------|--------|----------|------------|
| 1986 | 1985 | | $ THOUSANDS | $ THOUSANDS | $ THOUSANDS |
| 1 | 1 | Federal Nat'l Mortgage Ass'n (Washington, D.C.) | 100,406,000 | 10,540,000 | 183,000 |
| 2 | 2 | American Express (New York) | 99,476,000 | 14,562,000 | 1,250,000 |
| 3 | • | Solomon (New York) | 78,164,000 | 6,789,000 | 516,000 |
| 4 | 3 | Aetna Life & Casualty (Hartford) | 53,013,471 | 9,606,349 | 454,349 |
| 5 | 4 | Merrill Lynch (New York) | 53,013,471 | 9,606,349 | 454,349 |
| 6 | 6 | CIGNA (Philadelphia) | 50,015,800 | 17,064,100 | 817,300 |
| 7 | 5 | First Boston (New York) | 48,618,206 | 1,309,765 | 180,555 |
| 8 | 7 | Travelers Corp. (Hartford) | 46,299,600 | 16,046,600 | 545,800 |
| 9 | • | Morgan Stanley Group (New York) | 29,190,361 | 2,463,484 | 201,250 |
| 10 | 8 | Bear Stearns Cos. (New York) | 26,939,440 | 1,188,951 | 89,474 |
| 11 | 9 | E.F. Hutton Group (New York) | 25,921,257 | 3,504,927 | (90,286) |
| 12 | 11 | American Internation Group (New York) | 21,022,868 | 9,704,119 | 795,827 |
| 13 | 10 | Loews (New York) | 10,024,309 | 8,625,988 | 545,503 |
| 14 | 12 | Student Loan Marketing Ass'n (Washington, D.C.) | 18,232,065 | 1,376,785 | 144,559 |

| 15 | 15 | Lincoln National (Fort Wayne) | 16,243,838 | 5,998,713 | 284,392 |
|---|---|---|---|---|---|
| 16 | 13 | Transamerica (San Francisco) | 16,181,783 | 7,119,688 | 267,541 |
| 17 | 14 | Paine Webber Group (New York) | 14,725,750 | 2,384,720 | 71,599 |
| 18 | 16 | Continental (New York) | 13,623,225 | 6,002,273 | 449,632 |
| 19 | • | Household International (Prospect Heights, Ill.) | 13,206,600 | 3,825,400 | 208,600 |
| 20 | 21 | Fleet Financial Group (Providence, R.I.) | 11,690,346 | 1,207,513 | 136,744 |
| 21 | 17 | Kemper (Long Grove, Ill.) | 9,735,091 | 3,329,897 | 201,110 |
| 22 | 19 | Fireman's Fund (Novato, Calif.) | 9,178,000 | 3,699,000 | 228,000 |
| 23 | 20 | USF&G (Baltimore) | 8,935,993 | 4,336,783 | 296,330 |
| 24 | 23 | General Re (Stamford, Conn.) | 8,676,600 | 3,175,200 | 328,700 |
| 25 | 22 | St. Paul Cos. | 7,627,082 | 3,181,587 | 217,114 |

Source: *Fortune*, June 8, 1987 p. 204

This financial control provides opportunity for centralization on a much broader base, far beyond those of monopolistic industries. A financial group is well capable of coordinating policies of all firms it controlled for the purpose of maximizing profits as a whole. Such control, of course, further erodes the role of competition within the economy. Thus, to understand the extent to which the whole economy is controlled one needs to find out the extent of monopolized control by financial institutions.

Monopoly capitalism did not become established in the United States until the end of the nineteenth century and beginning of the twentieth. This transformation from competitive to monopoly capitalism became effectuated by concentration of economic power in a small number of productive industries enabling them to dominate the economy.[1]

Concurrent with this process of industrial concentration there occurred also a concentration of power in the hands of a small group through the control of ownership. We may appropriately term this group the monopoly capitalist class. Monopoly profits which provided the basis for rapid and enormous accumulation of wealth tended to concentrate economic power in a few families whose individual fortunes exceeded one billion dollars but were in control of hundreds of billion dollars of corporate assets. The Rockefellers, Mellons, DuPonts, Morgans, and Gettys are examples of these monopolistic class families. Though there were thousands of other multi-millionaire capitalists, it was the monopoly capitalists group which dominated the economy and determined its direction.

In the United States today, there are two major opposing views about control of large corporations. The first is the financial control concept, according to which financial institutions are the most important controlling force over major non-financial corporations concerned with production of goods, services, and distribution. According to this view, two or more financial institutions combining together their capital power form a financial group. This group in turn, through various means at its disposal establishes controlling authority over one or more large production or distribution corporations.

The second view is the managerial control concept. This view holds that, on the one hand, because of wider dispersal of stockholding in large firms in recent decades, the stockholders have lost their collective controlling power. On the other hand, the high profits trend in the modern large corporations has tended to free them from dependence on external sources of financing. Both of these trends have caused a steady weakening of the power and influence of financial institutions over these large production and distribution firms.

As a consequence, the top management in each firm, which has been gradually able to free itself form the yoke of the financial firms and mandate of the stockholders, has become the major policy-making body and has taken over the operation as well as the direction of the corporations. However, these managers who have climbed up from the lower echelons of the corporation executive hierarchy, in general, do not own a significant size of the corporation's stock; their assets are mainly their authority under their top executive position, their technical knowledge and experience in administering a large specialized corporation. Accordingly, this view holds that this top management group of large corporations have come to form a new leading component of the monopoly capitalist class.

62 / Technodemocratic Economic Theory

According to this management control view, large corporations, in general, tend to operate independent from one another.  Whereas, under the financial control view, the control power over these production and distribution firms are further centralized, concentrated and consolidated under the domain of a large and powerful financial group.  The monopolistic collusion among large corporations leads to a rapid process of centralization of capital through mergers during which the financial institutions make their entry and tend to establish their influence and control.  Recent evidence strongly supports the validity of the latter view.

## Historical Background

The nature of control over the modern large corporations cannot be fully understood without looking into its evolution from over a century of struggle between rivals within the capitalist class.

In the mid-nineteenth century when Karl Marx wrote his famous Communist Manifesto and later published the first volume of his classical essay *Das Kapital* the economy of advanced countries like Great Britain and the United States operated through relatively small, local firms.  The companies were normally controlled by a single individual or a small group of proprietors.  When the corporate form was devised the same individual or group controlled through ownership of a majority of the stock.

The consolidation and concentration took shape during the 1870's and 1880's.  In the United States great consolidations of many local railroads into larger entities took place during the 1880s.  Since railroad companies were not able to provide capital, from their own resources, for their rapid development, they turned to investment institutions for capital.  These institutions supplied capital to corporations by purchasing new bonds, stocks, and other long-term securities issued by the borrowing corporation.

The major U.S. investment institutions were located in New York and used the available European capital to finance railroad expansion. J.P. Morgan investment bank had access to the British capital market and Kuhn, Loeb and Company to the German.  Though the New York investment banks did not compete for one another's traditional clients, the railroads they financed followed an unrestrained competition causing waste and inefficiency. Rate-cutting wars resulted in substantial losses to all parties and were alarming to the creditor investment banks. Numerous efforts by the banks to create cooperation between the railroads, rather than competition, failed. When the Panic of 1893 occurred most of the large railroads which had become weakened by long rate-cutting wars could not survive the ensuing depression and went into receivership. This situation provided a golden opportunity for J.P. Morgan and Kuhn, Loeb and Company to take direct control of the railroads on behalf of stock holders they represented. They consolidated the railroads and established a cooperative, monopolistic system.[2]

## Financial Control of Manufacturing Industries

The late nineteenth century witnessed rapidly growing industries in raw materials, petroleum, agriculture and a variety of machineries. Soon these industries encountered cut-throat competition among rival industries and failed in cooperative attempts, similar to those which the railroads had faced previously. A very few, such as petroleum and tobacco industries, succeeded in limiting competition by merger. For many other industries competition continued until the 1890's depression, when the investment institutions were allowed the opportunity to interfere, and foster by financing mergers among the major competing firms.

Between 1898 and 1903 thousands of firms participated in the "Great Merger Movement".[3] Some seventy-eight of the trusts formed during this period obtained at least one-half of the market for their product. The advancement of control by the investment banks substantially increased the extent of monopoly power in the production industries. The institutions financing the merger received, on the one hand, a huge "promoter's profits", and on the other hand, a chance to share in the long-term profits ascertained by the resulting monopoly power.

The beginning of the twentieth century witnesses the emergence of strong financial groups which dominated the basic means of production and distribution, and the economy as a whole. These financial groups were formed by close association of two or more major financial institutions such as investment banks, commercial banks, life insurance corporations, with non-financial production and distribution firms. The center of control was the participating financial institutions.[4] By 1915 the leading financial groups and institutions had established control over most of the production, distribution and petroleum industries.

Though, by the start of the Great Depression of the 1930's, dominant individuals who had personified financial control passed away, the financial structure they had created remained active. During the 1920's, electric and gas utilities began to grow rapidly and issued a high volume of bonds. The New York groups, by using the device of a holding company, established control over them to the extent that by 1929 ten large public utilities holding company systems controlled about three-fourths of the electric power services in the United States.

However, the financial monopoly did not remain dominated by the New York groups. The 1920's witnessed a rising of new centers of financial powers in Chicago, San Francisco, and Cleveland. But during the Great Depression and World War II, the investment institutions faced hardships. The large production industries used very little external finance, since depreciation allowances were generally sufficient to finance the corporation's reduced level of production. Furthermore, when the economy prospered during World War II, the government, as an external source, supplied most of the capital for industrial expansion. As a result, thousands of investment as well as commercial banks went out of business; while the largest ones survived, their activities were sharply curtailed.

After World War II, industrial corporations returned to the use of external finance,[5] which caused a resurgence of power of financial institutions.

In recent decades there has been a transformation in the basis of power of the finance institutions. The power base has been shifted from control over the financing process to control over the stock of the borrowing corporations. This change has been mainly due to rapid growth of trust departments in commercial banks where the wealthy capitalists placed their fortunes in bank-managed trusts, and by means of which, they avoided taxation and prevented dissipation of the fortune through bad spending habits of heirs. The trust department of the bank invested and managed money placed in trusts. Often the money placed in trusts was in forms of stocks and bonds and other long-term securities, income from which generally went to trust beneficiaries but the capital remained under the bank's control often with the right to vote on stocks.

The importance and power of these trust departments was further magnified by gradually assuming control over pension funds. These private pension funds has increased phenomenally from under $2 billion in 1945 to about $157 billion in 1972. Most of these funds are managed by banks, which invest them largely in corporate stock and usually hold full voting rights over these stocks. Consequently, a huge amount of corporate stock, 25 percent by 1972, has been placed under the control of the leading banks.[6] It is expected that these holdings of corporate stock by financial institutions would reach 55 percent by the end of the century.[7]

Table 2-3 presents the overall result of a study of control over 200 largest non-financial corporations in the United States for 1967-1969.[8] Of a majority of 55 percent, 39 percent were found to be controlled by financial institutions, 21.5 percent by individual stockholders.

Table 2-4 indicates the extent of holding of the major financial institutions. The study reveals that financial control was most prevalent among the middle-sized corporations within the top 200. The very large corporations were so enormous that, in most cases, none of the financial groups could hold a sufficiently large amount of stock, or supply of sufficiently large amount of loaned capital, to obtain control. However, in many cases, these large corporations had representatives of several leading financial groups on their boards. It appeared that control over the large corporations could often be shared among several contributing financial groups and institutions. Several studies conclude that financial control has become the most important type of control over top corporations, and the amount of stock controlled by finance institutions is constantly growing.

## The Consequences of Financial Control

Economic concentration through mergers, and encouragement by the financial institutions of cooperative behavior among competing firms has enormously increased their monopoly power. The tendency toward collusion, in many industries in order to maintain cooperation and avoid competition, has further strengthened the position of financial firms. Today, their power is an important force for fraud and

## 66 / Technodemocratic Economic Theory

**Table 2-3 Summary of Control Over the 200 Largest Nonfinancial Corporations, 1967-69**

| | COMPANIES | |
|---|---|---|
| CONTROL CATEGORY | NUMBER | PERCENT |
| Financial control | 78 | 39.0 |
| Owner control | 43 | 21.5 |
| Financial or owner control* | 110 | 55.0 |
| Miscellaneous** | 5 | 2.5 |
| No identified center of control | 85 | 42.5 |
| No suspected or confirmed center of control | 61 | 30.5 |

*There is overlap between these categories in 11 corporations. Hence, the figure 110 is less than the sum of the first two categories.

**This category includes control by a foreign corporation and by a self administered fund.

Source: Edwards et al, "The Capitalist System", *op. cit.*, p. 154.

**Table 2-4. Number and Assets of Corporations in the Top 200 Controlled by the Leading Financial Institutions, 1967-69**

| CONTROLLING FIRMS | NUMBER OF COMPANIES CONTROLLED | ASSETS OF COMPANIES CONTROLLED ($millions) |
|---|---|---|
| Chase group | 21 | 29,966 |
| Morgan group | 15 | 22,417 |
| First National Bank, Chicago | 6 | 10,953 |
| Mellon group | 5 | 14,278 |
| Lehman-Goldman, Sachs | 5 | 7,262 |
| Kuhn, Loeb & Company | 3 | 8,930 |
| First National City Bank, New York | 3 | 6,198 |
| Cleveland Trust Company | 3 | 3,383 |

Source: Edwards et al, "The Capitalist System," *op. cit.*, p. 154.

collusion against competition. The implication of finance institutions' drive for monopoly power is less certain only when rival groups control different major corporations in the same industry. This situation may even lend to rivalry and competition among the production industries under their control. The financial institutions played a very significant role in the great merger movement of the 1960's.[9]

Major financial groups may control corporations that have potential buyer-seller relationships to one another.[10] Such relationships, for all practical purposes, replace the open market relationship with a primitive form of planning, a non-market relationship, which evolves strictly around the interests of the financial group as a whole.

The economic power of the financial institutions is far more centralized than the usual concentration ratio suggests.[11] Therefore, the leading banks can determine, or, at least, influence capital allocation over a significant sector of the economy as well as the operation process.

One further item needs to be added here. Financial institutions have been used by super capitalists to facilitate maximization of their profits.

A particular industry, regardless of size may decline in the long run as a result of technological or other factors; an investment bank, on the other hand, is not attached to a particular industry but to many, directly or through its trust department. Thus, if a capitalist allows the banks to invest his money for him, he receives several advantages. First, he can shift his main sphere of investment over time or diversify it for more profits and better security. Second, operating through a bank allows the capitalist access to other people's capital, those of thousands of working and salaried individuals who deposit their income with the bank through their checking or savings accounts. Third, investment through a trust allows the capitalist to escape taxation in a substantial part of his overall income. All these add to and expand the control power of the financial institutions.

## Growth of Monopoly Capital

Though, in modern technological society large corporations dominate the economy, small firms and their owners remain a significant feature of the economy. This is the competitive sector of the economy where, because of competition, new technologies are widely introduced. The result is decline in prices, benefit from which accrues to consumers. In contrast, in the monopoly sector, when new technologies are introduced, prices are not reduced but maintained the same through the monopoly power of large corporations, therefore, causing higher profits to the firms.

The dynamics of accumulation is different in each sector, based on the existing specific conditions. Monopolistic firms are the most dynamic sector of the economy. Their huge accumulated profits when reinvested create enormous change far more significant than their size, or their percentage of employment that their market share may imply.

The enormous changes occur in technologies used in production and marketing, in the kinds of products, and in required skills and relocation of positions. In all these areas, competitive corporations, though striving for technological innovations, tend to be more stagnant because of their limited financial and technological resources. In practice, they survive in the markets left alone by the big corporations. In order to survive, many competitive firms are left with no choice but being totally dependent on the monopoly firms, either as main suppliers or customers. Accordingly, the development of the economy as a whole is heavily affected by the investment decisions of monopoly corporations.

The following tables illustrate the phenomenal increase in the assets of financial and non-financial firms within a span of only ten years, 1971-1981.

Among industrial corporations (Table 2-5) the assets of 20 top corporations increased by 260.6 percent which in money terms meant $314,477 million. This reveals an average annual accumulation rate of 26.06 percent.

The 20 largest commercial banks (Table 2-6) increased their combined assets by 261.6 percent ($568,309 million) with an annual rate of accumulation of 26.16 percent.

The assets of the 20 largest diversified financial companies (Table 2-7) increased by 359.2 percent, amounting to $166,423 million with an annual rate of 35.92 percent.

The top 20 life insurance companies (Table 2-8) increased their assets by 148.6 percent or $181,138 million with an annual accumulation rate of 14.86 percent. Table 2-9 reveals the enormous capital accumulation of 1,112.35 percent by the 20 largest utility companies amounting to $265,618 million with the highest average annual accumulation rate of 111.235 percent.

Finally, the assets of the 20 largest retailing companies (Table 2-10) increased by 230.1 percent amounting to $53,692 million with an average annual rate of accumulation of 23.01 percent.

Table 2-11 while listing these data for the 20 largest companies in each of these six categories for the decade of 1971-1981, presents that this very small group of monopoly firms, 120 only, had a combined 10-year capital accumulation of 395.4 percent amounting to the phenomenal sum of $1,549,657 million with an astonishing annual capital accumulation rate of 39.5 percent.

Furthermore, the higher rate of accumulation accelerates the process of concentration and centralization of capital within the monopolistic sector. As evidenced from the above statistics monopoly corporations have much larger returns to reinvest. This power to reinvest is further significantly magnified by their easy access to credit from financial institutions. The opportunity for rapid accumulation of capital and reinvestment allows them to expand into remaining competitive industries causing the steady diminution of this sector.

In the financial scene outside the United States, the size of the corporations is enormously larger than those of the United States. The top 100, in 1986, had total assets of 7,382 billion against the U.S. top 100 assets of only 1,937. The top 20 had 55 percent of the assets, 41.6% of the deposits, 41 percent of the loans (Table 2-12). The enormous power of foreign banks can be visualized by considering that the U.S. top 20 commercial banks are in assets, deposits, and loans, respectively 27.66, 29.30, and 36.86 percent of the foreign top 20. Only 14 American commercial banks would fit into this top 100. Within the top 25, against 17 Japanese banks, there is only one American (Citicorp), 4 from France, and one from West Germany and Britain each (Table 2-13). Table 2-12 also presents the comparative situation. It demonstrates the extraordinary financial control capability of the foreign banks, those of Japan in particular.

In relation to the top 500 industrial corporations, Table 2-14, the difference is not so sharp, yet both sales by foreign companies and their assets substantially exceed those of the United States.

70 / Technodemocratic Economic Theory

## TABLE 2-5: ASSETS AND CAPITAL ACCUMULATION
## The 20 LARGEST INDUSTRIAL CORPORATIONS

| RANK | | COMPANY | ASSETS (million) | | ACCUMULATION | |
|---|---|---|---|---|---|---|
| 1971 | 1981 | | 1971 | 1981 | Million | % of 1971 assets |
| 1 | 1 | Exxon | 20,315 | 62,931 | 42,616 | 209 |
| 2 | 2 | General Motors | 18,241 | 38,991 | 20,750 | 113 |
| 7 | 3 | Mobil | 8,552 | 34,776 | 26,224 | 306 |
| 5 | 4 | International Business Machines | 9,576 | 29,586 | 20,010 | 208 |
| 3 | 5 | Texaco | 10,933 | 27,489 | 16,556 | 151 |
| 18 | 6 | E.I. DuPont de Nemours | 3,998 | 23,829 | 19,831 | 496 |
| 9 | 7 | Standard Oil of California | 7,513 | 23,680 | 16,167 | 215 |
| 4 | 8 | Ford Motor | 10,509 | 23,021 | 12,512 | 119 |
| 12 | 9 | Standard Oil (Indiana) | 5,650 | 22,916 | 17,266 | 305 |
| 10 | 10 | General Electric | 6,887 | 20,942 | 14,055 | 204 |
| 6 | 11 | Gulf Oil | 9,465 | 20,429 | 10,964 | 115 |
| 15 | 12 | Shell Oil | 4,464 | 20,118 | 15,472 | 333 |
| 14 | 13 | Atlantic Richfield | 4,704 | 19,732 | 15,028 | 319 |
| 16 | 14 | Tenneco | 4,565 | 16,808 | 12,243 | 268 |
| 55 | 15 | Standard Oil (Ohio) | 1,815 | 15,743 | 13,928 | 767 |
| 8 | 16 | International Tel. & Tel. | 7,630 | 15,052 | 7,422 | 97 |
| 11 | 17 | U.S. Steel | 6,408 | 13,316 | 6,908 | 107 |
| 25 | 18 | Dow Chemical | 3,078 | 12,496 | 9,418 | 305 |
| 28 | 19 | Sun | 2,813 | 11,82 | 9,009 | 320 |
| 24 | 20 | Phillips Petroleum | 3,166 | 11,264 | 8,098 | 255 |
| | | Totals | 150,464 | 464,941 | 314,477 | 260.6 |

Source: Calculated by using data available from Fortune (May, 1972) pp. 190-206 and Fortune (May 3, 1982) pp. 260-279.

**Table 2-6: Assets and Capital Accumulation The 20 Largest Commercial Banking Companies 1971 - 1981**

| RANK | | COMPANY | ASSETS (million) | | ACCUMULATION | |
|------|------|---------|---------|---------|---------|---------|
| 1971 | 1981 | | | | | % of 1971 |
| | | | 1971 | 1981 | Million | assets |
| 1 | 1 | Bank America | 33,985 | 121,158 | 87,173 | 256 |
| 2 | 2 | City Corp. | 29,320 | 119,232 | 89,930 | 306 |
| 3 | 3 | Chase Manhattan Corp. | 24,509 | 77,839 | 53,330 | 217 |
| 4 | 4 | Manufacturers Hanover Corp. | 14,277 | 59,108 | 44,831 | 314 |
| 5 | 5 | J.P. Morgan & Co. | 13,615 | 53,522 | 39,907 | 293 |
| 9 | 6 | Continental Illinois Corp. | 10,080 | 46,971 | 36,891 | 365 |
| 7 | 7 | Chemical New York Corp. | 12,624 | 44,916 | 32,292 | 255 |
| 8 | 8 | Bankers Trust New Yrok Corp. | 10,828 | 34,213 | 23,385 | 215 |
| 11 | 9 | First Chicago Crop. | 9,196 | 33,562 | 24,366 | 264 |
| 10 | 10 | Security Pacific Corp. | 9,765 | 32,999 | 23,234 | 237 |
| 13 | 11 | Wells Fargo & Co. | 7,804 | 23,219 | 15,415 | 197 |
| 14 | 12 | Crocker National Corp. | 6,496 | 22,494 | 15,998 | 246 |
| 12 | 13 | Marine Midland Banks | 9,189 | 18,682 | 9,493 | 103 |
| 15 | 14 | Mellon National Corp. | 6,433 | 18,447 | 12,014 | 186 |
| 18 | 15 | First National Boston Corp. | 5,099 | 16,809 | 11,710 | 229 |
| 20 | 16 | Northwest Bancorp. | 5,056 | 15,141 | 10,085 | 199 |
| 19 | 17 | First Bank System | 5,073 | 14,911 | 9,838 | 193 |
| 47 | 18 | First City Bancorp. of Texas | 1,882 | 14,291 | 12,409 | 659 |
| 24 | 19 | Bank of New York Co. | 3,384 | 11,462 | 8,078 | 238 |
| 27 | 20 | Seafirst Corp. | 2,817 | 10,747 | 7,9330 | 281 |
| | | Totals | 221,414 | 789,723 | 568,309 | 261.6 |

Source: Calculated by using data available from *Fortune* (May, 1972) pp. 210-211 and *Fortune* (July 12,1982) p. 134.

**Table 2-7: Assets and Capital Accumulation The 20 Largest Diversified Financial Companies 1971-1981**

| RANK | | COMPANY | ASSETS (million) | | ACCUMULATION | |
|---|---|---|---|---|---|---|
| 1971 | 1981 | | 1971 | 1981 | Million | % of 1971 assets |
| | 1 | Federal National Mortgage Assn. | NA | 62,095 | | |
| 1 | 2 | Aetna Life & Casulty | 10,865 | 39,630 | 28,765 | 264 |
| 4 | 3 | American Express | 5,213 | 25,103 | 19,890 | 381 |
| 2 | 4 | Travelers | 7,829 | 23,982 | 16,153 | 206 |
| 13 | 5 | Merrill Lynch & Co. | 2,867 | 17,682 | 14,815 | 516 |
| 12 | 6 | INA | 2,997 | 11,028 | 8,031 | 267 |
| 7 | 7 | Great Western Financial | 3,814 | 10,646 | 6,832 | 179 |
| 21 | 8 | First Boston | 1,419 | 10,314 | 8,895 | 626 |
| 11 | 9 | First Charter Financial | 3,303 | 9,750 | 6,447 | 195 |
| 10 | 10 | Lincoln National | 3,322 | 9,047 | 5,725 | 172 |
| 6 | 11 | Transamerica | 3,935 | 9,042 | 5,107 | 129 |
| 18 | 12 | Imperial Corp. | 1,735 | 8,500 | 6,765 | 389 |
| 15 | 13 | American General | 2,178 | 8,075 | 5,897 | 270 |
| 5 | 14 | Continental | 3,935 | 8,071 | 4,136 | 105 |
| 31 | 15 | American International Group | 930 | 7,957 | 7,027 | 755 |
| 16 | 16 | Beneficial | 2,094 | 6,340 | 4,246 | 202 |
| 30 | 17 | Walter E. Heller International | 979 | 6,256 | 5,277 | 539 |
| 14 | 18 | Household Finance | 2,374 | 5,927 | 3,553 | 149 |
| 47 | 19 | Golden West Financial | 462 | 5,541 | 5,079 | 1099 |
| 29 | 20 | Gibraltar Financial Corp. of Calif. | 988 | 4,771 | 3,783 | 382 |
| | | Totals | 61,239 | 289,757 | 166,423 | 359.2 |

Source: Calculated by using data available from *Fortune* (May, 1972) pp. 214-215 and *Fortune* (July 12, 1982).

**Table 2-8: Assets and Capital Accumulation**
**The 20 Largest Life Insurance Companies 1971 - 1981**

| RANK 1971 | RANK 1981 | COMPANY | ASSETS (million) 1971 | ASSETS (million) 1981 | ACCUMULATION Million | ACCUMULATION % of 1971 assets |
|---|---|---|---|---|---|---|
| 1 | 1 | Prudential (Newark) | 31,159 | 62,498 | 31,339 | 100 |
| 2 | 2 | Metropolitan (New York) | 29,163 | 51,757 | 22,594 | 77 |
| 3 | 3 | Equitable Life Assurance | 15,395 | 26,758 | 21,363 | 138 |
| 6 | 4 | Aetna Life (Hartford) | 7,803 | 25,158 | 17,355 | 222 |
| 4 | 5 | New York Life | 11,268 | 21,041 | 9,773 | 86 |
| 5 | 6 | John Hancock Mutual (Boston) | 10,603 | 19,936 | 9,333 | 88 |
| 8 | 7 | Connecticut General Life | 5,668 | 15,103 | 9,435 | 166 |
| 9 | 8 | Traveler's (Hartford) | 5,043 | 14,803 | 9,760 | 193 |
| 7 | 9 | Northwestern Mutual | 6,453 | 12,154 | 5,701 | 88 |
| 15 | 10 | Teacher's Insurance & Annuity (New York) | 2,596 | 11,439 | 8,843 | 340 |
| 10 | 11 | Massachusetts Mutual | 4,566 | 10,022 | 5,456 | 119 |
| 18 | 12 | Banker's Life (Des Moines) | 2,250 | 8,765 | 6,515 | 289 |
| 11 | 13 | Mutual of New York | 3,946 | 8,388 | 4,442 | 112 |
| 12 | 14 | New England Mutural | 3,751 | 7,273 | 3,522 | 93 |
| 14 | 15 | Mutual Benefit (Newark) | 2,697 | 6,619 | 3,922 | 145 |
| 13 | 16 | Connecticut Mutual (Hartford) | 2,922 | 5,818 | 2,896 | 99 |
| 17 | 17 | Lincoln National life (Fort Wayne, Ind.) | 2,363 | 5,038 | 2,675 | 113 |
| 16 | 18 | Penn Mutual (Philadelphia) | 2,512 | 3,963 | 1,451 | 57 |
| 35 | 19 | State Farm Life (Bloomington, Ill.) | 902 | 3.759 | 2.857 | 316 |
| 25 | 20 | Phoenix Mutual (Hartford) | 1,446 | 3,352 | 1,906 | 131 |
| | | Totals | 152,506 | 333,644 | 181,138 | 148.6 |

Source: Calculated by using data available from *Fortune* (May, 1972) pp. 212-213 and *Fortune*( July 12, 1982) p.136.

**Table 2-9:  Assets and Capital Accumulation The 20 Largest Utilities 1971-1981**

| RANK | | COMPANY | ASSETS (million) | | ACCUMULATION | |
|---|---|---|---|---|---|---|
| 1971 | 1981 | | 1971 | 1981 | Million | % of 1971 assets |
| 1 | 1 | American Telephone & Telegraph | 18,510 | 137,749 | 119,239 | 644 |
| 2 | 2 | General Telephone & Elec. | 3,836 | 21,112 | 17,277 | 450 |
| 9 | 3 | Southern Company | 821 | 12,415 | 11,594 | 1,412 |
| 4 | 4 | Pacific Gas & Electric | 1,260 | 12,366 | 11,106 | 881 |
| 12 | 5 | American Electric Power | 748 | 11,567 | 10,819 | 1,446 |
| 6 | 6 | Commonwealth Edison | 989 | 11,196 | 10,207 | 1,032 |
| 10 | 7 | Southern California Edison | 802 | 8,728 | 7,926 | 988 |
| 25 | 8 | Middle South Util. | 506 | 8,318 | 7,812 | 1,543 |
| 3 | 9 | Consolidated Edison | 1,313 | 7,732 | 6,419 | 488 |
| 27 | 10 | Texas Utilities | 483 | 7,306 | 6,823 | 1,412 |
| 8 | 11 | Public Service Electric & Gas | 885 | 7,277 | 6,392 | 722 |
| 31 | 12 | Virginia Electric & Power | 413 | 7,057 | 6,644 | 1,608 |
| 16 | 13 | Consumers Power | 651 | 6,872 | 6,221 | 955 |
| 19 | 14 | Detroit Edison | 599 | 6,607 | 6,008 | 1,003 |
| 28 | 15 | Duke Power | 451 | 6,531 | 6,080 | 1,348 |
| 18 | 16 | Philadelphia Electric | 608 | 6,304 | 5,696 | 936 |
| 26 | 17 | Florida Power & Light | 484 | 6,122 | 5,638 | 1,164 |
| 24 | 18 | General Public Utilities | 507 | 5,054 | 4,547 | 896 |
| 45 | 19 | Pennsylvania Power & Light | 300 | 5,010 | 4,710 | 1,570 |
| 16 | 20 | Carolina Power & Light | 255 | 4,715 | 4,460 | 1,749 |
| | | Totals | 34,421 | 300,039 | 265,618 | 1,112.35 |

Source:  Calculated by using data available from *Fortune* (May, 1972) pp. 220-221 and *Fortune* (July 12, 1982) p. 126.

**Table 2-10: Assets and Capital Accumulation The 20 Largest Retailing Companies 1971 - 1981**

| RANK | | COMPANY | ASSETS (million) | | ACCUMULATION | |
|------|------|---------|------|------|------|------|
| 1971 | 1981 | | 1971 | 1981 | Million | % of 1971 assets |
| 1 | 1 | Sears Roebuck | 8,132 | 34,509 | 26,377 | 324 |
| 3 | 2 | J.C. Penney | 1,923 | 6,216 | 4,293 | 223 |
| 5 | 3 | Federated Department Stores | 1,279 | 4,069 | 2,187 | 220 |
| 8 | 4 | Safeway Stores | 964 | 3,390 | 2,726 | 282 |
| 4 | 5 | F.W. Woolworth | 1,580 | 3,141 | 1,561 | 98 |
| 14 | 6 | Dayton Hudson | 748 | 2,555 | 1,807 | 241 |
| 13 | 7 | Kroger | 756 | 2,405 | 1,649 | 218 |
| 9 | 8 | May Department Stores | 951 | 2,387 | 1,436 | 150 |
| 10 | 9 | Allied Stores | 951 | 2,179 | 1,228 | 129 |
| 21 | 10 | Carter Hawley Hale Stores | 485 | 1,741 | 1,256 | 258 |
| 27 | 11 | Southland | 326 | 1,677 | 1,351 | 414 |
| 18 | 12 | Associated Dry Goods | 539 | 1,557 | 1,018 | 188 |
| 23 | 13 | Lucky Stores | 364 | 1,524 | 1,160 | 318 |
| 15 | 14 | R.H. Macy | 615 | 1,479 | 864 | 140 |
| 19 | 15 | Jewel Companies | 518 | 1,379 | 861 | 166 |
| 7 | 16 | Great Atlantic & Pacific Tea | 978 | 1,308 | 330 | 33 |
| 26 | 17 | ARA Services | 330 | 1,137 | 807 | 244 |
| 39 | 18 | Melville | 209 | 1,134 | 925 | 442 |
| 38 | 19 | Winn-Dixie Stores | 230 | 924 | 694 | 301 |
| 34 | 20 | Grand Union | 249 | 781 | 532 | 213 |
| | | Totals | 22,127 | 75,819 | 53,692 | 230.1 |

Source: Calculated by using data available from *Fortune* (May, 1972) pp. 216-217 and *Fortune* (July 12, 1982) p. 140.

**Table 2-11: Combined Capital Accumulation of the 20 Largest Financial and Non-Financial Companies, 1971-1981**

| Classification | Accumulation (million) | % of 1971 Assets | Annual Rate (%) |
|---|---|---|---|
| Industrial Corporation | 314,477 | 260.6 | 26.0 |
| Commercial Banking | 568,309 | 261.6 | 26.1 |
| Diversified Financial | 166,423 | 359.2 | 35.9 |
| Life Insurance | 181,138 | 148.6 | 14.8 |
| Utilities | 265,618 | 1,112.3 | 111.2 |
| Retailing | 53,692 | 230.1 | 23.0 |
| Total | 1,549,657 | 395.4 | 39.5 |

Source: Calculated from the available data in Tables 2-5 through 2-10 above.

**Table 2-12 The Largest 100 Commercial Banks (Billions) Outside U.S. & U.S.**

| | OUTSIDE U.S. | | | U.S | | |
|---|---|---|---|---|---|---|
| | TOP 100 | TOP 20 | % OF 100 | TOP 100 | TOP 20 | % OF OUTSIDE 20 |
| Assets | 7,382 | 4,060 | 55.0 | 1,437 | 1,123 | 27.66 |
| Deposits | 5,949 | 2,474 | 41.6 | 1,346 | 725 | 29.3 |
| Loans | 4,755 | 1,953 | 41.0 | 1,218 | 720 | 36,86 |
| Employees | 2,36 | 626,483 | 26.5 | 1,012 (million) | 0.525 | 83.85 |

Source: Extracted and calculated from *Fortune*, August 3, 1987, pp. 242-46; *Fortune*, June 8, 1987, pp. 200-203.

## Table 2-13: The 25 Largest Bank in the World (ranked by assets)

| RANK | | COMPANY | COUNTRY | ASSETS[1] | DEPOSITS | LOANS[e] |
|---|---|---|---|---|---|---|
| 1 | 1 | Dai-Ichi Kangyo Bank | Japan | 251,533,301 | 183,566,900 | 145,933,839 |
| 2 | 2 | Fuji Bank | Japan | 219,924,600 | 161,926,239 | 121,705,578 |
| 3 | 3 | Sumitomo Bank | Japan | 214,399,190 | 159,419,605 | 119,402,229 |
| 4 | 4 | Mitsubishi Bank | Japan | 209,304,645 | 149,783,388 | 116,158,562 |
| 5 | 5 | Sanwa Bank | Japan | 200,339,313 | 147,896,981 | 115,217,629 |
| 6 | 6 | Citicorp | U.S. | 196,124,000 | 114,689,000 | 129,206,000 |
| 7 | 11 | Industrial Bank of Japan | Japan | 167,147,204 | 130,173,009 | 93,864,056 |
| 8 | 8 | Caisse Nationale de Dredit Agricole | France | 156,295,970 | 129,386,232 | 116,411,228 |
| 9 | 7 | Banque Nationale de Paris | France | 143,606,020 | 121,763,010 | 114,325,409 |
| 10 | 15 | Tokai Bank | Japan | 142,485,151 | 111,900,790 | 83,874,616 |
| 11 | 16 | Mitsui Bank | Japan | 140,147,716 | 104,348,792 | 82,055,031 |
| 12 | 18 | Norinchukin Bank | Japan | 139,375,130 | 124,212,613 | 63,624,195 |
| 13 | 13 | Beutsche Bank | W. Germany | 133,726,588 | 120,358,172 | 104,886,178 |
| 14 | 9 | Credit Lyonnais | France | 133,691,709 | 115,171,444 | 114,873,353 |
| 15 | 20 | Mitsubishi Trust & Banking | Japan | 132,478,581 | 110,525,520 | 64,030,243 |
| 16 | 17 | Long-Term Credit Bank of Japan | Japan | 125,773,294 | 98,642,371 | 76,831,480 |
| 17 | 21 | Sumitomo Trust & Banking. | Japan | 124,548,591 | 110,133,061 | 52,854,836 |
| 18 | 10 | National Westminster Bank | Britain | 123,529,312 | 107,868,182 | 106,203,335 |
| 19 | 23 | Taiyo Kobe Bank | Japan | 120,949,666 | 91,237,324 | 74,113,411 |
| 20 | 12 | Societe Generale | France | 117,431,577 | 99,030,369 | 88,547,705 |
| 21 | 14 | Barclays Bank | Britain | 117,046,340 | 96,826,522 | 98,547,705 |
| 22 | 22 | Bank of Tokyo | Japan | 115,879,206 | 58,731,120 | 58,670,417 |
| 23 | 26 | Mitsui Trust & Bkg. | Japan | 115,491,681 | 98,916,067 | 60,990,489 |
| 24 | 29 | Daiwa Bank | Japan | 105,450,398 | 88,293,132 | 52,896,566 |
| 25 | 31 | Yasuda Trust & Bkg. | Japan | 103,851,655 | 85,898,471 | 50,348,967 |

Source: Extracted and calculated from *Fortune*, August 3, 1987, pp. 242-43; and *Fortune*, June 8, 1987, p. 200.

Table 2-14  The Largest 500 Industrial Corporations (Billions)

|  | FOREIGN | | U.S. | | |
|  | Top 500 | Rate of Income | Top 500 | Rate of Income | % of Foreign |
| --- | --- | --- | --- | --- | --- |
| Sales | 2,092 | 2.47 | 1,723 | 3.77 | 82.36 |
| Income | 51.6 | - | 64.94 | - | 126.0 |
| Assets | 2,254 | 2.29 | 1,560 | 4.16 | 69.21 |

Source: Extracted and calculated from *Fortune*, August 3, 1987, pp. 214-23; and *Fortune*, April 27, 1987, pp. 364-83.

# The Capitalist Class

A class is a group of individuals sharing a common position in the mode of production. Capitalists have in common the condition that they own capital, which they either lend (finance) or use to purchase the means of production, including labor and technology (investment). Their return from finance is in the form of interest, and from investment in the form of profits.

Members of the capitalist classes come from all levels of production and investment. A great majority are small operators. They employ few workers, face fierce competition, are insecure in their business prospects, and receive a relatively modest return. At the other extreme are a small group of super-capitalists with access to enormous capital and secured giant profits. To understand the magnitude of the power of this very small group, one may take note that in the United States only about ten percent of the population under contemporary standards could be categorized as capitalists. But super capitalists consist of only four tenths of one percent of the population. They control the majority of wealth and investment capital and all monopolistic private enterprises. One study shows that one percent of the population owned more than half of all stock.[12] Another study has estimated that appropriation of monopoly profits during the twentieth century has been under the exclusive domain of this small group through which it has more than doubled its share of wealth otherwise not possible.[13] At the very top, approximately 1.6 percent of the population own 30 percent of all capital stock, 100 percent of all state and municipal bonds, and 88.5 percent of all corporate bonds. In nearly every major industry a few giant corporations control from 60 to 98 percent of the sales.[14]

Some 200 top corporations out of nearly 200,000 industrial firms, which is controlled by this small group of capitalists, account for about 80 percent of all resources used in manufacturing. The largest 100 alone account for over 54 percent of these resources. Among the financial institutions, five commercial banks alone (Chase Manhattan, Citibank, Bankers Trust, Morgan Garanty Trust, and the Bank of New York) hold controlling shares of stock in seventy-five percent of the top 324 corporations.[15] One percent of all food corporations control nearly 80 percent of all the corresponding assets and about 40 percent of the profits, and only three companies control about 70 percent of all dairy products. Ninety percent of all grain shipped in the world market is handled by only six multinational corporations.[16]

Table 2-15 illustrates the phenomenal concentration of assets of manufacturing firms in the top 100 manufacturing corporations during the last three decades. It is particularly interesting to notice that while the second 100 largest firms are all giant corporations, they share a small fraction of the total assets.

The situation becomes more acute when the top 500 manufacturing corporations are taken into account. As evidenced from Table 2-16 the assets held by the top 100 firms account for 71.4 percent of the total. They appropriate 72.5 percent of profits and employ 63.4 percent of the total labor force.

The point about the concentration of control on the top is further clarified if the top 500 manufacturing firms are compared with the second 500. As shown in Table 2-17, in 1981, the ratio of sales between these two groups was 14.7 to one, profits were 14.8 to one, and assets 14.1 to one.

All these and other giant economic institutions are controlled by a very small group of capitalists. Yet, a small fraction of this tiny group of capitalists, one hundredth of one percent of the adult population, form what we may term super-capitalists. A few thousand in number, they are the major beneficiaries of monopolistic profits, and besides their immense personal wealth, they are in control of an enormous size of investment capital contributed and owned by others.

Personal wealth alone, however, does not guarantee economic power. The deciding factor is the size of corporate capital that one has under control. To achieve this purpose one must occupy top positions in large corporations which enable one to be able to establish control over huge corporate assets. If we combine the whole personal wealth of America's top 400 centimillionaires, it will amount to not more than 280 billion dollars,[17] but, if we look at their combined control of corporate wealth, we are then talking about some 4600 billion corporate assets.

Each of these few super capitalists sits on the board of directors of several giant industrial and financial institutions creating "family enterprises" of colossal size. For example, the Rockefeller family, with a combined personal wealth of about 4 billion dollars, has control over some 300 billion (75 times the family's personal wealth) corporate assets, which extends into just about every major industry within every state in the United States and every nation in the non-socialist world. They control five of the twelve largest oil companies and four of the largest banks in the United States.[18] They have substantial holdings in chemicals, steel, insurance, sugar, coal, copper, tin, computers, utilities, television, radio, publishing, electronics, agribusiness, automobiles, airlines, every major natural resource and manufactured commodity and service.[19] At times, members of the family or their close associates have occupied the offices of the president, vice-president, Secretaries of State, Defense, Commerce, and other cabinet posts and key government positions, the Federal Reserve Board and the governorships of several states.[20]

Another example is the DuPont family. It controls eight of the largest defense contractors. It grossed over 15 billion dollars in military contracts during the Vietnam War. It controls ten corporations each with assets over one billion dollars which includes such multibillion dollar corporations as General Motors (45.6 billion), Coca Cola (5.23 billion), and United Brands (3.8 billion). DuPonts own about forty manorial estates and private museums in the state of Delaware alone.[21]

It may come as a real surprise to many to note that a very small group of this super-capitalist class, only a little over 7000, occupy top positions in all major institutions of American society and run the system. These individuals possess the authority to formulate policies, direct and manage programs, plans, and activities of the major American corporate, governmental, educational, informational, legal,

**Table 2-15: Largest Manufacturing Corporations: Percent Share of Total Assets Held, 1950 - 1987**

| YEAR | 100 LARGEST (%) | SECOND 100 LARGEST (%) | 200 LARGEST (%) |
|------|------|------|------|
| 1950 | 39.7 | 7.5 | 47.2 |
| 1955 | 44.3 | 8.8 | 53.1 |
| 1960 | 46.4 | 9.9 | 56.3 |
| 1965 | 46.5 | 10.2 | 56.7 |
| 1970 | 48.5 | 11.9 | 60.4 |
| 1975 | 45.0 | 12.5 | 57.5 |
| 1980 | 46.7 | 13.0 | 59.7 |
| 1985 | 70.3 | 14.8 | 85.1 |
| 1987 | 71.4 | 14.1 | 85.5 |

Source: *Statistical Abstract of the United States 1980* (Washington, D.C.: U.S. Government Printing Office, 1980), p. 568, Table 953; *Statistical Abstract of the United States 1984* (Washington, D.C.: U.S. Government Printing Office, 1984), p. 538, Table 905; *Statistical Abstract of the United States* 1989, p. 536, Table 885.

**Table 2-16: Comparison of the Top 500 Manufacturing Corporations and the Top 100 (1987)**

|  | TOP 500 | TOP 100 | PERCENT ACCOUNTED FOR BY TOP 100 |
|------|------|------|------|
| Employees | 13,144 thousand | 8,333 thousand | 63.4 |
| Sales | 1,879.5 billion | 1,306.9 billion | 69.5 |
| Net Income | 90.6 billion | 65.7 billion | 72.5 |
| Assets | 1,705.7 | 1,217.2 billion | 71.4 |

Source: *Statistical Abstract of the United States, 1989* (Washington, D.C.: U.S. Government Printing Office), p. 536, Table 885.

# 82 / Technodemocratic Economic Theory

Table 2-17: Sales, Profits, and Assets of the top 500 Manufacturing Corporations, 1981

| | TOP 500 (BILLIONS) | SECOND 500 (BILLIONS) | RATIO OF TOP 500 IN 1979 | RATIO OF TOP 500 TO SECOND 500 IN 1980 | RATIO OF TOP 500 TO SECOND 500 IN 1981 |
|---|---|---|---|---|---|
| Sales | $1,773.4 | $120.9 | 13.1:1 | 13.8:1 | 14.7:1 |
| Profits | 84.2 | 5.7 | 12.8:1 | 13.5:1 | 14.8:1 |
| Assets | 1,282.8 | 90.7 | 13.1:1 | 13.5:1 | 14.1:1 |

Source: *Statistical Abstract of the United States, 1982-83* (Washington, D.C.: U.S. Government Printing Office, 1982-83), p. 543, Table 914.

civic and cultural institutions. Concentration, specialization and interlocking character of these large institutions further enhance the power of the individuals far beyond the capacity of the institutions with which they have direct contact. Table 2-18 illustrates 7,314 positions which collectively form the national ruling elite. In referring to Table 2-18, Professor Thomas R. Dye concludes that:

These top positions, taken collectively, control half of the nation's industrial assets; half of all assets in communication, transportation, and utilities; half of all banking assets; two thirds of all insurance assets; and they direct Wall Street's largest investment firms. They control the television networks, they influence news agencies, and major newspaper chains. They control nearly 40 percent of all assets of private foundations and half of all private university endowments. They direct the nation's largest and best-known New York and Washington law firms as well as the nation's major civic and cultural organizations. They occupy key federal governmental positions in the executive, legislative, and judicial branches. And they occupy all the top command positions in the Army, Navy, Air Force, and Marines.[22]

The supercapitalists associated with the giant corporations constitute the most economically and politically powerful segment of the capitalist class. They are, as a result, the most privileged. They command over vast economic, political, legislative, legal, educational, communication, and ideological resources. Because of self interest, they strongly tend to support and maintain capitalism as a viable societal system. Toward this aim they receive support from small capitalists, landlords and affluent classes; they manipulate labor and control the state, its law-making body in particular. Their interests and perspectives are mainly national, rather than local or regional, and they often extend into the international sphere with supportive state foreign policies.[23]

Capitalists who control monopoly corporations have increasingly come to control political and ideological trends within the capitalist society, mainly through control of information and legislative systems.[24]

## Capitalism and the Working Class

The second aspect of capitalism concerns the working class and social relations of production. Under monopoly capitalism, the character of the working class differs significantly from Karl Marx's description of the mid-nineteenth century proletariat. The enormous concentration, centralization and expansion of capital, a characteristic of monopoly capitalism, has caused great expansion in the size of the working class and corresponding changes in the conditions as well as the nature of the labor force. Along with continuous transformation of the labor process, the working class has gone through evolution and has become extensively diversified.[25]

### The Growth of the Working Class and the System of Control

Since the mid-nineteenth century the number of self-employed small property holders has steadily declined and the number of the wage-labor has increased, gradually transforming the independent small operators into dependent, salaried workers at the expense of surrendering control over their labor power, their authority over their products and manner of production. The term "wage-labor" under modern technological production refers to any person who sells his labor power for a determined amount of periodic pay and who is not involved in major goal oriented policy-making processes.[26]

The labor force has not escaped the impact of the accelerated changes in the forces of production during the past few decades. Its structure and quality has gone through a dramatic transformation in response to the changes in the forces of production.

The decline in significance of the small firms and the corresponding middle class and independent proprietors has been counterbalanced by the appearance of a new middle class of white-collar workers, increasing in number with a much greater pace than blue-collar workers. As a result, the modern technological capitalist society has tended to embody a large and crucially needed class of white-collar "proletariat" consisting of engineers, lawyers, administrators, all kinds of top and middle rank specialists, and computer experts. The main task of the institutions of higher education has shifted from providing for general knowledge for the good of humanity, to training specialists of all kinds in order to satisfy the demand of the high technology production process for the ultimate benefit of the small super-capitalist class.

This tremendous expansion of the labor force in number as well as variety is one of the most striking and significant features of monopoly capitalist development. Increase in number has been due to the capital accumulation and reinvestment process. Expansion in variety has been the result of scientific and technological development where the working class has become by necessity better educated, scientifically and technically skilled, embracing both white-collar and blue-collar forces. Besides specialists such as engineers, lawyers, executives, sales experts, accountants, etc., the white-collar labor embodies also a large number of skilled and semi-skilled clerical workers. Table 2-19 illustrates different categories of this labor force and its tremendous increase since the beginning of the twentieth century. According to these statistics, while the size of blue-collar workers has decreased only by 4.1 percent, the size of white-collar workers has nearly tripled, and among this class, the size of clerical workers has multiplied over six fold. The spectacular decline has occurred among farm workers, from 37.5 percent in 1900 to only 2.8 percent in 1980.

A distinctive change in the characteristics of the labor force has occurred by the continually increasing number of women entering the

Table 2-18:  The National Institutional Elite Positions

| CORPORATE SECTORS | NUMBER OF LEADERSHIP POSITIONS |
|---|---|
| Industrial corporations (100) | 1,475 |
| Utilities, communications, transportation (50) | 668 |
| Banks (50) | 1,092 |
| Insurance (50) | 611 |
| Investments (15) | 479 |
| Total | 4,325 |
| Public Interest sectors | |
| Mass media (18) | 220 |
| Education (25) | 892 |
| Foundations (50) | 402 |
| Law (25) | 758 |
| Civic and Cultural organizations (12) | 433 |
| Total | 2,705 |
| Governmental Sector | |
| Legislative, executive, judicial | 236 |
| Military | 48 |
| Total | 284 |
| TOTAL | 7,314 |

Source: Thomas R. Dye, *Who's Running America?* 4th ed., Englewood Cliffs, N.J.: Prentice-Hall, 1986), p. 12.

labor market. Table 2-20 illustrates the situation. While the size of the total labor force has multiplied three times since 1900, the size of women workers has increased nearly eight times. The highest increase has been in the clerical class, from 4 percent to 35.1 percent, and the sharpest decreases have been in the blue-collar class, from 27.7 percent to 13.8 percent, and in the farm workers class, from 19 percent to only 1.2 percent. Overall, since 1900, women have moved from either sectors of the work force into the white-collar class. Today, over 65 percent of working women are within this class.

The growth of this new labor force and the employment of scientific marketing techniques by capitalists have brought about substantial changes in the nature of production and work in the modern capitalistic system.

In modern capitalism, the expansion of surplus value through continually revolutionizing of the working process has produced far-- reaching changes. The individualized craftsmen's work of the past has been replaced by a mass production system where each worker on the production line carries out only a designated repetitive work unit often each to be completed within a prescribed short span of time. The work has been standardized and scrutinized in order to minimize costs of production and increase productivity to the extent that workers are rendered "interchangeable parts" often totally abstracted from the product and process of production involving them. The result has been the creation of what Marx described as the "abstract worker."

Workers have had, progressively, more years of education but only a small proportion of their knowledge and skills are generally utilized in the production process.

The management and upper echelons of the hierarchy have not escaped this standardization. Besides vast departmentalization of the tasks, decision-making functions have been placed into scientifically developed routine processes of particularly described and often prescribed steps and stages.[27]

As corporations have grown larger and more complex in their organizational structure, the organizational techniques to control the work process has become systematized and more sophisticated. The individualized decision-making process has been replaced with a giant bureaucratic system of rules, procedures, sanctions and incentives, forming an institutionalized machinery by which the invisible power of capitalists is firmly established under the apparent process of rationality and fairness.

This complex bureaucratic hierarchy has not been the unavoidable outcome of advanced technology but a cool system of control, institu- ted primarily to stratify the workers, induce competition among them, and to tighten control on different levels of management. The use of expanded organizational techniques has made the *social relations of production* more elaborate as well as complex. Out of these has emerged the institution of hierarchical job structure with the purpose of offsetting the increasingly organized power of the workers against the production system.

### Diversity and Unionization Among Workers

Possibly, the greatest flaw in Marx's projection toward the future was that he believed in the power and unity of the labor force. That exploitation of the workers, as a strong common ground, will bring different sectors of the labor force together and unify them in their struggle against capitalists, which would ultimately lead to the overthrow of the capitalist system.

This prediction has not materialized at all. With the advancement and tremendous expansion of technology, the labor force has become increasingly fragmented. Not infrequently, different groups competed against one another to the extent that today, despite several decades of struggle for unionization, the labor force is highly fragmented and only a minority of it has come to be unionized. Yet, unionization does not mean unity. Instead of tending to unify different labor groups together, often it has created groups with rivalry and competition relating to conflicting benefits and goals. Despite a dramatic increase in the number of workers as well as occupations, the American working class has remained heterogeneous and divided against itself.

In general, labor forces associated with large corporations have become unionized, such as automobile and steel industries. Through union power within the corresponding industry these workers have been able to extract, compared to the non-unionized sector, higher wage rates, pension, health plans, and other fringe benefits not available to the majority, non-unionized workers. These have often created sharp division between the two sectors since the non-unionized labor, with their lower wage rates, has had to pay for higher product prices to accommodate the higher wage rate and fringe benefits received by the unionized labor. In addition to these industry unions, there have been a large variety of independent craft unions such as carpenters, plumbers, electricians, etc. with diversified and special interests. There have been, furthermore, diversified public employee unions with ever increasing importance.

Table 2-19: Major Occupation of Employed Persons: 1900 - 1980 (1000)

| Major Occupation Group | 1980 | 1970 | 1960 | 1950 | 1940 | 1930 | 1920 | 1910 | 1900 |
|---|---|---|---|---|---|---|---|---|---|
| | | | | Both Sexes | | | | | |
| Total number | 97,270 | 78,626 | 66,681 | 58,999 | 51,742 | 48,686 | 42,206 | 37,291 | 29,030 |
| Percent of total | | | | | | | | | |
| White-collar workers | 52.2 | 48.3 | 43.1 | 36.6 | 31.1 | 29.4 | 24.9 | 21.3 | 17.6 |
| Professional and technical workers | 16.1 | 14.2 | 11.2 | 8.6 | 7.5 | 6.8 | 5.4 | 4.7 | 4.2 |
| Managers officials, and proprietors | 11.2 | 10.5 | 10.6 | 8.7 | 7.3 | 7.4 | 6.6 | 6.6 | 5.8 |
| Clerical workers | 18.6 | 17.4 | 14.7 | 12.3 | 9.6 | 8.9 | 8.0 | 5.3 | 3.0 |
| Salesworkers | 6.3 | 6.2 | 6.6 | 6.9 | 6.7 | 6.3 | 4.9 | 4.7 | 4.5 |
| Blue-collar workers | 31.7 | 35.3 | 36.3 | 41.1 | 39.8 | 39.6 | 40.2 | 38.2 | 35.8 |
| Craftsmen and foremen | 12.9 | 12.9 | 12.8 | 14.1 | 12.0 | 12.8 | 13.0 | 11.6 | 10.5 |
| Operatives | 14.2 | 17.7 | 18.0 | 20.4 | 18.4 | 15.8 | 15.6 | 14.6 | 12.8 |
| Nonfarm labores | 4.6 | 4.7 | 5.5 | 6.6 | 9.4 | 10.9 | 11.6 | 12.0 | 12.5 |
| Service workers | 13.3 | 12.4 | 12.5 | 10.5 | 11.7 | 9.8 | 7.8 | 9.5 | 9.0 |
| Farmworkers | 2.8 | 4.0 | 8.1 | 11.8 | 17.4 | 21.2 | 27.0 | 30.9 | 37.5 |

Source: U.S. Bureau of the Census, Historical Statistics of the United States, Colonial Times to 1957 (Washington, D. C.: U.S. Government Printing Office, 1960), p. 74; U.S. Bureau of the Census, Statistical Abstract of the United States: 1971 (Washington, D.C.: U.S. GPO, 1972), p. 222; and Statistical Abstract of the United States, 1981 (Washington, D.C.: U.S. Government Printing Office, 1981), p.401, Table 673.

Table 2-20: Major Occupation of Employed Women: 1900 - 1980 (1000)

| Major Occupation Group | 1980 | 1970 | 1960 | 1950 | 1940 | 1930 | 1920 | 1910 | 1900 |
|---|---|---|---|---|---|---|---|---|---|
| Total number | 41,283 | 29,667 | 22,196 | 16,445 | 12,574 | 10,752 | 8,637 | 7,445 | 5,319 |
| Percent of total of Total Labor Force | | | | | | | | | |
| White-collar workers | 65.6 | 60.5 | 54.6 | 52.4 | 44.9 | 44.2 | 38.8 | 26.1 | 17.8 |
| Professional and technical workers | 16.8 | 14.5 | 12.2 | 12.2 | 12.8 | 13.8 | 11.7 | 9.8 | 8.2 |
| Managers officials, and proprietors | 6.9 | 4.5 | 5.0 | 4.3 | 3.3 | 2.7 | 2.2 | 2.0 | 1.5 |
| Clerical workers | 35.1 | 34.5 | 30.0 | 27.8 | 21.5 | 20.9 | 18.7 | 9.2 | 4.0 |
| Salesworkers | 6.8 | 7.0 | 7.6 | 8.6 | 7.4 | 6.8 | 6.3 | 5.1 | 4.3 |
| Blue-collar workers | 13.8 | 16.1 | 16.4 | 22.4 | 21.6 | 19.8 | 23.7 | 25.7 | 27.7 |
| Craftsmen and foremen | 1.8 | 1.1 | 1.0 | 1.5 | 1.1 | 1.0 | 1.2 | 1.4 | 1.4 |
| Operatives | 10.7 | 14.5 | 15.0 | 20.0 | 19.5 | 17.4 | 20.2 | 22.9 | 23.8 |
| Nonfarm labores | 1.2 | 0.5 | 0.4 | 0.9 | 1.1 | 1.5 | 2.3 | 1.4 | 2.6 |
| Service workers | 19.5 | 21.7 | 24.7 | 21.5 | 29.4 | 27.5 | 23.9 | 32.4 | 35.5 |
| Farmworkers | 1.2 | 1.8 | 4.5 | 3.7 | 4.0 | 8.4 | 13.5 | 15.8 | 19.0 |

Source: U.S. Bureau of the Census, Historical Statistics of the United States, Colonial Times to 1957 (Washington, D. C.: U.S. Government Printing Office, 1960), p. 74; U.S. Bureau of the Census, Statistical Abstract of the United States: 1971 (Washington, D.C.: U.S. GPO, 1972), p. 222; and Statistical Abstract of the United States, 1981 (Washington, D.C.: U.S. Government Printing Office, 1981), p.401, Table 673.

Thus the working class within modern capitalistic society is highly divided and diversified both in its objective conditions as well as its subjective consciousness. Despite these changing conditions, workers in general have no choice but to sell their labor and surrender control over their production. They still have no voice in determining what to produce, how to produce and what to do with the product after it is produced.[28]

It has taken several decades of hard struggle, particularly since the turn of the century, for labor forces, to become unionized and be recognized as such by the capitalists.[29] Many capitalists then, as they do now, actively resisted the organizing efforts of labor.[30] Militancy and active struggle was necessary for the labor forces to gain some minimum bargaining power.[31] However since World War II, unlike in other industrialized capitalist societies, the labor unions in the United States have been transformed into highly conservative entities. Left-wing militant unionists have been expelled and the right to strike has been limited by legislative actions.[32] Furthermore, there has been certain degrees of accommodation between the capitalists and organized labor union leaders. There has been certain kinds of implied "social contract" according to which capitalists would recognize the unions and go along with the legitimate demands to negotiate increases in wage rates corresponding to increases in labor productivity; unions, in turn, would place their demands for such wage rate increases within a framework of limitations and exercise disciplinary authority over their members who do not abide by the established terms of negotiated contracts.

This accommodation has tended to promote stability in the production process allowing greater scope for long range capitalist planning on the one hand, and eliminating militant radical anticapitalist elements from the labor unions on the other. In times of prosperity, such as those of the 50's, this "social contract" has worked fine, but in hard times, such as those of the 70's, it has tended to create discontent among the rank and file of the labor unions causing antagonism toward the union leaders who have been unable to negotiate contracts acceptable to the members. Such rank and file resentments have developed during recent years by workers who have been able to organize in small groups among themselves within each factory in counter-planning against the management plan of production. Thus, increasingly, workers have been able to substitute the rational plans of management with entirely different plans for carrying out certain particular production functions. Among such substitutions have been a complete alternative break system, alternative systems of executing work, shutdown, plant-wide sabotage of different kinds, etc.

Presently, there is in co-existence two distinct sets of relations, two modes of production, and two power structures in many plants. With increasing organization and innovation of the workers to gain free time during working hours, this co-existence is the object of constant strife and turmoil. It is a struggle of losing and gaining ground between management and the workers. Management is under constant threat by the assertion of an alternative plan of action by the workers. The social relations of production is distinctly moving toward an era which may be termed post-unionism. A crucial point to focus on here is the differentiation of this new form of struggle from the previous one which took place under the drive for mass unionization.

These new independent forms of workers' organization appears to be the foundation for a new social relation of production with a potential to seize power in a crisis situation providing for a new societal direction. This new mode of production is gradually emerging out of the old as a result of increasing contradictions.

## NOTES

1. For more details see David M. Katz, "Finance Capital and Corporate Control," in Richard C. Edwards and others, *The Capitalist System* (Englewood Cliffs, NJ: Prentice-Hall, 1978), pp. 148-157.

2. For more details and other information see Lewis Corey, *House of Morgan* (New York: G. Howard Watt, 1930).

3. J.P. Morgan consolidated many of today's well known companies such as U.S. Steel and International Harvester. These mergers were called trusts. Morgan usually named the directors of the trusts he created and through his influence, encouraged collusive actions among the trusts.

4. For example, the Morgan group consisted mainly of J.P. Morgan and Company and the First National Bank of New York. It encompassed the three largest life insurance companies, American Telephone and Telegraph, and dozens of railroad

## 92 / Technodemocratic Economic Theory

and manufacturing firms. The Rockefeller-Stillman group, which was also based in New York, consisted of John D. Rockefeller, who had accumulated phenomenal wealth from the operation of Standard Oil, and James Stillman of the National City Bank of New York. It encompassed numerous railroad and production companies including the Union Pacific Railroad and Amalgamated Copper. The Mellon group, based in Pittsburgh, and Kuhn, Loeb and Company were two other major financial groups. For a detailed description of the major financial groups of the early twentieth century, see U.S. Congress, House Banking and Currency Committee, *Report of the Committee Appointed Pursuant to H.R. 429 and 574 to Investigate the Concentration of Money and Credit, 62nd Congress, 2nd Session, 1913.*

5. They obtained from 40 to 45 percent of their total funds from external sources during 1946-52, the large companies obtained about 34 percent of total funds from exterior sources during 1949-54. For more details, see John Lintner, "The Financing of Corporation," in E. Mason, ed., *The Corporation in Modern Society* (New York: Atheneum, 1969); S. Creamer, S. Dobrovolski, and I. Borenstein, *Capital in Manufacturing and Mining* (Princeton, NJ: Princeton University Press, 1960), and the *Economic Report of the President* (Washington, DC: GPO, 1974).

6. *Trusts and Estates*, March 1974, p. 145.

7. Robert Soldofsky, *Institutional Holdings of Common Stock 1900-2000* (Ann Arbor, MI: University of Michigan, Division of Research), 1971, p. 209.

8. David M. Katz, "Finance Capital and Corporate Control," in Richard C. Edwards, Michael Reich, and Thomas E. Weisskopf, eds., *The Capitalist System*, 2nd. ed. (Englewood Cliffs, NJ: Prentice-Hall, 1978), pp. 153-157.

9. For details on this subject see *U.S. Congress, House Judiciary Committee, Investigation of Conglomerate Corporations, Staff Report of the Antitrust Subcommittee, 92nd Congress, First Session, 1971.* For example, it was found that the Chase Manhattan Bank facilitated the acquisition plan of Gulf and Western Industries; and Lazard, Freres and Company, an investment bank, was instrumental in ITT's merger program.

10. For example, Chase Manhattan controls three airlines and two aircraft corporations.

11. For example, the Chase Manhattan group alone controlled over ten percent of the 200 top non-financial corporations.

12. J.D. Smith and S.D. Franklin, "The Concentration of Personal Wealth, 1922-1969," *American Economic Review* (May, 1974), Table 1, p. 166.

13. W.Comanper and R. Smiley, "Monopoly and the Distribution of Wealth," *Quarterly Journal of Economics*, 1975.

14. See Michael Parenti, *Democracy for the Few*, 4th ed., (New York: St. Martin's Press, 1983), pp. 11-12; for more details in corporate America see Thomas R. Dye, *Who's Running America?*, 3rd ed. (Englewood Cliffs, NJ: Prentice-Hall, 1983); Ferdinand Lundberg, *The Rich and the Super-Rich* (New York: Lyle Stuart, 1968); also Mark Green and Robert Massie, Jr. (eds.), *The Big Business Reader* (New York: Pilgrim Press, 1980).

15. "Corporate Data Exchange," *Washington Post*, May 2, 1980.

16. James Hightower, "Food Monopoly," *The Big Business Reader, op. cit.*, pp. 9-18.

17. "Index to the Forbes Four Hundred," *Forbes 400*, Oct. 1, 1984, pp. 194-208.

18. Parenti, *op. cit.*, p. 14.

19. For more details, see Peter Collier and David Horowitz, *The Rockefellers: An American Dynasty* (New York: Holt, Rinehart and Winston, 1976).

20. Parenti, *op. cit.*, p. 15.

21. Ibid., p. 14. For more details, see Gerald C. Zilg, *DuPont: Behind the Nylon Curtain* (Englewood Cliffs, NJ: Prentice-Hall, 1974).

22. Thomas R. Dye, *op. cit.*, pp. 14-15.

23. For more details, see "The American Ruling Class" by Paul M. Sweezy, in Paul M. Sweezy, ed., *The Present History* (New York: Monthly Review Press, 1953); see also Morton Baratz "Corporate Giants and the Power Structure," *Western Political Quarterly*, (9 June 1956); and Peter Drucker, *The Concept of the Corporation* (New York: John Day, 1946).

24. For more facts and analyses, see William Domhoff, "State and Ruling Class in Corporate America," *The Surgent Sociologist*, IV, No. 3 (Spring 1974) and T.R. Dye, *Who Rules America?*, 3rd ed. (Englewood Cliffs, NJ: Prentice-Hall, 1983); and Michael Parenti, *Democracy for the Few*, 4th ed. (New York: St. Martin's Press, 1983).

25. For more details see Richard C. Edwards, M. Reich and D.M. Gordon, *Labor Market Segmentation* (Lexington, MA: D.C. Heath, 1975).

94 / Technodemocratic Economic Theory

26. For more details see Michael Reich, "The Development of the Wage Labor Force," in Richard C. Edward and others, *The Capitalist System* (Englewood Cliffs, NJ: Prentice-Hall, 1978), pp. 179-85.

27. For more details see Richard C. Edwards, "Systems of Control in the Labor Process," in Richard Edwards, Michael Reich and T.E. Weisskopf, *The Capitalist System*, op. cit., pp. 193-200.

28. For more detailed analysis see Harry Braverman, *Labor and Monopoly Capital* (New York: Monthly Review Press, 1974).

29. However, until 1933 only about 5 percent of the American workers, less than three million in number, were organized into unions. For detailed data on unionization see Department of Labor B.L.S. Bulletin, *Directory of National Unions and Employee Associations* (Washington, DC: U.S. Government Printing Office, 1973).

30. Before the 1930's organized employer resistance, often violent and repressive and supported by the military and police forces, attempted to block industry-wide unionization.

31. For example, the massive sit-down strikes of 1936-37 during which tens of thousands of workers successfully occupied factories, at times for weeks, until the employers recognized their unions as legitimate bargaining bodies. For workers active resistance see William Watson, "Counter Planning on the Shop Floor," *Radical America*, Vol. 5, No. 3, May-June, 1971.

32. See for details Stanley Aronowitz, *False Promises: The Shaping of American Working Class Consciousness* (New York: McGraw-Hill, 1973).

# CHAPTER 3.

# THE STATE UNDER CAPITALISM

The third aspect of capitalism concerns the relationship between the state and class conflicts, the state's role in class struggle and the impact of classes on the operation of government.

The ever increasing complexity of the capitalist system has caused the imposition of high demands upon the state. The main task of the state has increasingly become to protect and maintain the existing economic system. It has become the task of the state to discourage and prevent the development of any movement, factors, or forces that may contradict the existing forces of production and may tend to have adverse effects on the state of economic affairs.

To achieve this goal the government has armed itself with a variety of complex devices, such as regulatory agencies, instruments of fiscal policy formation and control, and a vast array of subsidization of the basic institutions necessary for the proper operation of capitalism such as education, transportation, highway systems, research and development etc. The military is maintained as the last resort for the enforcement of governmental policies. The increasing role of the state has become largely a response to the needs of the dominant capitalist class. The functions of the state have tended to coordinate with the capitalist class and to guard its economic interests. Where and when any conflict arises between individual capitalists and the capitalist class as a whole, the state plays the key role representing the collective interest of the class. Consequently, the modern technological capitalist society remains fundamentally capitalist and firmly established as a result of the major changes and enormous technological advances that have taken place in its history during recent decades.

The United States is the major power among all advanced capitalist nations while Japan takes second place. All these form an increasingly integrated capitalist system heavily influenced by the powerful status of the United States.

One should not be misled by assuming that these dramatic changes in the operation of modern capitalism has caused moderating changes in the capitalist mode of production. The fact is that dramatic changes have occurred in the manner of operation, production, and distribution, but the substance of the mode of production has remained, and continues to be capitalist with high concentration of economic powers in the hands of a few giant multinational corporations. These corporations strictly pursue their capitalist objective of maximization of profit and growth, more likely, at a more intense degree than ever before. Despite a large sector of highly educated white-collar labor, the alienation of labor, its separation from capital and its subjugation to the capitalist whims and wishes have not been eroded, but established more firmly than ever before, not only through the control of technology and capital but also by controlling education and informational systems. Though the relative size of the proletariat has significantly increased by the explosion in size of the white-collar labor, this enormous labor force has remained sharply differentiated from the small group of super-capitalists and their immediate managers who control the huge multinational corporations.

Most contradictions in capitalist society result most fundamentally from antagonism between the interests of capitalist and working classes. The capitalist class, seeking to maintain its position and privileges, attempts to ensure the continuation of prime factors prerequisite to the survival of capitalist social organization. Most important among these are private property relations, capitalist control over the means of production and distribution, and markets. Survival of the capitalist class depends on reproduction of capitalist social relations of production from generation to generation and continuation of a society that is essentially capitalist in nature, namely, it fosters conditions favorable to making profits and accumulating capital.

Thus the prime concern of the capitalist class is to provide for conditions favorable to accumulation. For this aim it is always seriously concerned with the degree of organization and militancy of the working class.

The working class, on the other hand, tends to resist conditions that create opportunities for high rates of return for the capitalists. Such conditions of high profits are typically possible when workers can be paid lower wages and when they cannot challenge the system for fear of losing their employment. The capitalist social relations of production that produces high profits is usually undermined by organized labor when it is able to effectively challenge—working conditions, demand higher wages, oppose the capitalists efforts to reduce taxes they have to pay, and when the costs of pollution or safety conditions relating to the workplace are ignored.

The struggle of the working class to maintain and improve its living and working conditions is, necessarily, in conflict with the capitalist interests; however, such struggle is crucial for defending its demands for higher wages, better living standards, reforms and fringe benefits. Contrary to the expectations predicted by Marx regarding the unity and power of the working class, these struggles do not directly threaten the capitalist system itself. While each union or group of workers is a threat and extracts concessions from its capitalist employer firm, the very diversity among worker groups undermine a collective challenge against the system as a whole. Therefore, the social conflict arising out of the capitalist social relations of production, being itself the consequence of class division and class struggle, rarely take the form of actual confrontation between the two classes of capitalists and workers as a whole. In practice, when important sectors of the working class concurrently confront capitalist institutions, the latter has been able to forestall such challenge by resorting to its predominant resources including state laws and law enforcement agencies.[1] However, when contradictions within the system are intense, and the systematic origins of various manifestations of class oppression are clear, these separate struggles may be transformed into class confrontation as a whole. In such situations, in general, capitalists have responded collectively as a class employing the mechanism of the state.[2]

## Capitalist Control of Democratic Process

After the present state became crystallized, it replaced feudal aristocracy as a result of growing capitalist power, it then tended toward the democratic form in advanced societies. The state structure which materialized as a result of this struggle tended to operate on behalf of capitalists and their economic interests.

In appearance, the democratic process itself was inherently a potential source of serious challenge to the rule by a small group of capitalists. The irony was, and still is, that while capitalists constituted an insignificant minority of the electorate they were able to control the electoral process as well as the state.

The secret of this control is in the capitalistic nature of the state. First, the economy is capitalistically organized. This simply means that state functions cannot be supported which impede the profits and accumulation process and cause problems to the operating capitalist order. It is the capitalists, not the state, that carry out the primary responsibility for the operation of the means of production and distribution. The state usually has no alternative but to adopt policies acceptable to capitalists who control these means of production and distribution. If the state policies are in conflict with the capitalist goals of profit and accumulation of capital, the capitalists will simply refrain from further investment which will cause the state to face economic crises. In the absence of strong public demand for an alternative to capitalism, the state can resolve the crisis only be abandoning its anti-capitalist attitudes. It is important to notice that these limitations on state power come not from the voting power of the capitalists but from their control of the basic means of production and distribution, including the information system.

Furthermore, the capitalists attempt for direct control of state policies and manipulation of the electoral process, through the use of their vast financial resources, necessarily hampers the operation of the democratic process in advanced societies. Persistent and pervasive antidemocratic practices are incorporated in the political process ranging from domination of election financing by the capitalist class, influence upon the bureaucracy and its decision-making process, measures to reduce government accountability to the public, corporate corruptive measures and bribing of public officials, discriminatory administration of justice, control and censorship of the media (radio and television in particular) to strong lobbying efforts. These undemocratic and abusive tendencies have gradually enhanced the power and influence of the capitalist class.

Finally, deep involvement of the state in supporting capitalist functions has gradually developed a strong and established ideology in support of the capitalist system which tends to inhibit any anti-capitalist challenge. Such challenges are particularly restrained when the exclusive property right is questioned. Such anti-capitalist or socialistic ideas are effectively prevented through capitalist control of the media, educational curriculum and process, and control over other ideological resources. Strong, well designed and overall public indoctrination in favor of capitalism from childhood all the way through adulthood, by employing the institutions of family, school, church and numerous other social organizations, have tended to successfully perpetuate capitalism as an ideology and as a legitimate societal system.

This capitalist ideology has been carefully incorporated in the national constitution and into a formal democratic process which in theory recognizes, by its incorporating document, equal private property rights, and for their protection installs "due process of law," and "equal protection under law."[3] But in practice, the state's defense of property ends up with more protection for those with the most property, namely the capitalist class. Thus the laws that are enacted confer upon the state legitimate power to act within the context of capitalist property relations. By this approach the state appears to be neutral and fair-minded in antagonistic relations between classes. The state recognizes individual legal rights for people in all economic classes including equal rights to protection of their person and property, equal freedom to dispose of their property as they wish, and equal electoral rights.[4] In this way, the state appears to represent public interest as a whole distinguished from a specific class or group interest. But, the commitment of the capitalist class to this democracy ends where state action threatens the established capitalist property relations.[5]   Democracy is abandoned where the so called "free enterprise system," namely the capitalists interest, is at stake.

## The Capitalistic Functions of the State

The prime concern of the state in a capitalist society has been to maintain the capitalist relations of property which also has been the highest priority of the capitalist class operating through the state. Toward this purpose, legitimation and maintenance of capitalist ideology has been the core in state activities.  This goal has been achieved by different means, including the influence of educational context, media, sponsoring beneficial research projects, propaganda and campaigns in favor of "free enterprise system" and against any conflicting ideology, communism and socialism in particular, actual and often violent and illegal repression of anti-capitalist elements and threats.

Furthermore, the state is quite instrumental for capital accumulation within the upper echelon of the capitalist class.  Despite the fact that the state has no capital accumulation function of its own, its functions directly help private accumulation through use of its revenues and nature of its expenditures.  The state's aid to capitalists is carried out in different forms:  subsidies of various kinds, tax credits, financial loans and credits, financing costly research and development projects, subsidized vocational and educational programs in order to provide for appropriately trained labor force to service the capitalists, massive military and other spending programs to increase aggregate demand and counteract stagnation.  The state insures adequacy of labor supply by imposing legal restrictions on welfare, minimum wage, and unemployment compensation in order to prevent these programs from interfering with the replenishment of unemployed reserves, to restrain labor unions power by enacting laws weakening their power vis-a-vis the capitalist employer.  This dual function of the state causes the state to face conflict.   On the one hand, the state has to maintain the capitalist system and, on the other, it has to facilitate the accumulation process.   Advancement on the latter may disturb the equilibrium necessary to maintain the former.  In general, certain accumulation functions may cause popular dissension, labor strikes or general uprisings.  In such a situation, the very existence of capitalism faces danger and by necessity, the capitalist class as a whole, turns in opposition to the group within the class which has been the particular beneficiary of accumulation, such as industries producing war materials or those controlling the production and marketing of energy, such as petroleum.

Such national conflicts has caused the state to develop and assume certain degrees of autonomy from the influence of special capitalist groups. The state has tended to give priority to and serve the collective interests of the capitalist class and avoid falling under control of its particular factions. To maintain and protect the capitalist system the state must appear to act on behalf of public interest and attempt, at the same time, to resolve conflicts among capitalist groups competing for accumulation.

Besides resolving conflicts within the capitalist class, the state also faces challenges and class confrontation from working and other lower classes. To defuse such dissent the state has been obliged to expand its public socio-economic programs and services. As a result, the state expenditures has been continually increased and the bargaining power of workers has been enhanced. However, intensifying international competition has obliged capitalists to assist the state in lowering taxes and demanding cheaper labor costs enabling them to compete and maintain their high profit rates. At the same time, unlike the crisis of the 1890's and 1930's, the rising power of labor through expanded organization and further unionization has increasingly imposed restriction on state options in dealing with the crisis.

From these explanations one additional factor becomes evident. That is, while the state has been a crucial element in class relations in the course of class struggles, the latter in turn, along with continuing centralization and concentration of capital, intrastruggle within the capitalist class itself, between powerful corporate and small capitalists, and the attempts made by workers to organize and unionize, have been effective factors in shaping and stimulating evolution of the state.

To illustrate this situation we look as an example, to the historical relations between class conflicts and evolution of the state in American society.

**The Effect of Class Conflict in the Evolution of the American State**

Under the British empire the colonial government grew out of royal charter, proprietorship and legal relations emanating from the British monarch. Within the colonies either British laws applied, or if local legislation were allowed, they could not be in conflict with the British laws. All economic policies were intended to foster British trade and economic superiority and to benefit the British crown.

However, growing economic importance of the colonies tended to cause conflicts between British imperial demands and developing interests of colonial manufacturers, planters, merchants, and financial institutions. British laws insured British merchants' control of colonial commerce while depriving development of a domestic market and excluding planters and colonial merchants from entering the international trade market. Restrictions were imposed on settling of the western lands which caused strong resentment among poor farmers striving to explore the interior for rich farmland.

All these restrictions brought about the American Revolution, and led to the establishment of the United States as an independent nation. Independence freed American capitalism from British dominance and established needed conditions for development of the indigenous American capitalist class.

The struggle for independence awakened liberating forces within American society and through legislation provided civil rights and personal liberties not available before. Ideas of social equality and government by popular consent gained widespread support and application. Induced by these trends, farmers, partisans and other lower class members formed political groups and became enthusiastically active in political life.

The new American society continued to be based, however, on the interests of the coalition of dominant classes consisting of rich merchants of the North, plantation owners of the South, large landowners and manufacturers. The Constitution of the United States was crystallized and shaped by members of these classes to accommodate their interests.

The American state made rapid transition to a full capitalist form during the years between the Revolution and the Civil War of

1860-65. While the government was controlled by the coalition of the above mentioned groups, the national government remained relatively weak since no single group was able to control it and none was willing to grant it broad powers.

Despite these facts, the state played a crucial role in establishing the conditions necessary for a capitalist system. It actively aided the process of primary accumulation by extension of territorial rights to the West which enormously benefitted land speculators, promoters and developers; by military campaigns against Indians to dispossess them from their homeland; concentration of assets aided by subsidies in the form of cash grants, exclusive franchise rights, and land grants for canals, roads, and railroads; by establishment of a National Bank and other national credit institutions to mobilize profits; and by state governments' bond issues among many efforts to accumulate capital.

On the negative side, in order to guarantee a smooth advancement of the accumulation process, the state effectively attempted to suppress challenges to its authority and to its capitalistic policies.[6]

Conflict between the governing classes became tense when tariffs were introduced as designed by the industrialists of the North to protect the domestic market against foreign competition. This raised the cost of production for plantations of the South and farmers of the West. When the extension of slavery to new areas, demanded by planters, was not granted, the security of planters continuing economic and political positions were endangered. The result was a break in the alliance and the Civil War by which the Southern aristocracy was smashed by increasingly powerful Northern bourgeoisie.

After the Civil War, the American State was firmly in capitalist hands. When the Reconstruction era ended in 1877, white Southern property-owners were readmitted to the governing alliance but only as a junior partner. The South remained open to capitalist penetration. The primary accumulation process further accelerated by massive Western land grants to railroad companies. In the industrialized North the state intervened on the side of capitalists to suppress militant workers and the capitalist production continued its momentum without formidable obstacles.

## The State and Monopoly Capitalism

During the era of monopoly capitalism, which started to crystalize with the turn of the twentieth century and continues to the present, the state has continued its two main tasks of protecting the capitalist system and easing the accumulation process. During this period, in direct response to increasing capitalist demand, the state has been obliged to stimulate, regulate, and coordinate the accumulation process. Accordingly, state activities have vastly expanded.

Furthermore, while small capitalists have continually declined, the working class has grown in size and power. Through organization and expanding unionization the working class has been able to increase its economic as well as political power and, consequently, gain more access to the state and obtain some reforms. Expanding workers demands has caused further expansion of state activities in many areas and has established a variety of new services and functions such as the social security system, unemployment compensation, antipoverty programs, wage bargaining, etc.

The state has also been forced into long-range planning concerned with major aspects of the economy such as energy supply, assessment of long-run capital needs, supervision of product pricing for the major industries, inflation, recession, eliminating discrimination in employment on account of race, sex, color or national origin, and so on. The accumulation process in monopoly capitalism has thus become increasingly politicized. The state budget has expanded to finance programs aimed directly at facilitating and aiding accumulation processes such as highway construction, regulation of transportation means,[7] basic research and development on new technologies, job training, etc. All these have contributed to overexpanding bureaucracy and its complexity at all levels of government.[8] Thus the state, through its policies as well as its institutions, has become involved in and, not infrequently, has been identified by conflict within the capitalist and working classes.

The sharpest class struggles have occurred during industrial strikes by industrial workers, and this tradition of struggle has continued to the present and has expanded further into other sectors of the working class,[9] such as farm-workers, state and municipal workers, clerical workers, truck drivers, air controllers, airline pilots and mechanics, school teachers, etc. The state has frequently used physical force to suppress workers opposition to capitalists. Often these interventions have been under legal facade by enforcement of either state statutes or court injunctions, both favoring employers' interests because of political systems being under control of the capitalists.[10]

There have been cases that official actions were obviously illegal.[11] In other cases, legal harassment and false arrests have been pursued, in order to cripple the organizations by immobilizing their leadership and deactivating their resources.[12] In any serious situation the state has not been reluctant to employ legal, extralegal, and even illegal and violent means to suppress and curb working class resistance.

Although suppression of workers by officially sanctioned violence may be successful at times but in the long run tends to expose suppressive class relations and breed more opposition. Understanding this, more forward looking sectors of the capitalist class have often advocated state involvement in establishing programs providing for necessary reform, accommodation and ideological attempts toward legitimizing the capitalist system and its representative state. Accordingly, larger state expenditures for military forces,[13] welfare, social security, pollution control, and environmental protection, antipoverty and food stamp programs, education[14] etc. were required to stabilize the capitalist social order.

The aim of these programs has been not only an attempt to deflect dissent but, more importantly, to reshape the state toward a more appropriate response to developing new means of monopoly capitalism.[15]

Unlike the rise of competitive capitalism which produce a laissez-faire economic ideology, the evolution of monopoly capitalism brought about a more interventionist government.[16] This ideal of a liberal capitalist social order was formulated, developed and effectuated for the most part, under supervision of the more sophisticated leaders of the largest corporations and financial institutions who enjoyed ideological and political hegemony.

More importantly, these corporate leaders were able to harness, toward their own ends, the desire of intellectuals and reformers and bring together "thoughtful men of all classes" in "a vanguard for the building of the good community."[17]

In any case, this tendency toward "progressive democracy" was designed to serve as a counterpose to the threat of the working class revolution.[18] Despite the fact that the purpose of liberal capitalists was mainly to design and effectuate a defense strategy for the capitalist social system, they also intended and sought to improve human conditions among working classes, though they badly failed in achieving the latter purpose. This, however, by no means should imply that capitalists are the only beneficiaries of state activities. Quite in a variety of areas and at times, non-capitalist classes of the nation also benefit from state activities such as welfare, medical care, research and development, low income housing programs, social security and many other entitlement programs. Though some of these programs have clearly resulted from demands of groups other than the capitalist class, they also are not reflected and, in some cases even supported by the capitalist class as stabilizing functions of the state in maintaining the capitalist social order.

Thus, in short, it may be stated that the capitalist state tends to regulate society in such a way as to serve, primarily, the capitalist class interest and maintain the capitalist social order in which capitalists, as a privileged class, benefit most from continuation of the system. In a politically democratic society like the United States, the monopoly capitalist class rules and allows freedom of action and competition only to the extent that it does not interfere with, or fundamentally affect, the maintenance and continuation of the capitalist social order.[19]

This control by the capitalists as the ruling class is implemented through three main processes. First, the process of ideological control, concerned primarily with the formation, dissemination and enforcement of concept, attitudes and assumptions which legitimatize the existence and stimulates or at least allows the continuation of the capitalist order. It creates social forces which serve to fortify and maintain the privileged position of the ruling capitalist class.

In this process of ideological indoctrination, the policy-planning organizations are carefully linked, not to government as in the policy process, but to a research and dissemination network consisting among others of research and discussion groups, public relations firms, advertising and policy councils, vast university and foundation programs, books, journals, pamphlets, speeches and mass media.

The enforcement of the capitalist ideological consensus is achieved through a multitude of ways, from more gentle methods of persuasion through legitimization of the concept, monetary inducement, influence, pressure, to intimidation and violence. Outspoken opponents are readily silenced, neutralized or deactivated by a vast variety of means including the state instruments.

The second process relates to control of policy-planning processes concerned with the development and implementation of policies important to the interests of the ruling capitalist class.

These policy-planning processes provide opportunities for the ruling capitalists:

1. To familiarize themselves with general issues and hear the corresponding ideas and findings of their hired experts.

2. To discuss, compromise and resolve their conflicts.

3. To receive appropriate leadership experience for occupying governmental positions important to maintain the interests of the ruling capitalist class.

4. To commission studies by experts on important issues and disseminate the results through books, journals, policy statements, speeches, etc. in order to influence public opinion in favor of specific issues in particular, and the capitalist cause in general.[20]

The third process related to the control of the electoral process to the extent that it insures the election of sympathetic candidates and their accessibility to the ruling capitalist class.

In the United States, political process is limited to the candidate-selection process. Political parties, unlike what may be expected from a fully developed political party in a democratic society, have little to do with policy-making or political education. American political parties have been largely restricted in functional scope to the task of filling political offices.[21] For all intents and purposes, the two American major parties do not exist. "There are only individuals (candidates) and professionals (consultants, pollsters, media advisors).[22]

Because of its individualistic issueless nature of the electoral process, it has come under control and domination of the ruling capitalist class mainly by means of campaign contributions. "Recruitment of elective elites remains closely associated, especially for the more important offices...with the candidates' wealth or access to large campaign contributions."[23]

These politicians come from the higher levels of social order. Nine of every ten of the political elite come from the wealthiest one-fifth of American families.[24] These are men who know how to go along and to get along, and belong to or work for the capitalist class and usually have no strong and conflicting commitments of their own and thus are open to suggestions put forth to them by the ruling elite or their experts.

Accordingly, democratic governments in a capitalist society like the United States do not properly represent the people, they are ruled instead by a capitalist elite and reflect, primarily, their interests. More than a century ago, Marx and Engels identified the state, correctly so, with the capitalist class when they stated that:

> The bourgeoisie has at last, since the establishment of
> modern industry and of the world market, conquered
> for itself, in the modern representative state, exclusive
> political sway. The modern state is but a committee
> for managing the common affairs of the whole
> bourgeoisie.[25]

Later on, Lenin made the same distinction by stressing that the capitalists used that state as a special repressive force against the working class and peasant insurgency.[26]

The capitalist economy imposes objective constraints on the state, regardless which party holds power or occupies the high public offices. Capitalists have dominated both major parties in the United States and the party programs are designed as alternative strategies advancing capitalist interests. However, in recent decades, since World War II in particular, industrial workers and more recently non-industrial and white-collar workers, through grouping and unionization have been able to gain some leverage in both parties, the Democratic Party in particular. They have been able to force certain reforms and increasingly present capitalist rule with potentially serious challenge. To counteract this increasing challenge capitalists have sought to restructure the state in a way that its apparent democratic form has been maintained despite the fact that its democratic essence and content has been substantially reduced. This forced reaction has given class struggle a new and more general feature, namely conflict between capitalism and democracy. Since these two systems by their very nature cannot coexist, one has ultimately to give way to another. We think the developing forces and conditions indicate and favor the future triumph of democracy unless capitalists resort to irrational forces through the use of state power and destroy the world including their own existence. The hope for the triumph of democracy over capitalism rests on the fact that capitalists' control over the state is far from complete and is increasingly challenged by the continuing demise of small proprietors' interests and increasing demands of a vast and expanding enfranchised working class.

By state involvement in this class conflict, the struggle moves more and more into the political arena. Thus the struggle continues against capitalists and against the structural constraints that capitalist relations of production has placed on the state. This political consciousness has become an important component of the struggle against the capitalist mode of production under monopoly capitalism.

## The Institutions of Technological Society

### The Political System

Before the establishment of the national state the countries were ruled under autocracy when often only one person governed. The ruler was the center of authority, and all governmental powers emanated from him downward within the bureaucracy. As political democracy forced its way into the system of government, legislative assemblies were created with limited but increasing authority. The judicial system also received its partial autonomy much later. All these were political infringements upon the power and authority of the monarch.

The American and French revolutions established the national state and installed the foundation of political democracy. Before this change, the state had practically no interference in the operation of the economy. The private sector took care of the economic affairs and the state took care of its operation through taxation. The modern system took power from the autocrat monarch and transferred it to the people;

the people were to elect governmental leaders and were made able to check them by intermittent electoral processes. Simply, people were to elect representatives and these representatives, forming the legislative body, were to rule on behalf of the people during a determined term of office.

The executive branch of the government operated according to and within the limitations of the laws made by the legislature. A national document known as the Constitution established the power relationships between these branches and theirs with the people.

In practice, however, this theory did not materialize. Though the rule by one person disappeared and the state power was shared by plurality of its institutions and people's representatives, powerful economic forces in the society increasingly influenced the electoral process. As capitalism approached its monopolistic stage since the turn of the century, the state became, to an increasing degree, the capitalist instrument and the protector of its interests. For example, consider the U.S. Supreme Court rulings against the establishment of minimum wage and maximum hours of work during the first three decades of the 20th century.

The traditional concept of economy describes forces of production consisting of land, labor, capital and technology. The question has always been the manner of realizing and then combining these forces together in different forms for the purpose of production. The last one hundred years has seen development of the corporation, the most fascinating way of combining and employing these forces of production in enormous scale for extracting profits. Probably, the most striking aspect of the corporation has been its entity as a legal institution having a prescribed form and processes of functioning.

Though, for centuries, the state had been reluctant in getting directly involved in commercial activities and had satisfied itself with collection of taxes, the last one hundred years has also seen increasing involvement of the state in economic activities. The last fifty years, in particular, has seen rapidly developing state activities in relation to production and commerce and the whole economic activities in general. As a result, the government's size and expenditures have multiplied many folds all geared for sustaining, and fostering the capitalist system, and to provide, through diversified avenues, the monopoly capitalists' access to public funds.

Table 3-1 illustrates an increase in the size of public institutions from 1950 to 1982. The total number of employees has increased from 6.4 to 15.9 million. Table 3-2 demonstrates public expenditures from 1950 to 1981. The increase in about three decades has been phenomenal, from 67 billion in 1950 to 1075 billion in 1981, or by fifteen folds. While size of the national bureaucracy has increased only a few percentages, the national expenditures have grown about fifteen-fold from 44 to 659 billion.[27]

Today, in technological capitalist societies, the state plays a very important role affecting directly the process of production and distribution. Besides many laws favoring the monopoly business, the state makes enormous amounts of capital available, in the form of cash or natural resources, to giant corporations. So, in actuality, the state has become an important institution, second only to the corporation, directly concerned with the process of production and distribution of goods and services.

Thus, from the state of laissez-faire we have come to the recognition of the state as an important and undisputed force in the sphere of economic affairs.

## The Economic System

Before the institution of corporations, the capitalist economy operated through small independent individual businesses, in a competitive market. The capital for operation came from the individual owner of the business or partnership. Invention of the corporation soon changed the picture. It created an economic institution with a legal impersonal entity of its own with enormous economic implications. Its structure and function were prescribed by a document known as its charter. According to this charter, the capital of the corporation was divided into small increments called shares, making it possible for owners of small capital to invest by purchasing certain numbers of shares. Thus, ownership was highly dispersed. The shareholder could be anyone in any place. Though the shareholders owned the corporation, they did not operate it. The power of operation was designated to a board of directors elected by the majority of shareholders, in an arranged meeting, each share having one vote.[28] Elections of the board members were to be

## 112 / Technodemocratic Economic Theory

repeated annually at the stockholders' convention, time and place of which were to be designated by the board of directors. The board, restricted to the policy-making process, were to appoint the executive body of the corporation responsible for execution of the board policies and day by day operation of the business.

Through its bureaucratic structure, this form of economic institution was able to assemble immense amounts of capital for operation through

**Table 3-1  Government Employment from 1950 to 1982 (in thousands)**

| Year | Federal Civilian | State and Local | Total |
|------|------------------|-----------------|-------|
| 1995 | 2,117 | 4,285 | 6,402 |
| 1960 | 2,2421 | 6,387 | 8,808 |
| 1970 | 2,881 | 10,147 | 13,028 |
| 1980 | 2,898 | 13,315 | 16,213 |
| 1982 | 2,862 | 13,071 | 15,933 |

Source: *Statistical Abstract of the United States, 1984* (Washington, D.C.: U.S. Government Printing Office, 1984), p. 303, Table 487.

**Table 3-2  Government Expenditures from 1950-1981 (billions of dollars)**

| Year | Federal | State | Local | Total |
|------|---------|-------|-------|-------|
| 1950 | 44 | 11 | 12 | 67 |
| 1960 | 100 | 26 | 27 | 153 |
| 1965 | 126 | 39 | 38 | 203 |
| 1970 | 206 | 69 | 60 | 334 |
| 1975 | 302 | 119 | 98 | 519 |
| 1980 | 564 | 213 | 156 | 932 |
| 1981 | 659 | 240 | 176 | 1075 |

Source: *Statistical Abstract of the United States, 1984* (Washington, D.C.: U.S. Government Printing Office, 1984), p. 272, Table 448.

millions of shares issued by the corporation and sold in the open market. It was widely adopted and its structure grew rapidly. Giant corporations of today have an immense and complex bureaucratic structure.

The corporation, thus, grew in structure very much like the state. Its vast body of shareholders substituted the electorate; its board of directors, that of the legislative branch; its executive body, that of the executive branch and its bureaucratic structure very much similar to that of the state bureaucracy.

A very important factor in favor of the corporation is that, unlike the state, it does not have any territorial barriers. Its power and operation can extend beyond national borders into the territories of other nations. A corporation has the potential of becoming a global entity. For this characteristic, a multi-national corporation becomes independent from the state, and immune, to a great extent, from its restrictive laws. It can protect its capital within a state by transferring it into a safer state; it can avoid payment of taxes through many instruments available to it, such as price and technology transfer and complex international bookkeeping systems, immune to a particular state inspection.

In functional terms, a multinational corporation is an independent institution more powerful than a state. It does not possess armed forces but it can induce the state or group of states to use military force for the protection of corporate interests. It does not have legislative power outside of its entity but can influence the state legislatures to pass laws favoring corporate interests, and hinder passage of legislation to the contrary.

## Capitalistic Corruption and Militarism

**Corruption:** Corruption is a *sin quo non* of capitalism. Because the basic function of capitalism is based on profits and its maximization. Profit is, in essence, a legalized and legitimized term for theft. Profit is what a capitalist actually steals from the work of labor through exploitation; and extracts from the consumer, through misrepresentation, which often easily borders deceit through legitimized misleading advertisement. In fact, the capitalist is a licensed criminal whose corrupt and corruptive practices from commercial bribery, price-rigging schemes to tax evasion and fraud against customers, are an active part of his daily occupation.

To the capitalist the cause of his crimes and the controlling philosophy is "produce for profit or perish." There are innumerable examples found in many studies regarding the subject matter.[29] In many instances "where bribes are not freely offered, they are often extorted."[30]

The extent to which a society is civilized is illustrated by the way it treats its criminals. From this viewpoint, considering the extent of corruption and lack of punishment, American society approaches barbarianism, where no millionaire goes to the electric chair; where neither the president nor any board member of a giant company go to jail even if he pleads guilty for a felonious crime or is convicted of it.[31]

A study of crimes committed by persons of respectability and high social status in 70 corporations showed that for these individuals "a violation of legal code is not necessarily a violation of the business code."[32] Sixty percent of the 70 corporations were considered "habitual criminals." Slightly over 97 percent of the corporations had at least two convictions. It concludes that "practically all large corporations engage in illegal restraint of tender, and ... from half to three-fourths of them engage in such practices so continuously that they may properly be called 'habitual criminals.'"[33]

A Harvard Business Review survey in 1961 reaffirmed these findings. 1700 executive readers of the Review replied to the questionnaire. Four out of seven believed that businessmen "would violate a code of ethics whenever they thought they could avoid detection." One-half agreed that the American business executive is preoccupied chiefly with gain.[34] By considering the outcome of some other studies of the subject, one may safely conclude that a businessman in his daily operation considers what is "normal practice," rather than what is the law. If it is normal practice, it is then ethical, though it may not be legal.

Bribing under capitalism is considered a normal part of "doing business." It takes many forms from contribution to political campaign funds, free gifts and transfers of intangible properties such as stocks and bonds, to cash under the table payments. Once bribe is considered a part of the legitimate operation of capitalism, it breeds corruption among public officials who are trusted with appropriate spending of billions of dollars of the taxpayers' money. Corruption then spreads from politicians, top bureaucrats, who have certain responsibility regarding economic policies, to public servants including law enforcement and judicial officers, whose very function is to find and bring before justice those who break laws.[35] For example, the commission which investigated the New York Police Department in 1971 found:

> ...a standardized pattern of corruption.
> Plain-clothesmen, participating in what is known in
> police parlance as a "pad," collected regular bi-weekly
> or monthly payments amounting to as much as $3500
> from each of the gambling establishments in the area
> under their jurisdiction, and divided the take in equal
> shares. The monthly share per man (called the "nut")
> ranged from $300 to $400 in midtown Manhattan to
> $1500 in Harlem. When supervisors were involved
> they received a share and a half ... almost every plain-
> clothesman in the division, including supervisory
> lieutenants, were implicated.[36]

Corruption among detectives assigned to general investigative duties was the same: collections, not infrequently, came to several thousand dollars. In narcotics enforcement, the individual payments known as "scores" were commonly staggering in amount. In the Commission investigation it went as high as 80,000.[37]

Uniformed patrolmen received regular payments from construction sites, bars, grocery stores and other business establishments. Sergeants and lieutenants participated in the same kind of corruption as the men they supervised. Officers above the rank of lieutenant often each used a patrolman as his "bagman" who collected for him and kept a percentage of the take.[38]

Courts and judges are not exceptions. The author and constitutional scholar Charles Ashman put it this way:

> American justice is choking on judicial pollution...it is
> no longer a question of occasional corruption, but a

> decided pattern of conflict of interest, chronic bribery, profound abuse of office, loathsome nepotism, infamous sexual perversions and pernicious payoffs. ...All the bribes paid or tendered in any one year could undoubtedly eliminate much of the poverty that breeds the crimes that outrage America... The black-robed Mafia is an even more mercenary intrusion in American justice than its Sicilian counterpart.[39]

We intentionally cite law enforcement and judicial institutions because these are considered the guardians of justice and protectors of people. In the case of judges, for example, the courtroom is his dominion; our lives and property are his jurisdiction. He presides and he listens. He punishes instantly for any minor deviation from the protocol of his sanctimonious court, to any statement he considers an insult to his person. He assumes an empirical air when he sentences. "No one in our society, including the President exercises summary powers or more censorial prerogatives."[40]

The American people believe, or at least claim to believe, in equality before the law. But those who have money or contact, exert a judicial pressure that destroys equality and promotes a double standard of justice. No corruption in any other societal organization can be as dangerous and as destructive of individual rights and liberties than the one in the system of law enforcement and justice.

## Militarism

To counter contradictions in a capitalist society the capitalist through its elements of state, resort for enactment of the protective laws and their implementation by force, if necessary. Therefore, force and coercion are the capitalist tools for domination and imposing of "tranquility." Military power is emphasized and maintained for two main purposes. First, to suppress dissent and cries for justice at home and provide for "domestic tranquility." Second, to suppress other less developed countries for the purpose of bringing about, and if

**Table 3-3 Twenty Big Ticket Military Programs**

| Weapon System | No. | Estimated Cost | Cost per weapon |
|---|---|---|---|
| **ARMY** | | | |
| M-1 Tank | 7071 | $20 billion | $2.8 million |
| Patriot missile | 6449 | $11.8 billion | $1.8 million |
| Bradley vehicle | 6908 | $11.3 billion | $1.6 million |
| Apache helicopter | 524 | $ 7.3 billion | $14 million |
| Stinger missile | 46,417 | $ 3.7 billion | $80,000 |
| **NAVY** | | | |
| F-18 aircraft | 1377 | $40.0 billion | $29 million |
| F-14A aircraft | 899 | $38.3 billion | $43 million |
| TridentII missile | 764 | $37.4 billion | $49 million |
| Trident submarine | 16 | $32.5 billion | $ 2 billion |
| SSN-688 submarine | 64 | $31.0 billion | $500 million |
| CG-47 Cruiser | 26 | $28.8 billion | $1.1 billion |
| DDG-51 Destroyer | 14 | $14.9 billion | $1.0 billion |
| Cruise missile (sea) | 4068 | $13.0 billion | $3.2 million |
| AV-8B aircraft | 334 | $10.0 billion | $30 million |
| **AIR FORCE** | | | |
| F-16 aircraft | 2659 | $50 billion | $18.8 million |
| F-15 aircraft | 1376 | $38.0 billion | $27.7 million |
| AMRAAM missile* | 24,489 | $10.8 billion | $440,000 |
| HARM missile* | 17,528 | $6.4 billion | $36,500 |
| Cruise missile (air) | 1787 | $4.5 billion | $2.5 million |
| Cruise missile (ground) | 656 | $3.7 billion | $6.6 million |

* Joint AF-Navy program

Source: Center for Defense Information, *The Defense Monitor*, vol. XIII, No. 4, 1984, p. 3.

**Table 3-4 Budget Shifts to the Pentagon ($ in billions, outlays)**

|  | FY1981 | FY1985 | %change |
|---|---|---|---|
| Military | $159.7 | $272.0 | +70 |
| Hospital/medical care for vets | 6.9 | 9.6 | +38 |
| Consumer and occupational health and safety | 1.0 | 1.2 | +12 |
| Ground transport/highways/ mass transit | 17.1 | 18.6 | +9 |
| Higher education | 6.8 | 7.2 | +6 |
| Food and nutritional assistance | 16.2 | 17.0 | +5 |
| Elementary, secondary and vocational education | 7.1 | 7.1 | +1 |
| Community development | 5.0 | 4.8 | -5 |
| Recreational resources | 1.6 | 1.5 | -6 |
| General revenue sharing | 5.1 | 4.5 | -11 |
| Pollution control | 5.2 | 4.2 | -19 |
| Veterans education, training and rehabilitation | 2.3 | 1.3 | -41 |
| Energy conservation | .7 | .4 | -44 |
| Training and employment | 9.2 | 4.9 | -47 |
| Energy supply | 5.2 | 1.6 | -70 |
| Conservation/land management | 1.2 | .3 | -73 |

Source: Center for Defense Information, *The Defense Monitor*, Vol.XIII, No. 4, 1984, p. 5.

necessary, imposing of "stability" which would allow safe operation of the capitalist agents and subsidiaries abroad. The enhanced military is also a source of revenue and phenomenal profit for the monopoly capitalist firms. Thus, the emphasis is on a larger and larger military budget. For 1985 it was over 300 billion, the largest in world history. Military budgets for 1982-89 will provide $2.6 trillion in eight years, exceeding the $2.3 trillion spent on the military in the preceding 35 years.[41]

**Table 3-5 The Top Ten Military Contractors ($ in billions)**

|  | FY83 | FY80 | Fortune 500# | Weapons |
|---|---|---|---|---|
| 1. General Dynamics | $6.8 | $3.1(1) | 46 | F-16, Trident subs, SLCM, DIVAD, M-1, M-60 tanks |
| 2. McDonnell Douglas | $6.1 | $3.2(2) | 42 | F-15, F-18, KC-10, AV-8B aircraft |
| 3. Rockwell Int. | $4.5 | $0.9(14) | 43 | B-1B, MX, Hellfire missile nuclear weapon components |
| 4. General Electric | $4.5 | $2.2(5) | 10 | Ship nuclear reactors, jet engines, ICBM re-entry vehicles |
| 5. Boeing Co. | $4.4 | $2.4 (4) | 27 | C-135, B-52 upgrades, ALCM, AWACS, E-3A aircraft |
| 6. Lockhead Corp. | $4.0 | $2.0(6) | 50 | C-5, P-3, C-130 aircraft, Trident missiles |
| 7. United Technologies | $3.8 | $3.1(3) | 18 | Jet engines, UH-60, CH-53, SH-60 helicopters |
| 8. Tenneco Inc. | $3.7 | $1.5(9) | 19 | Aircraft carriers, nuclear submarines |
| 9. Hughes | $3.2 | $1.8(7) |  | AH-64 helicopter, Phoenix missile, electronics, radars |
| 10. Raytheon Co. | $2.7 | $1.7(8) | 59 | Hawk, Sidewinder, Dragon, Sparrow missiles |

Source: Center for Defense Information, *The Defense Monitor*, Vol. XIII, No. 4, 1984, p. 6.

Presently, the Pentagon has hundreds of weapon systems in the pipeline. Eighty-seven of the larger programs are estimated to cost $750 billion combined. The twenty which total $413 billion are shown in Table 3-3.

In this regard, it is important to note that these estimated costs are certain to rise substantially. The General Accounting Office recently analyzed 97 major weapons systems from 1963 to 1983 and found that, on the average, they cost 32 percent more than the Pentagon estimated. Some of the systems listed in Table 3-3 have already doubled in unit cost. For example the F-18 aircraft was supposed to cost $16 million each and the M-1 tank $1.4 million a piece.[42]

It is immaterial for the capitalist that increase in the military budget causes reduction in amounts necessary for social welfare functions and services. Table 3-4 illustrates the situation by comparing the budget appropriations of FY 1981 and FY 1985. It shows an impressive 70 percent rise in the military budget over a five year period, at the cost of sharp drops on financing highly beneficial socio-economic programs.

Table 3-5 demonstrated the monopoly power of giant corporations over the military budget. Once the contract is given to a corporation, absolute monopoly of one corporation over the subject of contract is established. The result is an unbelievable rip-off of the budget accompanied with an enormous waste of taxpayer's money. Table 3-6 presents some examples of what Department of Defense paid for certain spare parts compared to what the standard price should have been, based on comparable material in the open market.

## Conclusion

Facts and evidences presented in the preceding chapters leaves little reason to believe that the United States, as a leading capitalist society, is a "pluralistic democracy" as claimed by some authorities.

As presented above, a few thousand capitalists, directly or through their appointees, control public as well as private policy-making process. Consequently, such policies favor large corporate interests at a substantial cost to the rest of the society. Thus, despite the increasing national wealth, there are more and more people living in poverty, with a continually widening gap between rich and poor. There has been increasing economic insecurity, substandard housing, pollution and environmental devastation, serious health care problems, severe deficiencies in the educational system, among many other advancing deficiencies.

More and more people suffer, more and more profits go to the giant corporations, with corresponding increased influence over the institutions of society and with resulting scarcity in public services. Big cities are on the verge of bankruptcy and in ruin, and money for social-service programs is being reduced while the needs are increasing.

While American society is not ruled by a monolithic elite, the various interest elites are anchored in the giant corporations and financial institutions, extending their links into Congress, the executive departments, the press, universities, the military and other vital institutions of society from national down to the local levels. It is the power of money and position that holds these elite groups together and maintains their common interest in preserving and fostering a system that assures their wealth and protects and advances their privileges.

The top corporate group occupies a strategic and controlling position within the economic system, which obliges government to organize the economy of the nation within the existing capitalist

**Table 3-6 Doing Business with the Pentagon**

| Item | Standard price | Price paid (overcharges) |
|------|----------------|--------------------------|
| Circuit breaker | $ 11.10 | $ 243.00 (22 times) |
| Push switch | $ 15.41 | $ 241.00 (15 times) |
| Semi-conductor | $ .04 | $ 110.00 (2750 times) |
| Resistor | $ .05 | $ 100.00 (2000 times) |
| Transistor | $ .24 | $ 75.00 (312 times) |
| Tube | $ 12.00 | $ 639.29 (53 times) |
| Case assembly | $6445.65 | $45,236.16 (7 Times) |
| Oil plug | $ 117.05 | $ 1050.31 (9 times) |
| Connector | $ 13.03 | $ 143.28 (11 times) |
| Soldering iron | $ 3.75 | $ 272.16 (73 times) |
| Tape Measure | $ 10.00 | $ 427.00 (42 times) |
| Hammer | $ 18.40 | $ 450.00 (24 times) |

Source: Center for Defense Information, *The Defense Monitor*, Vol. XIII, No. 4, 1984, p. 8.

structure and maintain an intimate relationship with this corporate group. Thus, national interest becomes identified with the prevailing capitalist interests. In summary, in a corporate capitalist system, profits produce capital through accumulation, which ultimately leads to concentration of corporate capital and entailing economic, social and political power in the hands of a few. The only remedy in favor of society as a whole appears to be the democratization of the ownership of capital by establishing a system which would gradually cause the transfer of capital from a few at the top of the economic pyramid down to its lowest levels.

## NOTES

1. The state is a societal institution with a legitimized monopoly on the use of violence through its laws. In a capitalist society the state is supportive and a protector of the capitalist system.

2. See G. William Domhoff, "State and Ruling Class in Corporate America," *Insurgent Sociologist*, Vol. 4, No. 3 (Spring, 1974); for further details see his *The Higher Circles: The Governing Class in America* (New York: Vintage Press, 1970).

3. See U.S. Constitution, 14th Amendment.

4. Ibid, Bill of Rights, the first ten Amendments.

5. For example, in the United States, this was demonstrated by the Palmer Raids of 1919-1920, the illegal suppression of the Black Panthers in the 1960's, illegal and violent FBI and CIA campaigns against American Socialists, CIA involvement in the overthrow of Dr. Mossadegh's government in Iran in 1953 or the democratically elected socialist government of Dr. Allende in Chile in 1974.

6. For example, George Washington's suppression of the "Whiskey Rebellion," a Pennsylvania farmers protest against the new whiskey taxes; the New York tenant farmers' refusal to pay rents to landlords; Shay's Rebellion in Massachusetts; artisan's attempts to organize trade unions; and textile workers' strikes for better working conditions.

7. See, for example, Payntz Taylor, *Outlook for the Railroads*, (New York: Wilson Co., 1960).

8. For details, see James O'Connor, "The Fiscal Crisis of the State" *Socialist Revolution*, I, Nos: 1 and 2, (Jan/Feb. and March/April, 1970).

9. For the history of police and military intervention in several labor struggles see Vincent Pinto, *Soldiers and Strikers: Counterinsurgency on the Labor Front, 1877-1970*, (Chicago, Ill.: United Front Press, 1972).

10. For example, the postal strike of 1970 which was declared illegal under the Taft-Hartley Act.

11. Such as the Cripple Creek incident, or government destruction of the Socialist Party in the 1920's.

12. Such as the government destruction of the Socialist Party in the 1920's, or the Black Panthers in the 1960's.

13. Maurice Dobb, *Capitalism Yesterday and Today* (New York: 1962). See specifically p. 75 for mobilization of economic resources for military purpose and its effect on the growth of capitalist state.

14. One reliable study shows that increased education accounted for over three-fifths of the growth of output-per-man-hour in the United States between 1929-1957. See E.F. Denison, *The Source of Economic Growth in the U.S. and Alternatives Before Us* (New York: 1962), p. 148.

15. For more details see James Weinstein, *The Corporate Ideal and the Liberal State* (Boston, MA: Beacon Press, 1968).

16. In the United States note the expanded state functions under liberal state programs such as the New Deal, the New Frontier, and the Great Society.

17. Sidney Kaplan, "Social Engineers as Saviors: Effects of World War I on Some American Liberals," *The Journal of the History of Ideas*, XVII (June, 1956), 347.

18. Ibid., pp. 354-55.

19. For a good essay in this regard see William Dornhoff, "State and Ruling Class in Corporate America," *Insurgent Sociologist*, Vol. 4, No. 3 (Spring, 1974).

20. Consider, for example, the enormous effect of Ford, Rockefeller and Carnegie foundations, among hundreds of others, in channelling hundreds of millions of dollars each year for research and publications.

21. Walter Dean Burnham, "Party Systems and the Political Process," in *The American Party Systems* by William Chambers and Walter Dean Burnham, eds. (New York: Oxford University Press, 1967), p. 279.

22. John S. Saloma III and Frederick H. Santag, *Parties* (Westminster, MD: Alfred A. Knopf, 1972) p. 295.

23. Burnham, *op. cit.* p. 277.

24. Kenneth Prewitt and Alan Stone, *The Ruling Elites* (New York: Harper and Row, 1973), p. 137.

25. Karl Marx and Frederick Engels, *The Communist Manifesto*.

26. For details see Vladimir Lenin, *State and Revolution, Selected Works*, Vol. 2, (Moscow: 1960).

27. The 1987 budget has reached one trillion dollars.

28. We have seen before how the initial members of the board perpetuate their position and power through manipulating the selection process by use of the proxy method.

29. See, for example, Irwin Ross, "How Lawless are Big Companies," *Fortune*, December 1, 1980. pp. 57-64.

30. Jerome H. Skolnick & E. Currie, *Crisis in American Institutions* 5th ed. (Boston: Little, Brown and Co., 1982), p. 492.

31. Consider, for example, during 1972, Presidential election year, several giant corporations contributed substantially to Richard Nixon's campaign fund. The act was a federal felonious crime and carried a sentence of up to 3 years imprisonment and up to $5000 fine. While all the parties which were caught pleaded guilty, each was fined $5000 and none received a jail sentence.
For some 20 years General Motors had been involved in purchasing and dismantling more than 100 electric transit systems and replacing them with GM buses. In April of 1949, a Chicago jury convicted GM of having conspired with Standard Oil of California, Firestone Tire and others to dismantle electric transit systems in many major cities and replace them with GM gas and diesel powered buses and to monopolize the sale of buses. The court imposed a sanction of $5000 on GM. The jury also convicted H.C. Grossman, treasurer of GM, who had played a key role in the motorization campaign and in dismantlement of the $100 million Pacific Electric system. Though the act was felonious and a major crime, the court fined Grossman the magnanimous sum of one dollar. See Brandford Snell, "American Ground Transport," in J. H. Skolnick and E. Currie, *Crisis in American Institutions*, p. 323.

32. Skolnick, *Crisis in American Institutions*, p. 555. The study was carried out in 1949 by Edwin Sutherland and published under *White Collar Crime*.

33. Ibid.

34. Ibid. See also some of the recent relevant significant criminal cases such as *Electrical Equipment Manufacturing Cases*, Feb. 6, 1961, which involved 19 corporations and 45 executives charged with price-fixing; *The Quinine Cartel*, 1966; and *Plumbing Fixtures*, 1969, which involved 15 manufacturers. For brief details see ibid., pp. 559-65.

35. See for example *The Report By the Commission to Investigate Allegations of Police Corruption in New York City*, Whitman Knapp, Chairman, August 3, 1972; for the excerpts of the report see Knapp Commission, "Police Corruption in New York," in Jerome H. Skolnick and E. Currie, *Crisis in American Institutions*, 3rd ed. (Boston: Little, Brown and Co., 1976), pp. 525-34.

36. Skolnick and Currie, pp. 525-26.

37. Ibid., p. 526.

38. Ibid., 526-27.

39. Charles R. Ashman, *The Finest Judges Money Can Buy* (Los Angeles: Nash Publishing, 1973), p. 3, 4, and 6.

40. Ibid., p. 4.

*Chapter 4.*

# TECHNOLOGICAL SOCIALISM

A brief reference to the theory of communism is necessary for two reasons. First, some aspects of communism, procedural as well as substantial, have relevance to our theory; second, very few people in capitalistic societies are properly knowledgeable about communism, its Marxist as well as Leninist versions. We are not here concerned with the recent developments, Glasnost and Perestroika, in the Soviet Union, or in Eastern Europe. This appears to be a stage of transition from the unworkable concept of Leninism to some kind of democratic socialism, where its true characteristics are not yet know and are in the stages of formation. However, it seems that regardless of transition to a democratic process, tendencies toward decentralization of the means of production and distribution, allowing certain degree of private ownership and operation, and experimenting with somehow limited market economy, the public ownership and operation of production and distribution will remain a dominant factor at least in the Soviet economy.

In this writing, we are concerned with two extreme economic models of capitalism and Marxism. We do not focus on communism because there is no such society in existence except that it is the objective of Marxism as a perfect society in the far future.

While we can claim that Leninism—dictatorship of intelligentsia—is dead, we cannot say the same about Marxism. We know that Leninism and Marxism are two quite different ideologies. Leninism is a dictatorship of a very small group of "intellectuals" taking over the operation of an underdeveloped society and forcibly attempting to accelerate its development toward communism by bypassing the stage of capitalism. This idea in itself is in contrast to Marx principle of dialectic materialism when capitalism is an inevitable stage of development proceeding that of feudalism and preceding that of socialism which is to be the result of proletarian revolution.

There is also two essential differences between Lenin's dictatorship of intelligentsia and Marx's dictatorship of proletariat. First, while the former occurs in an underdeveloped and mainly illiterate society, the latter can only occur in a highly advanced, well educated, and socially conscious society. Looking upon present state of labor forces in advanced societies we don't yet find general social consciousness among these forces to the extent that will tend to unify them against capitalist elite with a demand for economic equalization or economic democratization. It seems that the stage of development that Marx thought to be inducive for unified labor uprising has not been achieve at this time yet. We still cannot tell for certain that Marx was wrong in his prediction of the proletarian revolution. I have explained my personal reasons in this writing as to why I don't believe that such a revolution ever could occur. However, there is room for others to argue otherwise.

Second, there are a substantial difference between Lenin's dictatorship of intelligentsia and Marx dictatorship of proletariat. The former is the forced rule of a very small minority over the masses of population. The latter is the rule by vast majority of labor force and its allied groups suppressing a small group of capitalists. It may be considered a majority dictatorship; yet, if we consider that this is a highly developed, highly educated and socially conscious society we may doubt that such government will brutally eliminate the capitalist group. It appears that the capitalist will be stripped of his capital and ownership of the means of production and will be assimilated into the labor society. The purpose of the dictatorship seem to be the elimination of the remnants of capitalism rather than physical elimination of the capitalist elite. I would like to remind again that here we have a highly educated and socially conscious society where reason is supposed to dominate over emotions. Such society will not be capable of, or at least will not have, tendency toward physical brutality. Leninism,on the other hand, is synonymous with brutality simply because a minority government has to push a backward society to achieve impossible. To prove this we already have example of some 70 years experimentation in the Soviet Union, 40 years in Eastern Europe and China.

My main point is that these two forms dictatorship are not comparable at all. We should not assume the characteristics of Marx's proletarian dictatorship by using the results from that of Lenin's.

By reference to socialism in this writing, we are considering so called "Leninist-Marxist" systems as they exist or did recently exist.

In a socialistic system there is nearly a total public ownership of the means of production which is controlled by the government on behalf of the people. The whole economy operates under a centralized system and according to a national plan, the workers which comprise the whole population within working age, except for a negligible number, are public employees and are paid standardized salaries at different levels of occupation.

Communism and a communistic society as developed and visualized by Karl Marx is the basic goal of these socialist nations. The process by which they intend to reach this goal is not Marxist but takes its roots from the concepts developed by Lenin and labeled later as Leninism. It seems appropriate that we take a brief look at these two concepts which appear essential in understanding the operational conditions of the existing socialist systems prevailing over one-third of the world population, and has substantial influence on the rest of the Third World.

The term socialist in its strict meaning refers to societies with Marxist goals of communism. Other countries which are usually referred to as socialist such as Sweden or Switzerland do not fall under the term of socialist as far as our definition of the term is concerned. They are mixed economies of state-and-private-capitalism with extensive social welfare functions.

## Marx and Marxism

From a capitalist viewpoint, nothing is more devastating to the order of a capitalist society than Marx's idea of communism. Based on this conviction, Marx and his ideas are presented to be evil and dangerous for the well being of so-called "democratic-capitalist" society. In no country is this adverse feeling stronger than the United States. Thus, by this advocacy, the study, discussion and analysis of Marx's ideas are almost totally and systematically prevented. Except for a very small group of academicians, in philosophy and social science disciplines, who are briefly exposed to Marxism, the rest of the society, particularly the working class, is kept in total ignorance and misunderstanding of the works of a giant philosopher and his enormous contribution all intended for the well being of humanity and humaneness of societies.

For this reason and for proper understanding of the ideas presented in this writing, a brief explanation of Marx's ideas seems imperative. However, a study of the original writing of Marx is a must for those seeking consciousness regarding the evolution of human societies and trends toward their future, at least from Marx's viewpoint.

Among the three giants of the nineteenth century—Darwin, John Stuart Mill and Marx—one can quite assuredly choose the latter as being the most significant in shaping world history. Regardless of one's political or ideological orientation to the contrary, impartial attention to Marx' contribution to political philosophy is imperative for an understanding of communism and its place in the contemporary world arena.

There is no question about the magnitude of his unchallenged contribution to social sciences. Marx's genius is well recognized by economists by his development of a macroeconomic model long before John Maynard Keynes. The explanatory power of his method for delineating the operation of capitalism and the nature of social change is well understood by philosophers, historians, political and other social scientists. Based on his early writings many scientists and philosophers have come to view him as a great humanist.

Intentional efforts by capitalist scholars to denigrate Marx's scholarly contribution to intellectual history is still strong in the United

States. However, their credibility has been increasingly questioned as the study of Marxism has gained wider attention and fairer analysis.

In capitalist societies the complexity of Marx's personality has not been fully appreciated for two main reasons. First, because of distorted presentation of his ideas and motivations. They were misrepresented, misunderstood, and oversimplified. Second, because of his contradictory and paradoxical character; he was, at the same time, a brilliant scholar and a political activist, a philosopher and an ideologue, a Victorian gentleman and a revolutionary, an economist as well as an historian, a devoted father yet an agitator of the masses. For this reason it is important to have a glimpse at his life and personality.

Karl Marx (1818-1883) was born in Trier, Germany as the oldest son of a middle-class prosperous Jewish family. As a youth, he suffered the sting of German antisemitism and witnessed the hypocrisy of his father, a lawyer, in adapting Christianity for commercial reasons. He was disowned by his mother, an Orthodox Jew, upon learning that he had become an atheist.

In 1835, Marx entered the University of Bonn Law School, where, instead of studying, he spent much of his time with friends relaxing in beer gardens and writing poetry. In 1836, his father, dissatisfied with his academic performance, transferred him to the more disciplined and strict University of Berlin. The romanticist Marx soon became under two very powerful influences, Hegelianism and the thoughts of Ludwig Feuerbach (1804-1872).

Feuerbach, a student of George Hegel and the successor to Hegel's professorial chair at the University of Berlin, consistently criticized Hegel's idealistic thoughts. Going along with Feuerbach's criticism of Hegel, Marx rejected the giant philosopher's conclusion while maintaining the validity of his analytical dialectic method. Marx, however, criticized Feuerbach's ideas claiming that he did not give enough attention to social and historical elements in formulating his philosophy.

After completing his doctorate in philosophy, Marx, because of his radical ideas, found it nearly impossible to acquire an academic chair. In 1842, he finally secured a position as an editor of a radical newspaper, *Rheinische Zeitung*. Soon thereafter, in 1843, mainly because of his articles which were critical of the reactionary attitudes of government, the paper was closed down and he went into exile.

But Marx cannot be fully understood unless we acquaint ourselves with the conditions of his time.

## 1. Political Environment

Marx belonged to the post-Napoleon era. Napoleon's conquest of Europe had completely dislocated the traditionally established order, by eliminating the Holy Roman Empire, modifying territories, and replacing the hereditary monarchs with common people. As children of the French Revolution he and his soldiers spread throughout Europe the principles of that revolution—liberty, equality, and fraternity.

Napoleon's defeat and exile did not resolve the problem for the European leaders. People were openly demanding democratic reforms. The Vienna conference of the European leaders, skillfully led by the Austrian Prince Metternich (1773-1859), decided to establish autocratic monarch systems. The crowned heads of Europe cooperated in suppressing their people. They agreed to use force against any attempt to establish Democracy.

Despite this coordinated and often very brutal suppression, the demand for democratic reform was not silenced. Thorough repression of each rebellion made the next one inevitable. These were the conditions under which Marx grew up. Feeling the heavy hand of reactionary repression, he fled from one country to another in search of freedom.

## 2. The Scientific Environment

Marx was exposed to a scientific method which had reached its peak at his time. Science had revealed many unimaginable secrets leading to a growing confidence that it soon will reveal the mysteries of the universe. These scientific discoveries such as those of Isaac Newton and Charles Darwin led people to assume that since there were laws governing natural elements, there might also exist natural laws that govern human beings. Persuaded by this idea, Marx developed his theories of *scientific socialism* and believed that he had found the key to human social development.

## 3. The Industrial Revolution

The scientific method had crystallized a new frame of thought and had developed a new technology and mechanized production. People with capital employed the new technologies which tended to make old skills obsolete, forcing self-employed artisans to work in huge factories. Thus, not even being able to see the sun, depersonalized labor, worked 16 hours a day in summer and 13 1/2 hours in winter in dark, damp and unventilated factories. Many thousands died from asthma, tuberculosis and other diseases because the air they breathed was contaminated by steam, dust, smoke and filth.

The most desirable laborers were women and children because they were paid less and were least likely to resist the harsh conditions imposed upon them and cruelties brought on them. Small children were left unattended. Fathers were the first to be fired. They often had to depend on the earnings of their wives and children. Disgraced and humiliated, they often either got drunk or committed suicide.

It will not be difficult to understand Marx's radicalism under these conditions of political suppression, economic exploitation and the accompanying social evils. It seemed that nothing short of radical reform could remedy the situation.

Despite all these conditions, Marx was optimistic about the future of humanity. From an historical viewpoint, Marx believed individuals were destined for freedom and creativity. Prior to the Industrial Revolution, human productivity had not been sufficient to provide people with their basic needs and free them from forced labor. They had remained the slaves of these basic needs. The advent of capitalism along with industrialization allowed, for the first time, abundance of goods through mass production. Individuals now had the opportunity to devote more time to development of their own humanity. On this assumption Marx built his theories in order to guide the masses in this new venture toward a bright future which he thought was waiting for them.

A knowledge of the ideas of Marx through his original writings is virtually indispensable to an educated person in modern industrial society, because the thoughts of Marx have profoundly affected people's views about history, society, economics, culture, ideology, political science, and the nature of social inquiry. No other intellectual influence has so profoundly affected and shaped the mind of modern left-wing radicalism in most parts of the world and no other societal thoughts are developed and experimented more than those based on Marx's thoughts. Furthermore, from a purely intellectual viewpoint, classical Marxism expands one's knowledge by linking it to a greater intellectual tradition extending back into the eighteenth-century French Enlightenment, German post-Kantian philosophy, British political economy and early-nineteenth-century European Socialism.

Simply, in societies where its members are free and able to discuss the vital issues, by not being well grounded in the writings of Marx, one unavoidably is insufficiently attuned to modern thought, and self-excluded to a substantial degree from the continuing debate by which contemporary societies live in. As it will be clear, through this writing, there are only two basic ideologies in the world: capitalism, of which the United States is an example, and left-socialism, of which the Soviet Union pretends to be an adherent. No other literature than Marx's would provide for appropriate comprehension of these two extreme settings and those in between, as well as, would shed light toward man's future and his humanistic existence. A profound knowledge of Marx's writings by any member of modern industrialized society is imperative.[1]

In order to place Marx's ideas in appropriate perspective, they may be looked upon from three different viewpoints—humanistic, scientific and economic, and historical and philosophical.

## Marx and the Nature of Humanity

As a member of a diffuse group of young scholars known as the "Left-Hegelians," Marx considered Hegel's ideas too remote from real life experience.[2] This group's critique of Hegel's abstract idealism shaped Marx's early thinking, and the influence of one of its members, Ludwig Feuerbach, provided them with a definitive form.[3] To Marx, humanity was a species-being, meaning that people, as distinct from animals, focus their consciousness on the entire species through which societal interactions and labor become humanized. Marx rejects the idea that people are passive beings interested only in seeking happiness, as claimed by utilitarian writers of the nineteenth century. Marx asserts that people are makers and achievers; they realize their humanity through their labor not only by changing the material world but also by changing themselves.[4]

Marx continued to believe in the absolute essential quality of human labor. In fact, it always remained his central concern.[5] It was this commitment of Marx to the creative nature of human labor that obliged him to reject capitalism. Under capitalism, human labor is alienated and thus his very existence as a human being is threatened. Labor has no contribution in the creative aspects of production. He has no say as to what is to be produced and how it is to be produced. Labor is simply made an instrument of production. Alienation is the result to this separation of the idea of what is to be made from the mechanical process of producing It. Under capitalism, according to Marx, this alienation is the basic cause of most social ills. From a Marxist's viewpoint the same is true in modern capitalistic societies of today like the United States.[6]

## Marx as a Philosopher

From Marx's viewpoint, philosophy is not to understand history, but to change it. One ought to read his original works if one intends a true understanding of the depth and scope of his comprehension of history. In the evolution of his thoughts, while continuing the inquiry into the idea of alienation, Marx also pursued the understanding of the process of change and evolution in history. Marx's writings are reflective of his command of language, depth and originality of ideas, the course and evolution of history, the astonishing sharpness of mind and critical intellectual method of inquiry, unquestionable integrity and compassion.

Marx is the most important single figure in the development of the modern philosophy of communism. His human vision, profound creativity and his intense critical power enabled him to establish the theoretical base for social revolution and societal reforms which have continued to change the world for more than a century.

In 1844, when only twenty-six, he wrote the *Economic and Philosophical Manuscripts* which is considered his finest philosophical work, though he never published it in his lifetime.[7] Applying the Hegelian dialectic to social needs and circumstances, Marx points out the philosophical faults of capitalism of his time.

With his bitter and vivid criticism of this system and his vision of a new framework for future society, Marx presents the best account of his genuine humanism. These "manuscripts" are today the most common source of reference for Marxists.

## Marx as a Scientist

Like many other scientists of his time in Germany, Marx was strongly influenced by the dialectical philosophy of Hegel which dominated German intellectual thought. Marx, however, was not an undisputing loyal follower of Hegel. He accepted the idea that history moved in a dialectical manner with continual change. In order to understand the reality of this ever-present change, one had to understand the process of change, the manner by which the change occurred. Marx also accepted the idea that the process of change was progressive, not linearly but in a dialectical manner. This idea of progressive dialectical change simply meant that nothing was as it appeared to be, but all things (thesis) were constantly in the process of becoming something different. They were always in the process of producing contradiction, thus, "negating" themselves, tending to change into their opposite (antithesis) and taking new forms (synthesis). The cycle is then continued endlessly. On this base, the human condition was taken as one of constant unrest, denying what then was, and striving to be what was not yet.

These abstract Hegelian ideas, central to his philosophy, were adopted by Marx, lifted from the sterile atmosphere of academic abstraction and given vitality by relating them to everyday life experiences and societal struggle in historical perspective. By changing the Hegelian dialectic, Marx held that it is not ideas as claimed by Hegel, but the material conditions of life that shape humanity's destiny as well as human ideas. It is the material conditions of life that determine the nature of existence. There is a definite relationship between technology and organization of the material world and the nature of the social, political, and spiritual life.

In his study of historical materialism, Marx was primarily interested in the development of a modern mode of production and the relationships between the substructure and superstructure of modern industrial society.

Of particular interest to Marx and the core of his contribution was the discovery of the way the mode of production, and the social relations pertaining to that mode, conditioned and determined the superstructure of the social system. Marx describes this relationship as follows:

My investigation led to the result that legal relations
as well as forms of state are to be grasped neither
from    themselves nor from the so-called general
development of the human mind, but rather have their
roots in the material conditions of life...In the
social production of their life men enter into definite
relations that are indispensable and independent of
their relations of production which correspond to a
definite stage of development of their material
productive forces.  The sum total of these relations
of production constitutes the economic structure of
society, the real foundation, on which rises a legal
and political superstructure and to which correspond
definite forms of social consciousness.  The mode of
production of material life conditions the social,
political and intellectual life processes in general.
It is not the consciousness of men that determines their
being, but on the contrary, their social being that
determines their consciousness.[8]

### The Concept of Historical Materialism

For proper understanding of Marx's analysis of the societal system, it is utmost important to note that nothing discussed by him is static. Nearly all of his writings should be read and comprehended in terms of the operation of the dialectical process.  His method is an attempt to comprehend the nature of change, the transformation of all that is becoming, without losing the essence of what it is.  Living human beings are subject to factors within and shapers of material production.  Through their presence, they all effectuate formal economic, social, and political structures and their interdependence.

Historical materialism, thus, relates all changes in human and community relationships to development of material means and relationships on class struggle.  In his view, in every society since the beginning of human history, there have been two distinct classes—the ruling and the ruled.  The former has ruled through the control of production under a specified mode of production.  The latter has been ruled for the lack of control over the means of production.

For example, in the slavery mode of production, the two classes comprised of the master who ruled, by owning all the means of production including labor, and the slaves, who were ruled by their owners; in the feudal mode of production, the ruling class consisted of the landed aristocracy and the ruled class comprised of the peasants and serfs; in modern times, under the capitalist mode of production, the ruling class is the bourgeoisie, the capitalist, who controls the capital and technology, and the ruled class consists of the workers or proletariat as referred to by Marx.

Of course, this classification is very general and, in fact, each class is composed of several subclasses. Since here our attention is on the capitalist mode of production, it will serve our comprehension of the subject matter if we take a look at the stratification within each of the two classes of capitalist and proletariat in a modern industrial capitalist society like the United States.

The working class, or the proletariat, is composed of blue-collar workers or "commodity-producing" class, comprising about 40 percent of the total labor force; "white-collar" class, with advanced education and sophisticated skills, working in production related scientific or technical positions. This group which constitutes about 13 percent of the total labor force is also known as the "new working class" since it did not exist as such in Marx's time. Furthermore, there are service and clerical workers amounting to about 35 percent of the total labor force.[9] Added together, these three groups of workers approximate 88 percent of the total working population.

The remaining 12 percent constitute the capitalist or bourgeoisie class which is also subdivided. The largest sector within this class consists of the private entrepreneurs and the small businessmen, petite bourgeoisie as labeled by Marx. It comprises about three-fourths (9 of the 12 percent) of the capitalist class and tends to maintain the myth of competitive market.[10] Another group consists of the professional intellectual class, the legal and medical professions, who make up an enlarging sub-capitalist class, and who, through private practice, top administrative academic positions serve capitalism. It remains a very small but enormously significant group, the real capitalist class. Comprising about one percent of the working population, it controls the means of production and distribution. Yet, as presented in previous chapters, a very small segment of this small group, only about 7300, controls the major industrial firms, financial institutions, retail business, insurance, utility companies and government.[11]

There are other groups which do not fit into either of these two major classes of proletariat and bourgeois. Marx spoke of *Cumpenproletariat*—the pimps, prostitutes, and thieves—who do not have a suitable place within the social order. They are, mostly, the dregs of society, victims of circumstance. There is also another group called "humanistic intellectuals," which are left outside the class structure that is based on the capitalist mode of production. Thus, these "free floating" humanistic intellectuals remain outside of the class analysis under this mode of production. However, it must be noted that a large number of other skilled intellectuals do willingly serve the interests of the capitalist elite. Finally, as remnants of the past era, the landed aristocracy and peasants are also excluded from Marx's class structure.

Accordingly, Marx focuses on two main classes differentiated but related to one another. This relationship, however, is antagonistic and based on a power struggle. In order to play its historic role as an agent of change, each class must develop its own class consciousness. From Marx's viewpoint:

> Insofar as millions of families live under economic
> conditions of existence that separates their mode of
> life, their interests and their culture from those of
> other classes, and put them in hostile opposition to
> the latter, they form a class. Insofar as there is
> merely a local interconnection among...(them) and
> the identity of their interests begets no community,
> no national bond and no political organization among
> them, they do not form a class. They are consequently
> incapable of enforcing their class interests in their
> own name, whether through a parliament or through a
> convention. They cannot represent themselves, they
> must be represented. Their representative must at
> the same time appear as the master, as an authority
> over them, as an unlimited governmental power that
> protects them against the other classes and sends
> them rain and sunshine from above.[12]

As illustrated here, under ordinary conditions, isolation and illusion joined by alienation reflect a kind of material and social condition that is not inducive to the development of class consciousness. However, it is in times of sharp contradictions and crises that under increasing pressure of changing material conditions of the proletariat, circumstances for class consciousness are generated.

From this viewpoint class relations as a whole—economic, political and social—are not static but dynamic and fluid expressions of dialectic historical materialism which expands into social and political conditions causing the transformation of society as a whole. Thus, social transformation, according to Marx is both historical and a mass concept. Its two main objectives are freedom and material well-being for the masses, through the rational use of the material conditions of human life.

Marx's uncompromising character in regard to evolution of modern society may be attributed to the realism of his ideas in delineating power relations in a capitalist society, and to the recognition of the tenacity of class relations with both capitalism and socialism. He presents this tendency in contrast to the compromising character of social democracy:

> The peculiar character of Social-Democracy is
> epitomized in the fact that the democratic-republican
> restitutions are demanded as a means not of doing
> away with two extremes, capital and wage labor,
> but of weakening their antagonism and transforming
> it into harmony. However different the means
> proposed for the attainment of this end may be,
> however much it may be trimmed with more or less
> revolutionary notions, the content remains the same.
> This content is the transformation of society in
> a democratic way but a transformation within the
> bounds of the petty bourgeoisie. Only one must
> not form the narrow-minded notion that the petty
> bourgeoisie on principle wishes to enforce an
> egotistic class interest. Rather it believes
> that the special conditions of its emancipation
> are the general conditions within the frame of
> which alone modern society can be saved and the

class struggle avoided.[13]

One may argue that the purpose of social democracy is the restoration, rather than transformation, of social harmony and the avoidance of heightened class conflict. Marx considers these failing bourgeois revolutions distinguished from his idea of a successful proletarian one.

> Bourgeois revolutions, like those of the
> eighteenth century, storm swiftly from success
> to success; their dramatic effects outdo each
> other; men and things seem set in sparkling
> brilliance; ecstasy is the everyday spirit;
> but they are short-lived; soon they have attained
> their zenith, and a long crapulent depression
> lays hold of society before it learns soberly
> to assimilate the results of its storm-and-stress
> period.[14]

## Proletarian Revolution

According to Marx, one of the primary causes of the revolution was the continued exploitation of workers by the capitalist class. As described by him:

> ...in the fully developed proletariat, everything
> human is taken away, even the appearance of humanity.
> In the conditions of existence of the proletariat
> are condensed, in the most inhuman form, all the
> conditions of present-day society. Man has lost
> himself, but he has not only acquired, at the same
> time a theoretical consciousness of his loss, he
> has been forced, by an ineluctable, irremediable
> and imperious distress—by practical necessity—to
> revolt against this inhumanity. It is for these
> reasons that the proletariat can and must emancipate
> itself. But it can only emancipate itself by
> destroying its own conditions of existence. It
> can only destroy its own conditions of existence
> by destroying all the inhuman conditions of
> existence of present-daysociety, conditions which

are epitomized in its situation.[15]

According to Marx, this awareness by the working class of the conditions of its own exploitation tends to develop it from a class-in-itself to a class-for-itself:

Economic conditions had in the first place
transformed the mass of people into workers.
The domination of capital created the common
situation and common interests of this class.
Thus this mass is already a class in relation
to capital, but not yet a class for itself.
In the struggle...this mass unites and forms
itself into a class for itself. The interests
which it defends become class interests. But the
struggle between classes is a political struggle.[16]

In regard to this working class Marx later states that:

Of all the instruments of production, the greatest
productive force is the revolutionary class itself.
The organization of the revolutionary elements as
a class presupposes that all the productive forces
that could develop within the old society are in
existence.[17]

Of course, this is a dialectical process in which the proletariat assumes its own historic role in the continuing struggle between itself and the material conditions established and controlled by the capitalist class. The aim of the struggle is for the capitalist to maintain the existing mode of production and for the proletariat to transform it into another. Thus, it is a struggle over the direction of human history. From Marx's viewpoint, the transformation of society and mode of production pursuant to revolution resulting in a true victory was fundamental and irrevocable. This proletarian victory, however, did not mean domination by a new class. Marx elaborates:

Does this mean that the downfall of the old
society will be followed by a new class domination?
No. The condition for the emancipation of the
working class is the abolition of all classes,
just as the condition for the emancipation of
the third estate, of the bourgeoisie, was the
abolition of all estates and orders. The working

> class, in the course of its development, will
> substitute for the old civil society and association
> which will exclude classes and their antagonism,
> and there will be no longer any political power,
> properly so-called, since political power is precisely
> the official expression of the antagonism in civil
> society.[18]

As it is presented later, this statement of Marx is fully applicable to the advanced technological democratic society constituted by the full effectuation of the technodemocratic economic theory. In this society all classes will gradually and automatically disappear and a single class society will be crystallized in which capitalist and worker will merge into one entity.

Human emancipation was, from Marx's viewpoint, the explicit objective of all revolutions, that of the proletariat in particular. Human freedom required above all an awareness and conscious appreciation of one's own humanity as well as a means of daily application of that humanity. The necessary conditions to acquire freedom are produced by the material conditions of human work, social organization, and knowledge of their existence. Thus, the brutal conditions of labor exploitation and a class awareness of that brutality are the essential steps toward realization of revolution for human emancipation.

> Human emancipation will only be complete when
> the real, individual man has absorbed in himself
> the abstract citizen, when as an individual man,
> in his everyday life, in his work, and in his
> relationships, he has become a *social being*, and
> when he has recognized and organized his own powers
> *(forces propres)* as *social* powers, and consequently
> no longer separates this social power from himself
> as political power.[19]

This statement of Marx will also be true in a technodemocratic society with the application of our economic theory.

The economic collapse of capitalism, as a result of growing antagonism between laborers and the capitalists, is another underlying cause of revolution. From Marx's viewpoint there is an internal contradiction within the capitalist mode of production, evolving from the consistent tendency within capitalism for decline in the rate of profit and aspirations of the capitalist for profit expansion. However, as long as the increased investment in capital results in greater exploitation of labor, profits will not decline. But, as capitalism advances profit rates will decline because first, accumulated surplus is more and more reinvested in fixed capital without affecting labor productivity. This takes place for the reason of increased wages or necessity to replace obsolete machinery before they have earned back their initial investment as a result of discovery of new technologies by rival firms. Second, the demand for increased taxes to support the ever expanding apparatus of the state responsible for administering the capitalist society and maintaining capitalism. (In modern capitalist societies of today, different steps have been taken to counter the falling rate of profits.) Third, and the most important of all is the idea:

...that as social problems mount and capitalism
becomes increasingly obstructive to the solution
of these problems, a pattern of stregs within
the system will become more and more evident.
Just as feudalism had eventually to give way to
the regenerative forces of capitalism, so will
a moribund capitalism face its own demise...[20]
History is the judge—its executioner, the proletariat.[21]

These conditions are now present even under the operation of monopolistic capitalism in the United States.

However, the mere existence of these causes for revolution is not enough to materialize it. It must be planned and organized and properly executed. While Marx paid careful attention to explaining the primary causes of revolution he did not elaborate on plans and strategies necessary for its execution. Lenin is credited for this part, though not under conditions prescribed by Marx, which will be explained later. Despite this fact, Marx is very explicit regarding the objectives of the revolution and the extent of social transformation it was to achieve.

Both, for the production on a mass scale of
this Communism consciousness, and for the
success of the cause itself, the alteration
of men on a mass scale is necessary, an alteration
which can only take place in a practical movement,

in a revolution; this revolution is necessary
therefore, because the ruling class cannot be
overthrown in any other way, but also because
the class overthrowing it can only in a revolution
succeed in ridding itself of all the muck of ages
and become fitted to found society anew.[22]

The technodemocratic economic theory does not find the revolutionary process necessary. If there has developed enough
consciousness, the transformation can be achieved through the
democratic process and in the case of continuous resistance, by social
evolution through resorting to general strike.

## Communism, The Ultimate Objective

Marx's theoretical work along with his empirical inquiries led him
to the discovery of "scientific laws of development" illuminating stages
beyond capitalism. His theory relied on the concept of historical
materialism involving the analysis of the past as well as future
developments. His findings toward the future indicated that as
industrialization advances, continually better educated and more
conscious working class will rise and eliminate the capitalist class
structure replacing it by a monoclass society of proletariat. Further
advancement in technology and means of production will bring an
abundance of goods which will be equitably distributed based on
individual needs. After all remnants of capitalism are eliminated by
the ruling proletariat, the latter will also disappear, since there will be
no need for government, and humanity will reach its ultimate stage of
freedom and democracy—a stateless and classless society. Marx
presents the picture of this future communist society as follows:

Communism differs from all previous movements
in that it overturns the basis of all earlier
relations of production and intercourse, and
for the first time consciously treats all natural
premises as the creatures of men, strips them
all of their natural character and subjugates
them to the power of individuals united. Its
organization is, therefore, essentially economic,
the material production of the conditions of this

unity; it turns existing conditions into conditions
of unity.  The reality which communism is creating
is precisely the real basis for rendering it
impossible that anything should exist independently
of individuals, is so far as things are only a
product of the preceding intercourse of individuals
themselves...Only in community with others has
each individual the means of cultivating his gifts
in all directions; only in community, therefore,
is personal freedom possible.  In previous substitutes
for the community, in the State, etc., personal
freedom has existed only for the individuals who
developed within the relationships of the ruling
class.  The illusory community, in which individuals
up to now have been combined, always took on an
independent existence in relation to them, and
was at the same time, since it was the combination
of one class over against another, not only completely
illusory community, but a new fetter as well.
In the real community the individuals obtain their
freedom in and through their association.[23]

Marx accepted that communism will not materialize immediately
after the proletarian revolution, but defects of the capitalist society with
its inequities and injustices will persist for a while.

But these defects are inevitable in the first
phase of communist society as it is when it
has just emerged after prolonged birth springs
from capitalist society.  Right can never be higher
than the economic structure of society and its
cultural development thereby.  In a higher phase
of communist society, after the enslaving
subordination of the individual to the division
of labor, and therewith also the antithesis
between mental and physical labor has vanished;
after labor has become not only a means of life
but life's prime want; after the productive forces
have also increased with the all-round development
of the individual, and all the springs of

cooperative wealth flow more abundantly—only
then can the narrow horizon of bourgeois right
be crossed in its entirety and society inscribe
on its banner:  From each according to his ability,
to each according to his needs![24]

Regarding the ultimate disappearance of the state and class, Marx
summarized his position as follows:

When, in the course of development, class
distinctions have disappeared, and all production
has been concentrated in the hands of vast
association of the whole nation, the public
power will lose its political character.
Political power, properly so called, is merely
the organized power of one class for oppressing
another.  If the proletariat during its contest
with the bourgeoisie is compelled, by the force
of circumstance, to organize itself as a class,
and as such, sweeps away by force the old conditions
of production then it will, along with those
conditions, have swept away the conditions for
the existence of class antagonism and of classes
generally, and will thereby have abolished its
own supremacy as a class.[25]

These statements as quoted here are necessary for comparison of
society under the technodemocratic economic theory with that of
communistic society.  Though under the former, like communism,
there is no class stratification, and the state reaches a negligible size,
the structure of society is sharply different.  There is a total private
ownership and accumulation of personal wealth during an individual's
lifetime.

## The Concept of Marxism-Leninism

Of course, as it has been noticed by now, Marx's theory of communism, including its start with the proletarian revolution, is possible
only in a highly advanced industrial capitalist society.  This is the very
outcome of his theory of dialectical-historical materialism.  Thus,
Marx's proletarian revolution could not have occurred in any society

except in that of advanced technological capitalism. Certainly, it could not have happened in an underdeveloped feudalistic society such as that of Tsarist Russia.

The Russian revolution was not proletarian but something more like that of the French Revolution of the late eighteenth century. The difference was that the system was taken over by a group of Marxists headed by Lenin through organized uprisings of the workers and peasants.

We must take note that our world is not only what we have made it to be but also, maybe more so, a product of the accumulated efforts of earlier generations. This fact emphatically suggests that for full and proper comprehension of the present we must acquire a deep understanding of the past. The writings of the great thinkers were substantially influenced by the history of their past generations and experiences of their own time. The extracts were then put together in the form of new ideas by employing their unusual talent and intelligence. Locke, Rousseau, Bentham, Marx, Hitler, Mao and a score of others can fully be understood only in the light of their intellectual, historical context and prevailing political, social, and economic conditions and norms.

Vladimir Ilyich Ulyanov, known later as Nicolai Lenin (1870-1924), was born in the small town of Simbirsk[26] located in the central Volga Basin. His father was the regional superintendent of schools. Among his five brothers and sisters, Lenin was particularly fond of his oldest brother, Alexander, who was arrested as a revolutionary by the Tsar's secret police, tried and executed in 1887. Profoundly affected by this tragic event, Lenin turned into a dedicated activist.[27]

After graduating from high school, he was admitted to the University of Kazan from which he was soon expelled because of becoming increasingly involved in radical activities. However, he continued to study law and political science on his own, and in 1892, he took and passed the law examinations at the University of St. Petersburg. However, he continued his revolutionary activities which caused him to be arrested in 1895. He was imprisoned for fourteen months and then exiled to a Siberian village on the Lena river. While in exile he encountered and married Nadezhda Krupskaya, a fellow radical in exile.

As a radical from the upper class noble intelligentsia, Lenin was not subjected to the savagery and unspeakable torture used on the exiled revolutionaries and other offenders from the lower class.

Like other aristocratic intellectuals in exile, with a great deal of leisure time, Lenin asked and received books to read. From 1897 to 1900 in exile, Lenin devoted his time to an extensive study of Marxism as well as developing his own revolutionary thoughts. It was during this period that Lenin prepared himself for the future years and produced his first important work, *The Development of Capitalism in Russia*.

In 1900 Lenin left Siberia and went to Switzerland to join other Russian Marxists including Georgi Plekhanov (1857-1918) known as the father of Russian Marxism. The ideological debates between these two most brilliant Marxists polarized the followers, leading to the Bolshevik-Menshevik split. The Mensheviks followed Plekhanov's Two-Stage Theory and insisted that the dialectic had to run its course. This meant that the socialist revolution could not occur in Russia until Russia passed from the feudal stage to the bourgeois stage which could only cause the development and bring it to power. The Bolsheviks challenged this view arguing that under certain circumstances, the working class and the peasant forces could be brought together to take control of the system and transform it into socialism. Thus, the former view required the final revolution to be one of the masses involving the whole society. The latter suggested an elitist coup to seize power by organizing the labor and peasant forces together.

Unlike Marx who devoted most of his time and energy to analyzing capitalism, Lenin attempted to develop a revolutionary doctrine by applying Marxism to a real situation. Accordingly, Lenin (1) restored the revolutionary spirit of the early Marx, (2) modified the theory significantly, attempting to answer questions arising from real situations which contradicted Marx's theories (3) amended Marxism to apply to developing countries, and (4) adjusted it in a way that it would be practical in its application to a real situation. Thus, in reality, by these substantial changes, Lenin transformed Marx's original theories into a new ideology known as Marxist-Leninism.

Unlike Marx who thought that revolution would erupt automatically after the working class had developed consciousness, ending the bourgeois state, Lenin believed that violent revolution was the only action that would bring about a transformation. Rejecting Marx's conviction he argued that the proletariat would not develop class consciousness without the help of a revolutionary group which would stimulate the revolution.

Thus, for Lenin it was the test of the vanguard revolutionary group to overthrow the regime and establish a socialist state even before the working class's self-consciousness. Here lies the significant disparity between Marx and Lenin. Marx, as explained before, had concluded that the proletariat should rise only after it was clearly aware of itself as a class when it had become an overwhelming majority in society. On this ground, he believed that the dictatorship of proletariat would be for a brief period needed primarily to reeducate or eliminate the small group of non-proletarians necessary for the establishment of a classless society.

Contrary to this theory, Lenin argued that a small intellectual revolutionary group would bring about a revolution long before the self-awareness of the working class and then would impose a socialistic system which would embark in proletarianization of the masses. Accordingly, the dictatorship of this elite may last for quite a long time.

Lenin prescribed the required characteristic of this group as small, highly disciplined, and totally dedicated to the cause of revolution. From this viewpoint, Lenin's elitist approach was substantially different from Marx's more democratic approach. The result of this strict approach was the victory of 1917 and the collective dictatorship of the Bolsheviks in Russia since then. After nearly seven decades of dictatorship there is no indication as to when Soviet society would be prepared to enter the utopian stage of Marx's theory—a classless and stateless democratic and communistic society.

Lenin specifically prescribed the governing procedure for this small Bolshevik elite group which he named the Communist Party. He called the system *democratic centralism* which was based on three functional processes, two of them were to be democratic but the third centrist. First, the elections of party leadership had to be by membership from the bottom up; second, issues requiring a decision were to be placed before the membership and subject for open debate; third, after viewpoints of the membership were clarified during the debate, the policy decision for the party had to be made by the leadership alone and be accepted and executed by the membership without question. Even though democratic centralism did not work in practice as it was intended, it was applied with certain integrity under Lenin's leadership. Its democratic aspects for all practical purposes disappeared under Stalin. The idea continued to be an important part of the operational concept in the Soviet Union until the concepts of Perestroika and Glasnost were put into operation in the late 1980's under the leadership of President Gorbachev.

## Marxist Revolution in Less Developed Countries

By the turn of the twentieth century, Marxism was attacked and criticized by growing numbers of socialists. The course of capitalism did not appear leading toward a proletarian revolution which had constituted the core of Marx's theory. In fact, improving labor conditions in the industrial capitalist societies in addition to the lack of unity among the labor force had substantially undermined the materialization of revolution.[28]

Lenin had to find an explanation for this situation. The answer could be formed only by studying transformation in advanced capitalism since Marx's time. He made a thorough analysis and a clever conclusion. According to his findings, as monopolies developed, their financial needs grew along with their corporate size and their increasing need for a vast amount of capital. Unable to finance this phenomenal growth from their own accumulated surplus, the corporations became increasingly dependent on financial institutions. Through this process of financing, these financial institutions soon gained control of the monopolies. Lenin called this development, unforeseen by Marx, *finance capitalism*.

Under this new development the financial institutions, rather than industrial corporations, became the owners of the means of production. However, they contributed nothing to the productivity of the industrial firms they controlled, and yet appropriated enormous profits which rightfully belonged to the workers in those production firms.

Furthermore, the financial monopolizing of national economy, diminishing profits from the domestic market, and increasing demands from labor, all prescribed expansion of the market beyond national borders. Relevant to these events, Lenin argued that this new monopolistic capitalist class realizing the validity in the Marxist prediction of a proletarian revolution, were led to find new sources of cheap labor in other countries and *export their exploitation*. This was the initiation of *imperialist capitalism*. This international exploitation of labor and resources brought to the capitalists phenomenal profits, part of which they shared with their domestic labor force by increasing their wages and fringe benefits in order to subdue labor uprisings and relax tensions created by their previous exploitation of their domestic workers. In this way, the domestic proletariat's revolutionary tensions were calmed. However, by allowing themselves to be "bought off" by profits stolen from their fellow workers in other countries, the domestic workers corrupted their virtues and became partners in the capitalist exploitation of unfortunate fellow workers in colonial countries.

From Lenin's viewpoint, imperial capitalism was destined to self-destruction. When colonial resources were consumed by the individual capitalist state, searching for new sources of profit, these nations would turn against one another. This ultimately would end in a general confrontation among them. Thus, to Lenin, imperialism was the final stage of capitalism.

To justify his elite revolution in an underdeveloped Russia, Lenin argued that colonialism allowed the advanced capitalist countries a tremendous advantage in competing with less developed capitalist states. In order to be able to compete against cheap labor and raw materials available to their imperialist opponent, these less developed countries had to impose a much greater exploitation upon their own labor force. The resulting harsh conditions would force the working class in these countries toward revolution while their counterpart in the advanced capitalist countries were being bought off by the capitalists by using a share from the profits materialized through exploitation of colonial people. From this argument Lenin concluded that Russia, fitting the picture of one of these less developed non-colonial countries, was the **weakest link** in the capitalist chain, and thus, the Marxist revolution there was quite logical.

Leninism is mainly the outcome of the historical fact that the Marxists under his leadership were able to take over a state which had not advanced to the stage of capitalism but was feudalistic, underdeveloped, and mainly a peasant society. Marx's theories of a proletarian society where people were highly educated and technologically advanced, obviously, were not applicable to the underdeveloped Russian society. Lenin had no choice but to maintain Marxism as a goal and invent a process which would justify the Russian road toward communism. He thus bent Marx's process of historical dialectic by claiming that countries in the stages preceding capitalism, through the rule and guidance of a small intellectual elite, can bypass the stage of capitalism and move into the stage of socialism and from there to communism.

Based on his sharply modified concepts of Marx, Lenin prepared a blueprint for the practical application of Marxism and outlined the economic and political development course of the future working-class society. He labeled this system *State Socialism* according to which the state was to control all the means of production and distribution. As employees of the state, all workers would be exploited by the state. The resulting surplus value would be returned to society by instituting social programs for the benefits of individuals, government measures to protect the citizens, investments in industrial and productivity development and increase in consumer goods, all beneficial to social progress.

From Marx's viewpoint, the dictatorship was to produce a single proletarian class with a socialistic ethic which was to be attained by educating the masses, and removing non-conformists from society. Lenin added a third technique in order to achieve a single-class society.

Lenin thought that the socialist workers would be more productive than the nonconformists since they would believe in the value of labor. Thus, paying workers according to their productivity would reward the socialists while punishing the others. In this way, as more people joined the ranks of proletariat and socialism, class differences as well as strife within the masses would tend to diminish and ultimately disappear. With this process, the need for the state would "wither away," leading socialism to its ultimate state of communism. People share their labor while working according to their ability and share the fruits of their production while appropriating according to their needs. Under this utopian economic system people work and live in peace and harmony forever.

Lenin, unlike Marx, believed that, even at the utopian stage of communism, there would always be a small number of misfits, lumpen-proletariat, who would naturally be disciplined by the masses, eliminating the need for a police force.

To sum up, Lenin was more revolutionary than ideologic, thus more concerned with the applicability and workability of a process rather than a theoretical refinement. He left the theoretical inconsistencies to sort themselves out in practice. He disregarded the democratic spirit of Marx's theory by selecting an elitist revolution. He claimed that achieving Marx's objective of a communistic society by such revolution justifies its harsh and extreme means. He contradicted the dialectic theory of Marx by advocating and materializing an early revolution within a feudalistic society which necessarily required the establishment of a harsh elite dictatorship never envisioned by Marx. He developed the theory of imperialism, an advanced stage of capitalism not foreseen by Marx, and used it to explain why the revolution took place first in an underdeveloped country like Russia and did not occur, as Marx had predicted, in the highly industrialized capitalist societies. Finally, within the context of "state socialism," and in sharp contrast with Marx's proletarian system, Lenin incorporated and justified a new kind of total labor exploitation, returns from which he considered indispensable and necessary for the required social and citizen developments.

With all these modifications and alterations in Marx's theories, one should have no doubt in Lenin's devotion to Marxism. The revolution had already taken place in underdeveloped Russia. There had to be a justification for and accommodation of it within the context of Marxism. As a devout Marxist, Lenin never lost sight of its goal—a stateless, classless, communist society. He strived for the materialization of a just society: a society at peace with itself and characterized by human harmony, individual well being and prosperity.

### Applied Marxism-Leninism: The Soviet Union

The historical development of Marxist-Leninism is not our concern here, but what it has led to, in the Soviet Union. However, to understand the present we must have a glance at the past.

With the advent of the revolution Lenin told the workers to take over the factories and the peasants to possess the land. However, the pressure of the Russian Civil War (1918-1921) demanded centralization of the economy. The workers resisted in turning over control of the factories to the Bolsheviks. They wanted the factories to be run collectively through councils of Borkers. The government faced even stronger resistance from the peasants. By the end of October, 1917, any pretense of democracy was abandoned, popular preferences ignored, and human liberties stifled. The dictatorship of "intelligentsia" had started to function no different than any other dictatorship.

The brutality caused by the Russian Civil War was worse than the sufferings of World War I. White Armies wanted to maintain the people's control over the means of production and Bolsheviks wanted nationalization with centralization of authority. Both sides demanded incredible sacrifices from their followers and brutalized their opponents. Ultimately, the Bolsheviks were able to defeat the White Armies one by one, but the country faced economic disaster, By 1921, the industrial production was drastically reduced because of unwillingness of workers to produce, poor management, and disruptions by the war. The peasants resisting government confiscation slaughtered their herds and buried their crop. About five million died from the resulting starvation and some 30 million suffered from malnutrition. Forced to take drastic action, Lenin declared that the party was at error in its intentions to create a socialistic state. He then announced his *New Economic Policy* (NEP) and called the new system *state capitalism*. Under NEP all means of production except heavy industry, transportation and finance were returned to private ownership and to a capitalist market economy. The NEP, to Lenin, was a temporary emergency measure to restore the economy, and he intended to return to a socialized economy later.

During this period, however, the Bolsheviks under their new name of the Communist Party had tightened their political control over the country. Opposition parties were outlawed and then destroyed, and trade unions were brought under control. Political concerns and keeping order in the state had taken priority over all others; economic, social or cultural. Gradually the party lost its revolutionary focus and became bureaucratic. Personalities with ideological brilliance were replaced with those of mundane, administrative know-how.

After Lenin, Joseph Stalin (1879-1953) gradually took over the power of the state. First, by eliminating his major contender, Leon

Trotsky in 1928 and then his other rivals, even loyal friends, in his great purges of the mid-1930's.

Unlike Trotsky, Stalin did not go along with the idea of large-scale attempts to stimulate world proletarian revolution. He gave priority to developing and strengthening the Soviet Union. In this approach, he nationalized Marxist-Leninism and called it building *socialism in one country*.[29]

In materializing this concept in order to make the Soviet Union unconquerable, Stalin personalized the dictatorship and became the single, unchallengeable head of the state. After attaining this control, he revolutionized Soviet society by completing the socialization process postponed by Lenin. He dramatically increased production by demanding enormous sacrifices from the citizens and employing brutal means.

The system moved forward by the subsequent leaders after Stalin's death in 1953. Khrushchev embarked on a liberalization program which relaxed restraints, attempted reforms in industry, agriculture, and party structure and function. Brezhnev and those who followed him, while returning to the hardline position, maintained the moderate attitude, though somewhat more strict politically. Until 1988, from a broader viewpoint, looking upon the total operation of the system from the grassroots upward, the Communist Party, a small minority of the people, ruled the country. From a specific power-policy viewpoint, the party was ruled by a small group of some 300 persons forming the Central Committee, the production and administrative system was managed by some 4000 top technocrats, and the whole system was controlled by a handful of individuals forming the Politburo, the highest authority within the system. The three top leadership positions, those of the President, the Prime Minister, and the Communist Party Secretary, were filled by individuals selected by the Politburo from its own membership.

Since 1986, after the ascent of Mikhail Gorbachev, the system has been, and continues to be, drastically liberalized. The first free elections were held in 1988 and non-party candidates were elected to different public offices. The constitution was amended, substantially increasing the presidential powers. Small cooperative business and production ventures were allowed. Glasnost and Perestroika are moving forward slowly but steadily. By dismissal of top party officials

# 156 / Technodemocratic Economic Theory

in the production and distribution process the economy of the country is in a shamble, the future being uncertain.

The changes in Eastern European socialist countries have been even more drastic and their economy is in big trouble. The fundamental question is whether they should go backward into capitalism and forget about democracy or seek a new democratic economic system to take the place of the centralized order.

## NOTES

1. Marx's writings amount to thousands of pages; for those interested in acquainting themselves with his basic writings, I suggest Robert C. Tucker, ed., *The Marx-Engels Reader* (New York: W.W. Norton, 1972). For an excellent analysis of Marxism see Ernest Mandel, *Marxist Economic Theory*, Vol. I and II, trans. by Brian Pearce (New York: Monthly Review Press, 1970). To visualize how improperly Marxism has been employed in the Soviet Union see Mandel, Vol. II, Chapter 15, pp. 548-599.

2. For Hegel's ideas see George Wilhelm Friedrich Hegel, *Lectures on the Philosophy of History*, translated by J. Sebree (London: Henry G. Bohn, 1861).

3. For early writings of Marx see Karl Marx, *Early Writings*, trans. by T.B. Bottomore (London: Pitman Publishing, 1963); and Erich Fromm, *Marx's Concept of Man* (New York: Frederick Ungar Publishing, 1961); Karl Marx, *1844 Manuscripts: Early Texts*, ed. David McLellan (London: Oxford University Press, 1971). On Feuerbach's ideas see Ludwig Andreas Feuerbach, *The Essence of Christianity*, trans. by Marian Evans (London: John Chapman, 1854); on Feuerback see F. Engels, "Ludwig Feuerbach and the End of Classical German Philosophy," in L.S. Feuer, ed., *Basic Writings on Politics and Philosophy by Marx and Engels* (New York: Doubleday and Company, 1959).

4. See *1844 Manuscripts*, p. 139.

5. See for example his *Capital* (New York: International Publishers, 1967), p. 177.

6. For a detailed analysis see Harry Braverman, *Labor and Monopoly Capital*.

7. Karl Marx, *1844 Manuscripts*.

8. Karl Marx, *Preface to a Contribution to the Critique of Political Economy* (New York: International Publishers, 1968), p. 132.

9. These figures are extracted from Charles H. Anderson, *The Political Economy of Social Class* (Englewood Cliffs, NJ: Prentice-Hall, 1974), pp. 124-132; This modern proletarian class structure will be discussed in more detail in proceeding chapters relating to labor.

10. Manuel Castells, *The Economic Crisis and American Society* (Princeton, NJ: Princeton University Press, 1980), p. 156.

11. See various tables in Chapter 1.

12. Karl Marx, *The Eighteenth Brumaire of Louis Bonaparte* (New York: International Publishers, 1963), p. 124.

13. Ibid, p. 50.

14. Ibid, p. 19. For more details see Maurice Dobb et al., *The Transition From Feudalism To Capitalism* (New York: Schocken Books, 1978).

15. T.B. Bottomore, *Karl Marx, Selected Writings in Sociology and Social Philosophy* (New York: McGraw-Hill, 1956), p. 232.

16. Karl Marx, "Poverty of Philosophy," Ibid, pp. 187-88.

17. Karl Marx, Ibid, p. 239.

18. Ibid.

19. Karl Marx, "The Jewish Question," in T.B. Bottomore, trans. and ed., *Karl Marx, Early Writings* (New York: McGraw-Hill, 1963), p. 31.

20. Charles A. McCoy, *Contemporary Isms: A Political Economy Perspective* (New York: Franklin Watts, 1982), p. 29.

21. Karl Marx, "Speech on the Anniversary of the People's Paper," in David McLellan, *The Thought of Karl Marx* (New York: Harper and Row, 1971), p. 208.

22. Karl Marx and Frederick Engels, *The German Ideology*, ed. by R. Pascal (New York: International Publishers, 1947), p. 69.

23. Karl Marx and F. Engels, *The German Ideology*, pp. 70, 74-75.

24. Karl Marx, "Critique of the Botha Program," in McLellan, *The Thought of Karl Marx*, p. 224.

25. Karl Marx and Frederick Engels, *The Communist Manifesto* (New York: International Publishers, 1948), p. 31.

26. It was later named Ulyanovsk in Lenin's honor.

27. For a brief but very informative biography of Lenin see Nina Gourfinkel, *Lenin* (New York: Grove Press, 1961).

28. For a brief study of Lenin's thoughts see Thornton Anderson, *Masters of Russian Marxism* (New York: Appleton-Century-Crofts, 1963), pp. 1-89.

29. For more detail of this concept see Joseph Stalin, *The Foundations of Leninism* (Moscow: The Foreign Languages Publishing House, 1924), see particularly materials under "Revolution in one Country."

# PART II.

# DEMOCRACY AND DEMOCRATIC ECONOMY

## CHAPTER 5.

# THE BASIC CONCEPT OF TECHNOLOGICAL DEMOCRACY

### INTRODUCTION

Today, in a world of narrow specialists, more than ever we need to be creative philosophically and normatively. The main responsibility of philosophers, and other men of broad knowledge is, by taking into account the past theories of utopia, to recreate a long range vision for the world and adamantly to reembark in reenacting it. If, by employing the knowledge left for us by the past utopians, we don't succeed in providing a rational coordination of impulses and thoughts toward restructuring the past utopias, for probably centuries our civilization will be degenerated into a state of chaotic minor transformations.

Unfortunately, today the technological society as a whole, including nearly all its young people, is unable to conceive any vision of the future, though many are not satisfied with the welter of minor changes.

With over thirty years of university teaching experience behind me and with a background in technology, economics, law, political science and literature, I have been unsuccessful in getting a student's grasp on the speculative writing about Utopias by Plato, Bacon and Moore, or about Marx's utopia of communism which is the term students hear continually on radio and television programs and read over and over in magazines and newspapers, without a true comprehension of it.

For years I have repeatedly asked my freshman and sophomore classes the following two questions. First question: "Who dislikes communism?" In answering this question everyone raises his or her hand. Second question: "What is communism?" No one responds. Third question: "How can you dislike a concept or ideology when you don't know what it is?" After my insistence for response, one or two would respond that it is an evil system, a harsh dictatorship. What could be more away from the truth. It is not the students fault. It is the faulty and increasingly decaying system of education they have gone through.

I remember, when I finished high school in Iran, I already had two courses in philosophy and knew quite a bit about the ideologies of capitalism and communism. I also had studied three languages, and spoke them fluently. One was French in which, in a period of six years, I had read a great deal about Western philosophy and philosophers, writers and poets. Fifty-five percent of Russian elementary school children study English starting at fifth grade. How many of our student study Russian? My point here is not our lack of concern in teaching Russian to our children. It is through the knowledge of language that one has the opportunity to get acquainted with literature, culture, and socio-economic and political concepts of another nation and understands its values and meaning of its aims.

The response of the upper level classes to my questions has been no better. Except for about ten in a thousand that take a course in political theory, the rest has been plunged in the same total ignorance.

If they had studied the subject, they would have known that communism, though utopian, is the most perfect democratic society ever described. A super-developed, super-educated, stateless, classless society where everyone strives for self-perfection, everyone voluntarily works according to his or her best capability but receives, also voluntarily, only according to his or her needs. Of course, when I describe this to my students many eyes become wide open with a clearly apparent sense of disbelieve. They are not be blamed, they have never heard such a statement about communism.

When student talk of a communist dictatorship they are unaware that they are talking of the process of reaching the stage of communism: through proletarian dictatorship envisioned by Marx and through the dictatorship of intelligentsia as prescribed by Lenin. The latter is what has been presented to students as communism, mainly through media. None of these are relevant to communism which is the objective. In the early 1970's the people of Chile, through democratic election, chose Marxism as their objective, bypassing the dictatorship stage.

In Italy, the Communist Party, during the last two decades has taken over, one after another, the municipal government of several Italian major cities, all through democratic process. By its action the party has repudiated the dictatorship process of the ideology prescribed by Marx or Lenin and is proceeding toward Marx's communism through democratic means.

As technology advances, the need for proper ideological and futuristic concepts increases in exponential scale. Because, technology has greatly widened the span of options and at the same time, it has made the choice a necessity. while, through science and technology, we can realize the results of alternate choices, we could hardly find out what it is that we really want. We have almost lost our ability to decide, subjectively out of domain of technology, what we want. Thus, through science and technology we have created power to destroy our enemies with enormous efficiency, yet we have made no real effort to analyze as to what it is that separates us from Russians or, at least, develop a cost-benefit analysis of coexistence. The general public's ignorance may end up to be very costly, if not totally destructive of our civilization.

Only a nation conscious of its present can hope for a bright future. It is about time, before it is too last, we ask ourselves: why must per capita consumption always increase in order for us to be a healthy society? What do we get for it, except the depletion of our finite

162 / Technodemocratic Economic Theory

resources, a tremendous amount of junk and garbage, including the atomic and toxic waste which threaten the healthy continuation of our civilization? Are we really happier, healthier or closer to some ideal state of societal life? Shouldn't we ask ourselves why many of the early societies have remained in a relatively balanced relationship with the environment for many centuries? Why in these societies, was social life highly organized and rewarding; there was a lot of leisure time to devote to pleasurable pastimes such as conversation, literature, and art? Shouldn't' we use technology to provide us with such a pleasurable life rather that employing it for wasteful production and destruction of our environment? Shouldn't' we use technology for freeing men and women from dull, irksome, distasteful, and uninspiring work? Why not use it for enlarging opportunities for more cultivated, enjoyable and creative pursuits?

We may sustain the philosophy that man's spiritual welfare is closely linked to his material circumstances, and to perfect man we must perfect his material circumstances. but this concept by no means implies that we overproduce everything. The concept simply means the satisfaction of man's material needs. But, it is also unfortunate to notice that technology is used to overproduce, not primarily answer man's material needs, but to amass profit for its users. So it is used for a very unhealthy and wrong purpose. Isn't it time for us to pay attention to the fact that material abundance alone is not enough to create a healthy society, rather it is the equitable way by which wealth is distributed among members of a society? Over twenty four million people are very poor in the United States and over forty million lack essential needs even for a subsistence living. Yet, the United States is materially, the most abundant society. At the same time, this is a society with the highest rate of crimes, accidents, homicides and mental stress. Thus, material abundance alone, does not inevitably lead to spiritual peace of mind, happiness, and pleasure. A healthy society means a state of physical, mental and social well-being, and material abundance has not produced it. With emphasis on material production the technological human community has lost a good deal of what made social life worthwhile, warm, delightful, rich and human.[1]

A comprehensive, equitable, and satisfying concept of the future is badly and imminently needed. A concept which would provide an overall standard for judging the more obvious and immediate use of technology for societal equilibrium, with equitable distribution of its fruits among all. This aim cannot be achieved if technology is used primarily to profit a small group in its attainment of power and wealth. Because, it has already become clear that the material successes of the spirit of capitalism, enormously enhance by the use or more truly misuse of technology, has not been the outward and visible signs of inward and spiritual grace; it has not caused social justice. Technology in the wrong hands can be utterly dangerous to and destructive of human prosperity, happiness, dignity, and freedom.

### Democratic Organism and Its Components

Technological society is distinguished from all previous societies by the very presence of high technology affecting every aspect of life from home, transportation, work to leisure and recreation.

Technological democratic society is yet sharply distinguished from technological society, through another important and essential ingredient, namely the principle of equality of opportunity. Thus, there are at least three basic components which together form the organic structure of technological democracy: People, technology, and equality of opportunity. Elimination of either of these three components from life's process will cause the elimination of democracy. Simply, no single component can provide for democracy without full employment of the other two.

An individual is necessary to operate the system. Bus this is a special kind of individual. He is well aware of the other two components. He knows all about the essence of technology and its role; he is also deeply committed to the principle of equality of opportunity. This required span of knowledge makes him a high quality being that the world has never before encountered in masses. He is self-conscious, eager to learn, well informed of social and technological norms as well as democratic principles. His knowledge is not limited to the normative aspects of life but he knows how to employ, apply, and operate all these norms in practical aspects of life. Without these qualifications, no man can fully and meaningfully participate in materializing technological democracy and fully, or at least substantially, enjoy its fruits.

Technology as the second component of democratic organism is mostly a self-operating organ which facilitates and substantially helps the materialization of the contributions of the other two components.

One of the essential requirements for a democratic process is freedom of information. This can be only possible to a full extent through high-technology information-communication (Technodem) system. This is another reason that democracy in a large scale can be achieved only in a high-technology society. There is no need to mention the overwhelming importance and influence of electronic technology at the present time on the political electoral process. However, compared to the information system of the future and its role in bringing about democracy, the present systems are primitive. In a technological society, as it will be demonstrated later, a true democracy without high-technology is unthinkable as well as impossible. It is for this reason that technology constitutes an indispensable component of the democratic organism in modern society.

The third, and most important component of the democratic organism, is the principle of equality of opportunity. The simple meaning of the term is that every individual in technological society must have equal opportunity of access to social, economic, and political means. However, its application is not so simple, in fact it is quite complex and requires particular attention to the meaning of the term. As we progress in definition and analysis of our technodemocratic economic theory, we will receive gradually increasing knowledge of the meaning of equality of opportunity and a better understanding of it. Once we master ourselves through different applications of the term, it will become quite easy to grasp its meaning and its manner of application under each situation be it economic, social, political, or technological.

This principle does not intend to provide for a society of equals in the absolute sense. It leads toward and equitable society where each person is equal to another with the same level of knowledge, capability, and experience as those of his own. Its proper application eliminates social stratification and moves the society toward a single class structure.

As the highest principle and component of democratic organism, equality of opportunity is permanent and universally superior and, at all times, controls the exercise of any human authority whatever. All other principles of society concerned with human rights are derived from this superior principle. They are supplement to it and cannot alter it. These principles are to be obeyed only when they are consistent with the principle of equality of opportunity to which they are always subordinate.

By nature of this supreme principle and under the protection of its application, man has a right to preserve his life, liberty and property during the full span of his life.

Equality of opportunity is a sacred right which serves as a foundation for all other rights. When a man renounces this right, he renounces all his rights and liberty emanating from this right. It might be rightfully assumed that by doing so, he renounces his duty as a true human being. In a modern, non-bestial society such renunciation is incompatible with human nature, and freedom. It deprived him of his freedom as well as from developing essential moral norms. By doing so, he also renounces mutual obligation, which is one of the essential requirements of equality of opportunity, because it is not an individual principle but a reciprocal societal one. The application of equality of opportunity requires multiplicity of individuals. The opportunity of one has to be compared with and evaluated according to the opportunity of the other, and usually those of many others. Democracy can flourish when one respects this principle in his relations with other fellow workers or citizens. The common benefit to which each individual's rights are subordinate, is a benefit each person has a share. Each individual's good is a part from the common good. Equality of opportunity is thus a very important societal obligation in democratic society. During the early stages of technological democracy one may, based on his discriminating and exploiting character inherited from the previous ideologies to which he has been long subject, be obliged to follow and abide by the principle of equality of opportunity as the supreme law of the land. He may even be forced to comply. But, as democracy progresses and democratic principles become general and ordinary norms of society, individuals become acculturated and accustomed to these norms and not only tend to comply with their application but believe deeply in them and become ardent advocates of them including, of course, the most important of all principles, the equality of opportunity. In a democratic society, the fulfillment or full development of an individual's characteristic is possible not in isolation from but in association with all members of one's community. It becomes the persistent impulse of every rational being to move toward a life of harmony, rather than conflicts and contradictions.

The common good includes the good of every individual and postulates free scope for the development and perfection of every individual. This is the very outcome of the application of equality of opportunity.

In an advanced democratic society, the collective activities of an institution or community does not proceed by coercion or restraint, but as the result of freedom and general consent. It is based on voluntary association and willing participation. The common good of society and its members can be realized in its fullness only through the common will to adhere to the principle of equality of opportunity.

To make the rights and responsibilities of every citizen real and dynamic, and to extend them to the whole society, is possible through the effect of democratic organism and the contribution of its organic components to the fullest extent. Such fulfillment is only possible when members of a society, by their own feelings, are strongly drawn toward the system. In the organic conception of democracy, there's no room for the imperfect ideologies of the past—capitalistic, socialistic, communistic or else. It is only through a democratic system that the ideal society is conceived as a whole, a society which lives and flourishes by the harmonious growth of its component parts, each of which in developing on its own direction, and in accordance with its own characteristics tends to further the development of other components and society as a whole.

The progress of a society and its members are not separable from one another. The development of society is a result of the expression of deep-seated forces of democratic norms which come to materialize only by an infinitely slow and cumbersome process of mutual adjustments. A basic force in democratization is understanding that progress is not a matter of mechanical contrivance, but depends on the enrichment of mind and spirit in democratic principles and materializing them through meaningful and vigorous actions.

To gain and maintain equality of opportunity and ensure freedoms, man has no choice but to submit to democratic organism. It is the only hope of humanity to free itself from the yoke of powerful and tyrannical economic institutions which rule men and have created and maintained political and social organizations to subjugate them.

Democratic organism is not a system established by an agreement reached between members of a society. Its nature is absolute and ever existing. It is the ultimate system. A society submits to it by simply discovering it. It is a system under which all people live according to its norms and demands. The difference with other systems is that it is truly and totally democratic. It causes the flourishing of associations as a result of which the whole strength of society is enlisted for protection of the individual, community, property, and nature.

Though equality of opportunity is absolute and permanent as a component of democratic organism, it is also the primary source of utility and abundance for all. It embodies utility in the largest and broadest sense. The term utility does not correspond only to material things in life, but those nonmaterial as well. Equality of opportunity is not only the source of a broad spectrum of liberties for the individual, but also the source of happiness for him and for society as a whole. Its utility, in every direction of application, is always supportive of what is just, moral and good.

Equality of opportunity provides for many kinds of rights and freedoms for the individual. It affects all individuals within society. It thus serves the common good of all which is the outcome of collective effects of individual rights and liberties. Therefore, the individual rights and liberties are not, and cannot be, in conflict with the common good. Since the common good is inclusive of all individual rights and liberties, thus no individual rights and liberties can exist apart from it.

It may appear that the individual is being made too subservient to the principle of equality of opportunity. Though the values of equality and freedom, outside the principle of equality of opportunity can be argued and criticized, no such criticism can be reasonably sustained valid regarding the latter. Within the realm of reason, everyone would accept its universal democratic and beneficial effect. Equality of opportunity is per se neither equality nor freedom but it provides grounds for both, equality based on knowledge and experience, freedom so broad that it cannot be fully expressed, but possible to enjoy.

## Toward Technological Democracy

Apart from the United States and the countries with Marxist-Leninist systems, the rest of the countries which have advanced beyond the feudalistic system have a mixed economy. Of particular interest for our purpose are those in advanced industrial stages, such as those of Western Europe and Canada. The production process on those countries is capitalistic and based on maximization of profit. This is true regardless whether the capital is owned by the private sector in different production areas, as is the case in all of these countries, or owned by the public sector as is the case relating to some main industries in some of these countries. For example, coal production the largest industry in England, is publicly owned since its nationalization in the late 1940's. Its operation, however, is capitalistic since it is based on profit and its maximization. These industries may be characterized, at best, as *state capitalism*, where capital is owned by the public at large and is controlled by the state on its behalf, and where the operation is concerned primarily with making a profit and tending to maximize it, and where all the operation depends on the market economy. In general, countries identified as "socialist" are those which have adopted broad social welfare services, with emphasis on certain specified areas such as health care, education, housing, transportation, old age benefits, and unemployment compensation. Nearly all Western European countries fall within this category with varying degrees of socialization of these basic individual needs. Despite this fact, the basic characteristic of these nations remains capitalistic because of their capitalistic mode of operation. However, one may justifiably argue that by taking drastic steps in social welfare services, by using the surplus value received through their capitalist mode of operation, to maintain and enhance these services, these countries are moving gradually toward socialism. Therefore, since despite their progress in installing extensive social benefit programs, none of these countries have reached the stage of socialism and since capitalism is the prevailing mode of production,they may be called *mixed-capitalism* at best. One important positive character of these systems is their advancement primarily in political democracy, and to a certain degree, in economic and social democracy. Despite the above mentioned distinctions these countries remain within the sphere of the capitalist mode of production.

## Prevailing Power Systems

From the above explanation, it can be concluded that there are two dominant systems in the world today. First, the capitalist system exemplified by the United States and Japan, and to a lesser degree, by the Western European countries and Canada. Second, the socialist system represented by the Marxist-Leninist countries such as China. The Soviet Union and Eastern European countries which belonged to this system are all in the process of transition to a new system. Though unlikely, they may regress to capitalism.

Both systems, whether capitalist or socialist, are authoritarian in which the major public and economic policies are made by a very small elite group. In the United States, little over 7000 persons form the ruling capitalist elite, and as it has been demonstrated before, the political democracy practiced is geared to maintain and support the elite interests and is used as a facade for certain claimed freedoms, which are nonexistent in reality.

Under socialism, the system is controlled by a very small and select political elite. though there is more social and economic equality of opportunity than in the United States, it is not inherent in the system itself but granted by the ruling elite in accordance to the framework established by the Marxist-Leninist theory as interpreted by the elite.

Therefore, none of the two systems enjoy a true democracy where the operation of the system, social, economic, and political, will be in the hands of the people as a whole. One problem with, and essential requirement of, establishing and maintaining a true democratic system is that it can be possible only in a highly advanced and well educated society. Both Marx and Lenin visualized this fact. Marx's democracy was to be attained when a highly educated society, after advancing through a proletarian dictatorship, would reach its ultimate technological stage, which would be stateless and classless.

Our documented presentation and analysis in preceding chapters demonstrate that despite some two centuries of effort to establish a more just society through democratic means, today there is no single nation in the world where democracy has been established in its true sense.

During the last two centuries, political democracy has been the center of attraction by its practitioners for the main purpose of establishing a legitimate system to maintain property rights and capitalism. The U.S. Constitution was framed with this main purpose in mind.

It was not until after the Second World War that attention was given to the reality of the situation. It was during the past three decades that monopoly capitalism, which has its roots in the late nineteenth and early twentieth centuries, established its firm grip on the American economy and through that, on the economy of many Third World countries. Similar developments, though in a less dramatic manner, were followed by other industrialized countries of Western Europe.

The 1960s and early 1970s uprisings in the United States was the first organized reaction against the monopoly capitalist group and the state which protected its interests. The uprising failed for two different reasons. First, since it took a violent form, it legitimatized forceful and brutal state action to suppress it. Second, and more importantly, while the primary aim was to undo the existing "establishment," there was no other suitable alternative envisioned to replace it. Some had suggested socialism as a substitute, but it received no support for two main reasons. First, people were uneducated in regard to societal philosophical ideas and visualized socialism as another evil system. This feeling was of course enhanced by decades of indoctrination by the capitalist system about the evil nature of socialism. Second, socialism as practiced then by some Western European countries was not what the theory intended it to be. It was just another kind of capitalism, maybe not as bad.

However, the hold of monopoly capitalism on the economies of the United States and other countries during the last two decades phenomenally increased.[2] It has also been during these decades that different scientists and philosophers have paid increasing attention to erosion of individual rights and liberties under *technological monopolistic capitalism*. It must be noted, as it is presented in the preceding chapters, that technology which is controlled by the economic elite, has played a significant role in this process of subjugation.

Our attempt in this chapter is to introduce in brief a philosophy of the future society which as all trends indicate, all advanced societies are moving toward, and inevitably sooner or later will attain it. This is the theory of a true democracy never described before. This is a democracy as a system, embracing all aspects of societal life whether economic, social, or political. The theory is quite solid and valid. For any questions in mind, the reader will find a lead, even in this brief presentation, if he reviews the materials carefully and impartially.

Under technological democracy, the term democracy is looked upon as a system embracing not only the political components of society but also its social an economic spheres. The term democracy, in its true and full meaning, means political, economic and social democracies all put together as a system. All these parts are interdependent. If any of these component parts are missing, democracy is defective to that extent, and a true democracy does not exist.

In the United States, for example, there is no economic democracy and social democracy is substantially missing. This makes the existing political democracy highly defective, and in many respects, meaningless. The lack of economic democracy is evident by control of the economy by a small group of monopoly capitalists, by the exploitation of the workers and consumers and the economic class stratification. The lack of social democracy is visualized through the practice of racism, sexism, lack of appropriate educational opportunities, lack of health care, housing, transportation, adequate old age benefits, etc. Thus, there is very little meaningful democracy in the United States, if any.

In a socialized system, democracy is highly defective because there is no political democracy. The political system, despite its electoral process, is controlled by a small elite of party leaders. However, there is more economic and social democracy than in the United States. In the economic sphere there is a more equitable distribution of wealth despite the fact that people are exploited. But, apart from the defense expenditures, a substantial part of the surplus value gained is spent for the causes of socialism such as education, health care, housing, transportation, recreation and old age benefits. These are social benefits financed through the system that rules. People have nothing much to say and have no power to cause desirable changes. Democracy is thus highly defective.

Technological democracy, therefore, is a societal system by itself quite distinguished from the existing systems of capitalism or socialism. It extends to all aspects of the societal life. Its understanding is quite simple since its operation depends only on the application of one principle—equality of opportunity—to its other two components, individual and technology. Accordingly, it becomes utmost important to understand the meaning of this term.

## Democracy As a System

For decades and perhaps centuries, democracy has been emphasized as a process by which people freely select their leaders and, through those leaders, express their views and influence the formation of policies. Democracy has been considered a political process only and has never been defined in its totality as a system.

For over two thousand years, since the Greeks crystallized the idea of democracy, this concept has been surrounded by controversy. Throughout most of this period, kings ruled and subjects obeyed. When the idea of democracy was brought to life in seventeenth century England, it was limited to the socially privileged class. Even the framers of the American Constitution considered popular election as mob rule; and accordingly only one institution, the House of Representatives, was made subject to popular election with suffrage restricted to propertied adult males. In theory, the individual citizen had sovereign power but in practices, the power was safely guarded by those of greater economic means and stability.

Today, few Americans are deprived from exercising their voting rights, and the public in general considers the system democratic. But there is more to democracy than being able to vote for candidates, even if there is full participation of those eligible to vote.

Democracy as defined and applied during the last two centuries has meant a governing process, a political process tending to lead toward a substantive democracy in which political equality of opportunity is to be realized. However, this goal has never been materialized.

Today, except for Marxism, there is an absence of contemporary systematic philosophy which attempts to explain the whole socioeconomic and political situations through generalizations about man, institutions and his environment.

Despite many honest and earnest efforts by social scientists and philosophers, no attempt has been successful in defining democracy in its entirety as a system. There is no straight forward set of ideas universally agreed to be the philosophy of democracy.[3] There is no set of writing that can serve as democratic gospel.[4]

Looking at the theoretical and experimental developments of democracy, there was first the *natural rights theory*. Before Christ, Cicero wrote: "We are so constituted by nature as to share the sense of Justice with one another and to pass it on to all men."[5] Locke[6], Rosseau[7], Burk[8], and Jefferson[9] were the most eloquent proponents of the theory of natural rights democracy.

Second, there came the concept of *utilitarian democracy* or democratic liberalism whose ideas were initiated and developed with different variations by thinkers such as Bentham[10], Mill[11], Calhoun[12], Green[13], Hobhouse[14], and Dewey.[15]

Third, there are contemporary democratic thoughts attempted by contemporary thinkers among whom are George Bernanrd Shaw, Thomas[16], Hayek[17], Lindsay[18], Schumpeter[19], Mayo[20], Rawls[21], and Nozick.[22] Philosophers in this category, by the very nature of complex problems of modern societies, while concentrating on political democracy, have been forced to deal explicitly with the economic aspects of societal life. From a variety of economic orders that have been defended, two general trends have evolved. One is *democratic capitalism*, which recognizes the need for some state activity in economic affairs but emphasizes the primacy of individual economic liberty; it presents a conservative defense of the freedom of enterprise. The other is *democratic socialism* which emphasizes the need for radical socioeconomic reconstruction, greater range of community control, and the cooperative determination of planned economic goals.

Consequently, on one extreme stands the United States, where the political democratic process is used to provide justification for sustaining socio-economic discrimination and exploitation inherent in capitalism; in the middle of the road is Sweden where political democracy is attempted to maintain the unstable combination of state and private capitalism; and on the other extreme stands the Soviet Union, where, at least until recently, so called "democratic centralism" has been made a facade to justify state socialism. In none of these systems has a substantive political democracy been materialized. It cannot materialize.

In reality, democracy as an ideology has no relevancy to capitalism or socialism; it is incompatible with both. Democracy is an independent system by itself, of which political democracy is just a part. It has never been defines as a system. Furthermore the democratic system has an important inescapable ingredient, technology, which has not been considered and is not an inherent part of other less advanced ideologies such as capitalism or socialism. While technology has developed under the latter systems, because of disparity between the level of capitalism and then socialism with the higher level of technology, the latter has never been properly understood and has thus been abused and used to the detriment of itself, environment, as well as the society as a whole.

The term technological democracy, as it is used here, means democracy as a system. It embraces not only the political but also the social, economic and technological aspects of a societal life. It encompasses the interactions of society as a whole.

Democracy of this kind cannot occur in any society which is not highly developed and broadly educated. It requires that people understand the democratic principles governing the socio-economic, political and technological norms and processes of society. It also requires that they do comprehend the causes and effects of such norms and processes and the philosophy and reason behind them.

Furthermore, such a developed society is also highly advanced in science and technology. Thus, democracy and technology are inseparable and democracy as a system can occur only in an advanced technological society in which people are well educated in social sciences and humanities in order to understand and properly apply and maintain the required democratic principles and norms. Therefore, it would be appropriate if we label this democratic system as Technological Democracy.

## Substantive and Procedural Democracy

From the above explanations, it has became clear that what is being presented here is not purely an economic but a societal theory. In fact, as we know, the economic norms and processes though the most important component of the societal life, cannot be considered in isolation from its social and political components. In order to understand properly our economic theory it is imperative that we take a look at it and examine it in conjection with the social and political forces. For this purpose, first we need a brief examination of the societal system as a whole and then expound and concentrate on its economic components.

There are two parts to any democratic system: substantive democracy and procedural democracy or democratic goals and democratic process.

## Substantive Democracy

Democratic goals are those ends toward which society strives. The closer society gets to these goals, the more democracy it attains. There are three basic objectives of democracy. These are: *Equality of opportunity* from social, economic, political and technological viewpoints; *freedom*; and *individualism*. Table 5-1 illustrates the system.

However, the essential objective of democracy is to achieve equality of opportunity in its full and broad sense. Once equality of opportunity is established the other two objectives of democracy, namely freedom and individualism will be ascertained as its consequences. The quality and extent of expansion of these goals mark the degree of *substantive democracy* achieved.

Freedom has two components: freedom to choose and freedom to act upon the choice. If any one of the two parts is missing then there is no freedom. In the United States we often consider freedom analogous with freedom to choose. This is an illusion because if we choose to do something and we do not have the means to act upon our choice then we do not reach the goal of our choice, thus, freedom of choice becomes meaningless.

Individualism, as an outcome of the equality of opportunity, means that in a democratic society the individual is the measure of value. Operation of society is based on and is for ascertaining individual dignity, desire, aspiration and demands. The individual has socioeconomic security and is important as an indispensable component of democratic organism.

**Figure 5-1. Components of Technological Democracy**

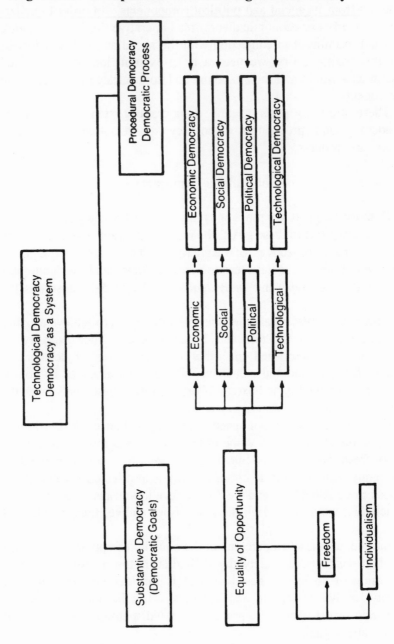

## Procedural Democracy

Procedural democracy is a process leading the society toward attaining substantive democracy and achieving democratic objectives. There are three procedures to follow: political, socio-economic, and technological.

### Political Procedural Democracy

The purpose of this process is to establish political equality of opportunity and to achieve political democracy. There are three requirements to establish this process: popular sovereignty, majority rule with minority rights, and limited government (Figure 5-2).

*Popular sovereignty* means people having full authority over the government. Equality of opportunity prescribes *free* and *frequent* elections to achieve popular sovereignty. There are at least six requirements for free elections: freedom to elect or be elected; freedom from financial burdens; freedom of information, expression, and organization for political purpose.

In the United States, though nearly every eligible person can vote, candidates are selected by the elite and people are manipulated through media and other campaign instruments to vote for them. Thus there is no freedom to elect or be elected.

Elections should be free from financial burdens. In the United States, money is the lifeblood of elections. No one can get elected without spending substantial amounts of money. Presidential elections require about sixty million dollars per candidate; senatorial and house elections from tens of thousands to over ten million. Therefore, there is no free election.

For free elections, there should be free access to information. Information is vital for evaluating and selecting proper policies and candidates. In the United States, first a substantial amount of vital information is classified, and second, the media of information, electronic information systems in particular, are censored at two levels; first at the top, by a very few financial firms which have controlling shares of the news media and second, by the business firms which sponsor each program. As we have seen before, five major New York financial firms have controlling share of the three major television

**Figure 5-2  Prerequisites of Political Equality of Opportunity**

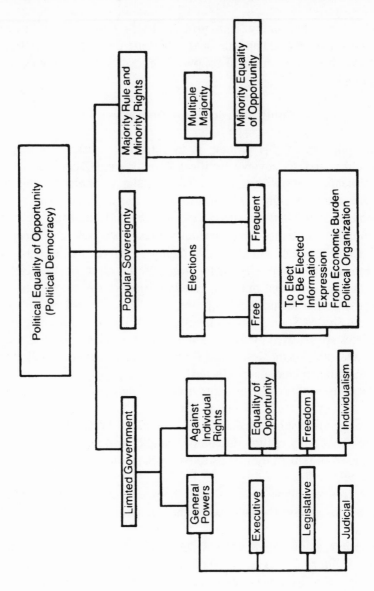

networks, and major radio stations. Thus to the extent the information is held from public access, controlled or distorted, free elections are absent.

Finally, for free elections there must be freedom for political expression and political organization. The former is quite available in the United States but the latter is defective since the U.S. political scene is dominated by two parties, both controlled by the economic elite. Both parties jointly would not allow any third party to reach a position of significance. Consequently, to this extent free elections are missing.

As we will demonstrate the electoral process through the use of Technodem in technological democratic society, free elections are totally guaranteed.

Elections must also be frequent so that no one person will remain too long in the public office which allows an opportunity to misuse the power of office.

The second requirement of political procedural democracy is the *majority rule with minority rights*. Majority rule alone will not guarantee democratic process, it may end in *majority dictatorship* which is the worst kind of dictatorship since it is a dictatorship with the appearance of democracy. Majority rule must accompany minority rights, namely, the minority must be given equal opportunity with the majority in participation, debate, expression, organization, and voting.

The third requirement for political procedural democracy is the *limited government*. In democratic society powers of government are highly limited in two ways. First, in the area of general powers namely legislative, executive, and judicial; second, in relation to individual rights which are protected by the principle of equality of opportunity. In technological democracy powers of government are minimal, both its size and power tending toward zero as the system approaches its advanced stage.

### Socio-Economic Procedural Democracy

Achievement of this process leads to socio-economic equality of opportunity or socio-economic democracy.

## Economic Equality of Opportunity:  Economic Democracy

As illustrated in Figure 5-3, economic democracy requires the application of equality of opportunity in four areas of capital, labor, state and technology. This is the heart of democracy. There cannot be any kind of real democracy without having first economic democracy.

## A. CAPITAL

To democratize the ownership of capital, the principle of equality of opportunity prohibits unjust enrichment. Unjust enrichment simply means that no one receives property or service without giving in return a comparable compensation. This is known as the principle of prohibition of unjust enrichment. Its application causes the following consequences:

1. **No inheritance.** Since anything received through inheritance is free and without comparable compensation, therefore, it is an unjust enrichment and thus prohibited. Inheritance, to the extent of wealth received, elevates the opportunity of the beneficiary to the detriment of others. It has been a very important cause of creating unequal opportunities. The proceeds from inheritance will go into the Public Consumption Fund which will be spent in providing vital services such as education and health care. The result is that as the rich individuals die, their wealth instead of going to their heirs, is transferred to the public treasury and spent for the public good. The consequence of this practice is that gradually wealthy families, which enjoyed a very high opportunity under capitalism, will disappear while their riches are used to enrich and enlighten the masses as a whole. In a span of a few decades, society will cease to have any multi-millionaires. The ruling capitalist elite will die and with it will disappears its dominating socio-economic and political powers.

In a technodemocratic society inheritance may be allowed to the extent that it will not disturb or contradict with the principle of equality of opportunity. This can occur only when every individual in society receives the same amount of inheritance. This limit is determined by the minimum amount of wealth left at the death of individuals divided by the maximum size of the family. This amount is determined

**Figure 5-3.** **Prerequisites of Economic Equality of Opportunity**

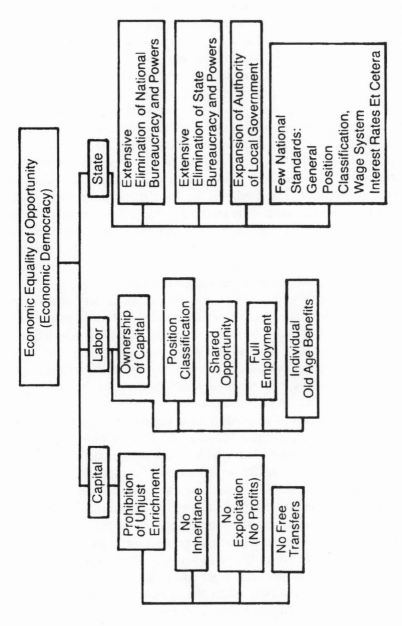

periodically from the national statistics ascertained through the Technodem. For example, if this minimum amount was $20,000, then every one will be allowed to inherit this amount. Since inheritance to this extent will not disturb the equality of opportunity, its exercise will be democratic. This level of inheritance will have its other benefits as well. For example, individuals will have opportunity to process the personal effects of their parents or some other items relating to the family or having particular sentimental values.

As the society advances toward the full state of technodemocracy, the amount of family wealth will tend toward general equalization. Accordingly, the amount of wealth left by most of the individuals, though not exactly the same, will be at the same level with some variations. There will be a few which may accumulate substantial amount of wealth. The result will be that the minimum wealth at the time of death will substantially increase. This will necessarily increase the level of allowable inheritance. The minimum allowable inheritance must be determined on the basis of the size of family. For example, if the minimum wealth left is $40,000 and the largest family size is four, then allowable inheritance will be $10,000.

If inheritance is allowed in a technodemocratic society, it will apply only to the immediate members of the family such as husband, wife, and children. It must be noted that the effect of inheritance is temporary and non-accumulative. When the receiver dies, all reverts to the public consumption fund. The next generation receives the minimum allowable from the total wealth of the deceased.

2. **No Profits.** As technodemocratic economy takes over, profits will be automatically eliminated. Profits materialize from two sources:

a. Through exploitation of workers. The capitalist appropriates to himself part of labor's work without compensation, hence unjustly enriching himself. If profits are eliminated, workers will receive the full benefit of their work. When the workers become also the owners, the profits ensuring from exploitation will be automatically eliminated.

b. Through exploitation of consumers. If the capitalist charges a price which is above the full cost of production, then he exploits the consumer to the extent of the price surplus. Both exploitation of the worker as well as the consumer is unjust enrichment and thus prohibited. Both adversely affect the equality of opportunity. As it will be demonstrated, with the advancement of technodemocratic economy, the exploitation of consumers will be also automatically eliminated.

It has been said that if profits are eliminated, there will be no incentive to work. Nothing can be further from the truth regarding this claim. In the first place, workers were those who worked and not the capitalist. Secondly, if the worker receives full return for his work, in contrast to partial return he received under the capitalist system, he will have far more incentive to work than before. It must be noted that in advanced technological society, the term worker applies to any working person within the productive system, from unskilled workers up to top managers.

3. **No transfer of property without just compensation.** Any transfer of property without just compensation moves its receiver to a higher level of opportunity producing unjust enrichment. Thus, for the sake of democracy and maintaining equality of opportunity, it must be prohibited. Certain minor gift items may be excluded from this rule.

The term property includes, among other things, any of the following:

a. Physical object or structure
b. Valuable claim such as stocks and bonds
c. Money or other means of exchange
d. Labor

## B. LABOR

There is a very basic distinction between capitalism and technodemocratic economy. Under capitalism the capitalist controls land, capital and technology, and employs labor from the market. Under technodemocratic economy the workers own and control the capital and all other means of production. Generally speaking, it can be said that all labor is collectively self-employed.

1. **Ownership of capital.** The principle of equality of opportunity controls the process of ownership of capital. It is through this principle that the ownership of capital is democratized, materializing the total private ownership of the means of production and distribution to the extent never achieved before.

The process of achieving this goal prescribes that the ownership of capital be gradually and systematically transferred from the capitalist to the workers. For this purpose while each worker receives a regular wage, he also receives with it a certain amount of the shares of the firm where he works. Thus, from the time he receives his first pay, he starts to become a part owner of his firm. As the years pass, the worker continues to accumulate capital and increase his share of ownership. As the big capitalists die, their share of stocks revert to the public treasury and from there are offered to the stock market for sale. These are purchased by different institutions, public institutions in particular, and gradually transferred to the workers along with their monthly pay.

After two or three decades, the capitalist class as we know today, disappears and the ownership as well as control of capital becomes wholly transferred to the workers.

From there on as the retired workers die, their share of stocks go to the public treasury, from there to the stock market and finally purchased by different institutions and gradually divided among the new generation of workers along with their pay. The worker receives cash pay, which is intended to take care of his and his family's living expenses. He also receives a share of stocks, which helps him to save and accumulate capital. Finally, he receives dividends from the share of stocks he owns, which continue to increase as he continues to accumulate more and more stocks.

2. **Position Classification.** Position classification is a technology developed for organization, classification and equalization of similar positions. It accompanies a corresponding pay system for its materialization. Under this technology, positions are classified vertically as well as horizontally. Details of functions and responsibilities for each position are determined and described. This system is applied nationally and universally to all available positions. The daily expansion of these responsibilities is calculated in a way that fills the daily hours required for full time work. Horizontal positions are those which require similar levels of skill to carry out job requirements. However, these positions may not be similar in the kind of functions and skills they require. For example, medical doctors, lawyers and top administrators all require a high level of professional skill, while functionally they are quite different from one another. However, they may be placed horizontally in one category and entitled to the same kind of pay. The same applies to clerical workers.

Vertical positions from the lowest level the highest. Vertically, while positions are divided into categories based on the nature to the required functions, each category is also hierarchically arranged. Thus vertically speaking, doctors, lawyers, and top executives belong to three different categories of health care, legal-judicial, and management. Vertically, in the health care category positions start from the lower levels of maids, nurses, paramedics, laboratory workers and other medical technician, to high levels of interns and doctors. Compensation for each level is determined within a minimum and maximum range according to the level of required skill, experience, and complexities involved. Technology of position classification was created primarily for the purpose of increasing and controlling productivity and also for providing equitable pay systems, similar pays for similar jobs.

This technology is not new at all and is being used in every industrialized society by its public sector and by all major, medium size and some small private institutions. However, each institution has its own independent classification of positions and corresponding pay system. The national government, each state government, major city governments, and giant corporations each has a position classification system of its own. However, there is no uniformity among these systems and there are injustices. Furthermore, a great variety of small institutions do not have such a system yet these are the institutions which employ the majority of the working class who are not subject to any standard of pay and are, generally, overexploited.

Under the technodemocratic economic system, all these systems are brought under one umbrella with the same standards of positions and corresponding compensations. However, such a monumental classification is not done in detail by a central office. This would be an impossible job. The national government through the Position Classification and Pay Commission, a branch of the National Economic Council, establishes a general classification of positions, a system somehow similar to the present national classification. Then it requires each institution, private or public, large or small, to establish its own position classification and pay system within the framework established by the national classification and pay system. A copy of this classification is conveyed through computer by each institution to the regional position classification council. The system is put into operation by each institution until it is objected by the regional council. The systems are reviewed each year by each institution as new technologies develop, certain positions are abandoned, new positions are created and functions of some positions are revised.

Position classification under one national system has several benefits:

1. It harmonizes and standardizes all available positions, private as well as public.
2. It equalizes the pay system, similar pay for similar jobs, regardless of whether a worker is a union member or not.
3. It eliminates union bargaining and thus eliminates unionization for economic purposes.
4. It simplifies position and pay classification at the institutional level since there will be a standardized and updated national model to follow.
5. It democratizes the work system by providing equality of opportunity in similar positions with similar pay.
6. It allows regional agencies to supervise the proper and uniform application of national standards.
7. It bestows discretion on each institution to go about establishing its own job and pay classifications.
8. It gives the worker an opportunity to evaluate his position comparing it with the national standard and petition first his institution and then the regional classification council in the case of discrepancy. In this way, position classification in each institution is scrutinized by its workers and brought to the level prescribed by national standards.

As it will be presented below, the pay system in an institution or a group of institutions, may be slightly reduced below the prescribed level by the use of the concept of "shared opportunity." However, such changes will be negligible.

3. **Shared Opportunity and Full Employment.** The very application of the principle of equality of opportunity requires that those having a higher level of employment opportunity share it with those lacking such an opportunity. Workers who have employment have a better opportunity, compared to workers without employment. If there is no employment opportunities for those unemployed, then those who have employment, in order to provide for equality of

opportunity, forego a small part of their employment opportunity by giving up a small part of their work, say one hour per week, and thus cause employment opportunity for their unemployed fellows. This is a requirement for materialization of equality of opportunity in the labor market and is known as *shared opportunity*.

For example, if there is a 100 million work force and each working person gives up one hour of his weekly work, nationwide, 100 million work hours, 2.5 million full time positions will become available to those who have no employment.

Therefore, those who were employed, by sacrificing one hour of pay per week, were able to provide jobs for all of the new workers looking for jobs. Of course in practice this is much more complex since there may be a demand for certain skills and a surplus of others; but these problems are easily resolved by an effective use of the forecasting and information system and by the very concept of supply and demand in the long run. People tend to move out from the areas of surplus into areas of demand through freely available retraining programs.[23] It is important to notice that unemployment in technological democratic society has a different character. Individuals don't wait to finish their professional or technical education and then look for a job. Every individual starts working when he reaches the age of fifteen and completes his professional or technical education while working. So work under technological democracy has a transitory character. Unemployment occurs when a person leaves his job or when a young person enters the labor market looking for a part-time job in less skilled areas which will not be difficult to find. More likely, more than 90 percent of the people looking for jobs will be those terminating their general education at the age of 15 and looking for a part-time job. The system always tends toward equilibrium.

By this manner, employment becomes an individual right and each person is able to secure employment. Sharing opportunities provides for continuous employment, causing stability in the market and thus eliminating a major cause for recession. Furthermore, the inflationary process will also be prevented since there will be no monopoly industry, no price increases to maximize profits. Giant corporations will automatically be divided into many smaller firms; international corporations will disappear, and competition in the market will be tense, more realistic and free. This decentralized and dispersed situation will be materialized because once workers receive controlling shares of a giant firm they will tend to eliminate the superstructure of the corporate bureaucracy which did not produce anything and also had then lost its unproductive use. Then desire to have voice in the operation will tend toward dismantling the giant corporation into smaller entities in which the policy-makers will be directly attached to production process and the worker can feel his voice and power over his institution. The same will happen to the branch or affiliated firms abroad. They would want to be independent especially when the superstructure in a domestic country becomes abolished. Thus the era of giant multinational corporations will become history as a stage of transition from monopolistic international capitalism to competitive technodemocratic economy. The old motto that "small is beautiful, small is controllable, small is more democratic," will become materialized.

4. **Old Age Benefits.** Unlike the welfare programs instituted under existing capitalistic and socialistic systems, there will be no retirement or general welfare system under the technodemocratic economic system. First, each individual will start part-time work when he reaches the age of fifteen. His hours of work increase each year, and in a few years he becomes a full-time worker. From here on, each individual is required to work full-time for at least 30 years in order to provide a sustained and sufficient income for his old-age period.

The process works as follows: Let us assume that a worker receives corporate stocks equivalent to 25 percent of his monthly pay. Individuals in public service receive stocks purchased by the government from the open stock market. This will not be a problem since the size of government is substantially decreased. As the individual's pay increases, so does his monthly share of stocks proportional to 25 percent of his salary. We can fairly assume that the value of monthly stock given to each worker to amount, on an average, to 400 dollars or 4800 dollars per year. In a period of 30 years he will accumulate a non-transferable capital equivalent to 144,000 dollars. At 10 percent return, this will provide a sustained income of 14,400 per year at the time of retirement. If he saves and accumulates returns from his stocks, after 30 years he will have an additional accumulation of over 160,000 dollars of transferrable capital. At 10 percent return, this will give him an additional annual income of $16,000.

With a combined income of nearly $30,000, a worker who retires at the age of 52 will have a quite comfortable life. However, he does not actually retire, but moves out of the general national work force. He may occupy himself with other income-producing functions. This retirement is mandatory in order to maintain equality of opportunity. It has three benefits. First, to provide vacancies to new workers entering the market; second, to provide the retired worker with many years of enjoyable and intellectually productive life; third, to provide for participation in the political process where required qualifications are high and the service is temporary.

Thus, this required retirement is technical. The individual who is highly educated and experienced at this stage of life, may get engaged in many different kinds of work such as art, music, creative writing, counselling, political activities, etc. He may also decide to establish a small specialty business of his own or in partnership with other retired workers. He has over 160,000 dollars in capital accumulated, which can be invested. It must be noted that the shares of stock he has received as part of his monthly pay are "non-transferable" stocks. This is simply to prohibit cashing these stocks and spending the proceeds. These stocks are to provide income for the worker's retired years so they are like retirement funds that the workers now pay to the government and their employers, with the expectation of receiving monthly payments when they retire. Under technodemocratic economy the individual worker is made responsible to hold and take care of his own retirement stocks. Furthermore, he is allowed to reap the benefits of holding them, by receiving annual returns from them during his working years.

As it will be analyzed later, the individual worker is far better off under this system. He is the direct owner of the means of production while he works and after he retires. When he retires, he is his own boss and a well-to-do person. He does not have to rely on monthly social security or retirement checks. His individualism and dignity are enhanced in the community because of his financial independence and his advanced and broad education. At this level of high competence he is also able to enter public life and serve and lead his society toward a better future.

Actually, nearly all elected public policy-making members come from this retired group since to occupy such positions of distinction requires high standards of qualifications and competence. Since top policy-making positions in regional and national government are temporary positions of four to six years, it might just as well fit into the plan for the post-retirement period. It would also discourage working people to run for political office since this will interrupt their working process and, financially have a negative effect on their future.

## The State Under Technodemocratic Economic System

In a capitalistic society, like that of the United States, as it has been presented above, the capitalist controls the economy. Through a continuous accumulation process, the capitalist increases its power and authority over the state to the extent that, under modern technological monopoly capitalism, the capitalist class controls or at least highly influences state activities directly concerned with capitalistic interests.

The matter of the power struggle has become more complex in favor of the capitalist class, where no single state has neither the authority nor the power to regulate or investigate the total operation of a multinational corporation.

Furthermore, while the state is responsible to its citizens and rules with their apparent consent, a multinational corporation is an autocratic system ruled, not by its shareholders as it should have been according to its charter, but by a self-appointed and self-perpetuating board of directors holding, collectively, only a small fraction of corporate shares.

Under a socialistic system, like that of China, the state is controlled by a single political party, that of the Communist Party, and the party is controlled in turn by its leadership. Like members of the board of directors in a corporation under the capitalist system, members to the party leadership are elevated to their position by the initial and senior members of the ruling body of the party.

The Socialist Constitution, prescribes a government by a democratic political process. But the execution of this electoral process is tightly controlled and supervised by the party through its instrumentalities. Consequently, the government ends up to be governed by a few who hold positions of leadership within the party.

In a socialist society it is this small political elite that, through holding the authority of the state, maintains control over the national economy. The continuing advancement of technology has provided the state by means of further tightening its control over the means of production and distribution.

Thus, it is the state that through its control of the means of production, determines what is to be produced, how it is to be produced and how the proceeds are to be appropriated or distributed. This mode of production is in direct opposition to the socialist fundamental principle that all means of production belong to the people as a whole, shall be used by them to produce, and these products shall be distributed among all to each, according to his needs.

In a sense, because of its dominance over the means of production, the socialist state appears to be more autocratic and more bureaucratic than the state under capitalism. Actually, under socialism, the capitalist and the state have merged as one and the workers are exploited to the extent desired by the state, with no recourse.

Of course, it may be claimed that under socialism, people receive a great deal of social benefits not available under capitalism, such as free health care services, free education, highly subsidized housing, transportation and recreation, as well as substantial old age and retirement benefits. But all these benefits, taken that are all provided, are granted at the pleasure of the state and not by a democratic process.

Consequently, under both capitalist and socialist systems, individual freedom has remained at the mercy of a very small group, which controls the means of production and distribution. Neither system has allowed the individual opportunity to develop according to individual desire but by subjugating him to the norms and requirements of the prevailing capitalistic or socialistic mode of production. In this manner, the state has increasingly imposed limitations on individuals' freedom of choice and action and thus has deprived him from full development of his faculties.

All this suppression has occurred because the individual, under either system, has been deprived of equality of opportunity. Under both systems, as illustrated in previous chapters, the state has played a substantial role in installing and maintaining the subjugation process. Individual life under either system is highly exploitive.

The main objective in a technodemocratic economic system is to allow opportunities for individual freedom and dignity in a way that no one is exploited economically, socially or politically. To accomplish this goal as we have seen, control over the means of production and distribution must be taken away from the small group that controls them and be returned to the individuals within the working class. This purpose is achieved through the application of the principle of equality of opportunity, and the prohibition of unjust enrichment. Through this process, capital and control of the mens of production are gradually transferred from the controlling capitalist or socialist group to individual workers. By application of the same principle, as we have also seen, any kind of exploitation becomes prohibited and is automatically eliminated. Accordingly, no profits are made through the use of productive means, and individual workers in each institution collectively, through their representatives, take over the policy-making process of production and distribution.

Consequently, under a technodemocratic economic system, the role of the state becomes quite distinguished from those under capitalism or socialism. The state, as any individual in society is obliged to abide by the principle of equality of opportunity.[24] As a result, first, the state cannot keep anything secret or confidential. Every individual has equal opportunity of access, mainly through the Technodem, to governmental achieves and information sources. If secrecy is allowed it would increase the opportunity of the state to the detriment of the public, which will be contrary to the principle of equality of opportunity. Accordingly, technological democratic society, as a result of the application of technodemocratic economic theory, has an open and very small bureaucracy. This openness extent to every corner of its operation, including that of the national security. This may seem very inappropriate and irrational under the present situation of international relations, but, such external relationships in technological democracy governed by the technodemocratic economic theory, cannot be anything but open. Any other way will be in conflict with the principle of equality of opportunity and will tend toward exploitation and subjugation of other nations as well as citizens. Second, under technodemocratic economic system, a major part of public functions are transferred down to the individual production firms. Other parts, such as maintenance of law and order and supervision and enforcement of the principles and standards governing the production process, are trusted upon local and regional governments; there is no line function left for the national government except for defense and foreign affairs. Defense establishment is also highly curtailed. Because in technological democracy, the essence of strength is not in military might and weapons but in the strength of its citizens' minds and commitments. No conquering force can rule a society governed by technodemocratic economic theory without being assimilated into its norms and culture in a short time. Thus, any conquering force will soon be conquered by the conquered society. In essence then, there is no need for military forces. Elimination of the military establishment will mark the disappearance of the greatest evil haunting humanity and its well being for centuries.

To many, this allegation may be idealistic and utopian. These are people who have failed to study and understand the essence of technological democracy governed by the technodemocratic economic theory; to comprehend the depth, force, and effects of its founding principles; and the causes which may induce military action under such circumstances. We cannot judge or evaluate the characteristics of technological democracy by employing our present values. We must rise and place ourselves on the proper plateau of knowledge and understanding before we start making judgement about the values of technological democratic society. Proper judgement requires a thorough knowledge of facts, which are ascertained through appropriate education and comprehension. Faulty judgements are often the result of haste and shallowness. One thus ought to be careful in making judgement, particularly when it concerns the future of humanity.

Consequently, if the state and its government have no line functions, there will be no need for the kind of vast, wasteful and expensive bureaucracy which presently characterizes the state under capitalism as well as socialism. The vast amount of capital used for its maintenance will be channeled for production purposes and, at the same time, citizens will be relieved from its dominance and burdens.

The state, while having new and extremely important functions, will be highly simplified, much closer to, and within easy reach of the people. Ultimately, its size will be minimal and negligible.

# 194 / Technodemocratic Economic Theory

## NOTES

1. Robert S. Morrison, "Vision," in *Technology and Man's Future*, Albert H. Teich, ed., 3rd ed. (New York: St. Martin's Press, 1981), pp. 7-22.

2. Carl Cohen, *Communism, Fascism, and Democracy*, 2nd ed. (New York: Random House, 1972), p, 394.

3. Ibid., p. 395.

4. De Legibus.

5. John Locke, *Second Treatise of Government, 1690* (London: Thomas Tegg, 1823).

6. Sir Ernest Barker, ed., *Social Contract: Essays by Locks, Hume, and Rousseau* (London: Oxford University Press, 1947).

7. T. Dundas Pillans, ed., *Forgotten Truths: Selections from the Speeches and Writing of the Right Hon. Edmund Burke* (London: Liberty Review Publishing Company, 1898).

8. Edward Dumbauld, ed., *The Political Writing of Thomas Jefferson* (New York: Liberal Arts Press, 1955).

10. Jeremy Beremy Bentham, *Principles of Legislation*, 1802.

11. John Stuart Mill, *Consideration on Representative Government* (New York: Harper, 1862); and John Stuart Mill, *On Liberty* (Boston: Ticknor and Fields, 1863).

12. John C. Calhoun, *A Disquisition on Government* (Columbia, South Carolina: State Printing, 1851).

13. Thomas H. Green, *Liberal Legislation and Freedom of Contract*, in *The Works of Thomas Hill Green*, vol. 3 (London: Longmans, Green and Company, 1888).

14. Leonard T. Hobhouse, *Liberalism* (London: Oxford University Press, 1911).

15. John Dewey, "The Future of Liberalism," *Journal of Philosophy* 32, no. 9 (April 25, 1935), also his other works.

16. Norman Thomas, *Democratic Socialism: A New Appraisal* (New York: League for Industrial Democracy, 1953).

17. Freidrich A. Hayek, *The Road to Serfdom* (Chicago: University of Chicago Press, 1944).

18. A.D. Lindsay, *The Essentials of Democracy* (Oxford: Clarendon Press, 1929).

19. Joseph A. Schumpter, *Capitalism, Socialism and Democracy* (New York: Harper and Row, 1950).

20. Henry B. Mayo, *An Introduction to Democratic Theory* (London: Oxford University Press, 1960).

21. John Rawls, *A Theory of Justice* (Cambridge: Harvard University Press, 1971).

22. Robert Nozick, *Anarchy, State and Utopia* (New York: Basic Books, Inc., 1974).

23. All these programs will be readily available through the Technodem.

24. For structure and function of the state and political processes see Reza Rezazadeh, *Technological Democracy: A Humanistic Philosophy of the Future Society* (New York: Vantage Press, 1990).

*Chapter 6*

# THE BASIC PRINCIPLES OF TECHNODEMOCRATIC ECONOMY

Since our main purpose is the presentation of a technodemocratic economic theory, here we elaborate further on the application of principles discussed in the preceding chapter essential for realization of an economic democracy. Primarily, it must be noted that in technological society there could not be a true economic democracy without democratization of technology, information-communication, technology in particular.

This democratized information-communication system is called the Technodem. It must be properly understood in order to comprehend the technodemocratic theory in particular. It is necessary to discuss this aspect of modern democracy in detail and we will attempt to achieve this in the proceeding chapters. Here we devote our attention strictly to the economic principles.

The manner property is produced, owned and used, determines the economic structure of society and to a substantial degree its social and political characteristics. Productive forces constitute land and natural resources, capital, technology, and labor. In modern industrial society, capital is the most important source of production. Though, by itself capital is not productive, through the use of capital one can employ all other forces, including labor, for productive purposes. Thus, those who have access to capital, to the extent of their access, hold power within the productive system as well as society as a whole. If most of this capital is owned or controlled by a few individuals or firms, then the production process and other superstructures in society are dominated by these few. If the capital as a whole is owned and controlled by the majority of the people, rather than by a few, then the other productive forces as well as the political and social system are governed by the majority of the population.

Therefore, one of the imperative conditions for democracy is the equitable distribution of capital among the people, along with highly dispersed control over its use.

How can we bring about the equitable distribution of capital? There are two principles which must be applied concurrently in order to achieve this objective.

The first thing required is the application of the principle of equality of opportunity. This principle, in an economic sense, means that no one in technological democratic society should gain opportunity over others through accumulated wealth except for savings he has made through his own labor. Based on this principle no one can be enriched through inheritance or through receiving material goods or capital without a comparable compensation. Such enrichment will disturb the equality of opportunity by increasing one's opportunity, without his personal efforts, over that of others. Any amount of wealth received through inheritance or bequest immediately places the receiver at a higher level of opportunity. The level of higher opportunity received by such enrichment is directly related to the amount of wealth received. Thus, inheritance or bequest of large amounts of wealth is the main reason which keeps wealthy families in control of the means of production for generations. Therefore, the application of the principle of equality of opportunity prescribes the *prohibition of unjust enrichment*. For example, if this principle is applied in the United States, in a matter of a few decades, as the members of wealthy families die, their wealth is transferred to the public treasury, and the economic and political powers of these families disappear. This principle of the prohibition of unjust enrichment continues to apply even when society has reached the stage of technological democracy, because any free transfer of wealth at any time upsets the concept of equality of opportunity. The application of this principle will eliminate the accumulation of wealth in any family since whatever is accumulated during a lifetime of an individual reverts to the public upon his death. It must be noticed that the concept does not prohibit individual accumulation of wealth.

Second, social surplus or profit is an unjust enrichment since the capitalist receives it without a compensation, but free, through the exploitation of labor as well as consumers. As we also know, appropriation of social surplus by the capitalist is the main source of accumulation of capital and wealth. Thus the application of the very concept of equality of opportunity prohibits the appropriation of social surplus by the capitalist, since such appropriation enhances the opportunity of the capitalist to the detriment of that of the labor. Accordingly, in technological society, profits as we know under capitalism, are not allowed. In actual operation of the market the price system will remain the same except that what was considered social surplus under capitalism will go now to the laborer who now owns the capital. On the other hand profits accrued from the exploitation of consumers under monopoly capitalism may still continue to exist in the early stages of transition. This may be particularly true in international trade when other nations have economic systems different from the technodemocratic system practiced in the domestic scene. However, as the society approaches to the mature stage of this economic system, and more and more countries follow the system, this kind of surplus will gradually decrease and ultimately eliminated.

It has been argued that profit is the main inducing factor in productivity and without profit there would be no incentive for productivity. This is a very false assumption because first, under a capitalist mode of production, the main producing factor is the labor force which is deprived of such incentive since laborers do not benefit from the profits. Those who do benefit from profits form a small minority class of non-producing capitalists. To increase productivity and thus the profits, they are obliged to impose inhuman and harsh pressures upon labor. Therefore, as a whole, there is no incentive in the capitalist mode of production but forced production in order to produce high profits for the capitalist. Simply, under capitalism the incentive relates only to maximization of profits benefiting only the capitalist minority. Labor is excluded. Second, a true incentive is a factor which induces the worker to produce more and better quality of product. If there is going to be no profit made by the capitalist, the laborer will receive, in addition to his wage, also what is labeled social surplus or profits. In other words, laborers will not be exploited for profit purposes. This factor alone, will necessarily increase the workers incentive to work harder. Thus, under technological democracy, there is a high level of incentive for productivity which in nonexistent under capitalism.

Consequently, by the prohibition of unjust enrichment in a capitalistic society like the United States, the accumulated wealth of the capitalist, monopoly capitalist in particular, tends to disappear in two ways. First, by prohibition of inheritance and other unjust enrichment, such as establishment of trust and free bequests. Second, the capitalist loses his main source of accumulation of wealth by the gradual disappearance of profits. He can no longer create and appropriate surplus values.

Thus, in the period of transition from capitalism to technological democracy the capitalist class tends to disintegrate and then disappear, while the wealth and its control tend to be distributed equitably among the working class. Along with these changes society tends to become more dynamic because of increasing incentives induced by the workers. The level of productivity and the quality of production tend to increase, reaching its maximum level when society reaches the stage of advanced technodemocratic economic system.

### Socialist System and Technodemocratic Economy

The application of equality of opportunity in a socialist system like the Soviet Union or China, would have a reverse effect on the ownership of the means of production. Under technodemocratic economic system, all of the means of production are owned and controlled by individuals. Under the Soviet socialist system, the means of production and distribution are nearly all owned by the public and controlled by a small group of ruling leadership. Thus, the individual worker is deprived of the ownership as well as control of the means of production, and his employment opportunity is dependent on the government "whim." Application of the principle of equality of opportunity would bring about several changes. The first and most important one, would be returning gradually the ownership and control of the means of production from public to private hands. The manner of this redistribution among the workers, and as to who gets what, is presented later through discussion of labor force and the transition process. Another change is the elimination of centralized bureaucracy, which is discussed when we consider the status of the state under technological democracy. A third change is the elimination of political dictatorship, which is being maintained now under technological democracy. A third change is the elimination of political dictatorship, which is being maintained now under the dominance of the Communist Party leadership despite some recent liberalizing movements in the Soviet Union.

One important and positive point relating to this transformation in socialist countries is that in these countries the control of the means of production and distribution, as well as natural resources, are already in public hands and they don't have to be taken away from the capitalist elite ownership, as the case is in the United States. Thus, while in a capitalistic society, like the United States, transformation to technological democracy will go through a period of transition which may stretch into several decades, in a socialistic system, like the Soviet Union, the whole transformation may take only a few years.

## Capital and Capital Accumulation

Capital will still be one of the important forces of production in technodemocratic economic system. However, its characteristic will be quite different from its counterpart in a capitalistic or socialistic system. In a capitalistic society accumulation is through appropriation of the social surplus and added surplus through exploitation of labor and consumers. In a socialistic society the accumulation is the result of exploitation of labor through forced appropriation of the proceeds of production by the government.

In a society under technodemocratic economy the accumulation of capital is a direct result of savings by the labor force. These savings are the result of surpluses left after each individual laborer spends his earnings to satisfy his and his family's needs. In other words, this accumulated capital is not the result of any kind of exploitive process, but the outcome of labor's work. Returns from its use also is not through exploitation. Furthermore, its ownership ends by the death of its owner. Thus, there is no continuing accumulative system since no accumulation extends beyond the owner's life.

Moreover, there is a very important distinction between the capital accumulated under a capitalist system and the one accumulated under a technodemocratic economy. The capital accumulated under a capitalistic mode of production is the result of the appropriation by the capitalist of the social surplus materialized through the exploitation of labor. This is, therefore, an "unfair accumulation" forming a "malignant capital" which tends to empower the capitalist further and subjects the workers for more exploitation. Whereas, the capital accumulated under technodemocratic economy is through savings by the worker from his earnings. It is a "fair accumulation" forming a "beneficial capital" which causes more prosperity and employment opportunity for the working class and provides income and security for their old age, after retirement. As we will see later on, under technodemocratic economic system there is neither retirement programs nor social security benefits for the retired and elderly people, except for those who are disabled or handicapped.

Therefore, since the capital accumulated by the working class, as a result of their own labor, is a "beneficial capital," it is justified if it receives reasonable returns from its investment which will directly benefit the individual worker holding the capital.

First, the capital could be loaned for which the owner receives a fixed rate of return similar to interest rate under capitalism. Second, it could be invested, for which the lender receives shares of ownership of the firm corresponding to the amount loaned. Returns from such accumulation could be used for the purpose of providing for more comfortable living conditions, could be saved for a better life after retirement, or could be reinvested. Each worker also has another automatically accumulating capital through the shares of ownership he receives each month along with his wage. The owner receives full benefits of ownership of these shares except that this capital cannot be transferred or expended. It can be exchanged in the stock market with other non-transferrable stocks. It remains intact until the owner dies. It then reverts to society to be used in the same way by the new generation. All these rules are scientifically reached by the application of the principle of equality of opportunity.

## Working Class Under Technodemocratic Economy

Technodemocratic economic system eradicates the gap between the capitalist and working classes. Actually, it eliminates distinction between these two classes and gradually molds them into one. For the first time in modern production history, the worker becomes involved in the whole process of production, having input as to what is going to be produced, how it is going to be produced, and what is going to be done with the product after it is produced. Alienation of labor, a major cause of social contradiction and struggle of masses, is eliminated.

This new democratic mode of production is attained by the application of the principle of equality of opportunity. First, the very concept of equality of opportunity does not allow any kind of exploitation, which is presently practiced under either the capitalist or socialist mode of production. By its very nature, exploitation of any kind increases the opportunity of its beneficiary to the detriment of the exploited. Thus, a continuous exploitation causes a continuous rise in the level of opportunity of the beneficiary, ever widening the gap between the level of opportunities of the exploiting and exploited parties.

To avoid this kind of exploitation the worker must receive full compensation for his work. This means that after the worker is compensated, there will be no social surplus left for the capitalist to benefit in the form of profits.

Second, there is no equality of opportunity when the form and process of production is decided without input from the part of the workers, and when without their participation in policy conception and formulation, they are forced to produce products they did not consent to its production. This, however, does not mean that in technodemocratic economic system all the workers in an institution should collectively participate and make decisions as to what they want to produce and how they want it to be produced. It simply means that these two decisions must be made by appropriate and qualified representatives of the workers who are also part owners of the capital of the firm.

In analyzing these situations we must bear in mind that equality of opportunity is not an abstract principle. As we have explained before, it is a principle subject to relativity, based on reason and reasonableness. Opportunities can be expected to be near exactly equal when the qualifications of two persons are exactly the same, including their intelligence, education and experience. This will be a rare case, if possible at all. Therefore, the equality of opportunity is judged, taking into consideration all productive qualities of the individuals with reasonable evaluation and nearest proximation.

Opportunity levels are of two kinds: *Initial* and *Gained*. The initial opportunity level is based on each individual's natural competence, without counting the effect of outside factors such as education and experience. From this viewpoint, the opportunity level for each individual is different from the other. This level is determined by the level of mental and physical capabilities of each individual at the time of birth. Thus, individuals are not born with equal opportunities. As they enter the world and face outside factors, educational opportunities in particular, and as by these contacts, they increase their knowledge, and thus competence, they reach a higher level of opportunity. This is a stage of *gained opportunity*. Therefore, even if a person is born with a lower level of opportunity, he may increase the level of his opportunity through seeking knowledge and experience. This makes the availability of education and experience imperative for increasing and equalizing of the opportunity levels. If the opportunity of education and experience is available to some and not to others, then the level of opportunity of the beneficiaries will rise faster than that of the others. Therefore, though individuals start life with unequal initial opportunities they can move up their opportunities to equalize them with those with a higher initial opportunity. However, each individual has a ceiling in his level of opportunity, based on the level of his initial opportunity and intelligence. This ceiling cannot be surpassed and can be attained only by the maximum use of one's capabilities. These different opportunity ceilings among individuals establish in each society what we may call *opportunity classes*. The crucial point in technological democracy is that everyone within each production opportunity class should fully enjoy the equality of opportunity with others within that class.

Thus, by full availability of educational opportunities, people are able to raise their level of opportunities to the level they may desire. This attained level may not be the optimum possible for each individual since one may not desire to reach his maximum level of opportunity. This means that the opportunity for further improvement was available but the individual, with his own free will, chose not to improve it further. This tendency may not be desirable in capitalistic society, but will be quite common under technodemocratic economic system where materialism does not dominate the life,and happiness in life is not determined in material terms. Consequently, individuals are classified according to the level of opportunity they have achieved based on their education, experience and personal desire. They form administrators, engineers, lawyers, accountants, computer scientists, technicians, economists, and different echelons of white- and blue-collar workers. Each individual's competencies are examined and certified by an appropriate institution. This certification determines the levels of opportunity available for each individual. Presently, there is this kind of certified classification though it is fragmented, disorganized, and often discriminatory. For example, there are elementary and secondary school certifications, college certifications (bachelors, masters and doctoral levels) in a great variety of areas and disciplines, certification in a wide variety of technical specialties, etc.

Let us see now how this class system of opportunities is transferred into the production process. In actual operation of production, opportunities have a hierarchical structure which is based on different levels of competence required to carry out a great variety of functions. There are positions for top, middle and lower level managers, professionals, technicians, specialists, skilled and unskilled workers. Each level within the individual opportunity class has a matching level of positions within the hierarchy of the production process. The competency and performance required for each of these positions have been prescribed in detail and all the positions are classified according to the level of competency required. Presently, there are such position classifications in both capitalist and socialist societies but it is fragmented and uncoordinated with an unequal framework of formulation. For example, in the United States, we have position classifications within the national as well as state bureaucracies. Also, many businesses and other institutions have their own position classification systems. For open positions the individuals are examined regarding their competence which also determines their level of opportunity. It is within each level of opportunity that equality of opportunity must apply in providing positions for all those within that specific level.

According to this process of application of the principle of equality of opportunity, there cannot be discrimination within each level of opportunity. Equality of opportunity in employment will apply whether the applicant is male or female, Black, Mexican American, native American or else.

Besides initial opportunity and gained opportunity, there is also what we may call *lost opportunity*. This occurs first, when a person is deprived or denied the opportunity to raise the level of his competence and consequently raise the level of his opportunity, such as if a person is deprived of or denied the opportunity to educate himself. This is one of the characteristics of a capitalist society, like the United States, where at the lower levels of education, elementary and secondary, the poor sectors of society are provided with educational opportunities far below those of well to do and wealthy sectors. As a result, poor and minority groups are denied the chance to appropriate high quality education, depriving them from raising their level of opportunity. Second, lost opportunity occurs when a person, because of exploitation, is not granted equal opportunity in employment. Again, this is a characteristic of a capitalist society like the United States. Poor and minority groups are denied employment opportunities granted to rich and non-minority groups. Suppose individuals A and B, both college graduates with the same academic achievements, look for employment. A's father is a wealthy corporate executive; B, on the other hand, comes from a poor or a minority family. A, because of his father's connections, will have a variety of available positions to choose from. B, however, will have difficulty finding a job, and if he is finally able to find it, it will be more likely, not within his specialty or a suitable one.

Third, the lost opportunity may be the result of wage discrimination. For example, women and minority members in the United States are paid much less than other workers for the same kind of job.

In each of these situations, when the discriminatory practice is carried out for an extended period of time, the continuous loss of opportunities widens the gap between the deprived group and the rest of the working class. It results in an undemocratic class stratification.

While lost opportunity is a major characteristic of a capitalist society, it does not exist under technodemocratic economic system. In the period of transition from capitalism to technodemocratic economy, it is up to the system to see that those subjected to lost opportunities be compensated, moving them gradually to other levels of opportunity. The intention must be to close the gap between the highest and the lowest levels of opportunity. The differentiation between the opportunity levels must tend to correspond to differentiation between the levels of competence.

In this process of change, during the transition period, the differentiation in the opportunity levels for employment must be based purely on competence and experience, and not on wealth and residually attained power and status. Once society reaches the advanced stage of technodemocratic economy, capitalists are automatically eliminated, their power and social status disappear and opportunities tend to be based strictly on competence and experience.

### Shared Opportunity and Employment Right

An outcome of the principle of equality of opportunity is the right of every individual to employment. This simply means that if an individual loses his job or is not able to find employment corresponding to his level of competence, he is denied the employment opportunity that he is entitled to, while his working fellows enjoy that opportunity. Under this circumstance, there is no equality of opportunity present between those who are employed and those who are not. To remedy the situation the system must provide the unemployed individual with an appropriate employment opportunity. By an "appropriate" employment opportunity it is meant that the person must have a position corresponding to his level of competency, so that his skills and experiences could be used fully and productively, and his pay schedule corresponds to his level of opportunity.

Shared opportunity signifies a situation where there are unemployed workers and there are no open positions available for their employment. By the very fact of being unemployed with no jobs available, their opportunity has been lowered, compared to their fellow workers who are employed. To equalize these two different opportunities, and bring about equality of opportunity, the working fellows must share a small part of their employment opportunity with their unemployed fellows. For example, looking upon this issue in general at the national level, let us assume that there are 100 million workers on the job and upon graduation from different educational and training institutions, an estimated 2.5 million individuals enter the job market. Let us consider the extreme situation and assume also that there is no job available on the market for any of these newcomers. If this happens in a capitalist society, like the United States, all the newcomers will remain unemployed, become welfare recipients, demoralized, and a burden upon the society. Under technodemocratic economy, if each of the working persons gives up one hour of his forty hours work per week, that is, if he works only 39 hours and receives pay for 39 hours instead of 40, there will be 100 million work hours released providing for 2.5 million new positions which will accommodate all the newcomers in the job market. Sacrifice of one hour's pay would hardly affect a worker's financial situation or daily family life and obligations, while it would provide a means of livelihood for 2.5 million new workers and their families. The workers who sacrifice that one hour, in actuality, do not lose all the pay for that one hour, because otherwise the government has to support 2.5 millon unemployed and their families through its welfare funds, available through the imposition of taxes on the working people. By using this process of "shared opportunity," the principle of equality of opportunity continues to prevail and full employment is maintained all the time. There is no need to tax working people in order to raise revenues to support millions of unemployed and their dependents. There is no lay off of workers during a sluggish market situation. By the application of the concept of shared opportunities, all the workers of a firm will remain on the job. Instead of lay offs the hours of work for each employee will be reduced with the corresponding pay. All workers will work several hours less than their full week work hours. In essence everyone will be partially laid off. For example, let us assume that a firm has 10,000 employees and has to lay off 1,000 workers or 10 percent of its total working force. If instead of laying off these 1,000 workers, the firm reduces the weekly work hours by 10 percent, it will not need to lay off anyone. If we assume that each worker works 40 hours per week, and the work load is reduced by 10 percent, each worker will work 36 hours and will get pay for 36 instead of 40 hours. As a result, there will be no lay offs and all the workers will keep their jobs. Doing it any other way will be contrary to the principle of equality of opportunity. At the time of recession, this will resolve the most serious problems of unemployment. In financial terms, this means that billions of dollars, which otherwise had to be used for unemployment compensation and welfare payments, will now be channeled into the production process to help the economy and recovery. This self nourishing financial process, tends actually to eliminate or make highly unlikely, the occurrence of recessions or depressions.

As we will see later on when we discuss market operation, inflations and recessions are very unlikely under technodemocratic economic system. Two of the main reasons for this optimism we already know. Under a democratic economic system since there is no drive for profits, prices remain quite stable and because of shared opportunities, there is always full employment. Application of the principle of shared opportunity is also eased by the fact that the workers are the owners of capital under technodemocratic economic theory.

## The Wage System

At every level of work hierarchy, compensation is based on the level of required competence and experience. Competence is determined by the level of education corresponding to the responsibilities of the position and experience is based on the relevant knowledge and expertise acquired through time at the work place. The general level of compensation is determined through a general position classification at the national level. The work system is divided into different classes and within each class into different levels.

There is a National Economic Council and under its authority, there is a National Position Classification Commission. As the operating tools of the system, this commission classifies all available positions provided by computerized data and establishes the level of competence and experience required for each position. This appears to be a difficult task. It is not so. Under a national computerized information system (Technodem) as discussed later, information about all jobs in the country, and duties allocated to each, are easily collected. An assortment of the positions and classification are all carried out through this computer system and made available to the commission. Of course this national position classification does not attempt to specify in detail every available position. The classification is general, yet thorough and specific, at each level. It also establishes the general level of pay and compensation for different classes of position within each level. This is all the commission needs to do. From there on, the system of positions and compensations are updated each year; nearly all the work is done by the computer. The commission's functions will relate partially to resolution of specific problems relating to classification and wages.

Each production or service institution establishes its own position classification and pay system, according to the general classification system established by the national commission, available to it through its computer terminal. A computerized copy of such document is submitted to the regional office of the National Economic Council. This copy is fed into the Technodem to check the accuracy of the classification and pay system, comparing it with the standards established by the National Economic Council. Any deficiency is reported and the corresponding institution is directed accordingly to correct its position classification and pay system. In more advanced stages of economic democracy, each institution will feed its position classification and pay system directly into the Technodem. They will be checked automatically against the nationally established framework and deficiencies, if any, will be pointed out by the computer which must be corrected by the institution. These deficiencies will be electronically reported to the regional office. The most important point with this system is that while the national authorities establish a framework for position classification and pay systems, they do not go ahead and do the actual classification or assign the actual compensation for each position. All these responsibilities are transferred to the local private institutions, which are better equipped to classify them with allocations of appropriate pay for each position. Thus, the enormous bureaucratic system of doing such work at the national or regional level is eliminated by transferring the task to individual institutions.

The execution of this system is much simpler and less burdensome than the system presently used in industrial societies. Its great benefit is that it provides for equality of opportunity through a uniform system of classification and compensation, and it eliminates the bureaucracies of the present civil service commissions (national, state, and local) and similar agencies within industries and other large institutions which operate such systems. A further benefit is that it extends the scientific classification system to every production institution in society, regardless of size, including those self-employed.

### Characteristics of the Pay System

With taking into consideration that pay for each position strictly corresponds to the level of competency and experience required for that position, the pay system under technodemocratic economy has two major characteristics. First, compensation for each position consists of two parts: a cash payment which we may call a wage, and payment in stocks of the employee's firm. However, the cash payment must be sufficient to provide the worker with a convenient living condition. Projecting this minimum pay to the present economic conditions of the United States, we may dwell in the vicinity of an annual income of $15,000, or about $7.50 per hour. Presently, the minimum wage in the United States is about $4.00 per hour. This amount to an annual earning of about $8,3000 about 60 percent of our proposed minimum pay. In addition to this $15,000 minimum wage, each employee also receives a certain number of the stocks of the firm. In order to determine the amount of stock that each employee must receive, it must be taken into consideration that the accumulated amount of these stocks within thirty years of employment will be appropriate to provide a return sufficient for sustaining a convenient living condition, at least at the level of the median wage paid. One must notice here that there is no likelihood of inflationary process in technodemocratic economy, so the value of the unit of money received will remain stable for years and more likely, for decades.

Stock allocations take place each month concurrent with the salary payment. The result is a gradual transfer of capital from capitalist to working class to the effect that, after a period of time, all capital is transferred to the workers and there is no capitalist involved in the production and distribution process.

Regarding the gradual transfer of ownership of a firm to workers, the question may arise whether there would be enough stocks of a given firm to satisfy ownership accumulation necessary for each worker to provide for a comfortable living condition after retirement. This will be dependent on the assets-per-employee ratio in each production firm.

First, let us consider the capital adequate to have returns sufficient to provide for a comfortable living for a retired worker. Let us assume every worker to accumulate $120,000 of capital by the time of retirement and after 30 years of work. For accumulation of such capital each worker needs to receive $4,000 worth of stocks each year or $334 per month. At a seven percent return, $120,000 will produce $8,400 annual return.

Second, if we assume that the return on the capital from the beginning is also accumulated, in a period of 30 years this will amount to over $140,000, which will produce an income of $9,800 at seven percent interest rate. These will give the retired worker a total annual income of $18,200. Considering that there will not be any kind of individual taxation, this amount will be equivalent, under the present conditions in the United States, to about $20,000. This will provide for comfortable living conditions, by considering the sharply reduced expenditures of life under technodemocratic economy. As will be demonstrated in the production process later on, first, two of the most expensive expenditures in life, namely, health care and education will be provided free of charge; second, the revolutionary process of marketing and shopping which will take place will cause substantial reduction in prices of commodities, such as goods, services, and electronics as well as live recreational programs; and third, individuals will tend toward a more simplified, though highly advanced, material life and a more intense intellectual and spiritual one. Furthermore, in technodemocratic society, during the retirement period, at least two people, more likely, will live together. This multiplies the combined income while reducing the expenditures.

Thirdly, it is very likely that the individual will have also personal assets accumulated from his savings, particularly during the later years of his employment when his income surpasses his expenditures. These savings will provide for additional income which we are not considering here. It could be quite a substantial amount.

To safeguard these benefits for the retirement period the share of stocks received by the worker during his working years and returns accrued from them are not transferable. Returns from the nontransferable stocks owned by the worker are issued to him also in the form of nontransferable stocks until the time of his retirement. From there on he receives cash returns for the total of his stocks. This is a substitute for the present retirement and social security benefits except that under the technodemocratic economy the worker has the ownership of and full benefits from his accumulated capital.

The assumed level of nontransferable stocks accumulation at $120,000 is based at the minimum level of assets-per-employee in the United States and other industrialized countries. Table 6-1 demonstrates an average assets-per-employee of $121,262 among the top 500 international industrial companies. In the United States the average of the assets-per-employee of the top 50 transportation companies and the top 50 utilities firms amounted to $122,799 and $419,393 respectively. It is definite that through advancement of technology the amount will sharply increase in the near future.

The situation is very different regarding the financial institutions. As Table 6-2 illustrates the assets-per-employee rate far exceeds one million dollars. More likely, this ratio will also increase in the future though not as much as those in industrial firms.

Therefore, the assumption of retirement capital accumulation at the level of $120,000 is quite conservative. It will likely go far above this amount providing for much higher retirement income. At the same time it is possible that there may be a small number of companies where the assets-per-employee ratio may be below $120,000 assumed in our retirement program. This situation may occur in certain labor intensive production firms. In such cases, in order to guarantee the capital accumulation appropriate for retirement benefits the company will be required to purchase from the free market stocks of other companies with higher than average assets-per-employee rate and transfer those to the workers in non-transferable form as part of their monthly pay. At any case, this will be a marginal situation and will not affect the soundness of the retirement system. It must be noticed that monthly transfer of shares to each worker is part of his pay package and under the national position classification it applies to every worker—a cash pay plus a share of stocks. If a worker receives cash wage but does not receive stocks, he is entitled to, then his total monthly income becomes to that extent less than the workers in other comparable positions who receive full benefit. This situation will disturb the principle of equality of opportunity, will amount to exploitation, and will endanger the retirement benefits of such worker. However, a close study of the operation of the technodemocratic economy will disclose that this situation will be very unlikely to happen.

In order to maintain the principle of equality of opportunity as well as to safeguard the control of each firm by its workers, certain requirements are necessary:

1. Stocks in public possession will have no voting rights. Since upon the death of every individual his or her holdings will go under public possession (Public Consumption Fund), until they are purchased

**Table 6-1.** Assets-per-Employee Ratio in Production Firms (1986)

| FIRMS | ASSETS (Billion) | EMPLOYEES | APE Ratio ($) |
|---|---|---|---|
| Top 500 International Industrial Cos. | 2,254 | 18,592,549 | 121,262 |
| Top 50 U.S. Transportation Cos. | 126.132 | 1,027,309 | 122,779 |
| Top 50 U.S. Utilities Cos. | 530,039 | 1,263,824 | 419,393 |

Source: Calculated from the figures in *Fortune*, August 3, 1987, pp. 214-33; and *Fortune*, June 8, 1987, pp. 212-15.

**Table 6-2.** Assets-per-Employee Ratio in Financial Firms (1986)

| FIRMS | ASSETS (Million) | EMPLOYEES | APE Ratio |
|---|---|---|---|
| Top 100 U.S Commercial Banks | 1,937,181 | 1,011,636 | 1,914,899 |
| Top 50 Diversified Financial Corps. | 903,493 | 708,459 | 1,275,294 |
| Top 50 Life Insurance Cos. | 670,371 | 422,156 | 1,587,972 |
| Top 50 Savings and Loan Corps. | 408,549 | 125,838 | 3,246,630 |

Source: Calculated from the figures in *Fortune*, June 8, 1987, pp. 200-205, 206-215.

in the open market by the corresponding firms or individuals, there always would be some stocks in the public possession. This rule is to keep the public institutions out of the production and distribution process.

2. Returns from the publicly possessed stocks will go to the Public Consumption Fund.

3. No production firm can own stocks of another firm except when they are purchased to be transferred to the workers of the firm and are kept for a short term for this purpose.

4. Candidates for the board of directors are elected from the workers of the firm. No persons from outside of the firm can be elected to any policy-making position. Top management which is not elective but appointive based on qualification remains outside of this rule.

One of the major distinctions between the capitalist mode of production and the democratic mode of production, is that under the latter, despite a total private ownership of the means of production, there is no separation between capital and labor. Labor owns the capital and thus governs the policy-making and management process, two important factors in the production process from which labor is totally detached under capitalism.

Monthly allocation of company stocks to workers has several purposes. First, it transfers ownership of the means of production from capitalists to workers. Second, it causes an accumulation of capital for each worker, returns from which bring additional income to the owner during his working years. This income gradually increases corresponding to the increase in the amount of stocks. Third, by the time of retirement, the income from the accumulated stocks and returns is sufficient to sustain a comfortable retirement life. The main purpose of this stock allocation is to provide each individual with an independent retirement and old age benefits. This is a substitute for the present social security and retirement benefits. The major difference is that under the American capitalist system, the control of social security funds are in the hands of the government and retirement funds are controlled by the leadership in private sectors. A retired worker depends on monthly payments from these two resources. Furthermore, while the worker is heavily taxed for this purpose during all his working years, the amount received is nowhere sufficient to provide for a comfortable living condition; nor is he guaranteed to receive payment during his retired life. Under technodemocratic economy each individual is the holder of his source of income for the duration of his retired life. He depends on no one for his support; he is the owner of the capital accumulated, not through exploiting others, but through his own labor. It is this capital that contributes to the demands of production while providing enough income for a dignified, individualistic and independent life for its owner, the retired worker. As will be explained later, this retirement is formal and actually the person never retired from being productive.

To protect this comfortable old age living for the workers, it is imperative that the stocks earned by each worker in addition to returns from them remain in his possession for the period of his life. For this very important purpose, these stocks and returns must be non-transferable. However, in order to diversify stock ownership, these non-transferable stocks are exchangeable with other non-transferable stocks available in the stock market. For example, a worker who works for company A and receives stocks of that company as part of his monthly pay, may desire to exchange part of his stocks with non-transferable stocks of company B and C. Since many workers working for different firms would also like to diversify their non-transferable stocks of their company, workers of company A will have no difficulty in exchanging their stocks with those of other companies in the open market. The value of non-transferable stocks of each company is determined by the value of transferrable stocks of the same company in the stock market. It must be noted that most of the stocks offered in the stock market will be of non-transferrable kind.

One may argue that since these stocks are non-transferrable, its ownership is not complete. Considering the purpose of these stocks, this argument is not valid. Because, these stocks are given to the workers, first, to transfer capital from the capitalist to the workers; second, to provide an additional source of income for the workers during their working years; third, and the most essential, to provide for a source of sufficient income for the workers after they retire. If these stocks were transferrable, it would have been possible for a worker to liquidate them in the market and spend the proceeds. In this way, he would have destroyed his source of maintenance during his old age. He would also have relinquished his ownership of capital. Since, under technodemocratic economic system, there is no welfare assistance, except for those who are disabled, if such a worker liquidates his stocks, he may not have sufficient income to maintain himself. Furthermore, public assistance to such a person would be contrary to the principle of equality of opportunity since by liquidating his stocks and spending the proceeds he consciously has harmed his equality of opportunity, and by receiving welfare assistance, he would be unjustifiably using the money earned by others for his support.

Finally, non-transferable stocks have all the benefits of ownership, except being transferable. The owners receive return from them and they are as valuable as transferable stocks of the same company. Furthermore, one must note that most of the investment capital will be in the form of non-transferable stocks and thus, most of the stocks in the stock market will be of the non-transferable kind. The philosophical idea behind this is that the capital, as a means of production, does not belong to anyone, but to society as a whole. Each person during his lifetime becomes the custodian of some of it and enjoys the benefits accrued from it. When the person dies, since there is no inheritance under technodemocratic economy, the capital he owns is transferred to the public treasury and gradually passed on to the next generation. Non-transferability of the stocks guarantees to every worker a share of ownership of capital; it materializes the equitable distribution of the means of production and distribution among all the members of the working class.

### The Work System

Under technological democracy, there is a general education program which every individual is required to complete. As it is explained later, when we discuss education, this general education is somehow similar in its structure, but not in is content, to the system of general education presently applied in the socialist countries like the Soviet Union.[1] It consists of a four year preschool education (age three through six), a four year elementary education, and a four year secondary education. We consider these grades one through twelve. This is the most important part of each individual's education and enormously effective in the future competence of the work force.

Work starts at the age of fifteen. However, the individual works only part-time. There are two sides to a worker's life. First, his development as a human being necessary to prepare him as a conscious participant in a democratic society. Here the purpose of worker's education is to develop and advance him as a *democratic person*. Such a person is deeply devoted to the principles of democracy, equality of opportunity in particular, in every aspect of the societal life. In order to achieve this high human quality the person needs a broad education in humanities, non-professional aspects of social sciences as well as natural sciences. A person needs a deep understanding of the purpose of being, truth, honesty, one's place and rights within the society, one's attachment and respect to the nature and environment, and one's unselfishness in social, economic and political spheres of life.

To develop as a democratic person one has to understand, through education, practice, and experience, the complex meaning and application of the principle of equality of opportunity. Because, it is only through the application of this principle that the socio-economic and political framework of each individual's life is determined, expansion of one's freedoms and their limitations are distinguished.

The core part of the education required to understand these democratic values is achieved through an individual's general education extending through the twelfth grade. However, in technological society education is continuous and extends beyond this initial level through all working years of each individual. As part of this continued education, along with technical and professional education, each worker will be required to take each year a certain prescribed number of courses in the areas enhancing his general and cultural knowledge, and updating his knowledge of democracy as applied in daily life.

The other side of a worker's life is related to his work, his professional knowledge, his proficiency, and productiveness. His education in this regard starts when he enters the labor market. There are two aspects to his education. First, a formal technical and professional education which will continue through one's working years until his retirement. For example, if a person wants to become an electrical engineer, he will start his formal higher education as soon as he finishes his twelfth grade general education. Each worker starts his professional education full-time when he starts to work and continues thereafter while working. For the first six years he works part-time and after that he works full-time for a period of thirty years, after which he retires from formal employment. As it will be illustrated later, by no means does this retirement indicate the end of an active and productive life.

During the first six years, after graduation from the twelfth grade, the individual continues his education near full-time; let us assume the equivalent of 30 college credits per year, including 8 weeks of the summer. Within six years, under the present higher education standards, this amounts to 180 credit hours of education, far beyond what is required now for receiving an engineering or other professional degrees. After this period of six years, when the worker assumes a full-time job, he is required to study at least the equivalent of six college credits each semester (two 3-credit courses). One of these two courses relates to his professional area in order to keep him up to date in his field and further expand his technical knowledge, and the other in the liberal arts area, to give him a better understanding of self and society and also to provide him with a better means of enjoyment of life.

This is the course of the individual's formal education which continues at least up to the time of retirement. It is considered as part of his weekly work load.

The other aspect of a worker's education is through experience. Experience at his work place teaches him how he can turn his scientific, cultural, and professional knowledge into efficient and productive action. Experience with the institutions of society outside of his work teaches him how to use his knowledge in the social sciences and humanities for better serving his fellow citizens and his society as a whole.

## Mobility

In technodemocratic society, an individual is free to terminate his employment in one institution and seek employment, within his level of competence, in another institution. Or, he may desire to move into another class of work or profession. For this purpose he must channel his continued education toward his desired field and complete the requirements for the level of competence necessary for his desired position. As it will be noted later on, education is provided free of charge through the Technodem, day and night. An individual desiring to change his field of occupation may be obliged to take courses, in addition to those required for continuing education from each worker, in order to achieve competency in his intended new line of work.

## Salary Range and Compensation

The minimum salary for a full-time job is based on the amount necessary not only to accommodate the basic needs such as food, housing, clothing, transportation and recreation, but to provide for comfortable living conditions. As stated before, based on the present standards, we may assume an income of $15,000 per person ($7.50 per hour) for this minimum pay. It is obvious that jobs requiring a higher and more specialized education, or harder physical work, would pay a higher salary. As the years of experience and further education is added to worker's initial level of competence for a full-time job, his salary increases accordingly. But at no time does a worker's pay exceed three time the minimum wage.

Let us assume, for example, that the minimum wage for full-time employment is $15,000; the highest salary would be around $45,000. This means an average salary increase of about 3.4 percent per year. The percent increase in salary will be higher during the early years of work tending toward zero by the end of the 30th year. This will cause younger workers to move faster toward a more convenient life. If we consider economic conditions as those of the United States at present, an annual income of $15,000 will be sufficient to provide an individual with a comfortable living condition as far as the basic needs are concerned. Consider there is no individual taxation under technodemocratic economy and no property tax to cover the cost of institutions. Thus a $15,000 income is equivalent to about $20,000 under the present federal, state, and local tax systems. One must also consider that there is no social security deductions and no expenditures for the workers' health care, his education and that of his children. Furthermore, each worker receives an equivalent of about $4,000 per year in company shares, from which he also receives benefits. On the other hand, a worker in his mid-career receives an income about $35,000 which would be sufficient to provide for a comfortable life with much higher standards. Here again, since the worker does not pay taxes and receives free health care and education for himself and his children, his $35,000 salary plus returns from his accumulated capital compared to the present standards in the United States, would be equivalent to nearly $50,000.

It is obvious that while nearly all workers start their full-time employment at the level of $15,000, there may be some with higher levels of opportunity which will enter the market at the level of their opportunity based on the extent of education and experience of each. These are usually entering the society from outside. Since through required continuing education and increased experience, the level of competence of a worker continually goes up, so does his level of opportunity and income. The extent of increase in competence determines the amount of increase in salary one receives. This principle applies to all levels of competency. Technical and professional learning can never stop, because in technological society one becomes easily obsolete without updating his knowledge. Remaining at the same level of knowledge is equivalent to decaying in competence. Such behavior will cause lowering of one's level of opportunity and thus the level of his income. This is why continuing education is necessary and required under the technodemocratic economy. Technological society cannot progress or even sustain itself without properly educated and conscious citizens.

## Retirement

When a worker reaches the stage of retirement, he is a very highly educated and well experienced person. Thus, by no means does retirement mean idleness, particularly when a person is in his early fifties and still has some 15-20 years of dynamic life to pursue.

First, as a person of high education in the liberal arts, years of experience in the operation of technodemocratic economy and in its social and political spheres, one would be highly qualified to fill political positions. As it will be explained later, the elected government officials are volunteers with no pay, only their expenditures are paid on a per diem basis. Elected line officials, such as governors, are exceptions. However, since these positions require high qualifications, a broad knowledge of society and deep acquaintance with the principles of technodemocratic economy, newcomers to the labor market are not qualified while retired individuals are well suited for the job. Since most of the elected political positions will be part-time, and the essence of the work will be carried out by full-time specialists and technicians, those at the later stages of employment, if otherwise qualified, may seek political positions by choosing to work part-time and spend the rest of the time on political matters. However, they will be reluctant to do so, since part-time work will affect their salary and retirement benefits.

Second, retired persons because of their high qualifications, will be in demand for lecturing and consulting, particularly, if they continue their education after retirement.

Third, again because of their high competency, retired workers may involve themselves in research and writing. They may concentrate on subjects in their technical or professional field. They may choose subjects relating to social or economic aspects of technodemocratic society, drawing from years of experience, as well as research.

Finally, a retired person may not wish to do any of these. He may desire to devote the rest of his life to art, music, literature, travel, or further study of nature and the environment; or, he may desire to start a business of his own by investing his savings and forming partnerships.

In doing any of these choices, with the exception of the latter, a retired person has plenty of time for travel, sports, and recreation since he is the sole determinant of his own time schedule. He may make his work and recreation plans as he desires. He has a steady income from his accumulated non-transferable shares, he is totally on his own as a truly free and independent individual. The retirement period is, in fact, a dream of life, with security, creativity, and freedom to do as one wishes with his money, body and mind. Furthermore, retired people are the holder of a good part of the investment capital in society through the ownership of their accumulated non-transferable and transferable stocks of production firms. In fact, the retired workers are the highest per capita owners of capital in the technodemocratic economy. All these put together make retired workers highly respectable individuals in the community. The slogan in technodemocratic society may well be that "I work and improve myself as an individual with the hope of arriving to the heavenly stage of retirement." This becomes even more desirable when individuals retire in their early 50s and have many years of dynamic life to look forward to. For some, this period may be more expanded than the period of their working years.

# NOTES

1. For a brief but very thorough presentation of Soviet education see A.I. Piskinov, "The Soviet School and Soviet Pedagogy in the Period of the Competition of Socialist Construction and Gradual Transition to Communism," *Soviet Education*, February–March, 1978, pp. 106-194.

*Chapter 7*

# ECONOMIC DEMOCRACY AND EQUALITY OF OPPORTUNITY

The application of the principle of equality of opportunity is a quite delicate matter. Some scientists in the past have tried to describe and analyze it. In describing his democratic "technotronic society", for example, Brzezinski characterized it by the application of the principle of equal opportunity for all but special opportunity for a talented few.[1] This appears to be a combination of a continued maintenance of the popular will with an increasing occupation of the key decision-making positions by individuals of special intellectual and scientific achievements. He argues that the educational and social systems will make it increasingly attractive and easy for those meritocratic few to develop to the fullest of their special potential. While it will be necessary to require everyone at a sufficiently responsible position to take, say, two years of retraining every ten years, the rest of the population will tend to develop a new interest in the cultural and humanistic aspects of life, which will tend to serve as a social valve, reducing tensions and political frustration.

Others argue that equality of opportunity as understood by the former group has little to do with creating a more egalitarian society in the technological age.[2] As they argue, equality of opportunity functions as an indispensable feature of the highly stratified society where equality of opportunity assures that talented individuals will be able to climb into the key decision-making positions, generating the success of new society and its cohesion against popular tensions and political frustration. Thus, in technologically advanced societies, equality of opportunity will function as a hierarchical principle, in opposition to the egalitarian social goals it is thought to serve. It will, indeed, become one of the main factors contributing to the widening gap between the cultures of upper and lower classes in technological society.

We intend to repudiate the approach of all these schools of thought to the application of the principle of equality of opportunity. But before doing this we find important to look, though very briefly, into the characteristics of an advanced technological society.

Some hundred and fifty years ago the concept of *laissez-faire* provided ground for identification of the interests of the institutions of entrepreneurial capitalism in the society which they dominated and profited from it. The laissez-faire taken as a capitalist ideology provided ground for the cultural as well as intellectual expression of the interests of a specific but small class.

In today's technological society, the concept of *laissez-innover* provides the same ground for expression to a specific class identified as technologists. It is a technological impulse in technological society providing opportunities for the institutions which tend to monopolize technology and profit from it. By free exploitation of technology this privileged class finds a guaranteed opportunity for wealth, status, and power.

This class creates a technological rationality which is as socially neutral today as market rationality was a century and a half ago. It encourages a political and cultural gap between the upper class, those who control the advanced technological systems, and the rest or those who are subject to control.

To understand the situation properly, we must consider the present status and the nature of technology. We must, first, consider technology as an institutional system. Today's relation of technology to monopoly capitalism is analogous to the relation of the latter to the free market (laissez-faire) capitalism of a century and half ago.

Second, the most important societal dimension of advanced technological institutions is social. If left alone, that is to say if we sustain laissez-innover, these institutions will tend to be instruments of highly centralized and intensive social control. Technology tends to conquer man and through him conquer nature. Even though there seems an absence of direct controls or coercion, technology demands a high degree of control over the training, specialization, mobility, and skills of the working class. Technical rationality is increasingly employed to organize physical objects as well as human services.

Third, there are very profound social antagonism causing contradictions much more intensive, sharper, and more fundamental than those ascribed by Marx to the conditions of the mid-nineteenth century industrial society. These contradictions are mainly the result of the control of technology by an elite class. The workers are overtrained, underutilized and their work is tightly controlled by technological means and processes. Technological progress requires a continuous increase in the skill levels of the workers while the advanced technical rationality in the production process does not provide ground for full use of the attained skills. Accordingly, in some sectors, the workers are obliged to be highly trained regardless how little of those skills is actually used in the work process. Unlike the nineteenth century industrial society, in advanced technological society, salary and wage increases lose their overriding importance once necessities of life are met and there are ample means of comfort and even luxuries available to the working class. While to get people to work harder requires growing incentives, the effect of traditional incentives such as money, status, and authority has been continually in decline.

If the present situation of class stratification continues, the advance of technology will tend to concentrate authority further in the hands of those who control technology and its managing group. But, the advance of technology, information technology in particular, while increasing the required skill, it also increases the educational levels of the population on a broader base. This creates first latent consciousness leading to open self-management both in the work place as well as in society as a whole. This is one important development in the contradictions inherent in technological advancement. It leads to a profound social contradiction between the highly stratified society of the present technological-capitalist system like the United States and the spread of educational opportunities among the masses. Thus, technology tends to create the basis for new and sharp class conflict in modern society quite analogous to the early industrialization era which created the working and owning class namely the proletariat and the capitalist.

Accordingly, drive for technological development by the elite—laissez innover—is the most powerful and influential movement toward the demands and program of the technological impulse in industrialized society which is rooted in its most powerful institutions—government and multinational corporations. More than any other development in the past, this impulse has succeeded in identifying and rationalizing the interests of the most authoritarian elite, which operate under the guise of democracy, in industrialized countries. They also exercise dominating expansion of their policies in the Third World countries.

In the life of Americans as well as other industrialized nations, many forces hostile to the democratic values are exerted by those who control the technology and its development. Understanding of this fact requires some comprehension of the fakeness of democratic values and processes in order to grasp the true fact of technological elitism and authoritarianism. The very comprehension of this fact is an important and significant step toward national consciousness leading to under-standing the malaise, irrationality, powerlessness, and official violence that characterize the life in the United States and other industrial nations. The result may well lead to a politics of radical reconstruction or social revolution.

## Application of Equality of Opportunity

In all discussions above, those who have directed attention and criti-cism to the application of the principle of equality of opportunity and its implications in causing a democratic society, have erred in several ways. The first and most important mistake has been the piecemeal application of the concept. In a highly undemocratic capitalistic society like the United States if one tries to apply the principle of equality of opportunity to one sector of operation of society leaving the other areas untouched, it is obvious that the outcome will still tend to comply with the norms of the basic system, in the case of the United States, capitalism. Within an elite-ruled society any partial reform would tend to comply with the elite norms. It will create a new elite, in those arguments technical elite, which will supplement the existing elite class and more likely to serve it.

The second error relates to the application of the principle of equality of opportunity to the existing system of operation which in itself it undemocratic. For example, in the area of education, they think in the advancement of the present system of education, which consists of a continuous education—elementary, secondary and college—toward achieving a professional status and then entering the work market and continue with periodical retraining and updating programs. An improper and undemocratic system creates improper and undemocratic consequences. Education in a technodemocratic society, as it has been explained before, is in no way similar to the system of education practiced in the United States as well as in other industrialized countries. Based on the requirements of technological capitalistic society education in these countries has built-in incompetency and substantial deficiencies.

The third error refers to the narrow interpretation and application of the principle of equality of opportunity. No one considers that technological democracy is a system by itself which is essentially based on the thorough application of the concept of equality of opportunity. There is no such system as technological democracy today. This system is independent and pure. It cannot coexist, within the same society, with undemocratic systems such as capitalism, socialism, or communism. It cannot be mixed with any of these systems without losing its democratic character. So, for the sake of democracy, it has to stand alone and be distinguished in its application to any society.

There are other errors in their approaches as well, but instead of going through those we try to explain the application of the principle of equality of opportunity in a technodemocratic society and let the explanation of the concept shed light upon the errors. First, we must try to understand that technological democracy is a system in itself substantially distinguished from the existing societal systems of capitalism, socialism and communism.[3] Under the requirement of the system it encompasses economic, social, political and technological aspects of the society. It encompasses the society as a whole, all its interactions, values and objectives.

This theory of democracy has never been described before since it has technology as its integral component. Here we refer only to some of its important aspects in relation to the application of the principle of equality of opportunity in an attempt, at the same time, to demonstrate the importance and complexity of the application of the principle.

## Social Democracy:  Healthcare and Education

Healthcare and education are the two basic and most important requirements for a progressive and advancing society.  No progress, specifically in the economic area, can be achieved without a healthy and educated population.

Technological society regardless of its form—capitalistic, socialistic or else—has its stresses of many kinds resulting from the complexities it creates in the daily operation of life.  Thus many diseases particular of technological society are mental.  Furthermore, in such a society because of excessive and widespread use of synthetic materials in food stuff and pollution of air and water, many physical diseases develop, varieties of cancer in particular.

These unhealthy conditions and phenomena, make health measures in technological society evermore important.  There can be no substantial progress in an advanced but unhealthy society.  If no proper health care is provided, such a society is doomed to failure and decay.  The negative effect of misuse or careless use of technology has an accelerating effect on this decay.

Consequently, a democratic healthcare program is imperative to maintain and improve the dynamism of the population as a whole, the working class in particular.

The only way the equality of opportunity in healthcare can be achieved is that it be accessible the same to all population, and the only way this can be materialized is when it is available to all, free of charge.  Thus, the healthcare services must be made available through a nationwide institution, not necessarily a governmental agency, to all the population.  It must be noted that by healthcare it is meant a preventive one.  This covers not only individuals and their physical and mental conditions, but also the environment tending to provide for a healthy life.  The environment includes not only the air, water, toxic and atomic waste disposal but also food and hundreds of products used in daily life.  It is obvious that if the causes harmful to health are diminished or eliminated, need for individual health care will be substantially reduced and so will the costs.

The total annual cost of health services in the United States was about 450 billion dollars in 1986 and predictions are that it will continue to increase and may likely reach 760 billion dollars by the year 1990.  To understand the incredibly enormous size of this cost, one may consider that the annual cost amounted to $1,700 per person in 1986 and will rise to $2,550 by 1990.[4]

In an expert's view, the United States is now in an indefinite stage of management and control, attempting first to determine the amount of money needed, and then directing it to appropriate destinations of health services' need and demand.[5]

In evaluating health care costs and sources of financial contribution, one must note that the federal government plays a substantial role and has a major influence relating to costs. It pays for about 50 percent of the hospital costs and more likely about 30 percent of the physician costs through Medicare. Within the private sector, there are hundreds of insurance companies bearing the costs. However, about 10 percent of these companies account for 75 percent of all payments by insurance firms. At the same time, of the 27 percent of all expenditures paid by insurance firms, about 80 percent are contributed by employers through payroll deductions.[6] Major problem is the very pluralistic nature of the health services. The plurality of sources of funds makes it difficult for proper administration of the services. On the public side of contribution, there is bureaucratic inefficiency and waste; on the private sector, there is a striving toward maximization of profits. Both factors together lead toward unjustifiably increasing high costs of health care. Looking realistically, as presented previously, insurance business has moved, as any other major business, toward monopolization. Today a few giant insurance firms control a substantial majority of services. As it is well known, monopoly capitalism is one of the causes for increased prices.

Despite substantial governmental and employer contributions toward health care services, still the great majority of Americans do not receive near adequate health care, and a substantial number receive practically none.

The solution seems to be in the unification of all health service funds under one system, eliminating both private and public sectors from interfering in the administration of this nationally vital service. Such a health institution can impose just prices for health services, including doctor's fees, hospital charges and medicine prices. It may require minor contributions from employers as per head of employees as well as from those self employed. All people then will benefit from such services and society will move toward equality of opportunity in relation to health care services.

Thus, in the area of health care the application of the principle of equality of opportunity prescribes that it be available to everyone with no obstacles, including the financial one. The very application of the equality of opportunity gives the health care agency authority to interfere in any production process that the agency experts find harmful to the affected public, such as coal mines, asbestos factories where the individual is directly exposed to harmful effects of the improperly kept work environment; or the operation of industries which pollute the air, water and other aspects of the environment and expose individuals living within that environment to its consequential hazards. In fact, those polluting institutions are infringing upon the equal opportunity rights of the population involved by subjecting them to an unhealthy environment, compared with the individuals living in other healthier environments. This intrusion in the equality of opportunity of the population involved, invests authority upon the health agency to interfere, punish and demand corrections. The structure, finance, and operation of this health agency is described elsewhere.[7]

## Education

Along with health care, the most important requirement for the advancement of a society is education. As demonstrated before, the education system, as well as programs in a technological society, are substantially different from the present systems practiced in industrialized societies.

Presently, formal education starts from age seven in noncommunist societies and from age three in the latter. It is then continued through high school. Education of the overwhelming majority of the population ends at the end of this level. Beyond this level some go to vocational schools and some enter institutions of higher education and continue full time toward receiving a college degree of a B.S. or B.A.; a much smaller number continue for a year or two toward a master's degree. A very few continue further toward a doctoral degree, which is the ultimate level of formal education. Though some study toward advanced degrees while working, the overwhelming majority get engaged in full time study to achieve the goal. A person graduating from high school is usually 18 years old. He is 22 when he receives his first college degree and at least 26 when he receives his doctoral degree. A person seeks employment after he finishes any of these stages. This means the majority enter the labor market at the age of 18 or sooner and a few continue studying until they are 26 or older before seeking employment.

This kind of education has at least four major defects. First, the continuous full-time education keeps students away from the labor market. Though some students work part-time, a great majority of them do not work. Thus, education becomes all expenditures without returning to the society the benefits of skills learned each year. It becomes a heavy economic burden upon the community, parents and society as a whole.

Second, in technological society, with the rapid pace of change and advancement, the knowledge received yesterday more likely becomes obsolete or of diminished value today. The present system of education has then built-in obsolescence.

Third, it is a one shot process; after it ends and the diploma is received it is considered completed for the purpose of employment. Yet changing conditions of work require continuous education to keep up with the changes and to be able to perform properly and efficiently.

Fourth, a very important defect of the present educational system is In its content. It emphasizes technical training to the detriment of cultural education such as history, philosophy, foreign and domestic languages and literature, music and arts. Cultural education is the kind of knowledge that creates a healthy society, intellectually speaking, where reason and wisdom prevail over force and brutality. Because of destructive potential of technological society, at no time in history such cultural education was needed more than the present. In fact, advancing cultural education along with technical training is a matter of urgency before it gets too late to save humanity from self destruction.

Education in technological society must remedy all these defects while, at the same time, making every individual a lifetime participant. It is divided into three phases as follows.

The formal education which is full-time and heavily cultural, involving social sciences and humanities, from the age of three to fourteen. From age fifteen each individual starts to work part-time while continuing his studies nearly full-time. He keeps at least one-half of his educational program, equivalent to nine credit hours per semester under present standards, plus three to six credits in the summer. From the age of twenty-two he works full-time, reducing his education to one-third of the full load or equivalent to six credit hours per semester. He then continues this required minimum educational program for the rest of his working years. It is more likely that a person so habituated to continual education will continue to do so also after his retirement at the age of 52. The method, content, and process of this education has been discussed elsewhere in this study and is no matter of concern here.

The period of full-time education which extends to twelve years, is the most important part and is rigidly structured for the purpose of conveying the most possible knowledge to the students during the daily time specified for education. It is during this period that the principle of equality of opportunity must be strictly applied. In order to give each child the type of education required to understand and comfortably live within the technodemocratic society, it is imperative that each child has the same opportunity for quality education as any other child in society. This very essential aim can be achieved only if education is available to everyone without any burden, financial or otherwise. Therefore the educational cost during this period must be afforded from the specific allotment for this purpose coming from the Public Consumption Fund.

From the date a person starts employment, one-third of his educational cost will be paid for by the employer and the rest from the Public Consumption Funds. Therefore, from this time on the public treasury will have a diminishing contribution to education. When the individual reaches the stage of one-third of time education, all his costs will be paid by his employer.

In actual process the money allocated for this purpose in each institution will be transferred to the Public Consumption Fund; the latter then will pay the workers educational expenses. By the use of the Technodem for educational purposes, the cost to the employer will be nominal in comparison to the cost of such education today.

Equality of opportunity is the most important constitutional right of every individual and it must be provided for, preserved and protected. Therefore, there can be no infringement against this right either by the institutions or other individuals whether education be for personal benefits or for attaining a better opportunity.

Accordingly, each individual has a positive right to equality of opportunity; it must be provided for him. Each individual has also a negative right to it; it cannot be abridged, denied to him, or taken away from him.

The most important aspect of this system of education is its social and economic equalizing powers. First, everybody starts education from the same level and more or less with the same quality. Thus, there is no classwise distinctive education. This is particularly effectuated by considering that under technological democracy, despite the fact that there is a total ownership of the means of production and distribution by the private sector and there is moderate accumulation of wealth, there is no ground for class stratification as it is evidenced under capitalism. Each individual's wealth goes to the public treasury upon his death and each person starts from scratch. This creates a fluid and mobile dynamic society which can be subject to no elite rule—technical elite or else. This is essentially an equalitarian and equitable society. The adherence to the application of the principle of equality of opportunity tends to keep this society essentially democratic and incredibly stable.

The other important aspect of this system of education is that it provides for highly qualified individuals to rule and guide the system in techno-political positions. Candidates come from the retired class because all positions in techno-politics are temporary with limited term and requiring very high qualifications.

Accordingly, this system of continuous education will provide a highly qualified personnel for elective offices by the time of retirement. Once elected, individuals will be responsible for proper operation of the system. Since the term of office will also be limited to one term, none of the elected officials can establish strong or lasting influence on the matters of the state, like those enjoyed by the elective officials under capitalism or other political systems. It must be noted that the one-term limitation applies only for the elective position held by the individual. He will be eligible to run for election in other political bodies. He cannot serve more than one term in each of these public bodies.

## Economic Democracy

After the two social requirements namely health care and education, both essential for having a progressive and dynamic society, the most important application of the principle of equality of opportunity relates

232 / Technodemocratic Economic Theory

to the economic sphere of society. Economic democracy is the most important aspect of the technodemocratic system.

This goal can be achieved only by proper application of the principle of equality of opportunity. There are several strong factors in capitalistic society which work against economic equality of opportunity. It is primarily in these areas that the principle must apply in order to lead society toward economic democracy.

## Accumulation of wealth through exploitation

As we have seen before, in a capitalistic society wealth is created and accumulated through the exploitation of labor and consumers. This is what a businessman calls profit and Marx has labeled it social surplus. Profit is what a producer earns by appropriating a part from the work of labor or charging extra, beyond the exploitation of labor, to consumers. In fact, in modern industrialized capitalistic society, profit is the result of double-exploitation. The result has been a phenomenal concentration of wealth and ensuing power in the hands of a very small class. This class, as a result, has been able to dominate the socio-economic and political spheres of activities, attain and sustain a highly privileged status. Thus, an industrialized capitalistic society brings into existence a society with a very high class stratification, the power being concentrated in the hands of a small, and enormously wealthy class. Consequently, there is no equality of opportunity in such capitalistic society and it can never exist. Those who have wealth, have a much higher opportunity than those who are considered poor.

## Accumulation of Wealth Under Equality of Opportunity

Appropriation of profit has caused the accumulation of wealth which has provided opportunity for power and privilege. Thus, one requirement for providing ground for establishment of equality of opportunity is to abolish profit and gradually return the ownership of the means of production to the workers and, thus, ultimately eliminate capitalism. Furthermore, the abolishing of profit would highly increase the moral values of the population since profits are nothing but cheating both the workers and the consumers, they cause sanctioned justification of fraud and corruption which will tend to disappear once profits are prohibited. As it has been discussed before, this prohibition will multiply workers incentive to produce which is not the subject of consideration here.

The elimination of profits entails the elimination of exploitation of workers as well as the consumers. But above all it eliminates the uncontrolled and free accumulation of wealth. This will be an essential step toward bringing about the economic equality of opportunity.

### Transfer of Wealth

The elimination of profit alone will not solve the problem of inequalities of opportunities that exist under capitalism. Those who have accumulated wealth, if allowed to transfer it to others can also transfer with it the accompanying power and privileges. Another word, anyone receiving wealth through transfer without paying a comparable price for it is being moved up in the hierarchy of opportunities, proportional to the size of transferred wealth. Such transfer, therefore, increases his opportunities to the detriment of the rest of the population. One of the most traditional and sanctioned transfers of wealth is through inheritance. If a person dies and leaves enormous wealth behind, it is transferred to his legal heirs enhancing their status, power, and privilege compared to other citizens. Thus, if a family is centi-millionaire, that family, short of a catastrophe, will remain centi-millionaire through inheritance, nearly perpetuating the power and privileges in the family members. It is by this way that the economic elite is created with dominating influence in society. The same is true not only with inheritance but with any transfer of wealth without comparable compensation.

If, upon death, individual's wealth is transferred to the public treasury, the children of the deceased have to start from scratch as any other citizen. They would be deprived from transfer of power and privileges accompanying the wealth of the deceased.

The result in the long run would be gradual elimination of all wealthy families tending to bring the wealth of society toward equitable distribution among its members. This is also an essential movement toward equalizing economic opportunities.

Since the size of official government in technodemocratic society is very small, a substantial part of wealth received, through such transfers, by public treasury will be spent in essential public services such as education and health care which will further enhance the equality of opportunity among citizens.

## Equitable Private Ownership of the Means of Production

As stated before, in technodemocratic society, all means of production and distribution are privately owned and operated. This becomes gradually materialized by allocating to each worker, in addition to his wages, a specific amount of share of ownership, primarily of the institution where he works. As a result, each worker from the very beginning of his work becomes, at the same time, a part owner of his institution. As he continues his work, his ownership share increases. As a matter of time the capitalistic ownership is eliminated and the workers become full owners controlling the system of production. The term worker in this study applies to anyone who works in production of goods and services. This encompasses managerial-professional members down to skilled and unskilled ones. In fact, under capitalism all these individuals work for the capitalist and thus are workers in real meaning of the term. This is a broad definition of the working class under monopolistic capitalism as well as technological democracy. Simply a worker is anyone who works.

The application of this system of ownership will gradually eliminate the influence of economic elite by transferring the power to the workers, enhancing the sense of responsibility and incentive among workers, and contributing substantially to the advancement of the equality of opportunity among the working class and stability and tranquility in society.

## Technological Decentralization

As the share of the working class increases by the passage of time it reaches a point where the workers take control of the board of directors. From this point on the institutional policies are made by the representatives of the workers rather than those of the capitalists. This change on the leadership automatically tends to decentralize large institutions. Suppose a large food production corporation which operates hundreds of supermarkets, scores of food processing and meat processing units. While the central management continue to remain in the hand of capitalists, these subsidiary institutions, one after another, fall under the direct control of the workers. After attaining this point, each institution tends to assume independence from the central office.

For example, once a supermarket unit operation is taken over by its workers, first it tends to make independent decisions which may be in conflict with those of the central office; second, the owners tend to operate independent from the mother corporation. The only thing the mother corporation can do is to restrain from supplying goods. If this happens, the supermarket may decide to operate like any other independent supermarket and buy goods from the competitors. It is more likely that the mother corporation will not resort to this policy since it will affect the marketing of its own products. Quite likely, it will go along with the independent operation of the supermarket in order not to harm its own size of the share in food marketing. The corporation may also think to stop relations with the supermarket and initiate a new one. Not likely, because of its cost and similar consequences a few years later. It also has to compete with its previous supermarket which now operates independently and which is quite familiar with the market and operation policies of the mother corporation. The same thing will happen also to other food processing institutions operating under the control of the mother corporation.

Consequently, this great movement toward equality of opportunity in the production process would tend to sharply decentralize the institutions of production and distribution. This decentralization will automatically cause decentralization or democratization of production technology. The latter is a great step toward democratization of society as a whole by taking control of technology out of the hands of a few who controlled it for the benefit of the capitalist elite and to the detriment of society as a whole.

### Shared Opportunity

As mentioned before, equality of opportunity may be positive or negative. Positive process refers to those that tend to enhance the opportunities of the masses of the working class to the detriment of the opportunities of a small privileged class. Negative equality of opportunity is when the opportunity of a small group of workers are increased to the detriment of the opportunities of the masses of the working class.

The latter concept, the negative equality of opportunity, is what we may justifiably call "shared opportunity." The purpose is first, to tend toward equalizing opportunities among the working class; second, to guarantee employment to every able citizen thus providing for full employment at all times.

It is very important to notice that new workers entering the market come nearly exclusively from those finishing their general education who are about fifteen years of age and are looking for part-time, low-skilled jobs. This actually does not disturb the employment opportunities at the other levels of the production system.

A very few may enter the work force at the higher levels of employment. These are specialists entering society from the outside or individuals within the work force who desire to change their line of work or profession. Since the number will be very small, its effect on the opportunities of other workers will be negligible. In any case, shared opportunity is a requirement in democratic society. Those who have a better opportunity share it with those looking for the same kind of opportunity while lacking it and at the same time being qualified to receive such opportunity. To accommodate this principle sometimes a minor structural revision of work may be required. But, as practice continues, its problems of application will gradually be resolved by innovating new processes and methods. These mostly will be helped by advanced technology and availability of electronic information through the Technodem in regard to the issue.

## The Essence and Meaning of Equality of Opportunity

Generally speaking, equality of opportunity is absolute. This means that every person has the same opportunity as any other person. From this definition it is also implied that the exercise of equality of opportunity by a person cannot infringe upon equality of opportunity of another.

More precisely, equality of opportunity is of two kinds: vertical and horizontal. Vertical equality of opportunity is universal. It means that the same equality of opportunity is enjoyed by everyone in the society. It mainly applies to those aspects of life essential for personal development and well being such as education and health care. It also applies to relations between individuals, institutions, and institutions with individuals such as speech, press, assembly, travel, access to information, justice, property rights, etc.

In the area of production of goods and services, public as well as private, equality of opportunity is based on the level of education and years of experience. This means that every person has the same opportunity as any other person with comparable education and experience. The reason for these prerequisites is the requirement and absolute necessity for competence which is essential for effective, efficient and creative production of goods and services.

In this respect, equality of opportunity exists horizontally within the hierarchical structure of the work place as well as nationwide among the working class. If it is understood that in a democratic society every able person works between the age of 15 and that of retirement, the full expansion of this horizontal equality of opportunity is visualized as follows. At the societal level, up to the age of 15, equality of opportunity is applied in its universal sense particularly in the area of education.

At the age of 15 each person enters the work force. From here on one's progress depends on one's advancement of knowledge and experience. So, at the age of 15 everyone starts work more or less from the same level, the lowest level of employment, and moves upward. From here on the application of equality of opportunity is horizontal. This means that all those having a comparable level of education and experience are entitled to the same level of employment as determined by the national position classification lists and receive the same pay and capital shares. As individuals educate themselves while working, their level of opportunity goes up, but not all at the same level or with the same speed. This depends on the programs of education that individuals choose for themselves, both at the technical-professional as well as the liberal arts levels. Consequently, each individual's advancement differs from another based on the individual's choice of courses offered through these two programs of compulsory education. It must be understood that while education is a continuous requirement for maintenance and improvement of competence, the selection of subject matters, area of specialization, and liberal art subjects are elective based on each individual's interest and desire. Though liberal arts education is very valuable in the decision-making process, and an important supplement to technical-professional knowledge toward becoming more efficient and creative, it is also a prerequisite for the realization, maintenance and betterment of a democratic system. Therefore, it is an indispensable part of each individual's education. Consequently, based on individual choices, certain individuals increase their level of horizontal opportunity much faster than some others and progress upward with a more rapid pace.

The pay system is based on technical and cultural education and experience. Every worker increases his years of experience as he continues to work. From this viewpoint, all those who work accumulate the same years of experience by the time of retirement. This leaves the pay increases primarily dependent on the other two factors, namely technical and cultural education.

A person choosing a highly technical area as his line of work will need a good deal of related education to keep him up-to-date as the years go by. He must sustain his high level of competence. Such a person will be obliged to devote one-half of his required continued education program to technical subjects.

Another person may not have interest in highly technical or professional work, but desires to become an artist or a poet. He may choose to work as a garbage disposal man which does not require much technical knowledge or upkeeping. He then may spend a major part of his required continued education in general and cultural areas and thus, enhance his knowledge in the non-technical areas he desires. As he increases his years of experience and pursues his required educational program, he climbs in the pay scale. However, since his job is not technical or professional, during the early stages of his career, his pay increases may not be as high as those in technical or professional areas. Therefore, a small gap develops between the two levels of work. Figure 7-1 illustrates the situation. Every person starts with the same level of pay when he enters the market as a part-time worker. The pay schedule and increments stay the same until the person assumes a full-time position at the age of 22. From there on, those in highly technical areas receive a little more pay increase than the others during the early stages of work. As the years of experience accumulate and education continues, the annual increases level off and during the last stage of working years, the pay increases become greater for those who had remained behind. At the time of retirement there are only negligible differences in income, if any, between the different sectors of the work force.

The reason for this equalization process in the later stages of work is that the person in non-technical work accumulates the same number of years of experience as the others and has the same amount of education. The difference is that others have more technical and professional education, useful for effective and efficient production in the early years, and those in non-technical positions have more cultural education capable of enriching society as well as the work process more than the others. The same will be true in the case of a worker who wants to stay at a certain level of work, does not want to climb upward, yet he continues his required educational program.

This will be very much possible, even desirable, in a technological democratic society where cultural rewards of life are very high and often may override small material gains received by technical workers.

In Figure 7-1, curve A represents the pay scale for highly technical positions and curve B shows the scale far positions with the least technical knowledge required. The rest of the positions fall between these two extremes. On the monetary scale shown here, the average annual pay increase during the 30 years of full-time work is around 3.4 percent. The high-tech positions receive little more than this, let us say 4 percent, while the lowest level receives 3 percent. This may continue during the first few years where the acquiring of technical knowledge has a high productive return (let us say until the time a person receives his Ph.D.). After that the pay increases approach one another and during the last years of the working period, non-technical workers receive little more of a pay raise than the technical. This higher pay increase becomes justified on two grounds. First, non-technical workers have accomplished more in cultural education, acquiring a higher quality as thinkers; second, the technical workers have approached the prescribed maximum level of wages and cannot get more substantial raises.

At the height of pay differentiation, the difference will be about 10 percent or $3,000. At the end of a career, this will tend to be reduced to about 4 percent or $2,000. For the whole period of a 30 year career, the difference will amount to about $50,000 or about one year's salary. Yet, those who received lesser pay, had more resourceful and enjoyable years of life than those with high-tech or professional positions.

**Figure 7-1**

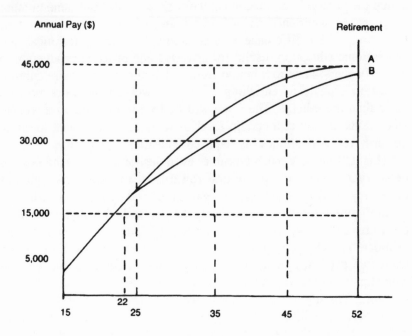

Another aspect of the pay system will be its accelerated increase during the first ten years and then leveling off and tending toward zero near the retirement time. The curve in Figure 7-1 presents the situation. The reason for this is two-fold. First, it is during the early years of professional and technical education that the production process will benefit the most from such knowledge. From there on the increase in knowledge will have diminishing returns. Second, it is during the early years of employment that the worker need more financial resources for establishing the family life and for providing initial necessities of life. To respond to both of these situations, it may be justified that, within the salary range of $15,000-$45,000, the employee's salary reaches near $30,000 by the end of the first ten years of work. By this manner, the salary increase during the first ten years will be the same as the salary increase during the remaining twenty years, each being equal to $15,000.

From one level to another, horizontal equality of opportunity moves upward in the hierarchical structure of production institutions until it reaches its highest level in each institution. This level of competence in one institution is comparable to the same class of competence in other institutions according to the requirements and responsibilities prescribed by the national position classification. Therefore, based on the national standards, not all top positions in every institution may be on the same level.

For a better comprehension of the application of the principle of equality of opportunity as an indispensable component of democratic organism, one must not forget that the equality of opportunity is absolute in both its vertical and horizontal aspects. It can never be disturbed. It is disturbed when one encroaches on another's equality of opportunity, when there are secret agreements, when effective information is withheld from free access, when there is transfer of property without comparable compensation, when profits are made, when required competence is disregarded in the employment or electoral process, etc. Therefore, the essential principle to govern absolutely the dealings of society with individuals and those of individuals with society is equality of opportunity. The sole purpose for which men are permitted, individually or collectively, in interfering with liberty of action of any other individual or individuals, is protection of equality of opportunity warranted to him or them by the community. No man alone can be the judge of equality of his opportunity when such judgement is in conflict and adversely affects the equality of opportunity of others related to that of his. It is also implied that equality of opportunity of no person can be taken away from him either by force or consent since this will lead to subjugation, servitude, or loss of opportunity affecting the present or future well-being of the individual.

Some of the important rights and liberties protected by equality of opportunity are as follows:

**A. Socio-economic:**

1. Right to employment, since those who have employment will have necessarily a better opportunity to employment than the person who is not employed, the latter acquires the right for the same employment opportunity.

Right to employment is one of the prime economic individual

rights in the society since unemployment adversely affects many other opportunities and liberties of the unemployed person particularly in the long run. Consequently, when the right to employment is in conflict with other individual rights or opportunities, it supersedes the others and thus receives priority.

The existence of democracy and its maintenance depends primarily on the economic operation of society toward the economic well-being of every individual on the basis of his knowledge, experience and capability, the latter being heavily based on the other two. Thus, the prime democratic component of a democratic system is economic. However, this should not be confused with materialism since the economic purpose of the democratic system is essentially distinct from that of a capitalistic system. It is not for the purpose of accumulation of wealth and the establishment of economic classes but, quite to the contrary, it is for the economic well-being of all members of society without economic class distinction. It is for this very purpose that employment is considered the prime right of the individual and the prime responsibility of the institutions, communities and society as a whole.

Accordingly, in cases where there are unemployed persons, in order to guarantee appropriate employment to them, the principle of shared-opportunities is used. This sharing is proportional to the level of unemployment and is shared equally by all those who are employed in positions corresponding to the qualifications of those seeking employment. This appears to be a complex process but under a computerized information system, the Technodem, it is quite practical. Since some 95 percent of positions sought are at the lowest entry level, the application of the principle is of no problem. In the case of the rest, similar positions can easily be searched areawide or nationwide, if necessary, and shared opportunities ascertained, new vacant positions determined for employment purpose.

Right to employment and its application by employing the concept of shared opportunities, has certain very fundamental effects in providing for a sound, stable, and healthy economy for the society. First, it eliminates unemployment which has been the source of many ill effects in a capitalistic society. Second, it provides for economic security of the individual and his family by guaranteeing employment until retirement. The positive psychological effect of this economic security on an individual's life and its effect on the stability of family should not be disregarded. Third, it eliminates the large welfare institutions established in a welfare state like the United States and other industrialized countries, thus releasing a vast amount of capital to be invested in productive purposes. Fourth, there are no individuals graduating from colleges or other higher educational institutions and then looking for appropriate employment. As explained elsewhere, based on the combined system of lifelong work and education, every person starts with general or less skilled work at the age of 15 and proceeds to move upward, while continuing his education in an area of his choice. He thus moves upward and later on horizontally, if he decides to change his line of work, leaving behind his previous position open for those following him. Continuity of education while working makes possible this orderly work system never experienced before. Individuals looking for employment will be primarily those terminating their general education at the age of 15 and entering the employment market.

2. Right to ownership of means of production and distribution. In a technodemocratic system, there is capital but not capitalist in the traditional meaning of the term. The nature of capital in a technodemocratic economy is sharply distinct from that of capital under a capitalistic economy. In the latter, capital formation is the result of accumulation of social surplus, namely profits through exploitation of labor and consumers. Capital, under, technodemocratic economy is the result of accumulation by each worker of savings from his wages. It is not through exploitation of labor. Also, since no profits are allowed in a technodemocratic economy, therefore capital accumulation cannot result from the exploitation of consumers.

The process of ownership is accomplished by two ways. First, the standard way, according to which every person who works in any societal institution, whether it relates to production of goods and services in private or public sectors, receives, as part of his monthly pay, a number of shares of production firms. If the firm has no capital and its purpose is not production of income but certain social or public services, the worker still receives as part of his income a certain number of shares which he is entitled to.

These shares are acquired by the employer institution from the stock market. Example institutions include government agencies, and educational institutions. Thus every worker, whether working for an income producing firm or not, from the time he receives his first pay check becomes part owner of the production and distribution means. As he continues work, his ownership of capital grows. By the time of retirement he has accumulated enough capital, providing him with sufficient income for his retirement life. As discussed elsewhere, these shares are not transferable, they constitute some kind of old-age insurance. However, they are interchangeable with other non-transferable shares in the stock market depending on the market value of the shares.

Accordingly, for the first time in modern society there is no separation between labor and capital, and one of the basic tenets of Marxism, struggle between capitalist and labor classes becomes nonexistent. Ownership becomes a right for the working class. For the first time, workers are in a position not only to produce whatever they desire to produce, but also manage the production as well as its marketing.

The second way of capital accumulation relates to purchase of stocks from the stock market by the money saved from wages. These shares of stock are transferable and can be bought and sold at will.

By relating capital and labor together, the industrial worker more likely for the first time, by finding himself the owner and worker at the same time, will sense a great incentive to produce. Under capitalistic production, he was nearly totally isolated from his production. The incentive was to survive, which was totally unrelated to the nature of his work.

In a technodemocratic economy, he suddenly and increasingly becomes the policy-maker, he or his representative sits on the board of directors and what he is producing he is a part owner. These factual situations tend to multiply his incentive to produce. Not only does he become an efficient worker but he also tends to become creative which is a very important factor in the effectiveness of production. All together, a highly dynamic process of production takes place, expanding from one firm to another and ultimately encompassing the whole society.

3. Right to education, since without an appropriate education

no society can progress. This is one essential individual right in democratic society. The process of education has been explained elsewhere. The National Education Council will provide for a model life-long program on liberal arts which will include minimum requirements in different areas of liberal arts and recommended electives. The program also will provide for several levels of certification with special titles such as BA, MA, Ph.D., PPh.D. (Post Doctoral). There will be no degrees such as B.S. since all educational programs will consist of at least 50 percent liberal arts education. Every normal individual will be able to receive his first advanced degree by the age of 22.[8]  He will be not only professionally well educated but more importantly, he will be a well rounded intellectual. In technodemocratic society every individual needs to have a profound understanding of humanity, human history, and nature, along with high technology. It might come as a surprise to many scholars in humanity but in a technodemocratic society, study of high technology and its effect on human and humane values will be an important part of studies in the humanities. We will be concerned, intensively, with areas such as technological humanity, technological moral values and philosophy, technological sociology and psychology expanding to technological literature and art.

4. Right to health care, since for progress not only is there need for an educated society but also for a healthy one. Furthermore, good health and education provide opportunities for a much enjoyable and pleasurable life.

Education and health care are two fundamental rights in a democratic system and, under the framework established through democratic organism, in order to provide equal opportunity of access to education and health care for each and every individual, they are made available free of charge and conveniently accessible to all.

5. Freedom of speech and press, which comprise freedom of conscience, thought, and feeling in its most comprehensive sense, freedom of opinion and expression of sentiment relating to any and every area of life and corresponding issues. These can only be materialized in full by the application of equality of opportunity. For example, in relation to freedom of speech or press, the application of the principle implies that there could not be any

246 / Technodemocratic Economic Theory

secrecy in speech or press when such speech or press affects any individual in any way. Thus, speech or press could not be classified or secret. It must be made public or freely accessible by the public. This is a very important aspect of freedom of speech or press in a democratic system. Benefits of access far exceed those of secrecy. The case is the same in international or foreign relations. There are no different standards for the same principle in democracy. In democracy people must have the opportunity to know exactly how their government policies are concerning all domestic as well as foreign issues and relations.

The only limitation is that freedom of speech and press cannot negatively affect the liberties and opportunities of others properly guarded by the principle of equality of opportunity. The Technodem is the backbone of freedom of speech and press.

6. Pursuit of happiness. Every person is free to pursue his own good in his own way, so long as his action does not deprive others of theirs or impede their efforts to realize it. The test here again is that an individual's action in pursuit of his life does not infringe upon the equality of opportunity of others.

Major factors in materializing happiness in a democratic society are good health, broad education, desirable employment, feeling of economic security, creativeness, accessibility of and desire for recreation, sportive as well as artistic. All theses are also prime concern and the technodemocratic system.

B. Political

The political system in a technodemocratic society is the least important, but yet necessary component, of the democratic organism. The following are its main requirements:

1. Popular sovereignty through free and frequent elections. Equality of opportunity requires freedom to elect and be elected, freedom from financial burdens, freedom of information public as well as private, freedom of expression and organization for electoral purposes.

2. Majority rule with equal consideration of minority rights. The principle requires that every member of a decision-making group be given exactly the same opportunity as any other in the decision-making process, including expression of views, participation in debate, access to information and all deliberations, voting, etc.

3. Limited governmental powers. First, in a democratic society the bulk of an individual's needs are taken care of through the institution where he works. The remainder is taken care of by the local government which is very close to the people. Regional government has certain law enforcement as well as supervisory power to see that national standards relating to equality of opportunity are properly carried out by the individual and institutions. Thus both the local and regional governments have a passive role and their general authority is extremely limited based on the application of the same principle to the extent that as the individuals move toward being accustomed to the principle of equality of opportunity and arrive to realize its importance for their pursuit of life, liberty, and property, the society automatically adheres to its application and need for a public institution to monitor its proper application tends to disappear. In the long run, the importance of government as an equilibriumizing factor will tend toward zero and society,will continue to function without need for governmental intervention. During the early stages of transition, the government's function will tend to be limited to establishing standards necessary to materialize equality of opportunity and provide for coordination and harmony among different regions of society. Thus, close to the mature stage of a democratic system, government tends to become invisible and nearly functionally speaking, will disappear from the scene of an individual's daily life.

Secondly, governmental powers are extremely limited regarding individual rights and liberties. These rights and liberties are materialized by the application of the principle of equality of opportunity, preservation of which is the prime task of government under a democratic system. Under this principle these rights are nearly absolute, and the government is made responsible for the realization of the equality of opportunity which determines the extension of freedom of individuals, institutions, including that of the government itself.

## NOTES

1. For example, see Zbigniew Brzezinski's concept of "Technetronic Society" and his application of the concept of equality of opportunity, in his article in *The New Republic*, December 1967.

2. See for example, John McDermott, "Technology: The Opiate of the Intellectuals," in Albert H. Teich, ed. *Technology and Man's Future*, 3rd ed. (New York: St. Martin's Press, 1981). For a more detailed account, see Theodore J. Gordon and Robert H. Ament, *Institute for the Future, Report R-6* (Middletown, Conn.: IFF, September, 1969).

3. The term communism in this essay, unless otherwise distinguished, refers to the existing socialistic systems with communism as the objective.

4. Odin W. Anderson, "Wisconsin: 2000 A.D.," *On Wisconsin*, University of Wisconsin-Madison, April 1987, Vol. 9:1, p 4.

5. Ibid.

6. Ibid.

7. See Reza Rezazadeh, *Technological Democracy*, op. cit.

8. By age 22 each person will accumulate at least 144 credit hours, entitling him for a B.A. degree. When he accumulates 72 more credits, he will be entitled to an M.A. degree. This will take about six years. A Ph.D. is received when 84 additional credits are acquired beyond an M.A. This will take about seven years to achieve including a creative work or writing in technology or liberal arts. PPh.D. is a post-doctoral degree which will be granted after an additional 72 credit hours of study and a creative work in any area of knowledge is completed (in about six years). The credit hours gained after each degree will be indicated after the degree symbol. For example, PPh.D. 48 means that the person had 48 credit hours of education beyond his terminal degree. The same presentation applies to other degrees. If a person has 54 credits achieved beyond his B.A. degree, his educational designation will be BA54. An MA100 means that a person has completed course requirements far beyond a Ph.D. but has not yet been able to receive his degree, because he has not completed the additional required creative performance and writing.

# PART III.

# THE OPERATION OF THE TECHNODEMOCRATIC ECONOMY

CHAPTER 8.

# TECHNOLOGY AND TECHNODEMOCRATIC ECONOMY

**Information-Communication Technology: Economic and Social Benefits**

There are a variety of socio-economic benefits to be gained as a result of advances in electronic information and communication technology. Among these are the coordination of socio-economic activities, reorganization of the industrial operation, unification of service systems and substantial progress in infrastructure. However, the most profound and significant benefits relate to socio-cultural aspects.

Commercial firms are already experimenting with computers to help them sell everything from paint and hair coloring to shoes and eyeglasses. Mass retailers, facing their toughest competitive environment in years, are discovering a new and incredible sales instrument, the computer. Major chains have already hired full time experts to search for ways to sell with computers. In the process, these mass retailers have added another term to the computer vocabulary, namely *transactional terminals*. It refers to computer screens that help close a business transaction as opposed to those that simply provided information. An explosion of computerized merchandising in retail stores will occur as soon as the price of new technology becomes affordable. It is the way of the future and by one estimate there will be 50,000 transactional terminals working in the marketplace by 1990.[1]

Given current population trends, retail sales are expected to grow at an excruciatingly slow pace in the next several years. According to Marketing Science Institute's study, the average retail sales growth through 1990 will be only 2.3 percent per year.[2] Furthermore, the marketplace has been flooded with new players, including "off price" merchants and specialty stores selling clothing and toys, as well as electronic products. One management consulting firm calculates that there is 50 percent more retail selling space in the United States than is actually needed.[3] That means that to survive, merchants will have to steal customers from their competitors. Computers may come in handy. For example, one cosmetics firm has taken its electronic make-up system to large stores in several major cities. The high-tech machinery has drawn far more new customers into the stores than typical promotions. The new electronic system overcomes the reluctance of many women to have their faces made over in the store. The work is electronically done on an image of the customer's face projected on the computer screen. On a split screen, the customer can compare four different suggested make-up treatments at one time. The system presently costs about $40,000 each.[4]

Another example, is a computer Magic Mirror that produces a full body image of a person standing in front of it. First, the reflection of the customer's face appears on the mirror. From the neck down the computer takes over, shaping a figure that conforms to that of the customer's and on which it projects any number of outfits the customer desires to see.[5] The customer can try on as many as ten different outfits in a time limit of one minute. Presently, after seeing several images, the customer narrows down her choices to one or two which she then tries on in a conventional manner. In the future, after consumers have developed confidence on computer projections, they may not deem necessary to actually try the outfit. This is the time that the computer order sales will flourish. Consumers can examine the outfits on the images projected in the screens of their home terminal, make selections, order and pay for the merchandise without the necessity of leaving their family room. But, such developments, though very possible, are years away. One recent experiment with this system showed an increase in sales of 700 percent.[6]

There are many other ways that computers have entered the marketing process. A computer can show a customer a graphic of every new model car put out by a company and let the customer compare any model he is considering with similar cars by other automakers and help the customer decide whether it is better to finance the purchase or pay cash. A paint company can use a computer that measures the light frequencies of a color sample and concocts a formula that allows a dealer to mix paint to match it exactly. For a selection of eyeglasses from among several thousand styles, a computer, after receiving a customer's facial characteristics and favorable colors, is able to narrow down the customer's choice to a relative few that the customer should try on. The use of computers in retail marketing expands to many areas of retail business. Presently, the cost is the main element preventing the widespread of its most advanced systems in trade. As the costs are reduced, more and more firms will adopt the use of newly developed systems to enhance the sales volume.

In France, citizens now bank, shop, read their morning papers and maintain anonymous friendships through Teletel. This is a national videotext system that has been transforming French business and culture since its introduction in 1981. Videotex is the process of sending and receiving texts and graphics primarily over telephone lines between a central computer and a terminal or personal computer. Videotext is not unique to France, but Teletel, a project created and operated by the French Postes Telephones Telecommunications (PTT), the state-owned monopoly that controls the nation's postal and telephone services, is the world's first successful mass-consumer videotext system.[7]

In a mere five years, desire for the videotext has swept France. Currently, there are over two million in use in households and businesses throughout the country. Each unit is known as Minitel and consists of a keyboard, screen and modem, an instrument that translates telephone signals into computer-readable graphics. The PTT owns the terminals and issues them free of charge to selected customers and for an 85-franc (about $12) monthly charge to business customers. For the French government and industry, the sophisticated Minitel network is a profitable enterprise with virtually unlimited growth potential.

Not surprisingly, commercial firms elsewhere are scrambling to follow the French lead in videotext. Several early forays into commercial videotext in the United States have failed. However, major American communication firms are continuing investment on videotext and redesigning the systems.

The greatest success of Minitel has, so far, been among some owners which have been drawn to the system by its most unusual feature, *le Kiosque*, which is the old name used for the corner newsstands usually located at the intersections.

In Paris, the modern Kiosque provides for more than 200 separate services which enable consumers to read updated news synopses, browse through paper and magazine headlines, and communicate with other customers, all without leaving their home. Users only pay for the time they spend on le Kiosque. The charge goes to their monthly telephone bill. The service providers keep about 60 percent of the revenue and the remainder goes to PTT. Services provided through le Kiosque account for more than half of the country's Minitel use.

Many of the services provided through the Kiosque are owned and operated by French newspapers and magazines. Initially, many newspapers voiced concern that Minitel would cut into their readership. However, it has worked as a publicity device, widening the recognition of the newspapers and increasing circulation. With its 24-hour operation le Kiosque has also proved to be complementary to the newspapers' conventional print operation. This occurs especially when important news misses the print deadline. It can readily be made accessible through le Kiosque.

The success of the Minitel has moved the French newspapers to not being content with offerings, ads, games, and news headlines, but going after developing new methods of employing videotext. For example, a discussion program on current issues, led by a well known expert or celebrity, where hundreds of individuals could participate simultaneously from their home.[8]

Satellites have become a mainstay of the information revolution which was triggered when the computer and telecommunication technologies gradually merged into one. They have become vital for long distance data transmission and broadcasting over large areas.

Presently, the U.S. Space Shuttle is the major means of launching satellites into space. However, the European Space Agency (ESA) has entered the competition. It has produced the Ariane rocket, which has opened up encouragement of commercial prospects for the European Ariane launches, produced and marketed by Arianespace and owned by shareholders from eleven ESA member countries. Arianespace began its commercial career in 1984 by putting an American satellite, the Spacenet-1, into orbit. It has booked a total of 24 launchings of some 30 satellites to be accomplished by the end of 1998. Over half of Arianespace's customers are non-Europeans, including many American groups.

French firms have dug in among the ranks of the world leaders in new communication technology. They have made their mark in areas such as digital public telephone exchanges, fiber-optic systems that transmit data by laser pulsars through a glass-core cable, and smart cards, now poised to revolutionize the retail banking industry. In a more artistic vein, INA[9] and its industrial partners are developing exciting new uses of computer-generated images (CGI) for television advertising and movie industries.[10]

France has also emerged as Western Europe's leading space power and the pilot of a joint European venture that has produced the Ariane satellite launches, the only significant commercial challenge to the U.S. Space Shuttle program. By 1995, the French, and their European partners hope to send their own space aircraft (code-named Hermes) on its first manned flight around the earth. It is designed to carry up to six astronauts with a 4.5 ton payload. It would be smaller than the U.S. shuttle because heavier payloads would be launched separately by the Ariane-5. France is driving for the third position in space, behind the United States and the Soviet Union.

France has already launched the first of four SPOT remote sensing satellites into a polar orbit from the Kourou space center in French Guyana. The SPOT is capable of providing more precise data for cartography and surveys of natural resources, environmental and land use than the U.S. Landsat, its only rival.[11]

A joint French-German direct broadcasting satellite (DBS) project is meanwhile setting the stage for an audiovisual revolution in France, which now has only six national TV channels. TDF, the French public broadcasting authority, has its first DBS satellite operational. It has doubled the supply available to 18 million French households with a total of 22 million TV sets. With agreement on new technical standards, this and its German counterpart should reach 200 to 300 million Europeans, offering programs with sound tracks in the language of their choice.

Television without frontiers is heralding significant change in geographically fragmented Europe, and the information revolution is breaking up old notions about distance and space. For example, Frenchmen are suddenly warming to armchair banking and shopping through the Minitel and smart cards. According to an official report, two-thirds of the French people are now enthusiastic about, or interested in, computers. The percentage far exceeds that of the United States. Experts link trend with a crash program initiated in the 1970's to modernize the French telephone network. This program has led to rapid expansion in the field of high-speed data transmission, including interactive videotext. The inexpensive Minitel has made this a mass consumption product. As a result, the videotext has expanded far more than in the United States or Japan.

French banks and the Post Offices have agreed on standards for credit cards. The Bull computer group's smart card, tested extensively in several small French, Norwegian, and American cities, has been a success. Home banking, now in an experimental phase, will soon be a reality in France. Using a secret identity code entered on the chip, bearers may make payments from their personal bank accounts through the Minitel, pay for their grocery purchases and make phone calls from public booths.

Experts in Europe and the United States believe that the French - invented smart card will have a bigger impact than the personal computer. The card is being tested by some American credit card groups.

However, there already is stiff competition between American, Japanese and European firms regarding all segments of the telecommunication market. French companies are also pushing the advancement of the art of computer-generated images (CGI). They are trying to develop high-quality, but cheaper, three-dimensional (3D) CGI for the television, advertising, and movie industries.

Interactive videotext, as a fantastic educational device, is attracting more attention. Efforts are being made to establish the world's first computerized data bank for radio and television broadcasting. This audiovisual medium now covers between 350,000 and 400,000 hours of French language programs, and sales of digital copies to several American TV networks is now a possibility.[12]

### Prospects and Possibilities During the Next Decade

The integration of digital technology has caused the unification of transmission and contents of information systems. On a nationwide electronic information network, digital integration will make available a wide range of activities to be coordinated irrespective of distance and complexity of required services. The use of online computers will vastly extend from their present uses in business and industry to other areas such as education, entertainment and most important of all to the services related to daily family life and general services. Socio-economic activities will closely be tied to and associated with the electronic information-communication systems.

Reorganization of the industrial operation based on digital electronic systems appears to be vital in a competitive market system. Even in a monopoly system, adherence to this technology will be a requirement. Automated production will go far beyond the present stage, which is primarily concerned with the mechanical production process, to include management and supervision, and individual services to the workers while at the workplace. An electronic workers grievance resolution process will be possible in which the workers grievances will be received by the grievance computer terminal, studied, analyzed by detailed and exact consideration of working conditions and responded back to the workers. The working conditions will be automatically corrected according to the findings of the grievance resolution system.

Of course, to improve productivity, a shift to advanced electronic technology will be required in order to minimize the resources and energy inputs and maximize added values. But technology will not be solely concerned with this aspect of production. It will also turn to the workers well-being at the work place. High technology will make it possible for reducing the full load of workers far below forty hours per week. This will allow the workers extra hours of leisure time while at the workplace, with creation of entertainment centers, which will nourish the workers mentally and physically and give them ample time for leisurely social acquaintances with one another at the workplace.

Unification of services as a byproduct of digital technologies enables identical processing of data and facilitates communications in various formats. Distinction between services that were once considered separate and different are disappearing; information and communication systems are being molded into one.

Regarding the effect of electronic information-communication technology on cultural development, one only needs to look at the revolution brought about in the entertainment area by the development of audio and video tapes. Historically speaking, each new development in information technology has caused the enhancement of culture in the affected society. The introduction of paper and the invention and development of printing methods was an era of revolution in information technology. The combined information-communication revolution underway, as a result of electronic technology, is incredibly powerful. Its consequences on cultural development appears to be beyond imagination.

Changes in industrial operation through technological development invariably results in certain workers becoming incompetent within the new system and thrown out of work. The question arises as to how to transfer workers from the old systems into the new ones. What comes to mind first is reeducation. Presently, this is a difficult and costly process. The reeducation process also is not appealing to many workers who otherwise would have liked to be reeducated. Computerized training is more likely to facilitate this training process. However, it requires training of the workers to use computers as training media. Such a reeducation process also needs upgrading available databases and creating new ones. Presently, information produced each day is far beyond the capability of society to digest it. But the problem is not that too much information is being produced; the sheer volume of production makes it quite difficult to locate the desired information under the present dispersed system. There is need for a centralized and easily accessible information-communication system, where each individual upon registration of the type of information he needs, can obtain precisely what is desired. Databases should be developed and upgraded with this concept in mind. The method should provide an easy access to desired information. There should be developed a unified and simplified process of search and screening of data not beyond the understanding and convenient use of common people.

Regarding the fusion of service systems, without appropriate legislation and regulation, users will benefit little from information technology that integrates different types of services. Here, we are talking about the choice between monopoly and equal opportunity of access to information. The concept of free competition will not solve the problem since giant corporations all have market factors to suppress competition by small firms. In a technological capitalist market there is no such thing as free competition. The lions kill and eat their prey and jackals take care of the leftovers. It is the job of legislation and the state to prescribe the framework for democratization of information-communication systems and enforce it. The government should strive to protect the public nature of the information-communication systems.

## Democratization of Information System

Technology can be devastatingly evil if controlled by a small group and operated for its benefit. It can be a tool of exploitation and subjugation never envisioned before. Its enormous power over the daily life of individuals can be turned against them and create an incredibly monstrous authoritarian society. Since a technological power system can be encountered only by a better technological system, rivalry and race for domination between the elite controlled technological systems tends to drag the human race to the brinks of extinction. Each system tends to tighten its domination over people, transforming society into an inescapable modern slavery system controlled by the means of technology. This technological slavery is of the worse kind. In appearance the individual may feel free, but in reality, he is hooked to the system from many directions. He has no way out if he desires to live within the technological society.

This situation happens when the information as well as the production technologies are controlled by a small elite. Under the present situation in advanced countries, the United States in particular, where the substance of technology is controlled by a small elite, society tends toward such a technological authoritarian system. For example, in the United States, as it has been demonstrated before, a small monopoly capitalist group controls the information system, such as television, radio networks and most of the published information materials.[13] It also has monopoly over production technology through controlling the giant production and finance institutions.[14] As technology advances, through its use by the elite as a suppression instrument, individual freedoms are systematically suppressed. Consider, for example, the electoral process before the first television debate of the presidential candidates in 1960 and those of 1968 and thereafter. The media works for the elite and informs the public in a manner acceptable to the elite and in conformity with its interests. The media supports only the candidates of the two major parties since both of these parties serve the interests of the elite and the difference between their candidates is mostly cosmetic and for public consumption. Every president in recent decades has been the servant of the economic elite if not a member of the group himself.

The only way, the sole hope for democracy, lies in the control of technology by the people as a whole rather than by a small group. Technology must be democratically owned, controlled, and used.

Capitalism was an era of societal development encompassing and enhancing the process of industrialization. Though it was highly undemocratic, exploitive and discriminatory, through the accumulation of capital, it caused the rapid advancement of technology. But, as technology progressed, the evils of capitalism became more stringent by the use of more advanced technology to tighten exploitation and discrimination.

When society passed through the stage of industrialization and reached the era of post-industrialization, capitalism became monopolistic. In order for the capitalist group to hold the status quo it had to resort to its technological power to control the capitalistic oriented socio-economic and political set up. But, the advance of technology and its operation also required better and better educated masses. Presently, though the elite tries through control of the information and educational system to prevent, or at least retard, the enlightenment process, public consciousness takes root mainly through activities and teachings of a small intellectual anticapitalist-futurist group. Consequently, as the pressure of the monopoly capitalist elite to maintain power increases, the public consciousness about the situation develops further. It comes a moment In history when capitalism has to leave the stage and technodemocratic economy take its place.

In a capitalistic society this transformation, more likely, occurs through a social revolution by the employment of the theory of general strike.[15] Since the capitalist elite and its instruments of power, including the state, control the use of technology, no violent uprising has a chance to succeed. It can be easily suppressed by the state military and local police forces, all at the service of the capitalists. But when people as a whole, stop working, the economic system immediately disintegrates and along with it goes the political system. A point in favor of this general strike is that in a highly advanced society, the production and distribution processes are highly specialized and the whole operation of economy depends on the supply of energy and available distribution systems. If through a general strike, workers in the energy and transportation areas or a specific sector of production stop working, the collapse of the economy is a matter of days. The government will be placed under no condition to persist or continue operation. People can then ask for a constitutional convention to get rid of capitalism and establish a new technological democratic system based on the principle of equality of opportunity.

The first requirement for the new system would be the democratic control of the use of technology in information, production, and distribution areas. There cannot be a true democracy without first achieving this goal. Once this goal is achieved socio-economic and political democracy will follow. The most important factor in helping to achieve technological democracy is the democratic use of information technology in a systematic manner. We have labeled this coherent information system the *Technodem*. What is being presented here is not extraordinary and needs not to wait for a decade or so to be invented and developed. The technology necessary for the operation of this fantastic system of information and communication, this pillar of modern technological democracy, is already in existence. What is really new about the Technodem is the way the existing information technologies are put together and managed.

The Technodem actually is a more systemized and nationwide system of data collection, processing, and dissemination. It is new in that it has been placed on public domain. On the one hand, information is fed into the system by every individual, public and private institutions; and on the other, everyone and every institution has access to all the information stored in and analyzed by the system. The Technodem is the backbone of democratic technological society. It is the information system without which technological society cannot properly function. It is the symbol as well as the instrument of democracy, provider of opportunity for all, grantor of freedom, protector of individual values, dignity and power, destroyer of giant public and private institutions, and a staunch instrument of decentralization and transfer of authority to individuals and local private and public institutions.

The present state of technology, the way it is used, controlled and abused in advanced societies, is regrettable. In capitalistic societies it has been controlled and directed by the monopoly capitalist production institutions and their supporting state agencies. Thus, technology has been used primarily for profit and for its maximization, and then, for stabilization of society through manipulation of information. We have already demonstrated the negative and ever-increasing destructive effects of the use and control of technology for profit purpose by the production elite, and by the state for the protection and preservation of the elite interests.

The situation is not much better under the socialist system. Here technology is controlled by, and used according to the wishes of a small political elite, which controls the means and the processes of production and distribution. Though technology may not be used primarily for profit-making and its maximization, it is however, used to secure and maintain the power and status of the political elite. Consequently, the negative aspects of technology, though somehow diminished, are by no means eliminated.

Under some of the existing advanced systems, capitalistic as well as socialistic, the working people and the public as a whole have nothing much to say about the use of technology. Technology controls not only the production process but also the daily life of every individual, and the elite—corporate elite under capitalism and political elite under socialism—control the use of technology.

With this technology's dominance over our daily life, as long as it is controlled by a small elite, no substantial progress toward a democratic way of life can be made possible. This is the main difference between an advanced technological society and those less developed. Whoever controls the technology controls the societal system. This is the modern type and the most monstrous elite rule. Through the use of technology, there is nearly an absolute tyranny in the economic sphere which expands to the social structure and ultimately encompasses the political process.

Thus democracy in a technological society is possible only when technology is governed by the people as a whole rather than by a minority elite. This is why the democratic system of the future may be properly called *technological democracy*, and its economic system, *technodemocratic*.

For moving towards a technodemocratic society, the control of technology must gradually move out of the hands of the monopoly capitalist group into the hands of the working class. Unlike monopoly capitalism, where a very small group of capitalists control and benefit from technology, the major beneficiary under the new system is the public as a whole and the working class in particular.

Now let us see how this change of hands and decentralization takes place. Once workers start to receive shares of ownership of the means of production in a manner explained before, technology, which is probably the most important factor among the forces of production, starts to be owned by the workers. As the workers continue to increase and accumulate their ownership shares of the means of production, they continue to increase their voice in the use of technology. Once they take over the majority of the membership of the board of directors and other decision-making bodies of their firm, the control of technology within the firm falls into their hands.

As it was demonstrated before, once the workers take the control of their firm of employment, they tend to run it independent from the parent company. For example, in the case of Safeway Food Corporation, its 2400 supermarkets, its food processing plants, etc. will all tend to become independent once the decision-making body in each of these component institutions falls into the hands of the workers. Thus, gradually, the large production institutions become highly fragmented. Decentralization of the production institutions necessarily entails decentralization of technology used by these giant institutions. Before decentralization, all available technology was directly or indirectly under the command of the parent company, in this case, Safeway Food Corporation. After decentralization, each newly independent firm takes hold of its own technology. Thus, high decentralization of technology is the outcome of the application of the principle of equality of opportunity to the area of capital and capital ownership. For the benefit of society and control of the negative effects of technology, this transformation is a very significant achievement. It is an achievement resulting from the application of a democratic theory with an enormous effect upon the environment and society.

Under the new system, control of technology is purely and totally in the hands of the private sector. It takes two different directions: a centralized, yet dispersed, national information system and a highly decentralized and dispersed technology of production of goods and services.

### The Societal Information System: The Technodem

The present possibility of a national or international information and communication system labeled here as the Technodem is no more a fantasy, a dream, or utopia. It can be realized with the presently existing information and communication technology and refined in a matter of one or two decades.

The Technodem is a nationwide network of electronic communication and information which can provide any desired information any place in the country and can connect individuals and institutions anywhere within the national or international territory it covers. It operates like the present telephone network except that it also supplies the desired information in written displays in the computer terminal or in audio-video forms on the screen. Development of various technologies have made the availability of this high-tech information and communication system possible.

The first development is the progress in electronics which has been increasingly and astonishingly shortening physical distance. For example, a single communications satellite launched into a geostationary orbit is capable of headlining communication over an area as large as about one-third of the earth's surface. Optical-fiber cables offer fantastic advantages compared to electrical transmission, by having a much wider bandwidth with much less loss of signal strength.[16]

The second is that of remarkable progress in digital technology with a trend toward digital integration of all kinds of communication and information systems. Quite similar technologies can now be employed to handle every kind of information and communication. The integrated digital systems that are now being developed and used offer the same degree of support for all kinds of communication whether it is a speech, written text, or even gestures. It is a revolutionary concept with the potential of handling all the modes of communication that human beings use when conversing face to face.

The third is the massive potential and storage capacity of computers, microcomputers in particular. Many complex and complicated tasks can now be carried out by microcomputers. Larger, ultra high speed super computers can carry out hundreds of millions of matrix calculations per second. Presently, these are used in information centers and are also available on a time-sharing basis for a variety of extremely complex and powerful uses.

The fourth is the availability of rapidly developing electronic information sources retractable through computers. It provides the users easy and immediate access to the data resources. The combined development of computer networks and databases will make it, not very far from now, possible for anyone anywhere to retrieve, feed into the system, or exchange any type of information desired.

The fifth is the rapidly developing office automation as a result of the availability of microcomputers at progressively lower prices. An outstanding feature of this process is that materials produced in a word processor in one office will no longer have to be printed and copied for mailing to another office. The material can be transmitted electronically from one word processor to another through a teletex system. The new electronic methods of producing, editing, storing, and transmitting information will be a normal way of working and doing business. This will substantially reduce the time, and paper work required, for the same results obtained under existing conventional systems of communication. One of the rapidly developing relevant areas is electronic publishing through the use of word processors. Today, it is already possible to produce, edit, and print sheet music in the same way other texts are produced in a word processor.[17] The publishing industry is going through a thorough revolution in its production process.

Of course, last but not least, is the introduction of electronic devices at home, including microcomputers which have been discussed before. As illustrated in Figure 8-1 the Technodem is a two-way information service system which is fully computerized. It is the most beneficial contribution of technology to human society. Continually useful, new and modified information is fed to the terminals within each unit of production of goods and services all over society. These are then automatically transferred to the local centers. They are checked against existing information, filtered, modified and then made accessible to the regional centers and from there to the central computer system. The central unit which has access to information of a similar nature or category nationwide, checks and verifies it. If it finds the information is new it then records it.

No computer unit in each production institution, which is located at the bottom of the information service hierarchy, would report anything which is already available through the Technodem. Because, each production unit has access to all information available through the Technodem. Any new information fed into the unit terminal, which is connected to the Technodem through local centers, will reject the information if it is not new; at the same time it will signify where such already existing information is stored within the system. Thus, if the "new information" is already available through the Technodem, it will be known and such "new information", which is not actually new, will be discarded.

Besides its use in production of goods and services, through local centers, every household is connected to the Technodem by a terminal computer. So a vast amount of information stored in the Technodem is available to every individual in society. At the same time, all data about each member of the family and information regarding the family as a whole, is available to the Technodem through each family terminal. Each household pays a small fixed monthly fee for the use of the Technodem to a local center, similar to what is presently paid to the telephone company. Figure 8-2 illustrates the structure of the local system of the Technodem.

The Technodem is a two-way system of information: "upflow and downflow."

## Information Upflow

Each individual, family, and each institution of production of goods and services carries a data disc about one-fourth of a square inch in size, embodied in a plastic, rectangular computer I.D. card (CID) with a specific computer code. Each disc embodies detailed information about the individual, family or the institution. Within each household, this information is fed to the terminal by inserting the CID card into a slot provided for this purpose. The same applies to each institution. In this case, the CID card contains basic information about the institution. Each time a CID card is inserted into the computer terminal, it is also automatically updated. For example, if a person had left one job and employed in another place, since this information is totally available to the Technodem, through the corresponding employers, the individual's CID card is automatically modified and his new employment and its specifics are added to his personal data disc. It is the same if the individual changes his residence, achieves certain educational goals or receives a promotion. Part of the information which is public record will be accessible to everyone. But personal data that is private, remains confidential, unless one has access to the individual's CID card. Similar to the Social Security number of each individual, or business identification number of each institution, each disc card carries a computer code. Without this code, even though personal data of each individual is stored in the Technodem, it will remain confidential and will not be accessible. Thus, in order to receive confidential information about an individual or institution, one has to give to the computer the name of the individual or institution and the pertinent code.

As information fed to the individual and institutional computers move upward to local, district, regional and national levels, it is analyzed, tabulated, processed and stored. This allows the person access to phenomenal statistical data at the local, district, regional and national levels. The Technodem thus becomes a source of vast information never achieved before and, more importantly, always updated and immediately available to the inquirer upon request.

Therefore, the upflow of information is highly, and nearly totally, decentralized as well as dispersed. It starts from each independent individual or institution at the bottom of the societal strata and moves upward to the center of the Technodem at the national level. The input of information is continuous, reflecting every change and interaction in society, and through the immediate availability of information it also, in turn, continually affects changes and interactions. This makes society as a whole highly dynamic, a stage never achieved before.

**Figure 8-1. The National Information System: The Technodem**

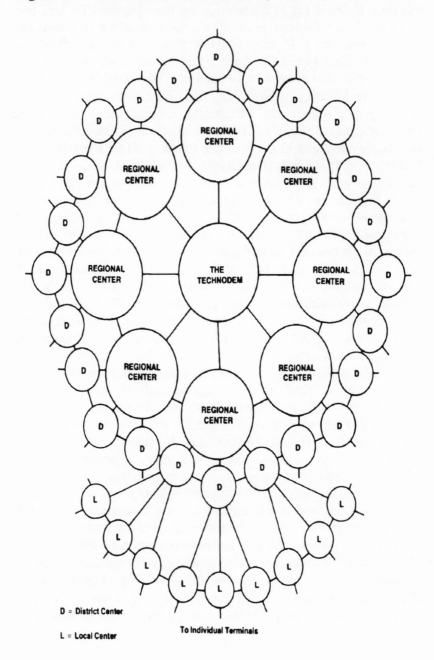

D = District Center

L = Local Center

To Individual Terminals

**Figure 8-2. Local Structure of the Technodem**

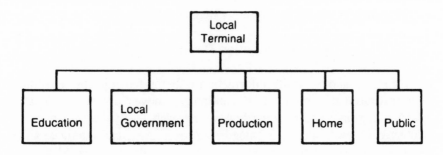

1 Central terminal in each educational institution connected to the terminals within the institution providing access to educational programs produced or available.

2 Central terminal connected to other terminals in different departments or offices providing information relating to local government functions, rules, and regulations, also providing for public participation in the decision-making process.

3 Central terminal in each production institution connected to terminals in different departments and offices within the institutions.

4 Personal terminals located in each home.

5 Terminals located in public places (similar to public telephone system) to be used by persons who need immediate access to a terminal.

Thus, in gathering information for public use, no single group or combination of groups or government agency has control or even influence over what is being gathered. This advanced technology of information system makes it highly democratic.

### Information Downflow

As stated above, while information is being fed into the personal and institutional computers, it continually moves upward to local, district, regional and national levels. At each level, the information collected on each subject is categorized, processed, and tabulated and ready to be used at that particular level. It is also transferred to the upper level, which is processed and tabulated at that level. Thus, at the national level, we have all kinds of national statistics and national information available through the central system.

For example, if we want to know the rate of exchange for a dollar in European countries, classification of a specific position and its salary ranges by the national office, number of children born during the past day, the text of a specific law just passed through the national legislative assembly, job availability on the market in a certain specific field or profession, and millions of other national level information, we can get it from the central system through our computer terminals at home or in the office.

Communication within this whole national system of information is very similar to the telephone system and the area codes we use for long distance calls, except that instead of an individual at the other end of the line, we deal with a much more knowledgeable machine, the Technodem. These communication code numbers are different from the CID card codes. The latter are confidential, while the former are available through a directory similar to that of the telephone, except that it is electronic and can be retrieved from the computer by dialing the name of the area, institution or the individual.

Therefore, each individual through his computer has access to all kinds of information available at any place in the country. By this computerized arrangement, no central office or group or governmental agency has neither control nor influence upon availability of any information to individuals or institutions. Everything is controlled and automatically processed by the system and made accessible to the inquirer by the computer.

Thus, despite the fact that the Technodem is a centralized information system, gathering of information and its dissemination is highly decentralized and dispersed. Here again, high technology makes this vital process in the daily life of individuals, institutions and society highly democratic, a stage of democracy never achieved or possible before. The Technodem is the foundation and backbone of *technodemocratic society*.

## NOTES

1. Pauly, David and Carolyn Friday, "Computers Take the Sale," *Newsweek*, Sept. 23, 1985, pp. 46-47.

2. Ibid., p. 47

3. Ibid., p. 46

4. The system is used by, and is available through, Elizabeth Arden, Inc.

5. The system is being used by L.S. Ayres and Co.

6. The experiment was carried out by L.S. Ayres by putting the entire Liz Clairborne spring collection on the system at three of its stores. The system was leased for $105,000. The Magic Mirror is a French invention and is distributed in the United States. Presently the high price of the system limits its use to very large firms.

7. Nadine Epstein, "Et Voila! Le Minitel," *France Magazine*, Nov. 4-5, Summer 1986, pp. 71 and 75.

8. Ibid., p. 75.

9. Organizations corresponding to abbreviations are as follows: ESA - European Space Agency; CNET - The National Telecommunications Research Center; France, INA - Institute National de la Communications; CNES - The National Center for Space Study (France); and DBS - Direct Broadcasting Satellites.

10. Marie Joannidis and Jan Kristiansen, "Telecommunications: Its Irreversible Impact," *France Magazine*, Nos. 4-5, Summer 1986, p. 69.

11. Ibid., p. 71.

12. Ibid., p. 72.

13. For more details, see Michael Parenti, *Democracy for the Few*, 4th ed., (New York: St. Martin's Press, 1983), pp. 182-83; Peter Brosnan, "Who Owns the Networks?", *Nation*, November 25, 1978, pp. 561, 577-79.

14. See Parenti, Chapters 2 and 3.

15. For more on the theory of general strike see George Sorel in Carl Cohen, *Communism, Fascism, and Democracy*, 2nd ed., (New York: Random House, 1972), pp. 297-302.

16. Hiroshi Inose, "Social Benefits of Information Technology," *Economic Eye*, March 1985, p. 407.

17. The system has been developed by a Stanford University group.

*Chapter 9*

# THE DEMOCRATIC USE OF
# THE TECHNODEM

It is practically impossible to enumerate the services available through the Technodem or try to describe its vital contribution to daily life, to individual, to economic and to societal development. The few examples described below illustrate the incredible magnitude of the capacity of the Technodem to serve socio-economic interactions and humanity. An interesting and unique aspect of this high technology is that the individual does not have to leave his home or office in order to get these services, whereas today he has to travel long distances to go to different localities to be able to get only a fraction of the service or information available through the Technodem.

## Education Services

Each household will have access to immense sources of educational information from pre-school all the way up to the highest educational level. For example, the outline of every course will be available to each individual through the home unit; a person may choose to start a course at the first grade level, eighth grade social studies, second course in physics, U.S. history, advanced algebra and thousands of other courses. While studying such a course, a student is able to ask questions from the Technodem and receive explanations. Of course, all educational materials are prepared by competent scholars and fed into the Technodem system. At a higher level of knowledge, different schools of thought in a field are available for comparison and analysis. This will particularly be true in the area of social sciences which is and will remain the most complex and increasingly important of all sciences. Furthermore, examinations for each course are carried out through the computer. They are corrected, graded and recorded in the individual's academic record stored in the computer of his local educational institution. Thus, each individual will have, in the possession of the computer, an accumulated record of his education and achievements coded to that individual and accessible to others only by permission from the individual through a temporary decoding process by the use of an individual's CID card.

This system will revolutionize the total educational process. First, it will make available to each individual, updated educational information at every level of knowledge or discipline, 24 hours a day. Thus, an individual may select his daily hours for learning according to his own choice. Second, the present classroom education and institutions will become obsolete and discarded. Laboratory work, for study or research purposes, will be carried out through the computer by using the latest available facilities. Experimental research work will still be carried through traditional research institutions, the results being continually fed into the computer and thus made available to the public and other scholars. Third, the system will be used by individuals as an enormous encyclopedia, covering every area of knowledge, updated at all times. Fourth, new educational institutions will be created, whose jobs will be to prepare courses on every subject area and at different levels within that subject area, and feed those to the computer, thus making the knowledge available to the public. Fifth, for the preschool and the first stage of general education up to the eighth grade physical institutions and instructors will be used. However, this type of education will be heavily supplemented by computer education, particularly in doing homework and seeking study aid. Sixth, the system will serve as an enormous library and provide the individual with all the services presently available through a modern library except that the services will be far more comprehensive, more extensive and easily accessible. This is a democratic educational system, providing equal opportunity for all, which never existed before and could be achievable only through the use of a high technology information system, such as the Technodem.

## Medical Services

A data bank regarding medical information, including preventive medicine, health and diet care will be provided and be continually updated by medical task forces, each consisting of experts in a specific area of medical knowledge, all will be made available to each individual through his home terminal. Each person may examine his own health condition by feeding into the computer symptoms of his illness or discomfort for the purpose of diagnosis. He then receives a response about his condition and possible alternatives, which he may continue to narrow down, by giving more facts and asking additional questions. For simple discomforts, allergies, etc., the individual may get prescriptions for drugs from the computer, and instruction about using them. The computer will also disclose the side effects of each drug. If the computer finds the situation serious, it will then suggest probable diagnosis and will advise seeing a physician. The computer will be equipped to respond to questions regarding the nutrient or other effects of fruits, vegetables, grains, etc. upon the body and health of the individual, particularly if the individual gives the computer his vital information such as age, height, weight, sex, blood pressure, etc. by inserting his or her CID card in the computer.

In brief, the Technodem will serve as an ever ready medical aid which keeps the individual conscious of his health condition and provides the individual with guidance in taking care of his health. The possibility of many illnesses will be discovered without reference to a medical expert and will induce the individual to see a doctor. The computer will also make an analysis of all drugs and outline their beneficial effects and negative side effects. The same will apply to all food stuff. The computer will also provide a list of physicians in the area, with their specialties. The individual will then receive a copy of the computer analysis from the printer of his computer and take it with him to the physician. The Technodem will be specifically useful for child care, the elderly and for those who shy away from seeing a doctor or are reluctant to disclose their physical ailments. It will also be an extremely valuable source of knowledge to physicians keeping them updated in every area of medical and pharmaceutical sciences.

### Legal Services

Most of the services presently rendered by attorneys will be available to each individual or institution through the Technodem. These will include information and commentaries about the laws, court decisions, and administrative rulings. The computer will provide a copy of any legal form needed by an individual such as a lease form, an affidavit, a financial loan, a corporate charter and thousands of other forms, with appropriate information about completing each form and procedures to be followed. It will also have a list of attorneys within the area, with their specialties. If the individual asks the computer about a certain illegal act, it will explain the law applied to the situation, including a previous legal history of such violation by others. It will also propose the steps to be taken to resolve the problem which may include seeing an attorney. The Technodem will also be extensively used by physicians, as well as lawyers, since it can supply all information available through a medical or law library and much more. Physicians will receive analysis and advice from the Technodem about the illness of their patients, drugs to be used and procedures to be followed to cure the illness. Lawyers, as well as judges, will receive all kinds of necessary information, even suggestions of decisions, from the Technodem about each specific case. This will be possible because the Technodem has the legal history for each offense, including past applications of pertinent laws, court interpretations, most recent rulings, etc.

## Product Services and Market Information

Under technodemocratic economy, the Technodem will be the prime tool of marketing as well as shopping and purchasing. One must pay special attention to understand the simplicity of highly complex processes of marketing and distribution effectuated through the Technodem.

## Marketing

Nearly all kinds of advertisement presently used will gradually be discarded, because through the increasing use of continually updated information available through the Technodem to the consumers, all advertisement will be outdated and obsolete.

As society moves toward technodemocratic economy and the Technodem develops, gradually production firms by necessity will desire to feed into the Technodem through their terminal the specifics of every item they produce. When a consumer asks for a product the computer will show the item on the home screen, and give specifications of the product and the price. Outside advertisement will be ineffective since people will refer to the Technodem in relation to their shopping.

Thus, the present system of commercial advertisement will lose its effect and become discarded. A substantial amount of capital, amounting to hundreds of billions of dollars, that is spent on advertising today will be saved, causing a significant reduction in product prices. This enormous amount of capital saved by abandoning advertisement will then be channeled toward production of goods and services. This will also eliminate the annoying commercials on billboards on the side of highways, in newspapers, radio and television. Because through the home computer, an individual for example, may investigate the kind of restaurants in the area, their specialty and their menu. He may then choose which one he desires to go to.

Each locality, based on size of the community, will have several public information centers each with several computer terminals where the newcomers and tourists can get information about hotels, restaurants, apartments and houses for rent, and many other needs.

## Shopping and Purchasing

This system of computerized shopping applies to retail as well as wholesale transactions.

For example, if a person wants to purchase a cassette player with special specifications, he will feed to the home terminal the name of the item and the specifications he has in mind. The computer will respond by listing different brands available on the market. Though specifications for each may not be exactly what the customer desires, he has to make a choice from among several presented to him. The individual may ask the computer that at his desired price range which one of those presented is the best buy and why.

He may then ask which stores in the area carry that item. The computer will list all local stores having the item available. The customer then calls the store and makes the purchase which is delivered.

In a technodemocratic society there also will be little use for money as we know it today. Most transactions will take place automatically through an advanced credit system which is transferred from the customer's computerized bank account to the seller's account. Each account holder will receive a monthly computerized statement which will show all transactions, deposits and transfers. In addition, through use of a CID each individual will have immediate access to his account, including recent deposits and payments, on the screen of his home terminal. He can then make any transfer of funds he desires which will be recorded in his monthly statement of account. For making payment for the purchased item, the consumer will give the computer the computer code of the store where he purchased the product plus his bank code and account number. The amount equal to the purchase price will then be transferred from his bank account to the store's account. In the advanced stage of technodemocratic economy, no monthly bank statements need be sent to individuals, since each individual will have access to his account statement through the computer.

## Entertainment

The Technodem will have in its library an immense collection of materials for entertainment, such as movies from its silent stages to the most recent productions; concerts, operas, ballets, documentaries of all kinds, whether historical or relating to the nature of things or outerspace; sports of any kind, with championship matches, etc. Each individual will find a variety of items according to his taste and for his enjoyment. These services constitute a substantial part of the national economy. As it will be demonstrated later, the Technodem plays a central role in providing for these services in production of which thousands of firms are involved.

## Job Market and Placement Service

Placement services available through the Technodem to every individual is unique and has never been possible to be rendered before. Every institution which has any open position, feeds it to the computer through terminals available to it.

An individual looking for a job or desiring to change his present occupation or place of work may ask the computer for open positions in his desired field and location. He immediately receives a list of such positions in the desired location. If there were none available in that specific area, then the computer will give openings closest to the desired area. Or the individual, if he has no preference of a specific locality, may check the openings on a regional basis. Each opening has a computer code number presented on the screen. The applicant, after selecting one or more of the open positions, gives the code number of the position to the computer plus inserts his personal computer data card (CID) in the computer.

Immediately, the terminal in the personnel department of the corresponding institution extracts and transcribes the applicant's personal data. The personnel department's computer then studies it, comparing the applicant's qualifications to those of other applicants. Then, using the applicant's CID, informs the applicant of the results and his ranking compared to all the others. The message is transcribed by the applicant's computer. An unusual benefit of this process is that the applicant finds out, immediately after his application for the job, about his position compared to the other applicants and thus the likelihood of getting the job. If his standing is not promising he may then apply for other sobs, without waiting for the final results from the one already applied. After the deadline for filing an application, the final decision is made by the institution and is communicated to the applicant in the same manner. The communication is transcribed by the applicant's computer. The institution may decide to interview the top two or three on the list. If the answer is negative, the applicant then applies to the place of his second choice and so on, until he is offered a job. If the applicant does not receive a response for his application within a reasonable time, using the code number of the position applied for, he communicates with the employer asking for an explanation.

Consider the tremendous amount of time, red tape and money saved compared to the present burdensome procedures which one has to follow while seeking employment.

## Production and Distribution Services

Presently, computers play a very vital role in the production process. Besides the electronic technology directly applied for the production of goods and services, the Technodem will play an essential role in the operational process. The operational results in every sector of a production firm will automatically be fed into the various terminals in different production departments. This data will become immediately available to all other production, sale, and distribution departments. This will enormously simplify the communication and decision-making process. It will save quite a bit of time, synchronize the operation, and enhance efficiency. Furthermore, the production firm, through the Technodem, will have up-to-date knowledge about the production processes and results in other institutions. This is of particular importance when the products from different firms are to be put together to produce the final product.

Each production firm also will have continuous access, through the Technodem, to information about the market situation—local, regional, national, and international—regarding its own various products and those that are similar. This information is vital in the production, planning and operational policy-making process.

## Library Services

Each terminal will have access to the Technodem's library. There is a vast variety of information stored in the Technodem, including areas of economics, production of goods and services, statistics, literature, history, science, technology, art, music, sports, etc. Imagine the information held today in the Library of Congress and expand it several times. Presently, such sources of knowledge are not available to everyone but to small groups of production experts, scholars, and researchers. Through the Technodem, everyone will have access to this information. As a result, the library systems existing now will become obsolete and gradually discarded. The new local and regional libraries will be electronic, and to that extent, a part of the Technodem.

The immensity of information available through the Technodem is beyond comprehension. If necessary, these can all be copied through an advanced VCR which is connected to the terminal set or can be transcribed through a word processor attached to it. However, there will be no need to copy any of the programs, since each will be accessible through the terminal anytime it is desired. Only materials to be used for research purposes, such as a bibliography, may need to be copied.

Of course, as it was described under education, the Technodem will make available to each person instruction on any subject matter at any level desired. This may be a beginner tennis instruction, high level physics, a course in biochemistry, or instructions regarding the maintenance and repairs of household items such as plumbing, electrical wiring, water softener, refrigerator, heating and cooling systems, etc.

## Communication System

There is no question that communication plays a significant role in the operation of business and production. The Technodem provides for a super communication system never available before. It substantially eliminates communication by the postal system as well as telephone. Though the individual is charged for each communication, the cost is much less than the postal or long distance telephone calls. The reason is that this is a nationwide centralized system capable of providing for a super advanced and instant interpersonal or interinstitutional communication, and furthermore, there is no profit to be gained. For example, if a person is sending a message and the receiving terminal is busy transcribing another message, this individual's message is stored in the memory of the receiving unit and transcribed when its turn arrives, a service that the present telephone answering devices are not able to render. A great advantage of this communication system to the postal services is that regardless of distance the message is received instantly, rather than in a day or more needed by airmail. Also consider the tremendous amount of manpower, buildings, materials, transportation and other resources that will be saved. All these can, then, be diverted to be used for more beneficial production of goods or services.

It must be noted that unlike postal communication, where the individual must know the exact address and zip code of the receiving party, or in telephone communication where the party must have access to a telephone directory, in the Technodem system the computer has the needed information for communication purposes. For example if A wants to communicate with B, he gives B's full name, and general place of residence to the computer. Immediately B's computer code number appears on the screen. By giving B's code to the computer, A is connected to B's terminal and can start communication. The individual may also store in the memory of his computer the names and the numbers of the individuals or institutions he usually contacts. This serves as a personal computer communication directory, similar to the personal telephone directory individuals use today. In these cases no search is required and the individual needs only to give the computer the area code and the code number of the person or firm he wants to get in contact with.

In the advanced communication system of the future, B will personally appear in A's screen and the communicating can be carried out orally. If B was communication with someone else, A can leave a transcribed message for B to contact him when he is available. This technology is not far off and will be available in a decade or so.

Thus, daily communication, personal as well as business, is a very important part of the Technodem services. Thinking of the enormous volume of such communication one may doubt in the capacity of the Technodem. To comprehend this, one needs to consider that in actual operation the Technodem is highly decentralized. For example, within a locality, e.g. Chicago, for local communication purposes people and institutions use only the local system. The rest of the Technodem is not involved. The same applies to regional communications, e.g. Midwest. In this case only the regional system is involved. The basic function of a regional system is simple. It connects the involved local systems together. For example, if a person or an institution in Chicago wants to communicate with a person or an institution in Detroit, the function of the regional system is to connect the Chicago system to the Detroit system. So the main functions of communication are carried out through the local systems. If the communication is inter-regional, then the Technodem makes the connection. Most individual communications are local such as contacts with the city government, schools, utility companies, shopping centers, local social, production, and service organizations, etc. Most of the production institutions' communication is also local. These are small service institutions and retail businesses. Most of the larger institutions' communication is regional. These comprise the bulk of daily communication and in none of these does the central system of the Technodem get involved.

Thus, when we say the Technodem is a centralized information system, we must make a distinction between the daily communication process, which is highly decentralized and the inter-regional communication when the Technodem gets involved and interconnects the regions in question. Thus, in this situation its only function is to connect the two regions together.

In fact, in operation, the system uses area codes and is quite similar to the telephone system presently used except that it is far more advanced and much cheaper.

In the areas of general information services of nationwide interest such as library, medical, legal, and educational services, the system is highly centralized. Yet, gathering of information for these services is highly decentralized and achieved through many expert task forces for accuracy and neutrality. This decentralized system also keeps information gathering out of the hands of the small elite, which may tend to manipulate the information. The system is highly centralized but not centrally controlled.

Thus, the central operation of the Technodem is purely a technical function and no employee is involved in dealing with substances of the information supplied by the system. This is simply because the important aspect of control relates to the preparing and feeding of information to the Technodem. In this regard, local or scientific information is prepared by the local individuals, firms, government or scientific task forces, each consisting of a carefully selected group of experts, by the academic or scientific institutions, on the related subject matter of information. Many vital statistics and data are gathered automatically as soon as information is fed to the system by an individual or an institution. These include areas such as population, elections, economics, production, housing, employment and thousands of other areas. Nearly all the data used is fed to the computer by individuals, institutions, or agencies at the local levels and then processed at the district, regional and national levels. This process makes an elite control or influence impossible.

Thus, the collection of data is highly decentralized, and after in each locality, the information is fed to the computer, it is the computer that tabulates them at the district, regional and national levels without any human function involved. And when the information is needed it is the computer, without human involvement, that provides it.

Furthermore, a substantial bulk of information is supplied by the production and distribution firms by feeding the operation data to their own computer terminals which becomes available to interested parties through the Technodem. This information must be verifiable by the company documents, files and accounts which presently in many companies are all computerized. Since the operation of the firms will also be electronic, this purpose will be achieved by connecting the firm's computers to the Technodem. This will be a necessary requirement in technodemocratic society as it will be discussed later. In this regard, hundreds of thousands of firms supply much vital information relating to production, finance, employment, positions, their classification and corresponding salary ranges, organizational structure and function, products, product description and prices, employment, ownership, work regulation and so on.

District computer centers tabulate and store all this information while making it available to regional and national centers. District computers also are able to give information requested by anyone regarding any or a collection of firms within the territory or a specific subject area. The same information will be accessible by terminals in other regions by going through the Technodem.

Thus, when we are talking about a highly centralized information system, we are not talking about a centralized control of information but a centralized system of electronically controlled information services. Even a great bulk of national information will be supplied to the Technodem not by one, but by a variety of the national institutions independently. For example, the Economic and Production Council will provide information relating to the frameworks established for position classification, pay system, capital distribution and return, natural resources and environmental use or preservation.

This information is regularly fed into the computer terminals of the Council and its subordinate agencies and through these they are automatically transferred to the Technodem. The information and data are continually kept updated.[1]

In the same manner, the National Health and Education Council provides information and data regarding the educational system, its structure and operation, curriculum, general rules and requirements. The same applies to health care and welfare rules, principles and framework of operation. The International Affairs Council and Foreign Affairs Department supply an immense volume of information regarding economic, socio-cultural and political aspects of other nations in addition to relations between the nations in each of these areas including the foreign relations of the United States. The Judicial Council supplies information regarding the national laws and regulations, final court decisions on matters of regional and national conflicts, criminal and civil punishments and information and data regarding prisons, prisoners, and prison work regulations. The National Legislative and Coordination Assembly provides information regarding the approval of reports submitted to it by all the above stated agencies, the legislative process, the latest status of bills under consideration and their passage or failure.

The same applies to all agencies of the national government including the Executive Council, Defense, Foreign Affairs, Finance and Judicial departments. Thus, collection of information at the national level is highly decentralized and dispersed, and out of the control or influence of a particular elite. Furthermore, there is no elite under technodemocratic economic system.

All this immense information is accessible to every individual through his home or local public terminals. The only thing he needs to do is to ask for his desired information through his computer terminal by using the specific code from the code directory or asking the computer for the desired code if he has no access to such code.

The role of the Technodem in political process is incredible. It is a fantastic achievement toward a true democratic process. A citizen's voice is heard and the vote is counted, regardless of where he is at the time of policy-making or election. No elite or pressure group can interfere or influence such an election or policy-making process.[2] Political parties, a kind of elite in themselves will become history.

Of course, this kind of true popular democracy is possible because of the availability to every citizen, the use of a high technology information system. This is what *technological democracy* is all about.

## The Technodem and the Pay System

In describing the services of technodem it is important to remember that not all the information is stored in the central brain but only those of general interest and of use to everyone regardless of the place of residence. Much information of local and regional interest will be stored only in local and regional information centers. However, since these are connected to the Technodem, they will be available to everyone within the whole system. Thus, if one wants to purchase a stereo set, and wants to know what is available on the national market, one will use the Technodem through his home terminal. After the choice is made, he will ask the local or regional information center in order to find the closest place that carries the chosen item. He will then, through his home terminal, get in touch with the closest store carrying the item and will order it. If one needs nursing service, he will need to use only the local information center. After the purchase is made he feeds his bank account code, the price of the item, and the company code to the computer. The cost of the item, including the delivery charge if any, will be transferred from his bank account to that of the company. The item will then be delivered. If no such service is available in that locality, the computer will indicate the closest locality which provides such services. The Technodem is supported by a monthly payment for each terminal set held by each household, business or other institution. This monthly payment will be similar to that of the telephone system we have now which is a very reasonable fee to pay for the free use of many available services and information. This will provide the Technodem with an annual revenue of tens of billions. Besides paying for its operational costs, a substantial part of the revenues will be allocated to research for further technological developments and innovations in order to advance and refine the structure and operation of the Technodem. The excess amount of the revenues will go to the Public Consumption Fund. These functions will be supervised by the Technodem Operation Council. The Technodem and its branches will also charge fees for businesses who want to feed into the Technodem their catalog of items for sale. There shall be a standard form for this e.g. description, prices, delivery cost, if any. The consumer is able to look at all similar commodities presented by different firms on the screen of his terminal set, compare qualities and prices, make a choice and order and pay through his set, the item will be delivered to his place of residence, or he may choose to go and see the merchandise and pick it up personally. All this will eliminate the need for printed, radio, and television advertising, printing and distribution of catalogs, etc. It will provide substantial savings for business firms. It will also save time for consumers, while allowing them access to all varieties of the item to be purchased in the market. Presently, a consumer does not have this chance. He either has access to a catalog of certain major companies or goes to the market searching different stores for the item he intends to purchase. The process will eliminate the creation of want in consumers, a characteristic of capitalism through advertisement. People will purchase whatever they need rather than being induced to buy things they don't need.

For entertainment the person will have access, through his set, to huge libraries of films, concerts, operas, comedy shows, plays, games, excursions, documentaries, etc. The payment for such access will appear on the corner of the screen. The viewer will allow, by giving his bank code and account number to the computer, the amount to be charged to his account. From the amount paid by the user, a certain pre-arranged percentage, e.g. 15 percent, will automatically go to the account of the Technodem and the rest will be transferred to the account of the owner of the program, show, or movie. This will provide first, for a prompt payment; second, eliminate billing, check writing, mailing services, etc. These and other services provided by the Technodem will cause the elimination of all television networks and stations for two reasons. First, the services and programs provided by the networks will be made available to the viewers through the Technodem; second, there will be no desire by the business to sponsor TV programs since consumers more likely will receive their information from the Technodem which will include not only the goods sold by one company, but by all companies selling similar products. However, the importance of television networks may remain in the area of the news and live programs. The question will be whether it will receive sponsors, and whether the network can sustain itself economically. Society may end up with either one or two public television networks to keep people in contact with the local, regional, and national news, and international affairs, despite the fast that all these can also be available through the Technodem. The advertising business will be extremely diminished in size. Their main job may be reduced to advise businesses as to how to present their items in the Technodem, or assist them in doing so. Because of all the media channels being available through the Technodem, all conventional antenna systems or cable TV industries will be eliminated. More likely, each community will have cable-antenna systems consisting of one large antenna system connected to all homes and businesses. A household may have more than one terminal or one terminal and several screens, the receiver having the capability to handle incoming of more than one program or information. Satellite systems will play a very significant role in this new network of communication, information, and entertainment.

For businesses, one central terminal in the industry or department may handle several office terminals. Society will also get rid of all advertising billboards, which now occupy all roadsides. Newspapers and magazines can feed the news and editorials to their computer to be picked up by the Technodem and through the local, regional, and national centers individuals can get hold of local, regional, and national news. Important local news of national interest is also sorted continually and instantly, and are incorporated in the national center for national consumption. This may tend to eliminate or sharply minimize the need for published newspapers or magazines causing substantial savings in human and natural resources, equipment, buildings and other facilities.

To have access to the news, the individual feeds to his computer the identity of the news center, e.g. Washington Post, by using a computer code which he can get from the code directory at home or through his terminal. Then immediately his computer is connected to the intended news center. He then asks for the kind of news he wants, e.g. Middle East situation, general national news, sports or specific news related to a specified date in the past. The requested materials appear on his TV screen. Or if he wants video news he may ask for, e.g. ABC news, using the same process and the proper computer code. More likely, the audio and video broadcasting networks will sharply change in their structure and functions to comply with the new high-tech information system of the Technodem.

Each time an individual connects his terminal to any of these centers, his own computer code is entered at the accounting sector of the destination, whether it is the Washington Post or ABC network, or any other entertainment firm. The individual is then charged for the use. As the individual uses the newspaper or video news center, the amount of charge appears at the corner of the screen and the viewer gives the computer his bank code and account number and the bill is automatically charged against his bank account. His monthly statement from the bank will show all the charges. If he does not desire to pay when using the service, at the end of each month he receives a computer printed bill that he pays in the same manner he paid the paperboy or his cable TV, or he may allow this to be charged to his bank account.

Furthermore, each time that he gets in contact with his desired news center, his balance of account with that center is shown on the corner of the screen. In the long run, as a result of acculturation, individuals will pay on the spot what they owe, allowing it to be charged to their bank account, and gradually monthly billings will be eliminated and the institutions will only bill those who are behind in their payments, e.g. beyond 30 days.

Financially, this will be beneficial to the news consumers because, presently, they pay for all materials in the newspaper. But through the Technodem, they pay only for the news they want and not for the whole cluster of news, in some of which they have no interest. Furthermore, the cost will be far less than the present because first, there will be no profits made; second, there will be no need for capital spending on the printing and processing equipment; third, there will be no physical distribution to individual customers and thus a very substantial cost of marketing and distribution will be eliminated; and finally, human resources previously used for these purposes can be averted to more beneficial and fruitful services.

## Music, Fine Arts, Sports and the Pay System

### Available through the Technodem

An immense amount of music, concerts, operas, and plays will be available through the Technodem and the user pays a very small amount for whatever he uses. Through the Technodem, part of this income is paid to the producers of the program used which is then divided among the producers of and participants in the program, as illustrated in explaining the salary and compensation. Those participating in the production of the programs, whether it is a rock concert, opera, play or baseball game, receive pay within the range specified by the national position classification system. The range of this pay, like in any other occupation area, is based on the level of education, skill, and experience. It never exceeds the level of the highest annual pay of, e.g. $45,000.

This is sharply in contrast with the present situation when an actor or actress may receive one or more million dollars for a movie, or a popular band may earn far over a million a year, or a top rank tennis player, baseball star, or football player amasses over a million dollars a year.

In technological democracy, none of these individuals will receive above the maximum wage prescribed by the national classification pay system. As we have seen in this equitable society, the highest pay is around three times more than the lowest pay. So, if the lowest full time pay is $15,000 per year, the highest pay will be $45,000.

This pay system embodies every position in society from garbage disposal men, actors, musicians, engineers, doctors, and lawyers, as well as famous sports personalities. That is why the cost of using the Technodem for recreational purposes will be far, far less than what people presently pay to see such programs, and in most cases they don't get the quality performances that they expect. The Technodem will offer such quality, with much wider variety and choices. The cost will be minimal. By the year 2000, over 75 percent of the national production will be in the service area.[3] Under the technodemocratic economic system most of this will be in entertainment areas.

## Live Programs

In the first place, live programs will be extremely popular since these will be the areas more and more people will choose as their profession, and since people will be well-educated in these cultural areas to enjoy them, their interest in such events will sharply increase. Secondly, people will have more leisure time since they will spend a good deal of time using the Technodem for the purpose of their daily needs, e.g. education, work, shopping, etc., they would like to get away from it and get out to see a live program or sport event.

Thirdly, when the present pay schedule is sharply reduced and more and more people seek to work in these recreational professions, the cost will be minimal. Instead of paying $10-25 for a concert or play as the case is now, one may need to spend only $1-4 to attend an opera or $1-2 to see a sports event. The rate of movie houses will be also sharply reduced to a fraction of the present rate since the participants in the production of a movie are compensated based on the amount of time they have spent in production corresponding to their salary schedule. For example, if a participating actress is famous and popular, her pay will be around the top bracket of the pay schedule, e.g. $45,000 per year. If she has spent six months in production of the program, she will receive only $22,500. The film company will receive what it has cost to produce the film. The company may do one of the two things, or both of them at the same time, in marketing its production.

The first choice for the film company is to market the product itself through renting it to the movie houses. Of course, in this case the company moves away from its artistic work and gets involves in advertising and marketing. If production is of high quality, it will bring money which may far exceed the total cost of production, marketing and distribution. In this case, through annual accounting reports, the excess amount is reported and paid to the Public Consumption Fund which is responsible for public services such as health care and education.

The second choice will be to make the film available by its computer terminal to the public through the Technodem. The cost will then be recovered by charging a fee to the users. Income beyond the cost will go to the Technodem. Finally, the company may choose to send the film to movie houses first and after a period of time to feed it into the Technodem. Or, it may decide to do both at the same time.

Considering the fact that through individual marketing and distribution the company occupies itself in a kind of function which has no extra income for it, the company may find it more convenient to sell the production to a distribution company and go about producing another program.

Naturally, as a result of sharply reduced costs of production, the rate of movie houses will be sharply reduces. The rate must be enough to pay for the cost of operation plus a small amount paid to rent the program. The rental rate of films will sharply be reduced in proportion to the reduction on the cost of production.

Consequently, for all these reasons, there will be a phenomenal surge in attending fine arts and sports events which will create employment for a large sector of the population. It will also demonstrate the high civilized quality of the nation and exert liveliness and dynamism into the nation's cultural life.

## Technological Equality of Opportunity

In a technodemocratic society, the most important means to bring about socio-economic and political equality of opportunity is technology and the manner it is used.

We have already discussed the status of technology in previous chapters. Here the purpose is a systematic but brief presentation of its role in the democratic system and its effects in materializing equality of opportunity in all other aspects of life.

The first step in this direction is to bring equality of opportunity into the sphere of technology. Figure 9-1 presents the effect of such achievement upon all aspects of life.

## Information Technology

From a democratic viewpoint, the most important aspect of technology relates to the information-communication area where the Technodem plays the predominant role. We have already discussed the democratic operation of the Technodem. In this regard, we know that feeding information into the system is through millions of sources and no single group or groups have influence in information gathering. We also know that the system is centralized yet highly dispersed to the extent that all individuals and private or public institutions have equal opportunity of access to all information stored in the system, with the only exception of personal data, which are not a matter of public record at least in the early stages of technodemocratic society.

## Economic

In the economic area, this includes all kinds of production data and designs often vital for production purposes. These are all relevant information fed into the Technodem by all production institutions in society. They relate to production of goods as well as services.

The next area is policy data and its analysis. Policies made by an institution or a variety of firms which have been successful can be studied and analyzed for the formation of new or better ones. There is no question about the importance of availability of such information to other production institutions.

Marketing is a vast and important part of the production economy and we have seen the vital role the Technodem plays, not only in presenting the products to consumers, but also in analyzing the qualities of products in relation to their prices.

Purchasing is another important area of economic activities which relates to marketing. We already know that the consumers can electronically seek many kinds of a product they want to purchase and go about investigating its quality, compare prices, make a final choice and purchase or order through the Technodem.

The banking operation will see a major change. Consumers will be able to pay through the Technodem from their bank accounts, for the purchase of goods, and have continuous access to their account statements and balance of their account. Monthly bank statements will be a matter of the past. The same transition will occur between financial institutions themselves, and between them and production institutions. The banking system can become nearly fully automatic through computerization and its connection to the Technodem.

Research and development, vital to production progress, will be substantially achieved through the Technodem. In no other place can the researchers have access to such an enormous volume of data, up-to-date information to relevant inventions, innovations or developments, and more importantly the analytical power and capability of the Technodem.

**Figure 9-1. Technology and Equality of Opportunity**

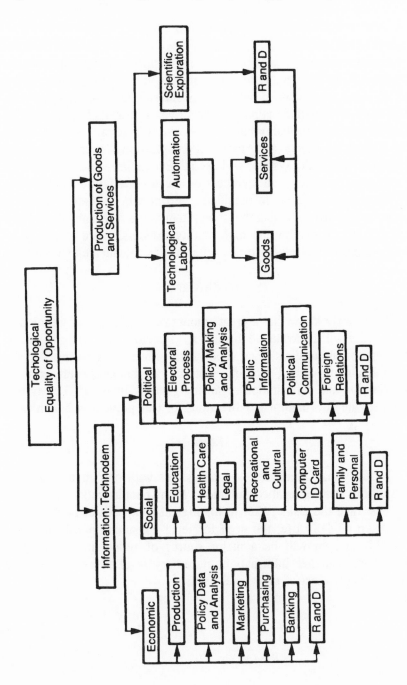

# Social

## Education

In the social area, possibly the most important contribution of the Technodem to the equality of opportunity is in the sphere of education, which has been discussed before. Considering the continuity of education, especially beyond the first 12 years of formal education, the Technodem will probably carry the heaviest burden. Nearly all the population in society and, more likely, millions in other countries having access to the system, will use it. Education, which is now very costly, will be free to all members of society and will either be free, or for a nominal cost, to outsiders. From this favorable economic situation and from the fact that the system is the reservoir of the best, up-to-date information and high quality teachers, there is no reason why people should resort to any other means to educate themselves.

## Health Care

We already know that a great amount of information in relation to health care will be available through the system. Among these will be information about diets, food, body care, effects of all aspects of the natural, chemical, and synthetic materials on human health, medical information and consultation regarding general illnesses. The system will provide information and directions for true preventive health care.

## Legal

Today, most interactions of individuals with one another or with institutions require legal consultation. Many people who cannot afford the cost take the risk. With technological complexities of the future operation of daily life, the need for legal consultation will increase. The Technodem will be a major source of relief since through it individuals can get information, necessary legal forms, as well as directions for most of their legal needs.

## Recreation and Cultural

Today among the industrialized countries, the United States in particular, a small minority is educated enough culturally to enjoy artistic presentations, performances or exhibitions. Even so, in many areas in the United States there are no such performances—operas, ballets, plays, classical concerts, etc.—available. Those few who are knowledgeable and desire to enjoy, have often no such opportunity. In large communities such as New York, there are some available but the opportunities are very limited; first, because of cost; second, because of space, since in large communities a much larger minority are educated enough to enjoy such cultural events; third, the quality of many performances is quite low, because of the lack of public education in this regard there is not much encouragement and support for development and refining of artistic skills.

Continuous cultural education in technodemocratic society will elevate the cultural events to the level of national consciousness. They will flourish and develop enormously. First, the Technodem will play a significant role in this area of education; second, it will make accessible to the people a wide variety of first class performances. The public cultural consciousness through the Technodem, will also enormously enhance the creation of opera houses, concert halls, play houses and art galleries all over society. On one hand, this will provide for the majority of the population an opportunity of access to live performances; on the other, this will be one of the major sectors of economic functions employing a large portion of the workers.

The area of sports and other recreational functions will see similar developments.

## Computer Identification Card

The nature and content of this card has been discussed before. It will be a vital companion to each individual. It will be needed in the electoral process for voting purposes as well as determining the candidates qualifications. It will be needed for employment and any purpose that requires an individual's identification. It will be needed in banking, purchasing, renting, and using of the Technodem for many social and economic needs.

## Family and Personal

This encompasses a broad area of information including all aspects of technological housekeeping, food preparation, gardening, planting, child care and a vast area of information that a member of the family may desire for his personal or family use.

# Political

We have already seen the enormous role of information technology in the political and electoral process. It also plays a very important role in the governmental decision-making process; particularly in establishing economic and social standards such as position classification, wage system, interest rate, educational standards and health care requirements. The same importance also applies to the use of the electronic-communication system in relation to international affairs and foreign policy process.

The government is also one of the important sources of information. All kinds of information coming from all the public agencies including decisions, standards, laws, regulations and judicial rulings, are immediately fed into the Technodem and become accessible to the public.

Another area is political communication, which includes involving the public in the governmental decision-making process or receiving public response to certain decisions made by the government, and finally, educating the public about governmental policies and programs and receiving inputs from the people.

The last but not the least area concerns relations with other nations. The role of the Technodem in providing for equality of opportunity in international relations has been discussed before. It extends to the expansion of the use of production technology abroad with educational assistance through the Technodem.

# Technology and Production

The second area of application of equality of opportunity relates to production technology. Unlike the technological information system which is highly centralized, technology relating to production of goods and services is highly decentralized. As we have explained before, giant corporations will break into its component parts, each becoming an independent entity by itself. This corporate decentralization process will be the main cause of decentralization of production technology. While in the information area each industry, large and small, is hooked to a highly centralized system of the Technodem, benefiting it and benefiting from it, its production technology is independent from other similar technologies.

Technology in the production area is of two kinds; human technology and machine technology. The labor in technological democratic society will be highly trained and advanced. It won't be inappropriate to call him a "technological person." This level of individual technological knowhow will be one of the three determinants of the level of opportunity of the individual and necessary for his high performance and understanding of technological society and life. No person can work and function properly in this kind of society without the required advanced technological knowledge.

A very important contribution of human technology relates to production processes and corresponding innovations. The process of production, whether it is crystallized and put into effect directly by human hands or computer programs, is initiated by the human mind. Regardless of how far modern computerized technology may develop, the human mind will have the upper hand in establishing the work process. Modern technology will widen and strengthen human minds' contribution to the production process but never totally replace it, except as prescribed and programmed by the human mind. With our lack of knowledge today, in relation to the human mind, we are only fractionally aware of the power and capability of it. With further tools of knowledge and control we will attain a greater awareness as to our mental capability. It will dramatically increase and we will have substantial use of our mental power, which has remained more or less idle for centuries. Equality of opportunity to educate ourselves about ourselves and our relations with our work and environment will elevate all citizens to the level of a technological person.

The other aspect of production technology relates to machines. Machines are instruments created by humans for production of goods and services. Of course, humans have been able to create machines that create machines. This is done through a process known as automation. Today, in most areas of production, automation helps human workers in the production process. In more advanced systems, automation has taken over most parts of production. It will be possible that in the future many production processes will be totally automated through appropriate and detailed systemwide programming. For example, as we look at the operation of the Technodem, except for the input of information, the rest of the operation which is immensely wide and complex and involves thousands of areas, is automatic. Yet the system's hardware, software, communication and energy devices are all produced by the production sector.

Future possibilities in the automation area are fantastic where it is imaginable. One promising area related to robotic technology. Yet, there are probably areas which are unimaginable today. All these developments will enhance the equality of opportunity of each individual in a technodemocratic society.

A very significant area of production technology relates to scientific research and development. This will be a fascinating area from understanding the secrets of creation and life to space science. For the first time in human history, man will start to look upon the universe as a single entity and will start to study, discover and understand the fine design of the universe and the exact role of every component in its operation and sustenance from atoms, bacteria, plants, humans to planets, galaxies, material universe and beyond, which in the language of many religions is known as God or the Creator. The great secret of the universe will be known when we discover the essence of the Living Universe upon which all the rest depends, from which all receive life, and into which all dissolve and transform.

Less fascinating, but by no means less important, of this scientific venture will relate to research and development relating to production of goods and services.

## NOTES

1. For the structure and function of government under a technodemocratic economy see Reza Rezazadeh, *Technological Democracy: A Humanistic Philosophy of the Future Society* (New York: Vantage Press, 1990).

2. Ibid.

3. "The Service 500," *Fortune*, June 8, 1987, p. 194.

*Chapter 10*

# THE SOCIETY UNDER THE TECHNODEMOCRATIC ECONOMIC SYSTEM

## Democracy and the Meaning of Life

Spiritual achievement, not materialistic successes, are signs of greatness of a society. One must never forget that other civilizations of far greater significance than the United States from the standpoint of spiritual achievements have appeared before, flowered forth in magnificent products of spiritual expression and have disappeared again, engulfed in the shadows of oblivion and covered by a few layers of sand or by the triumphant vegetation in the wilderness. Each advanced civilization has plunged gradually into the dark ages until the flourishing of another one.

A new dark age is still possible, and it will dawn upon our civilization soon enough unless we discover a meaning for life, a different purpose than the drive for materialism and satisfaction of senses, and finally, a new goal for human efforts which, presently, is so implacably frustrated by the emptiness, the vacinity, and the futility of the goal which is tried so desperately and still so vainly to reach.

It is the possibility of such a dark age which technodemocratic economy will try strenuously but successfully to stave off by teaching people anew the truth that is needed to visualize and to appreciate a deeper reality lying behind and beyond the immediate and closely bound world of the self, toward a desire to find peace, achieve salvation and restore dignity and purpose to life.

It may not be so obvious to common men, but this is an extremely critical time in history, and the fate of a whole civilization is at stake. Technodemocratic economy can take up the challenge and to the perplexing, age-old query, it can answer emphatically that besides materialism life has a meaning, that it has a purpose and a goal, and that it has worth, dignity, and beauty. Material means are needed to the extent to achieve the spiritual goals in life.

When individuals become aware that their individuality is truly and fully realized, then they become aware of the great significance and the deep importance of the democratic philosophy of life. Democracy prescribes in effect that the meaning of life is found only in the realization of a full spiritual life; that this realization in turn is achieved only when the individual's spiritual needs, aspirations and longings are rooted, integrated and nurtured within the organism of democracy. One should not confuse the meaning of spirituality as employed here with the spirituality related to different religions. The latter is external, artificially induced, based on certain dogmas. Spirituality as employed here refers as the individual's self, a deep committed inner feeling, independent of external factors. It is mainly the result of self consciousness through self education, through seeking the truth by studying self, others, the natural environment and the meaning of life.

Within the context of its organic being, technodemocracy is also a philosophy. It relates to a process of human life and institutions within the organic system of democracy. This is to say that democracy per se is not a philosophy or a theory but a living institution with its organic structure and norms. What happens to individuals and in- stitutions that live and operate under this democratic system, their personality traits, tendencies, aspirations, outlook in life, attained socio-economic cultures all together form the democratic philosophy of life.

Organism refers to the functional body of thing which is made up of parts that are quite distinct from one another, where removal of one part destroys or substantially alters the operation of the rest. It must be noted that democracy as an organism is timeless and absolute and thus its existence is not contingent upon the individual will or action. The system exists and the question is whether or not men discover it and subject themselves to its domain and to its benefits as a result.

Within the democratic organism, through the democratic philosophy of life, individuals rise to the capacity of a true spiritual being. They find something which expresses the fundamental continuity of their human experience without determinate limits of space, and the fundamental unity, despite individuality, which is at the very root of the democratic way of life. In democracy, they find an organism which offers limitless scope to the expression of their spiritual life, to the full play of their activity, the full extent of their freedom and equality of opportunity, and the full recognition of the same to their fellow beings. In democracy one's life flowers forth in an expression of great spiritual achievement with visualization and admiration of a deeper reality than the immediate materialistically oriented and closely bound world of self.

## Democracy and the Conduct of Life

The conduct of life under democracy rests upon three great, unalterable principles: authority, duty and productivity. The principle of authority refers not to any individual ruler or governmental institution but to the democratic organism of which the individual is the main part. It refers also to the authoritative states of democratic principles and their implementation within the society. The national supervisory councils establish the foundation and operation of society in strict accordance to these principles. The regional institutions supervise their implementation; individuals and production organizations become responsible for the full implementation of those principles. Thus governments have very little to do with direct implementation of democratic principles. Implementation remains mainly the individual's task along with the institution where he works. Any dispute regarding the principles are resolved by the appropriate high council and ultimately by a supreme judicial system.

Duty is the second principle affecting the conduct of life. Though democracy as a system cannot be destroyed, democratic philosophy of life can be infiltrated by non-democratic norms and actions, and can be abused. If such infiltration is allowed the very existence of democratic life will face danger. Those who attempt to destroy the democratic nature of life by disobeying or twisting democratic principles must be distinguished and singled out by the individuals and subjected to authoritative investigation. Punishments must be harsh relating to intentional abuse of basic principles. The principle of equality of opportunity does not allow death penalty in a democratic society, but there is a strenuous educational and rehabilitation process. The individual faces hard labor and education to undo the wrong done and to understand the importance and benefits of democratic principles and the consequences of abusing them. An individual committed to the democratic way of life will automatically respond to duty to protect the system from destructive interference. This duty is concerned with harmful action and by no means related to speech or press, which are free. It is the outcome of adherence to the principle of equality of opportunity.

The third principle of democratic life is productivity. The principle of equality of opportunity prescribes that each individual must be productive in life to the best of his ability. He must not make himself a burden upon the labor of others. He must contribute, though his activities and participation in the productive process, to the well-being of his society. The extent of a person's material benefits from democratic society depends on the scope and level of his participation in the production process. There is no place for laziness or inactiveness in a democratic society. Society helps only those who, for physical or mental deficiencies, are not able to produce and sustain themselves. A person who is productive below his individual capacity does not use his equality of opportunity to its full extent and thus remains behind compared to those with the same opportunity.

Equality of opportunity is the invisible tie that binds together the destinies of all people in a democratic society and is a ruling guide in the application of the above stated three principles relating to the conduct of life. It is the most important and most essential principle sustaining the democratic organism. It is one whose consequences are the most far-reaching in the life of a society. It is the foundation of durable and satisfying socio-economic life in which the good of the whole is dependent upon the material and spiritual welfare and intellectual well-being of the individual. Each individual, group, private and societal institution, and society as a whole operates and prospers by adherence to the indisputable norms of the organism of democracy whose entity is absolute and thus its characteristics are absolute and not subject to alteration. The democratic system is a living organism, independent from people who live under it. The degree of adherence to the organism determines the extent of approach to a full democratic way of life.

Never before had a socio-political system advanced such penetration to the inner world of man, and never before had men experienced a combination of knowledge and understanding leading not only to their individual happiness and joy in life, but also to those of the society as a whole. Life, as thus conceived by the democratic organism is free, serious, austere, spiritual, and pleasant; its development takes place in a world sustained by the just and responsible principles of the organism. He who subscribes to the ensuing rules of conduct, with their exacting claims upon individual will, lives a satisfactory sensual life. He is ready, willingly and pleasantly, to sacrifice a fraction of his own well-being in order to enhance the well-being of others toward the level of his own. He volunteers to share his opportunities with those less fortunate. Thus, though he learns and works primarily for his personal benefit, he thinks of himself as a part from the whole, namely his other fellow human beings, related institutions, and the environment. He holds the unity of his community to be a sacred means for realization of the true good of life, for his efforts, to be just and true, and for the supreme test of high qualities required by the system which has provided him with opportunities for knowledge, economic and spiritual comfort and wisdom.

The individual in a democratic society does not use his freedom and opportunity solely for the satisfaction of his instincts and desires but also for the well-being of his community and society as a whole, of which his is an indispensable part, though individually independent.

Under a technodemocratic economic system, the meaning of freedom expands beyond pursuing of one's own passion, ambitions, or desires. It extends to discovering and maintaining what is true, good and just at all times, in all cases. This is the realization of the true mission of man. Personal liberty allows the individual to follow the call of one's own nature and one's own faith; to think, act or speak according to the dictates of one's own mind; to earn, spend, or save. It causes men to strive for wealth, health, happiness, and pleasure; it also provides that all be enjoyed within the framework of the principle of equality of opportunity. No exercise of freedom is democratic if it hinders or encroaches on the equality of opportunity of others or is an impediment toward its realization. Here, the individual is the center of whole society but he must realize that every other individual is so too. The relationship, therefore, is prescribed by the principle of equality of opportunity. Without application of this principle, the individual would not know the framework of his societal life and how to use his freedom in a just manner. He will consider it unjust if it is used for the satisfaction of one's personal instincts and desires contrary to democratic norms and processes. Under democratic organism, the individual is brought back to the vision of his true place in society and the universe. He must sincerely, tirelessly, try to learn how to curb and master his self in realization of the democratic way of life.

A true and great spiritual life cannot take place unless democracy has risen to a position of pre-eminence in the society of men. Maximum liberty coincides with the maximum strength of democracy. A man's liberty is interrelated, interactive, and interrestrictivs in relation to the liberty of others. It finds its maximum realization in the fullest expression of democracy and fully established equality of opportunity.

The democratic organism is not a term denoting the authority underlying a complex system of relationships between individuals, classes, organizations, etc. It is an organism of far greater import and meaning; it is not a state, it is not a government, it is a societal entity, a well and justly structured societal system. It is there to bring mankind back to the true visions of the relative worth of the individual and of the system. It is an organism of which each individual is an integral and essential part.

Gone forever will be time when it was possible to find a way to the heart of man by appealing to the mystic side of his nature through a religious commandment; through his devotion to his unalienable natural right; or through so called utilitarian—political—democracy masking grave economic injustices. It will be time when it is possible to illuminate the reasoning powers of man's mind with the light of ideals whose existence and whose reason of being for his well-being can be proved through the powers of reason.

What is needed is a societal consciousness through learning, debating, and understanding the technodemocratic economic system, its organism as well as its operation, in order to progress slowly but surely toward the comprehension of its worth, its beauty and significance.

Though democracy is an organism, its power and operation is conditioned to the will of the people as one of its integral components. However, democratic organism is unique and unalterable in its structure  There are no different kinds of democracy, there is one and only one kind.   As such, democracy is above individuals, organizations, classes, interest groups, and ambitions. It is also above the state; the public sector is but a small component of the organism. There is no welfare of the state, but only that of the individual. The triumph of democracy means, in fact, that the role of the people is finally brought to its highest importance which it assumes when considered in its proper relation to the other components of the system. The normative components of the organism determine the role and manner the individuals have to assume for full realization of democratic norms. Thus, the power to operate rests wholly on the people. The organism provides only the method and process by which people govern themselves the best.  Structurally speaking, under this system people are governed the least. The government is minimum in its initial state. It continues to diminish further in size tending toward zero as the operation of society moves to a closer association with the organism and approaches the closest adherence to its fundamental principles.

When it is claimed that the democratic organism as well as its three major components—individual, technology, and equality of opportunity are permanent and absolute, it does not mean that their nature, value and characteristics cannot be discussed, argued, or criticized.  The very existence of the organism is based on freedom of information, striving for knowledge based on reason, seeking the true purpose and meaning of life, and the extent of the manner of human participation in its conduct.

## The Essence of Technodemocratic Economy

In a capitalistic system the betterment of life is understood to be on increased production and increased profits. In the case of the working class, advancement toward happiness is thought to be based on increased income and capability of purchasing more goods. Simply, under capitalism, progress is based on the upward movement of material gains heavily based on production and sale.

The outcome is that those able to subjugate technology and workers accumulate immense wealth and those who do not have access to production means produce for those who have, for a meager return relative to the value of their work. The result of this materialistic concept is a highly stratified, power concentrated, and unjust society.

In the technodemocratic economy, materialism leaves its prime importance and becomes responsive only to the average needs of the individual for a comfortable living condition. Its essence from maximization of profits shifts to satisfaction of needs. Profit resulting from exploitation of workers and consumers becomes automatically and gradually eliminated. Therefore, progress is not based on the economic upward movement but relates to improvement of the individual characteristics and upward movement of human values. The economic class stratification disappears and social distinction becomes based on the individual's knowledge, experience, and humane concerns. Economic hardship does not present backwardness as long as there is an equitable distribution of income. So, based on the economic conditions, individual income may go up or down. It is considered an ordinary consequence of operation of the economy, yet there is no unemployment at any time, regardless of the state of the economy. There is lifetime security of a job and income for every individual, except those incapable of participating in production for physical or mental defects, whose life and security is guaranteed by the community. While under capitalism, concentration of wealth creates power through exercise of which individuals or groups tend to control, or at least influence, operation of the societal systems; in technodemocratic society there is no concentrated source of power. This occurs because there is no sustained power structure in the first place. All production institutions are decentralized and dispersed; all information systems are mainly responsive to the people as a whole and are fed by the whole society—individuals, public and private institutions; it directly feeds the society without any individual or group influence or interference; all important governmental agencies or offices are ruled by elected people whose term of office is limited without offering an opportunity to anyone to build a political or economic powerbase. The only meaningful influence in technodemocratic society will be that of intellectuals, whose effect and influence in the form of ideas may last for generations. Therefore, the technodemocratic society, in its matured stage, is essentially a classless and nearly stateless society. This is a radically different concept of economy and society and must be studied carefully in order to be properly understood. It can occur only under a technodemocratic economic system.

The establishment of a technodemocratic system will produce one of the most painful, because of radical adjustments to be made, but the most promising characteristics of modern existence. Through a new form of consciousness, men will come to sense that their education is utterly inadequate. They will come to assert that they have a right to be properly educated, meaning that it must be social as well as technical, general as well as special, free from indoctrination and based on reason, aimed to free men rather than to subjugate them, all geared toward consciously structured democratic norms, values and processes. It will also be understood that in order to improve productivity as well as knowledge, education must be continuous, a lifetime responsibility. It is under this kind and system of education that men will come to realize the irrational and utterly unjust aspect of capitalistic economy, disapprove it, and be determined for its transformation to technodemocratic economy.

Any other prevailing economic system, whether communistic, socialistic, or mixed will become subject to the same rationalization relating to its unjust aspects. The Marxist-Leninist economy, for example, though it provides for a more equitable distribution of income, is state controlled where the individual worker, though he receives more equitable benefits, is subject to state authority. All his conditions of work and economic life are subject to state made policies.

Education is a prerequisite for democracy, democracy is a stimu-lator and contributor to education. Under a democratic system, economy may achieve its own form of excellence, but the more important human excellences are achieved elsewhere. Economy, though still important, leaves the driver's seat and the individuals are able to define the important ends of life in their own voluntary pursuits, free from economic pressures. Democracy brings different qualities to an individual's life. It nourishes his mind, imagination, and conscience, providing for a strong democratic attitude, vast domain of freedom, variety, and self-consciousness.

Democracy, by requiring extensive and continuous education, makes individuals wiser and more virtuous. It invites man to think of alternatives consciously and rationally, to reduce the barrier of class, cast, and inherited economic and power privileges. It adds to the variety of individuals and occasions one meets. It places greater pleasure on one's capacity to adapt to the new and different norms and conditions.

Technodemocratic economy stands as the nemesis of all economic doctrines and all economic practices of both the capitalistic and the communistic systems. In a technodemocratic society:

1. The economic life of man, though independent, cannot be abstracted and separated from the societal life. The economic aspect of life is not the most important but remains in balance with the intellectual and spiritual aspects of life.

2. The economic life of man is structured upon and influenced by democratic principles as components of democratic organism.

3. Economic progress is the outcome of concerted efforts of individuals who, by acculturation to technodemocratic norms, have come to know how to overcome their egotistic tendencies and ambitions for their own gold and the good of society as a whole.

4. Economic initiatives are not based on profit motives or arbitrary decisions. They are based on efficiency, effectiveness, and fair return for the individual's efforts. They are based on the democratic collective decision-making process of production and distribution.

5. Open competition is the backbone of the democratic market, but it becomes free of fraudulent and propagandic advertisement. Exact specifications of the product are stated and left to the consumer to make a choice.

6. The wealth of a society is the sum total of individual wealth plus all natural and other resources. The important part of the wealth of society is not economic but technological in the form of knowledge, expertise, and means.

7. More important than the production of wealth is its equitable distribution among the working class, subject only to the level of expertise and experience.

8. In a technodemocratic system, there is no class structure or class distinction. The differentiation is only at the work place, based only on the level of expertise and experience.

9. The proper function of the state is to establish, maintain and periodically revise the standards required by the principle of equality of opportunity, particularly relating to division of labor and compensation. National government has no domestic line functions except some supervisory authority in the areas relating to the national consumption fund such as education, health care and corresponding standards.

10. Since there are no classes, there is no class struggle in technodemocratic society.

11. Private wealth totally belongs to the individual. It is a wealth initiated, created, and accumulated through an individual's own labor.

12. Public wealth mainly constitutes the society's natural resources. It belongs to the society as a whole, thus proceeds from it go to the national consumption fund and are used for the society's benefit as a whole, such as education and health care.

13. A prime distinction of the economy under a technodemocratic system with that of other systems, is that there is no separation between capital and labor; thus workers receive full return for their productive labor. There is no social surplus and thus no profits.

14. A worker's wage is paid in two parts; one part in cash and the other in capital (stocks and shares). Thus each laborer starts with no capital ownership and builds up capital through the time of his retirement. However, this capital is a public resource belonging to the society as a whole, except for the new capital produced by the worker through his personal savings. Despite this fact all gained capital remains his absolute property during his lifetime and then it is added to the societal capital after his death. The public capital is distributed among all workers through the pay process and each worker has the full benefit of his share of it during his lifetime. Since it is a societal property, it reverts to the public treasury at the end of an individual's life.

15. Except for handicaps and those disabled, there are no public assistance programs of any kind. It is not needed. There is also no social security or retirement plan. When retiring, the individual has sufficient wealth accumulated to provide him with a comfortable life.

These fundamental tenets of the technodemocratic economy are derived essentially from the principle of equality of opportunity and its proper implementation. Equality of opportunity is the supreme principle and the supreme law of the land. The result is that under a technodemocratic economic system there is no single economic interest dominating others; there is no monopoly of any kind; there are also no conglomerates or giant economic institutions. The very application of the principle automatically and necessarily breaks down giant institutions into independent component parts.

16. Supervision of the operation of equality of opportunity within the framework of democratic organism is primarily the responsibility of local and then regional governments. Enforcement will be according to the standards established by responsible national organs.

17. The primary responsibility of the application and implementation of equality of opportunity within the framework established by the national organs rests upon each production institution, large and small, all the way down to the self-employed. No public agency interferes with this process except when it is not properly applied.

18. Thus the total policy-making and operation of a production system is under the command of individuals within each production institution. The individual is the master of his own destiny and responsible for that of society as a whole.

19. Equality of opportunity is an invisible but strong tie that binds together the destinies of the people, of a society, and ultimately the world. It causes joys and pains experienced by individuals to be shared, thus enhancing the joy and reducing the pain of society as a whole. The terms wealthy and pauper, capitalist and worker, employer and employee, lose their antagonistic meaning and the distinctions actually disappear. The individual worker, through and within his institution, dictates the extent and manner of the relationship between capital and labor, employer and employee, landlord and tenant.

20. The production and distribution of goods and services become harmonized to the actual needs of the individual and society as a whole. The system tends toward coordination of all economic forces of the society under one principle, thus providing a material life for the people free of struggles, strikes, unemployment, too much wealth or poverty.

21. Operation of the system makes unnecessary the unionization of labor, thus from an economic standpoint, eliminating all kinds of labor unions, syndicates, and guilds. There are no class wars between capitalists and labor, and no need for the protection of material welfare of the workers. Duties and compensation for every position is

determined by the working firm, according to prescribed national standards, and every worker gets the same pay for the same job, regardless of the place of his work. Simply, in place of the unions and capitalist employers who determined the duties and compensation for each position in their firm according to their own norms, now there is a national position classification norm that the firms must follow in assigning the duties and compensation for each position within the firm. Now, all the working citizens of society are brought by an all-comprehensive national manifestation into the framework of one superior and far reaching organization which has for its purpose the material welfare of the whole nation. This brings the egotistic tendencies of the individual, particularly during the early years of technodemocracy, under discipline of the nation toward realization of not only the guarantee of individual well-being but also that of the society as a whole.

22. Within each production firm the interest of producers and consumers, employers and employees, individuals and groups are inter-locked and integrated in a unique way by bringing all types of interests under the aegis of the firm. Necessarily, interests of the workers are protected and preserved since each firm is governed by the workers themselves who are also the owners.

23. The technodemocratic economy, unlike those under other ideologies, is heavily affected by ethical principles mainly generated through the application of the principle of equality of opportunity. It is a translation of ethics into economics. It is a totally new form of economics. It is an economy without exploitation of neither the labor nor the consumer.

24. Unlike capitalism, where an economic elite ruled the system sf production and distribution, under technodemocratic economy the individual is the ruler. To carry out this responsibility he is required to properly educate himself, not restricted to knowledge concerned with the production process alone, but also that of developing mental and intellectual capabilities. For proper participation in the decision-making process, he must be able to develop an inner vision to the very heart of things; to discover the truth, and to translate his inner thoughts into deed and action. Each individual in technodemocratic society is a hero on his own account. He must prepare for and make himself capable of acting like one. His heroism is an integral part of that of others and all together they create a heroically dynamic society.

## Essential Characteristics of the Technodemocratic Economic System

Toward technodemocratic economy, the task is not just to reformulate the traditional ideals of "democratic capitalism" or "democratic socialism," but to establish a totally new system, that will give life and society a concrete content through norms and institutions that are democratic as well as practical in a highly industrialized and densely populated society with a rapidly changing environment. The economic and technological means of extraordinary dimensions must be directed by all men, each according to his capability, to the benefit of each and all.

The concrete needs of individuals in a technodemocratic system are best met in the long run, by close adherence to democratic norms and proper functioning within the framework of democratic organism. The social goal and common purpose for which society is to be organized, concerns itself in providing equality of opportunity for everyone. In such an accomplished society:

1. Everyone starts life from scratch.

2. Everyone receives free and general education up to age 15.

3. Everyone starts to work at age 15, starting with part-time and proceeding to full-time by the age of 22.

4. Everyone continues his education part-time after the age of 15 until retirement. Such education is a balanced combination of technical and cultural subjects. It is reduced to two courses on each subject per year after the age of 22.

5. Everyone receives free healthcare from birth until death.

6. Everyone, starting from zero, gradually becomes a part owner of the means of production and distribution. These ownership shares are destined for the old age support and thus are not transferable.

7. Everyone works full-time for 30-35 years or equivalent of it.

8. Equivalent to one-fourth of the working hours are allocated to education. So, for a 40-hour a week work, the person will work for 32 hours and study for 8 hours.

9. Promotion is based on the level of education and years of experience, cultural education having the same importance as the technical or professional.

10.  The age of retirement depends on the supply of young labor force for the purpose of allowing them equal opportunity for employment.  However, to guarantee a comfortable retirement life no capable person works for less than 25 years full-time before retirement.  The general retirement occurs after 30 years of full-time work.

11.  After retirement, which more likely will occur when individual is in his early 50's, he has enough capital accumulated to give him returns sufficient for a comfortable life.

12.  All elective public positions will:

a.  Require very high qualifications relating to education as well as experience.

b.  Be temporary.  No one could be elected to the same office for more than one term.  Besides other benefits, this is also to allow opportunities to a greater number of well qualified citizens to hold public offices.

c.  These two requirements will allow retired individuals a better chance of being elected to public office since they are better educated and also are not looking for a permanent position.  They are still young but matured and thus capable of fruitful participation in the public policy-making process.

13.  As a result of the democratic norms and technological developments, family life is transformed from its traditional form into a democratic unit; parents being responsible, though in a different manner, for upbringing of the children up to age 15, after which the person, who is considered an adult, will enter the labor force and will become independent.

14.  By the time of retirement, the family, more likely because of voluntary birth and population control, will have no children to take care of and the couple, if they desire to remain together, will have a very fruitful, still productive, and enjoyable life.

15.  After death, individual's wealth will return to society, to the public consumption fund, to sustain free services including health care and education for the newcomers who will also start from scratch.

16.  Though some individuals will accumulate more wealth than others, the difference will not be so great as to cause class distinction.  Such difference is only for the life of the person and will disappear after his death.  In reality, this will be a single-class or classless society.

17. An individuals' obligatory relationship is in his family and workplace. Outside these, he remains free to enjoy life with a great many things accessible in an infinite variety of combinations.

The moral boundaries of democracy are very broad and centers around the principle of equality of opportunity. No common ethical code can be comprehensive enough to cover the nearly boundless domain of these moral possibilities. It will be impossible for any mind to comprehend the infinite variety of individual freedoms and good deeds ensuing from this concept of technodemocratic morality. It is impossible to even vaguely define the boundaries. Whether one's interests center around his own well-being, or the welfare of others, regardless how broad and expanded these interests may be, the ends that he may concern himself with will always be only an infinitesimal fraction of what could be possible under a technodemocratic system. It is within these nearly limitless confines that the individual pursues his life, liberty and pursuit of happiness within a technodemocratic society.

## Individualism

Democratic organism materializes the kingdom of the individual. The whole operation of society is geared toward well being, freedom and happiness of the individual. The individual is the center of attention in all societal interactions. His integrity, honor, individuality, independence, opportunities and liberties all are flourished, sustained and protected under the technodemocratic system. The organism provides only the tools and means to achieve these. The individual is the operator, initiator, sustainer, and protector of all these conditions and values. The operation of society and its regulation starts from the bottom, namely the individual and his immediate production institution; it then extends to local, regional, and national levels. However, as the organization moves upward from the individual to the national level, the concern with and involvement in operation of the system diminishes, the national level having the least. The situation becomes very clear when the detailed structure and operation of the system is studied and understood.[1]

## Religion

None of the present world religions will survive under the technodemocratic system because, first, as they are practiced, none is democratic; second, all are superficial; third, they are the glorification of personalities rather than rationalization of creed.

Any religion that intends to subjugate individuals through a set of commands, e.g. Ten Commandments, and a set of rituals, cannot be considered democratic. Christianity, Islam, and Judaism, as well as other major religions, as they are practiced, fall under this characteristic. Their undemocratic nature, therefore, makes them unfeasible to come under or to survive within a technodemocratic system.

These major religions are artificial in existence and in practice if not in their essence. For example, both Christianity and Judaism prescribe that Thou Shall Not Kill. Yet, Christian as well as Jewish societies have been the cause and initiator of bloody wars during this century, let alone the past history. Capitalism, in reference to teachings of Christ, is the most un-Christian act, yet, it has developed, flourished, and advanced in Christian and Jewish societies and sustained by them. Capitalism is identified by exploitation of workers and consumers, cheating, dishonesty, brutality, colonization, and lack of concern to human life. All of these qualities are utterly un-Christian as well as anti-Islamic. These are good examples of artificiality of all major religions of today in practice.

Major religions are associated with glorification, organization of specific persons in order to force subservience and compliance with the rules and obedience to religious authorities who have been able to place themselves as representatives of so-called "Holy Spirit." Religion, in its essence, is not and cannot be external to human. True religion relates to the individual's inner feeling, it is his faith If it is induced, by conditioning or indoctrinating the individual's mind, it is not then real but artificial and imposed. A true religion which conquers the inner self of the individual has to be rational, subject to inquiry, analysis, and verification. In a technodemocratic system, there can be room only for this kind of faith which is developed by individual deliberation, resulting in adherence to certain norms. Even if they relate to the supernatural, they are within the reach of reason. It must be remembered that in every aspect of life, material or spiritual, individual is the king, a conscious, curious, knowledgeable, and humane ruler of his life and concerned the same with the life of his other fellow beings. Technodemocratic society is the union of many kings, conscious of well-being of others as that of their own.

In a technodemocratic society, man is the seeker of his own religion. In his continuous analysis of self, and search for the truth, he is the person to succeed or not to succeed in establishing relations with his creator. Once he reaches this stage of accomplishment, he believes deeply in what he has discovered. Religion relates to his relation with his creator within the realm of self and through his own self-consciousness. To him it is a discovery based on reason, a belief resting on a solid foundation. In this regard, he has no external relationship, his religious privacy is complete and is sacred to him. Of course, his acculturation to human and humane values through his democratic life will be an important factor and guidance in his efforts to discover the secret of the universe and the truth about it and life.

This kind of individualized religion, apart from outside interference, suggests that in a technodemocratic society there will be neither a place for, nor use for, traditional or new religious institutions. The society will rid itself from these kind of reactionary and wasteful institutions and each individual, based on the extent of his personal efforts and convictions, will establish his relations with the spiritual world and his Creator. Since everyone will be seeking the truth based on reason, the outcome will be a faith through consensus and unanimity of those who reach the same conclusion. However, religion will remain individualized without institutionalization. This will show one true aspect of individual freedom, freedom from dogmatic beliefs and pressures.

## Conclusion

Becoming acculturated to all technodemocratic norms, man will enter into the realm of timeless and true reality and will become able to translate his vision of good into deeds and to act automatically according to the dictates of his conscience which demands from him nothing but good. There will gradually develop a sincere and deep belief that man lives a true human life only when his life is devoted to and, if necessary, sacrifices for the triumph of the ideals of democracy, and that only by living such a life can he ever find true happiness in the world. Through enlightenment, by continually studying society and humanity, in seeking the true meaning of life, he will come to realize that by his democratic deeds he is answering the call of history in delivering a message of hope, trust, and faith by devotion to materialize a new way of life, a life capable of leading man out of his present miserable and unhappy state. As an example, through his words, actions, influence, and his whole being, he will demonstrate a true and sincere being who lives according to the very democratic messages he is delivering to his fellow citizens and his children.

Nothing good and great, nothing of any value or of any meaning to humanity can ever be accomplished in the world, if all fear of and temptation toward the known and unknown hostile, belittling or derisive forces are not banished from the heart and mind of man. To achieve this, man needs sincerity, courage, and belief. In order for society to be actually and effectively changed through an individual's own efforts, he must believe in democratic norms, in his own destiny, in the rule which he is destined to play on the stage of life and in his own individual capacity, capability, and power.

Man, burning with the great flame of goodness that he has carried and still carries deep within, strives to bring forth that inner flame, to follow the call of destiny without being aware of exactly what that destiny expects from him. He only dimly, in a blurred vision, perceives the image of some great and good thing shaping itself in the mist, calling, leading, and drawing him toward a yet unknown but delightful end. As he proceeds, the mist enveloping the vision, haunting his dreams since the early days, is finally lifting, the contours of his vision tend to become sharp, distinct and clear. Ultimately, the image of the great, democratic and equalitable society becomes revealed.

It will not be easy for him to reach this ultimate stage of life. It will need consciousness leading toward a complete revolution of all thoughts, all feeling, all sensations, taking his soul by storm and forcing him to examine critically his whole past, revise all his beliefs, fashion for himself a new creed, the democratic creed, a creed that a whole society, a whole continent, the whole civilization is in need, is waiting to see, and desires to embrace. At this stage of enlightenment, he will then have the true vision of the present society, sunk in the mire, seeking light, pleading for help.

On the one side, there stands decaying capitalistic-materialistic organization of society; on the other, authoritarian socialism and abjection. It will become imperative for him to choose another way of life in tune with his soul's aspirations, in accord with his conscious enlightenment, and a way from his animal nature's desires. It will be then that the dumb, inchoate historical forces which shape the destinies of man will find suddenly a true purpose; it is then that centuries of thought and action will be brought suddenly to a climax by such a purpose; it is then that the people themselves will suddenly acquire the purpose so earnestly, and yet so vainly, they had sought.

Technodemocratic economy actually expresses and explains in words what remained unexpressed in the innermost heart of the people; it translates into action what laid dormant in a potential state within the very nature of the people.

## NOTES

1. For detailed study of the structure and operation of governmental system see Reza Rezazadeh, *Technological Democracy*.

*Chapter 11*

# TRANSITION FROM SOCIALISM AND CAPITALISM TO TECHNODEMOCRATIC ECONOMIC SYSTEM

Generally speaking, as envisioned by historical evidences, people always think that their societal institutions are essentially appropriate. When problems arise, they try to solve them through efforts toward reforming or modifying their existing systems. They do not favor fundamental transformations affecting the basic foundation of the existing system and societal life.

But, as societies develop, new technologies and processes are introduced; the level and nature of knowledge, education, desires, and demands of people change; new consciousness regarding unavoidable defects of the existing systems is crystallized; and the increasing destructive effects of these defects on the ecosystem, including the human species, become undisputable evident. The situation reaches a point where reforms and modifications do not resolve the problems, and a fundamental transformation in societal norms and processes becomes necessary. In an awakened society it becomes mandatory to look for a fundamentally new societal system whose institutions, under new democratic norms and processes, will be able to accommodate the needs and demands of the new technological age.

After the collapse of Leninism in Eastern European countries sweeping changes in the Soviet Union and the end of the party monopoly, the conditions necessitate a fundamental change in every aspect of society, the economy in particular. There is an imminent need for a solid but humanistic societal philosophy to replace the old regime, create a clear perspective, and thus induce individuals to pull the nation out of its present chaotic order. Such societal philosophy must be democratic, dynamic, and responsive to the needs of modern society. It also must be rational and scientific, presenting the people not only long range objectives but also directions as to how to get there. The theory and processes presented here accommodate all these requirements.

It is regrettable to see that Eastern European countries and the Soviet Union, instead of looking for an appropriate and democratic new system, are regressing into capitalism which has proved to be one of the most undemocratic economic systems and the most destructive of the environment and natural resources in the long run. It is true that capitalism, at the expense of the environment and depletion of natural resources, has created temporary abundance of goods, but its development has reached a point that its destructive and exploitive effects substantially surpass its overall benefits. This is not to say that there is no need for the abundance of goods and services; it is the way these are produced at the expense of other vital necessities to sustain human life and those of other species in this fragile little planet. What is really desperately needed is not capitalism but a societal system which will provide for equality of opportunity for all the people in every aspect of life—economic, social, and political—regardless of race, color, gender, religion, or national origin.

The study of the technodemocratic economic theory makes it clear that it can be fully materialized in a society which is highly educated and super advanced in technology, information—communication technology in particular. There is no such society in existence today. However, there are societies that have a better capability of moving toward attaining the state of technodemocratic economy. Here, we divide the societies of the world into three general categories of advanced socialist, capitalist, and less developed. Since the transition process is different for each of these categories, each is discussed separately. The recommendations for transition to technodemocratic economy are general, and each society may modify them according to its specific situation and facts.

## Transition from Socialism

This process applies to countries like the Soviet Union and those of Eastern Europe. They have the alternatives of either regressing to capitalistic market system and importing its evils to their society, or accepting a new, long range technodemocratic economic theory with its democratic norms and advanced free market system.

These socialistic systems have the potential of advanced technology and a better background in liberal education. The latter part is important since, as it has been demonstrated, education in technodemocratic society, besides its professional and technological content, contains a substantial component in liberal education. Despite some distortion of facts, socialist countries appear to have more of this kind of education in the early stages of their educational programs than the capitalist countries like the United States, where technical and professional training are emphasized to the detriment of intellectual contents. No democracy can be materialized without corresponding social consciousness, and this can be realized only through substantial liberal education. Socialist countries comparatively have this advantage.

It was this kind of liberal education and ensuring consciousness that caused general mass uprisings in Eastern Europe against Leninist dictatorial and centrally controlled regimes. Now that the old regimes have been toppled, the societal institutions have been almost totally upset. What is needed is a well-planned, long-range objective based on new democratic philosophy and a proper policy for transition period. To initiate personal and group dynamism and incentives, such philosophy and its essential components must be well understood by the people. To progress toward a socio-economic development, people must know and understand the long-range objectives and have a clear direction in moving toward achieving them. The technodemocratic economic theory presented here provides for both. It points out the principles and scientific ground for them; it also gives detailed directions for achieving them. Countries with lesser technological know-how must adopt the technodemocratic economic principles without being much concerned with needed high technology. This approach properly establishes the stage of transition. The technology can be gradually incorporated into the system as it becomes available. In establishing this initial stage of transition, the socialist societies have certain very substantial advantages over the capitalist ones.

*Equality of Opportunity.* This is the very basic principle and the foundation of the technodemocratic economic system. It has been much more present under a socialist system than under a capitalist regime. Its nature and application must be studied carefully.

*Ownership of the Means of Production and Distribution.* Under technodemocratic economic theory, all the means of production and distribution is owned and operated by the private sector based on the concept of equality of opportunity. The most outstanding advantage in a socialist system is that the means of production and distribution have already been under the control of governing regime. The only important step toward establishing technodemocratic economy will be to return to the workers all the means of production and distribution. However, this must be done gradually, according to the process presented before, by the application of the principle of equality of opportunity, in an orderly and scientific manner. We also know the reason why all these transfers of ownership must be in the form of nontransferable stocks, namely the owners will not be able to cash them in the market.

In transitional societies the appropriate way appears to be a two-stage transfer method. During the first stage, which will take effect immediately, 30 percent of the total means of production and distribution will be transferred to the workers based on the length of employment. By this way about one-third of the total assets will be transferred to the workers, and the government will still control the other two-thirds.

The second stage, which will also start immediately after the initial transfer of 30 percent, will consist of a gradual transfer of the rest of the means of production and distribution to the workers by allocating to each, through the method prescribed in the text, a monthly share of nontransferable stocks primarily from the assets of the institution where the worker is employed.

The benefits of this two-stage transfer process are manifold. First, by the initial transfer of substantial part of the capital to the working class, individual interest and incentives are induced. Second, the workers, through their elected representatives, will occupy 30 percent of the membership of the board of directors. This will give the workers opportunity of participation in management and receiving experiences by being exposed to policy-making process. Third, and most importantly, the government holding the majority of the capital in every institution will still keep the control of management and policy-making process. This is necessary from the standpoint that in a socialist country, because of a centralized economy, workers have not been able to acquire managerial experiences in order to be able to operate their institution effectively, efficiently, and properly. But this control by the government will not last very long because each month, along with wages, more shares of production firms will be transferred to the workers, and in a few years they will gain the majority of shares and consequently the control of the firm. However, these few years of control by the government will keep the production firms from falling into a chaotic state, while at the same time giving opportunity to the workers to be trained and experienced in management and decision-making skills. Initially, it will eliminate 30 percent of the party bureaucracy concerned with the production process, and at the same time will prevent apathy by the rest of the government members of the board since now 30 percent of the membership by the workers, as part owners of the institution, will insist on efficiency and will disclose inappropriate behavior of the public members of the board. This will initially diminish and ultimately eradicate the inefficient bureaucratic operation of the production firms.

As soon as the first stage of capital transfer is completed, the central economic and production planning must be abandoned. Each institution must be managed independently despite the fact that the government will have controlling share of stocks and the majority of membership in the board of directors of every firm. The total process of planning for production and marketing will be independent from interference by the central government. The production system must tend toward market economy based on open competition, supply and demand, not as practiced under a capitalistic system, but according to the prevailing principles of technodemocratic economic theory.

In the early stages of transition and until the substantial development of the Technodem, it might be necessary to resort to advertisement. There may also be unavoidable profits. But as the system of Technodem develops, and marketing and purchasing are increasingly done by the use of it, both advertisement and profits will diminish and tend to disappear. However, in the area of international trade with capitalistic societies, there may still be some profits made. Profits in this area will be automatically eliminated as the other societies, one after another, adopt and establish technodemocratic economic systems.

*Prohibition of Unjust Enrichment.* The application of the principle of equality of opportunity also requires the prohibition of unjust enrichment. As it has been illustrated, this prescribes the prohibition of inheritance, profits, and any major transfer of property without comparable compensation.

The application of prohibition of inheritance, while very difficult in a capitalistic system, is much simpler in socialistic societies since, unlike in capitalistic society, the means of production and distribution are not owned by private individuals and families. The same applies to prohibition of free transfer of property. Furthermore, in a socialist society individuals and families, unlike those in a capitalist one, do not possess substantial assets and properties to transfer to one another. As discussed before, a limited amount of inheritance my be allowed as long as such free transfers do not disturb or go contrary to the principle of equality of opportunity.

As far as the prohibition of profits are concerned, in the initial stage when the workers own 30 percent of the means of production and distribution, the government receives 70 percent of the revenues. These revenues will be necessary for the government to finance some basic social services such as education, health care, old age benefits, and other expenditures of the transition. As is has been discussed, education and health care are provided free of charge under technodemocratic economic system, and there are no old age benefits payments.

At the same time, during the same initial stage, workers, beside their wages, will also receive 30 percent of the institution's revenues. As the ownership is gradually transferred to the workers, percentage of revenues appropriated by the government decreases, and that of the workers increases. When the ownership is ultimately totally transferred to the workers, they receive all the benefits, and the government appropriates none. There is no capitalist since the workers are the owners. Thus, there is no social surplus to be appropriated by any source, whether public or private, and profits ar automatically eliminated.

*Full Employment.* The application of the concept of shared opportunity in order to guarantee full employment will also be simpler in a previously socialist system where the production was not based on maximization of profits, and employment was guaranteed to all the workers. Under capitalism, maximization of profits frequently requires substantial lay-offs of workers.

The application of this principle becomes more essential and needed during the period of transition where otherwise vast numbers of workers may lose employment. Shared opportunity guarantees full employment even though the earning of some workers may be reduced by reducing their weekly hours of work in order to sustain the employment of some others. Everyone loses a little for the benefit of all, for the dynamism of economy as a whole, and for assisting public treasury and well being of society. Without the use of the concept of shared opportunity the system may fall under the unaffordable economic pressure if a large number of workers becomes unemployed as a result of transition.

*Position Classification.* A national position classification for all work positions in the society will also be much simpler in a previously socialist system since in such a system nearly everyone worked for the government and all the positions were classified by the latter in one manner or another. The system will definitely require modification in a scientific manner as presented in this study. Position classification guarantees that the workers receive the same pay for similar positions.

*Technology and the Technodem.* The most important operational component of the technodemocratic economic system is the *Technodem.* It will be much easier to establish this instrument of progress and democracy in a socialist society than in a capitalist one. The main reason is that in such society all the means of information and communication were already under government's control. They can be gradually democratized and collected together as a national system. Its operation becomes then autonomous and independent of any outside interference or influence including that of the government. This will constitute the basic body and foundation of the Technodem, a very important progress in itself toward democracy and economic well being. The future developments of the Technodem will depend on the advancement in the use of electronic technology, popular use of microcomputers by the government agencies, businesses, families and individuals all hooked to the Technodem. With conscious planning in

Eastern European countries, this progress may be achieved within two decades.

At the level of production firms, this development can start with one or more computer terminals within each firm which will be connected to local terminals and through them to regional and national units of the Technodem. All computer terminals in governmental agencies will also be connected to the Technodem system. By this way the main operational structure of the Technodem will be established.

It must be noted that the formation of the basic operational structure of the Technodem in socialist countries will be a great advantage in accelerating technodemocratic economy. This will move these countries ahead of the capitalist system since in the capitalist countries the information-communication technology is controlled by the monopoly capitalist elite, and it will take a great deal of efforts from the part of the people and a longer time to take this technology away form the elite and attempt to democratize it to serve the benefits of society. Another word, the formation of the Technodem in capitalist societies is at least some forty years away.

Presently, the big deficiency in socialist countries is the lack of electronic culture and the use of microcomputers at home and business. Computerized society is the cause for the advanced socio-economic system. Special attention must be devoted to computer education and popularization of its use. The technodem is a necessity for the future democratic socio-economic development. It is the backbone of the technodemocratic economy. Without the Technodem the application of this economic theory will be complex and incomplete. Its initial establishment and continuous development must receive prime attention.

*Education and Health Care.* Dynamism and progress in every society depends on the level of education and health. Under a technodemocratic economic system education and health care are available to all for life and free of charge. In a socialist society both of these have been available to the people almost free of charge. This is another significant advantage that a socialist system has in moving toward establishing a technodemocratic economic system. both the education and health care systems may require certain modifications in content and process to comply with the principle of equality of opportunity. The very important thing is that basic national structure for both are already in existence.

As the system of the Technodem develops and advances, more and more educational programs should be made available through this system. Education through the Technodem may be made first accessible in educational centers and be used concurrently with the traditional methods of instruction and gradually extend to homes and other societal institutions. Education is one of the essential instruments of progress and yet very expensive. The use of the Technodem for educational programs will sharply reduce the costs while facilitating access to educational programs. It will save billions of dollars each year.

It must be emphasized that the democratic nature of the system depends on the extent of the adherence to and application of the principle of equality of opportunity. Its nature and application in different areas of the societal life and workplace must be properly understood as presented and discussed in this study. The socialist society has a great advantage here since its theoretical structure has been based on equality. The full application of the principle may not be possible in the initial stages of transition, but it is essential that development of its application be given primary and continuous attention until it is fully operational.

As it is noted from the text, the technodemocratic economic system, when fully developed, tends toward a classless and nearly stateless society.

Finally, it must be remembered that continuous education is the heart of the success of technodemocratic economy. this continuous education, which occupies one-fifth of the workers weekly working hours, is particularly essential in the period of transition in order to provide for the necessary skills at different levels of production, at the management level in particular.

## Transition from Capitalism

Capitalism, as perceived in this study, is a stage of development toward technodemocratic economy, but in the process of societal development, it precedes the stage of social democracy.

Social democracy, as assumed in this study, is a societal system where the operation of economy is mainly capitalistic while certain basic means of production are nationalized, and where people are provided with substantial welfare services which are rendered either free or through heavy subsidies from the public treasury such as education, health care either direct or through a national health insurance, transportation, unemployment compensation and so on.

Thus to proceed from capitalism directly into the stage of technodemocratic economy will require the bypassing of the social democratic stage. this will place a heavy burden on the process of transition. In its advanced stage, namely monopoly capitalism, the efforts by the system is to alleviate or at least diminish the effects of rising contradictions tending to undermine the stability of the capitalist system.

To achieve this purpose, the educational programs and information-communication media are carefully manipulated in all relevant aspects in order to keep people ignorant of the depth and breadth of the negative effects of and injustices caused by the monopoly capitalism. The system is idealized as the free enterprise, democratic and the guardian of freedom and dignity. The substantial negative aspects of capitalism such as exploitation, alienation, discrimination, racism, sexism, poverty, homelessness, indignation, lack of health care or old age benefits, and ever widening class stratification are hardly given serious attention.

When socio-economic conditions have tended to cause discontent and instability with possibility of explosions and uprisings against the system, the ruling elite has tried to deflect the situation by legislating necessary concessions such as unemployment compensation, anti-poverty programs, medicaid, etc. It must be noted that these handouts have never been a financial burden on the ruling elite. These have been paid through the taxes collected, mainly from the working middle class. Accordingly, development of public consciousness about injustices and inequalities caused by the capitalistic operation of society has been systematically contained. The effects have been that, despite all injustices which are the characteristic of capitalism, the American people have been conditioned to think favorably about the system, to associate it with democracy, free enterprise, freedom, and equality of opportunity. Concurrently, Americans have become increasingly apathetic about political democracy to the extent that today only 30 to 40 percent of the eligible voters participate in congressional elections and over one-third of the voters who bother to vote, are independent and do not belong to any of the two political parties. Also, as it has been demonstrated before, the system has always tended to eliminate successfully the development of any third party with an ideology critical of the American capitalism.

All these circumstances collectively cause the public authority to fall in the hands of several major groups, including the two major political parties, which are all controlled or manipulated one way or another by the tiny ruling elite.

All these factors combined together make public consciousness about democracy extremely difficult. When there is a deeply rooted misconception as to what democracy is all about, the road toward inquiring into and understanding of the true meaning of democracy becomes rocky and full of conceptual obstacles. Social democratic system provides grounds for development of such consciousness and gradually leads toward realization of a technodemocratic economic system. The capitalistic system, being one stage farther behind, requires intensive public education about the true nature of democracy, economic democracy in particular. As it has been demonstrated before,in a capitalistic society like the United states, this goal cannot be achieved through the existing educational system. It must be done, if at all, by the individuals or organization outside the formal educational process. The very development of such consciousness will face a brute confrontation and harsh reaction from the system.

In the United States, unlike Western or Eastern Europe, transition to technodemocratic economy requires a substantial transformation of the societal concepts and structure. The capitalistic economy is far divorced from democratic norms. Any transformation toward economic democracy will face fierce opposition. It will require societal uprising. It could happen in one of the two ways if there is sufficient national consciousness.

First, it is possible through the formation of a national constitutional convention. According to the United States Constitution and precedence, such convention, once formed, will have authority to amend the Constitution as it sees fit. To form such a convention at least two-thirds of the state legislatures must petition the U.S. Congress through a resolution asking for the formation of the convention. When this step is achieved, Congress will be obliged to call for the formation of the convention. Once the convention meets and amends the Constitution or writes a new one, it must be submitted to the states for ratification. It must be ratified by the state legislatures or state constitutional conventions. The National Constitutional Convention determines which of the two methods will be used for ratification. The amendments or the new constitution must be ratified in three-fourths of the state in order to become effective. after such ratification, it will go into effect and the new societal system will begin to crystalize. It is obvious that the success of this process will require a broad national consciousness about the purpose and consequences of the change.

Such consciousness is very unlikely to take place in the United States. So, while the socialistic and other less capitalistic societies like some of the Western European countries move toward technodemocratic economy, the United States will fall behind. However, the development of technodemocratic economy in European societies will have awakening effect on the United States which hopefully may accelerate their move toward economic democracy.

The second method to achieve technodemocratic economy is through the employment of the concept of *general strike*. The theory first advanced by George Sorel has been effectively used in recent years. The idea is that when the majority of workers in a society go on strike the existing system falls apart. The concept was effectively employed in 1979 by the Iranian people which toppled the Shah's government in a few weeks despite his command of the strongest military force in the Middle East. Thus the Iranian revolution of 1979 succeeded through general strike. More recently, resorts to general strike were quite successful in several Eastern European countries.

The more technologically advanced a society is the easier it is to succeed through the use of general strike. Smooth and proper operation of the system in an advanced technological society depends on cooperative and coordinated functioning of many specialized organizations. Even if one of these organizations such as Teamsters Union controlling the highway transportation, communications workers, or railroad employees go on strike, the economy will plunge into a chaotic state. The point is that in a technologically advanced society, because of interdependence, the stoppage of any major sector of technology will cause breakdown in the proper operation of society as a whole and will bring response to demands for change. There will be no need for real general strike where nearly all working class must stop working.

As soon as the government is subdued, the leading groups will ask for the formation of the National Constitutional Convention to rewrite the nation's constitution. It seems apparent that under economic pressures created through the strike state legislatures will petition congress for the formation of such convention. The constitution will then be amended under the leadership of the strikes to contain the basic principles for the establishment of the technodemocratic economy and corresponding political and social institutions.

## Steps Required for Transition

The transitional process in a capitalist society is much more complex compared to that of a socialist one. The following steps are some major requirements.

1. Total prohibition of transfer of property without comparable compensation. Simply, there shall be no unjust enrichment. Among these, the prohibition of inheritance is the most essential one. Without elimination of inheritance no class stratification can be eliminated; neither can the principle of equality of opportunity be effectuated. However, a minimum amount of inheritance may be allowed as long as everyone can inherit that much and the equality of opportunity is not disturbed. In transitional society, however, this minimum will tend toward zero since there will be poor people in the society who will receive none. On the other hand in the advanced technodemocratic society this limit may be quite high since the level of wealth of the individuals at the time of death will not be substantially different from one another. The main scientific rule here is that the inheritance should not disturb or go against the principle of equality of opportunity.

Prohibition of inheritance is very essential in a capitalistic society since it is by this way that a very substantial part of class stratification is eliminated. When wealthy individuals die their assets are transferred to the public treasury and from there they are gradually returned to the people as a whole either in the form of services or stocks.

It must be noted that the abolition of inheritance automatically eliminates all existing trust funds and other similar arrangements.

Without abolishing inheritance there cannot exist economic democracy and, as it has been demonstrated, without the latter there can be neither political nor social democracy. Abolition of inheritance is the very foundation of transition to technodemocratic economic system. Once inheritance and free transfer is prohibited the rest of democratization of the means of production and distribution will be just a matter of time as the assets are gradually transferred to the public treasury and from there to the workers.

2. Nationalization of the major means of production and distribution by paying just compensation to the owners as determined by the government within a short but determined period of time.

Actually, it does not matter how much compensation is paid for these means of production and distribution because unjust enrichment will be prohibited, in a few years upon the death of the receives their assets will return to the public treasury.

The nationalization process is for the purpose of accelerating the transfer of capital to the workers. Otherwise, the system can wait without nationalization. As the capitalist owners die their share of stocks goes to the public treasury and from there to the market, then gradually acquired by the companies, and transferred to the workers. This is not advisable since it will take much longer time for the transfer of ownership to the workers and will lengthen the period of transition.

3. Immediately after nationalization the process of gradual return of the ownership to the workers must be established and effectuated. To create incentive and a sense of ownership, about one-third of the assets had to be transferred to the workers at once based on the length of service.

Initially after the nationalization, the government will own a substantial percentage of the stock of various major firms. This situation will continue for several years until the capital is gradually transferred to the workers. This government ownership will be beneficial since it will provide funds for the expenditures necessary for the initiation and continuation of the transition. Two of the major expenditures will be providing for free education and health care. Also, by sharp reduction in national and state bureaucracies there will be need to provide employment for quite a large number of ex-government employees. If no other way of employment is possible then the concept of shared opportunity will be used to provide employment for public employees becoming unemployed.

4. The amount of gradual monthly return of capital to the workers should be calculated according to the method presented before so that the annual return from its accumulation in about 30 years will be enough to provide for a convenient old age living standard.

5. After nationalization of the major means of production and distribution and immediately after the initial transfer of 30 percent of assets to the workers in the nationalized firms, the nationalization of lesser firms will take place in several stages starting with the largest and moving down to the smallest.

Again, it must be noted that the compensation paid to the owners of the nationalized firms will eventually return to the public treasury as these owners pass away.

Transferring of nationalized assets to the owners of each pertinent firm will follow the same procedure. About thirty percent will be transferred initially and the rest gradually.

The assets of much smaller enterprises which may not be nationalized on time will go to public treasury as soon as the owners or its shareholders die. This does not mean that these enterprises will cease functioning upon the death of their owners. Only the ownership will be transferred temporarily to the public hand and from there to the workers of each enterprise as prescribed above. The enterprises will continue to operate.

6. In the period of transition, there will be workers who will retire without being able to accumulate enough capital to provide for post-retirement living expenses. They will have some capital accumulated and will receive return from it, the balance will be paid from retirement trust funds of the previous enterprises and available social security funds and if necessary from the public consumption fund. This situation is of course temporary.

Another choice is that after nationalization a major part of the assets be transferred to the workers based on the length of service according to the formula presented in this study. The remaining part of the assets will be then transferred monthly as prescribed by the formula. By this way a person having 30 years of service and retiring will have enough return from his accumulated capital to sustain him. In this case all retirement funds of the firms will revert and added to the assets of the corresponding firm in the form of stocks to be transferred to the workers in the future. This method seems much less burdensome, less bureaucratic, and less costly. However, since more shares will be initially transferred to the workers, the initial revenues of the government from the ownership of the rest may diminish substantially. This may produce certain shortage of funds necessary for the period of transition.

7.   Elimination of profits will be the last stage and will be accomplished fully once all the national assets are transferred from the capitalist class to the workers.   Since there will be no capitalist, there will be no exploitation of the labor, no social surplus and consequently no profits in traditional capitalist concept.   However, under a monopoly capitalism where the market prices can be arranged and rearranged, an additional profit comes not from the exploitation of workers but that of the consumers.   this part of the profit will also be gradually eliminated as the giant corporations and conglomerates disappear by automatic decentralization of the production firms and change in the attitudes of the working class as a result of advanced education.

8.   Providing for full employment will be a big problem during the transition period.   A large sector of the government bureaucracy will become unemployed as many governmental agencies are discarded including all regulatory agencies; all agencies dealing with entitlement programs, social security, and subsidies; and all major departments except defense and state (foreign affairs).   There will be over a million federal employees losing their jobs and about twice as many at the state level.   Initially, only the number of local government employees will increase.

All these unemployment problems will be resolved through the application of the concept of shared opportunity.   All unemployed workers will be placed within the production system according to their qualifications and experience.   It may be required to reduce the weekly work hours of some workers to provide employment for some others.   Every worker will benefit the same from work opportunities and will lose some income as it may be required to maintain equality of opportunity for all and sustain full employment.

It should be noted that the term of worker applies to anyone who works including the management and professional employees such as lawyers and physicians.   Equality of opportunity requires that all opportunities be shared without exception.

9.   Position classification is an important step toward democratization and equalization of the work system.   It is one of the things to be initiated and fully developed during the early stage of transition.

In the United States it requires the modification and further expansion of the national position classification by using the existing classifications within the major firms. This will not be a difficult thing since all these are computerized and after combining these, the computer will do most of what is required to establish a national position classification framework. The individual firms will be required to do their own detailed classifications within the framework established by the national government. Since all the firms use computers in the United States, the government supervision of position classification done by individual firms will be simple once their computers are hooked into the national system, the Technodem. the doctrine of equality of opportunity requires the same compensation for positions with similar responsibility.

10. Establishment of the Technodem is another prime concern in the stage of transition. The Technodem is a substantial step toward establishing a technodemocratic economic system and great facilitator of the process. In the United States as ell as the Western European countries nearly all the components for establishing the Technodem are present. First, the government itself has a sophisticated system of information and communication. Second, each giant firm has its own computerized information system often expanding beyond the national boundaries. Third,nearly all middle level and smaller firms use computers extensively and have their own electronic information system. What is needed is to bring all these systems under one by connecting them together systematically under a centralized method presented in this study.

First, after nationalization of the giant firms, the government will have access to their vast electronic information-communication systems. Combining these with those of the government will form the main body of the Technodem. Second, as the lesser firms become nationalized, their systems will also be hooked to the national system. Third, all this centralization by no means implies that the government gets the ownership and control of these vast information systems. Each system remains under full control of the corresponding firm but hooked to the Technodem. The same applies to the government's systems. In fact all the firms and public agencies lose exclusive control of their information. All the information becomes accessible to anyone with a computer terminal. Forth, after these initial steps when a vast array of useful information including marketing and purchasing becomes available to the consumers through the Technodem, all the firms and personal terminals will be voluntarily hooked to the Technodem. In a few years the system will refine itself as the most important instrument in materializing and maintaining the technodemocratic economic system. Democracy then will expand further to political and social spheres of life.

## The Less Developed Countries

The advanced global electronic and satellite communication systems make possible to less developed countries to connect their electronic information systems to those more advanced. They become continually and extensively informed of developments and changes that take place in the advanced societies. The result is enormous rising expectations and ensuing desire to catch up with the advanced societies through the acceleration of socio-economic and political development processes.

There are several impediments for establishing a technodemocratic economic system in less developed countries. Among these, two problems are the most significant. First, there is a high level of general illiteracy and quite low level of education and lack of corresponding educational means. Second, there is a quite low level of technological development. Because of the latter, these societies must be initially directed toward democratic economy which is quite distinct from the technodemocratic economy. At the same time, they must be guided toward technological development as more advanced technologies are introduced, adopted, and incorporated into the system.

The first fundamental question to be answered would be: Should the road chosen for transition need to be democratic or some specific kind of authoritarianism? Can democracy materialize in an overwhelmingly illiterate society? The experience for certain shows a direct relationship between literacy and democracy. Democracy requires an informed and conscious society which can be materialized only through proper education.

There are also other essential and particular issues which must be decided based on the conditions of literacy and the level of technological development within each specific society. For example, the transitional system chosen for South Korea or Taiwan needs to be quite different from the one aimed for Saudi Arabia or Nigeria. Furthermore, it is of no question that traditional ways of life prevail in many of the less developed countries. Accordingly, recommendations presented here for the process of transition are in general terms. They may require substantial adjustments and rearrangements in order to become applicable to each particular societal setting.

The stage of transition for the less developed countries is much more prolonged, burdensome, and complex. It must be noted that many of these countries are still at the stage of feudalism or early capitalism. Under the ordinary process of development, they are to move into stage of capitalism, then to democratic socialism, and from there to technodemocratic economic system. By implementing an accelerated process of transition from feudalism to technodemocratic system they must shortcut the process of normal development by attempting to bypass the stages of capitalism and socialism in order to reach the stage of technodemocratic economy.

This will be a rocky road with innumerable obstacles. There is already a good example of such experimentation which has ended in failure. Leninism attempted to move from feudalism to communism by attempting to shortcut the distance by bypassing the stage of capitalism and proceed toward the highly advanced technodemocratic communistic system and a classless, stateless society.

There is no question that this experimentation, despite it past failure to achieve its goal, provides opportunity for research and studying of the seventy-year transitional process, with an attempt toward discovering the causes of failure and learning of lessons from the experimentation. Such studies and findings might prove fruitful to less developed countries which have the intention of establishing and implementing accelerated development plans that will bypass the stage of capitalism, coming directly into democratic socialism and from there to technodemocratic economic system.

It has been already presented that the initial establishment of a democratic system in a less developed country is impossible because of the lack of elements required for the operation of such system. A certain kind of guided system, until the appearance and establishment of the instruments of democracy, is needed for the sole purpose of democratization of the society.

This, as a matter of fact, will be a certain kind of authoritarian, not necessarily dictatorial, system. The question will be: first what kind of authoritarian system should be chosen for the initial period of transformation and transition? Second, what would be the nature and duration of such system before democracy is installed?

One lesson to be learned from the past experiences is that the nature of authoritarianism must allow room for and foster democratic norms such as freedom of speech and expression. It must place prime importance on democratic education and education for democracy. It must recognize that this is a transitory stage and authoritarianism has been chosen for the sole purpose of providing ground for democracy and systematically accelerating socio-economic and political democratization processes.

Such system, if properly employed, will stay in power only for a few years, until the concept of equality of opportunity is understood by the people and its implementation in socio-economic spheres has substantially advanced. By this time, the population has become sufficiently educated in democratic process and can take charge of the political system as well and move forward. Apparently, Lenin had this kind of authoritarianism in mind and saw appropriate placing the full responsibility for transformation in the hands of the country's small group of intellectuals. However, the idea was not followed in practice and was totally abandoned by Stalin. Less developed countries contemplating an accelerated transformation to democratic economy should learn the lessons from this valuable experimentation in order to avoid repeating its mistakes. They must always keep in mind that the purpose of every plan, every move is to approach the state of democratic economy.

Within the bounds of this authoritarianism, democracy must be always kept in mind. No governmental action must be inhibitive of moving toward socio-economic democracy. The establishing of a socio-economic democracy must be the sole purpose of the government.

## Steps Required for Transition

All ten steps suggested for the transition of a capitalistic society to technodemocratic economic system are recommended also for the process of transition in less developed countries. However, proper adjustments must be made based on the specific socio-economic conditions of each particular country. It is obvious that steps requiring high technology must be postponed or be proceeded by slower pace. The Technodem will be the last to be developed.

In less developed countries the emphasis must be on establishing a democratic economy rather than a technodemocratic one. The prime and initial attention must be fully devoted to understanding and application of the principle of equality of opportunity in the socio-economic spheres. As it has been presented in the text that economic democracy is the heart of democracy. All other aspects of democracy depends on the success of economic democracy.

# Bibliography

## Books

Adams, Henry. *Democracy*. New York: NAL Penguin, Inc., 1983.

Adams, Richard M. *Energy and Structure: A Theory of Social Power*. Austin: University of Texas Press, 1985.

Akin, William E. *Technocracy and the American Dream: The Technocrat Movement, 1900-1941*. Berkeley: University of California Press, 1977.

American Academy of Arts and Sciences. *Appropriate Technology and Social Values*. Ballingers: AAA and S, 1980.

Amin, Samir. *Accumulation on a World Scale*. New York: Monthly Review Press, 1972.

——. *Imperialism and Unequal Development*. New York: Monthly Review Press, 1977.

Anderson, Walt. *A Place of Power: The American Episode in Human Evolution*. Santa Monica, California: Goodyear, 1976.

Arendt, Hannah. *The Human Condition*. Chicago: University of Chicago Press, 1970.

Atkinson, A. B. *The Economics of Inequality*. New York: Oxford University Press, 1975.

Bachrach, Peter. *The Theory of Democratic Elitism*. Boston: Little, Brown, 1967.

Baran, Paul A., and Paul M. Sweezy. *Monopoly Capital: An Essay on the American Economic and Social Order*. New York: Monthly Review Press, 1966.

Barker, Sir Ernest, ed. *Social Contract: Essays by Locke, Hume, and Rousseau*. London: Oxford University Press, 1981.

Bauer, P. T. *Equality, the Third World, and Economic Delusion*. Cambridge, Massachusetts: Harvard University Press, 1981.

Bell, Daniel. *The Coming of Post-Industrial Society.* New York: Basic Books, 1973.
——. *The Cultural Contradictions of Capitalism.* 2nd ed. Eexeter, New Hampshire: Heinemann Educational Books, 1979.
Bellamy, Edward. *Looking Backward 2000-1887.* New York: Modern Library, 1951.
Bentham, Jeremy B. *Principles of Legislation.* 1802.
Bereano, Phillip L. *Technology as a Social and Political Phenomenon.* New York: Wiley, 1976.
Bernard, H. russell. *Technology and Social Change.* New York: Macmillan, 1972.
Bernstein, Eduard. *Evolutionary Socialism.* Translated by E. C. Harvey-B. W. Huebsch, New York: 1909.
Berry, Brian. *The Human Consequences of Urbanization.* New York: St. Martin, 1974.
Bettelheim, Charles. *Economic Calculation and Forms of Property: An Essay on the Transition Between Capitalism and Socialism.* New York: Monthly Review Press, 1974.
Biddle, Derek. *Human Aspects of Management.* Brookfield, Vermont: Renouf, 1981.
Blumberg, Paul. *Inequality in an Age of Decline.* New York: Oxford University Press, 1980.
Bock, Kenneth. *Human Nature and History: A Response to Sociobiology.* New York: Columbia University Press, 1980.
Bookchin, M. *The Ecology of Freedom.* Palo Alto, California: Chesire Books, 1982.
——. *Post-Scarcity Anarchism.* Berkley: Ramparts, 1980.
Borchert, Donald M., and David Steward (eds.). *Being Human in a Technological Age.* Athens: Ohio University Press, 1979.
Braverman, Harry. *Labor and Monopoly Capital: The Degradation of Work in the Twentieth Century.* New York: Monthly Review Press, 1976.
Bork, Alfred. *Learning with Computers.* Bedford, Massachusetts: Digital Press, Educational Services, Digital Equipment Corporation, 1981.
Bretton, H. L. *The Power of Money.* New York: State University of New York Press, 1980.
Brown, Bruce. *Marx, Freud, and the Critique of Everyday Life: Toward a Permanent Cultural Revolution.* New York: Monthly Review Press, 1972.
Bruce-Briggs, B. *The New Class.* New Brunswick, New Jersey: Transaction Books, 1979.
Buchanan, James M. *Democracy in Deficit.* San Diego, California: Academic Press, 1977.
Burke, John G. *The New Technology and Human Values.* Belmont, California: Wadsworth Pub., 1967.
Burke, John G., and Marshall C. Eakin. *Technology and Change.* San Francisco: Boyd and Fraser, 1979.
Burnham, James. *The Managerial Revolution.* Bloomington: Indiana University Press, 1960.
Calhoun, John C. *Disquisition on Government.* Columbia, South Carolina: State Printing, 1851.

Callenbach, Ernest. *Ecotopia.* New York: Bantam, 1977.

Caraellil, M. Dino and John G. Morris (eds.) European Colloquy for Directors of National Research Institute in Education. *Equality of Opportunity Reconsidered: Values in Education for Tomorrow.* Netherlands: Swets and Zeitinger, 1979.

Carnoy, Martin, and Derek Sheafer. *Economic Democracy: The Challenge of the 1980s.* White Plains, New York: Middle East Sharpe, 1980.

Chapman, G.P. *Human and Environmental Systems: A Geographer's Appraisal.* New York: Academic Press, 1978.

Chester, Robert. *Equalities and Inequalities in Family Life.* San Diego: Academic Press, 1978.

Clecak, Peter. *Crooked Paths: Reflections on Socialism, Conservatism, and the Welfare State.* New York: Harper and Pow, 1977.

——. *Radical Paradoxes: dilemmas of the American Left, 1945-1970.* New York: Harper and Row, 1974.

Clontz, R. C., and E. K. Tarlow. *Equal Credit Opportunity Manual.* 3rd ed. New York: Warren, Graham and Lamont, 1980.

Cnudde, Charles F. and Deane E. Neubauer. *Empirical Democratic Theory.* Chicago: Markham, 1969.

Cochran, Thomas C. *Social Change in Industrial Society: Twentieth Century America.* London: St. Anthony's Press, 1972.

Coggin, P. A. *Technology and Man.* Oxford: Pergamon Press, 1978.

Cohen, Carl. *Communism, Fascism, and Democracy.* 2nd ed. New York: Random House, 1972.

Cohen, Marshall. *Equality and Preferential Treatment.* Princeton, New Jersey: Princeton University Press, 1976.

Coleman, James S. *Equality of Educational Opportunity.* Totowa, New Jersey: Littlefield, 1973.

Commoner, Barry. *Poverty of Power.* New York: Knopf, 1976.

Conley, Patrick T. *Democracy in Decline.* Providence: rhode Island Publications in Society, 1977.

Coser, Lewis A., and Irving Howe, eds. *The New Conservatives: A Critique from the Left.* New York: New American Library, 1977.

Curti, Merle. *Human Nature in American Thought: A History.* Madison: University of Wisconsin Press, 1980.

Coulter, P. *Social Mobilization and Liberal Democracy.* Lexington: Lexington Books, 1975.

Croley, Herbert. *The Promise of American Life.* Hamden, Connecticut: Anchor Books, 1914.

Daniels, Norman, ed. *Reading Rawls.* New York: Basic, 1975.

Davis Gregory H. *Technology: Humanism or Nihilism: A Critical Analysis of the Philosophical Basis and Practice of Modern Technology.* Lanham, Missouri: University Press of America, 1981.

Davis, William, and Allison McCormack. *The Information Age.* Reading, Massachusetts: Addison Wesley Publishing Company, 1979.

DeNevers, Noel, ed. *Technology and Society.* Reading, Massachusetts:

Addison Wesley Publishing Company, 1972.

Denitch, Bodgan, ed. *Democratic Socialism: The Mass Left in Advanced Industrial Societies.* Allanheld: Osmun and Company, 1981.

DeVore, Paul W. *Technology: An Introduction.* Worcester, Massachusetts: Davis Publications, Inc., 1980.

Diggins, John P. *The Bard of Savagery: Thorstein Veblen and Modern Social Theory.* New York: Continuum, 1978.

Dizard, Wilson T., Jr. *The Coming Information Age.* 2nd ed. New York: Longman, 1985.

Doel, Hans Van Den. *Democracy and Welfare Economics.* Cambridge, Massachusetts: Cambridge University Press, 1979.

Dolbeare, Patricia, and Jane Hadley. *American Ideologies: The Competing Political Beliefs of the 1970s.* ed. Chicago: Rand, 1973.

Dolota, T. A. *Data Processing in 1980-1985.* New York: Wiley, 1986.

Dorsey, Gray. *Equality & Freedom, International and Comparative Jurisprudence: Papers of the World Congress on Philosophy of Law and Social Philosophy.* Dobbs Ferry, New York: Oceana Publications, 1977.

Douglas, Jack D., ed. *The Technological Threat.* Englewood Cliffs, New Jersey: Prentice-Hall 1971.

Drucker, Peter. *Technology, Management and Society.* New York: Harper and Pow, 1977.

Drucker, P. F., and others. *Power and Democracy in America.* Westport, Connecticut: Greenwood Press, 1980.

Dudek, Louis. *Technology and Culture.* New York: New American Library, 1975.

Dumbauld, Edward, ed. *The Political Writings of Thomas Jefferson.* New York: Liberal Arts Press, 1955.

Dunn, Peter D. *Appropriate Technology: Technology with a Human Face.* New York: Schocken Books, 1978.

Durbin, E. F. M. *The Politics of Democratic Socialism.* London: Routledge and Kegan Paul, 1940.

Dye, Thomas R. *Who's Running America? The Conservative Years.* 4 ed. Englewood Cliffs, New Jersey: Prentice-Hall, 1986.

Edison Centennial Symposium, 1979. *Science, Technology, and the Human Prospect.* Elmsford, New York: Pergamon Press, 1980.

Edmunds, Stahrl W. *Alternate U.S. Futures.* Santa Monica, California: Goodyear, 1978.

Edwards, Richard C., Michael Reich, and Thomas E. Weisskopf. *The Capitalist System.* 3 ed. Englewood Cliffs, New Jersey: Prentice-Hall, 1986.

Ellul, Jacques. *The Technological Foundation of Law.* New York: Seabury Press, 1969.

———. *The Technological Society.* Translated by John Wilkinson. New York: Knopf, 1964.

———. *The Technological System.* Translated by Joachim Neugroschel. New York: Seabury Press, 1980.

Elsner, Henry, Jr. *The Technocrats: Prophets of Automation.* Syracuse, New York:

Syracuse University Press, 1967.

Encel, Solomon. *Equality and Authority*. London: Tavistock Publications, 1970.

Etzioni, Amitai. *Technological Shortcuts to Social Change*. New York: Russell Sage, 1973.

Eulan, Heinz. *Technology and Civilization*. Stanford, California: Hoover Institute Press, 1977.

Feinberg, Walter. *Equality and Social Policy*. Champaign: University of Illinois Press, 1978.

Feldman, Anthony. *Technology at Work*. New York: Facts on File, 1980.

Ferkiss, Victor. *The Future of Technological Civilization*. New York: Braziller, 1974.

——. *Technological Man: the Myth and the Reality*. New York: Braziller, 1969.

Fields, G. S. *Poverty, Inequality, and Development*. Cambridge, Massachusetts: Cambridge University Press, 1980.

Forbes, F. W. *Technology and Utilization Ideas for the 70's and Beyond*. San Diego, California: American Astronautical Society, 1970.

Forcey, Charles. *The Crossroad of Liberalism: Croly, Weyl, Lippmann and the Progressive Era 1900-1925*. New York: Oxford University Press, 1961.

Freedman, Robert. *The Marxist System: Economic, Political, and Social Perspectives*. Chatham, New Jersey: Chatham House Publishers, 1990.

Fried, Jacob. *Technological and Social Change*. Princeton, New Jersey: Petrocelli, 1979.

Friedman, Milton. *Capitalism and Freedom*. Chicago: University of Chicago Press, 1962.

Fromm, Erich. *Revolution of Hope: Toward a Humanized Technology*. New York: Harper and Row, 1974.

Fuller, R. Buckminster. *Utopia or Oblivion*. New York: Overlook Press, 1969.

Galbraith, John K. *The New Industrial State*. 3rd ed. Boston: Houghton-Mifflin, 1978.

Garvin, A. P. *How to Win with Information or Lose without It*. Washington, D.C.: Bermont Books, 1980.

Gehlin, Arnold. *Man in the Age of Technology*. Translated by Patricia Lipscomb. Irvington, New York: Columbia University Press, 1980.

Gendron, Bernard. *Technology and the Human Condition*. New York: St. Martin, 1977.

Gibbs, Jack P. *Sociological Theory Construction*. Hinsdale, Illinois: Dryden, 1972.

Goddard, J. B., and A. T. Thwaites. *Technological Change in the Inner City*. London: Social Science Research Council, 1980.

Gold, Bela. *Technological Change: Economics, Management & Environment*. Elmsford, New York: Pergamon Press, Inc., 1975.

Goodman, Paul. *The New Reformation and Notes of a Neolithic Conservative*. New York: Random House, 1970.

Goodpaster, K. E., and K. M. Sayre, eds. *Ethics and Problems of the 21st Century*. Notre Dame, Indiana: University of Notre Dame Press, 1979.

Graham, Otis L. *Toward a Planned Society: From Roosevelt to Nixon*. New York:

Oxford University Press, 1977.

Gray, Francine du Plessix. *Divine Disobedience: Profiles in Catholic Radicalism.* New York: Random House, 1971.

Green, Thomas H. *Liberal Legislation and Freedom of Contract.* 1880.

Guerin, Daniel. *Anarchism: From Theory to Practice.* New York: Monthly Review Press, 1971.

Gurwitch, Aron. *Human Encounters in the Social Work.* Pittsburgh: Duquesne University Press, 1971.

Gutmann, Amy. *Liberal Equality.* Cambridge, Massachusetts: Cambridge University Press, 1980.

Gutman, Herbert. *Work, Culture and Society in Industrializing America.* New York: Random House, 1977.

Haksar, Vinit. *Equality, Liberty and Perfectionism.* Oxford: Oxford University Press, 1979.

Hale, Matthew, Dr. *Human Science and Social Order.* Philadelphia, Pennsylvania: Temple University Press, 1980.

Hamilton, David. *Technology, Man and the Environment.* London: Faber, 1973.

Hammond, Kenneth R. *Human Judgment and Decision Making.* New York: Praeger, 1980.

Hansot, Elizabeth. *Perfection and Progress: Two Modes of Utopian Thought.* Cambridge, Massachusetts: MIT Press, 1974.

Harrington, Michael. *Socialism.* New York: Dutton, 1972.

——. *The Twilight of Capitalism.* New York: Simon and Schuster, 1977.

Harris, Anthony B. *Human Measurement.* New York: Heinemann Ed., 1978.

Hartz, Louis. *The Liberal Tradition in America.* New York: Harcourt Brace Jovanovich, 1962.

Hayek, Freidrich A. *Constitution of Liberty.* Chicago: University of Chicago Press, 1960.

——. *Road to Serfdom.* Chicago: University of Chicago Press, 1949.

——. *Social Justice Socialism and Democracy.* Terramurse, Australia: Center of Independent Studies, 1979.

Heilbroner, Robert L. *An Inquiry into the Human Prospect.* New York: W. W. Norton, 1974.

Henkin, Alice H. *Human Dignity.* New York: Aspen Institute for Humanistic Studies, 1978.

Herrington, Michael. *Socialism.* New York: Dutton, 1972.

——. *The Twilight of Capitalism.* New York: Simon and Schuster, 1977.

Hess, Karl. *Community Technology.* New York: Harper and Row, 1979.

Hetzler, Stanley A. *Technological Growth and Social Change.* New York: Praeger, 1969.

Hickman, Larry, and Azizah Al-Hibri, eds. *Technology and Human Affairs.* St. Louis: Mosby, 1981.

Hobhouse, Leonard T. *Liberalism.* London: Oxford University Press, 1911.

Hodges, Wayne. *Technological Changes and Human Development.* Ithaca, New York: ILR Publications, 1970.

## 344 / Technodemocratic Economic Theory

Holoein, Martin O. *Computers and Their Societal Impact.* New York: Wiley, 1977.

Howard University. Institute for the Study of Educational Policy. *Equal Education Opportunity.* Washington, D.C.: Howard University Press, 1978.

Hughes, John F. *Equal Education.* Bloomington: Indiana University Press, 1973.

Hunt, G., ed. *Writings of James Madison.* New York: G. P. Putman, 1910.

Hurst, Charles E. *The Anatomy of Social Inequality.* St. Louis: Mosby, 1979.

Information Industry Association. *The Business of Information Report.* Washington, D.C.: Information Industry Association, 1981.

Jackman, Robert W. *Political and Social Equality: A Comparative Analysis.* New York: Wiley, 1975.

Jantsch, Reich. *Technological Planning and Social Futures.* London: Associated Business Programmers, 1974.

Joseph, Keith and Jonathan Sumpton. *Equality.* London: John Murray, 1979.

Judson, H. F. *The Search for Solutions.* New York: Holt, Rinehart and Winston, 1980.

Kanowitz, Leo. *Equal Rights: The Male Stake.* Albuquerque: University of New Mexico Press, 1981.

Kaplan, Max, and Phillip Bosserman, eds. *Technology, Human Value and Leisure.* Nashville: Abingdon Press, 1971.

Kariel, Henry. *The Decline of American Pluralism.* Stanford, California: Stanford University Press, 1961.

Kaufman, Arnold. *The Radical Liberal.* New York: Simon and Schuster, 1970.

Keating, T. J. *Politics, Technology, and the Environment.* New York: Arno Press, 1979.

Kheel, Theodore W. *Technological Change and Human Development: An International Conference.* Ithaca, New York: Cornell University, ILR Publications Division, 1970.

Knight, T. J. *Technology's Future: The Hague Congress Technology Assessment.* Melbourne, Florida: Robert E. Krieger Publishing Company, Inc., 1976.

Kolki, Gabriel. *Wealth and Power in America.* New York: Praeger, 1962.

Kozol, Jonathan. *Illiterate America.* Garden City, New York: Anchor Press/Doubleday, 1985.

Kranzberg, Melvin. *Technology and Culture.* New York: New American Library, 1975.

Kuhns, William. *The Post-Industrial Prophets: Interpretations of Technology.* New York: Weybright and Talley, 1971.

Kumar, Drishan. *Prophecy and Progress: The Sociology of Industrial and Post-Industrial Society.* New York: Penguin, 1978.

Laing, Neil F. *Technological Uncertainty and the Pure Theory of Allocation.* Bedford Park, Australia: Flinders University of South Australia, 1978.

Langone, John. *Human Engineering: Marvel or Menace?* Boston, Massachusetts: Little, 1978.

Lawless, Edward W. *Technology and Social Shock.* New Brunswick, New Jersey: Rutgers University Press, 1977.

Lecky, William E. H. *Democracy and Liberty.* Indianapolis, Indiana: Liberty Fund,

1896. Reprint, 1981.

Leiss, William. *The Domination of Nature.* New York: Braziller, George, Inc., 1972.

——. *The Limits of Satisfaction.* Toronto: University of Toronto Press, 1976.

Lenski, Gerhard. *Human Societies.* New York: McGraw-Hill, 1974.

Lerner, Daniel. *The Human Meaning of the Social Sciences.* Magnolia, Massachusetts: Peter Smith, n.d.

Lindsay, A. D. *The Essentials of Democracy.* Oxford: Claredon Press, 1929.

Locke, John. *Second Treatise of Government.* London: Thomas Tegg, 1823.

Loscerbo, J. *Being and Technology: A Study in the Philosophy of Martin Heideger.* Boston: Klurver, 1982.

Lothstein, Arthur, ed. *The Philosophy of the New Left.* New York: Putnam, 1975.

Lovings, Amory. *Soft Energy Paths: Toward a Durable Peace.* Cambridge, Massachusetts: Ballinger Publications, 1977.

McDonald, J. Ramsay. *Parliament and Democracy.* Manchester, England: National Labour Press, 1920.

Machlup, Fritz. *The production and Distribution of Knowledge.* Princeton, New Jersey: Princeton University Press, 1962.

MacPherson, C. B. *The Political Theory of Possessive Individualism: Hobbs to Locke.* New York: Oxford University Press, 1962.

McKinlay, John b. *Technology and the Future of Health Care.* Cambridge, Massachusetts: MIT Press, 1981.

McNeill, William H. *The Human condition: An Ecological and Historical View.* Princeton, New Jersey: Princeton University Press, 1980.

Mae Kay, Donald. *Human Science and Human Dignity.* Downers Grove, Illinois: Inter-Varsity, 1979.

Magdoff, Harry, and Paul M. Sweezy. *The Deepening Crisis of U.S. Capitalism.* New York: Monthly Review Press, 1981.

Marcuse, Hubert. *One Dimensional Man.* Boston: Beacon Press, 1964.

Martin, James. *Design of Man-Computer Dialogues.* Englewood Cliffs, New Jersey: Prentice-Hall, 1970.

Marx, Leo. *The Machine in the Garden: Technology and the Pastoral Ideal in America.* New York: Oxford University Press, 1967.

Masi, Dale A. *Human Services in Industry.* Lexington, Massachusetts: Lexington Books, 1981.

Mayo, Henry B. *An Introduction to Democratic Theory.* New York: Oxford University Press, 1960.

Meissner, Martin. *Technology and the Worker.* San Francisco: Chandler Publishing Company, 1969.

Miles, Rufus E., Jr. *Awakening from the American Dream: The Social and Political Limits to Growth.* New York: Universe Books, 1977.

Miliband, Ralph. *The State in Capitalist Society.* New York: Basic, 1978.

Mill, John Stuart. *Considerations on Representative Government.* New York: Harper, 1862.

Miller, A. R. *The Assault on Privacy.* Ann Arbor: University of Michigan Press,

1971.

——. *Democratic Dictatorship.* Greenwood Press, 1980.

Montgomery, John D. *Technology and Civic Life.* Cambridge, Massachusetts: MIT Press, 1974.

Moor, Wilbert E. *Technology and Social Change.* Chicago: Quadrangle Books, 1972.

Muedler, Eva. *Technological Advance in an Expanding Economy: Its Impact on a Cross-Section of the Labor Force.* Ann Arbor: University of Michigan, Institute for Social Research, 1969.

Mulford, Siblely. *Nature and Civilization: Some Implications for Politics.* Itasca, Illinois: University of Notre Dame Press, 1977.

Naidbitt, John. *Megatrends: The New Directions Transforming Our Lives.* New York: Basic Books, Inc., 1979.

Nash, George T. *The Conservative Intellectual Movement in American Since 1945.* New York: Basic Books, Inc., 1979.

NATO. *Advanced Study Institute on Perspectives in Information Science.* Leyden: Noordhoff, 1975.

Noble, David. *America by Design: Science, Technology and the Industrial Revolution.* New York: Knofp, 1977.

Nordliner, E. H. *On the Autonomy of the Democratic State.* Cambridge, Massachusetts: Harvard University Press, 1981.

Norman, C. *The God That Limps.* New York: W. W. Norton, 1981.

Nozick, Robert. *Anarchy, State and Utopia.* New York: Basic Books, Inc., 1974.

Odum, Howard D. *Environment, Power, and Society.* New York: Wiley, 1971.

Ogburn, William F. *Technology and the Changing Family.* Westport, Connecticut: Greenwood, 1976.

Ophuls, William. *Ecology and the Politics of Scarcity: Prologue to a Political Theory of the Steady State.* San Francisco: W. H. Freeman, 1977.

Parat, Marc Uri. *The Information Economy.* Washing, D.C.: Government Printing Office, 1977.

Parenti, Michael. *Democracy for the Few.* 4th ed. New York: St. martin's Press, 1983.

Parsons, Harold L., ed. *Marx and Engels on Ecology.* Westport, Connecticut: Greenwood Press, 1977.

Pascarella, Perry. *Technology—Fire in a Dark World.* New York: Nostrand Reinhold, 1979.

Pavitt, Keith. *Technical Innovation and British Economic Performance.* New York: Macmillan, 1981.

Phillips, Derek L. *Equality, Justice and Rectification: An Exploration in Normative Sociology.* London: Academic Press, 1979.

Pillans, T. Dundas, ed. *Forgo These Truths: Selections for the Speeches and Writings of the Right Hon. Edmund Burke.* London: Liberty Review Publishing Company, 1898.

Plamenatz, John. *Democracy and Illusion.* New York: Longman, 1977.

Preston, Ronald H., ed. *Technology and Social Justice.* 1st American ed. Valley

Forge: Judson Press, 1971.

Pyke, Magnus. *Our Future.* New York: Hamlin/America, 1980.

Quarles, Hohn. *Cleaning Up America.* Boston: Houghton-Mifflin, 1976.

Rae, D. W. *Equalities.* Cambridge, Massachusetts: Harvard University Press, 1981.

Rand, Ayn. *The New Left: The Anti-Industrial Revolution.* New York: New American Library, 1971.

Rescher, N. *Unpopular Essays on Technological Progress.* Pittsburgh, Pennsylvania: University of Pittsburgh Press, 1980.

Rezazadeh, Reza. *Technological Democracy: A Humanistic Philosophy of the Future Society.* New York: Vantage Press, 1990.

Rhodes, Harold V. *Utopia in American Political Thought.* Tucson: University of Arizona Press, 1967.

Rink, Evald. *Technical Americana.* Millwood, New York: Draus International, n.d.

Ritterbush, Phillip C. *Technology as Institutionally Related to Human Values.* Washington, D.C.: Acropolis, 1974.

Rosenblatt, Samuel M. *Technology and Economic Development.* Boulder, Colorado: Westview, 1979.

Ryan, W. *Equality.* New York: Random House, 1982.

Sanford, Charles L. *The Quest for Paradise: Europe and the American Moral Imagination.* Urbana: University of Illinois Press, 1961.

Schumacher, E. F. *A Guide for the Perplexed.* New York: Harper and Row, 1977.

——. *Small is Beautiful.* New York: Harper and Row, 1973.

Schumpeter, Joseph A. *Capitalism, Socialism, and Democracy.* New York: Harper and Row, 1950.

Schuster, Edward. *Human Rights Today: Evolution or Revolution.* New York: Philosophical Library, 1980.

Silver, Harold. *Equal Opportunity in Education.* New York: Methuen, Inc., 1979.

Sinai, I. Robert. *The Decadence of the Modern World.* Cambridge, Massachusetts: Schenkman, 1977.

Slusser, Dorothy M., and Gerald H. Slusser. *Technology—the God that Failed.* Philadelphia: Westminster Press, 1971.

Skinner, B. F. *Beyond Freedom and Dignity.* New York: Bantam, 1972.

Smith, D. M. *Where the Grass is Greener.* Baltimore, Maryland: John Hopkins University Press, 1982.

Smith, Sharon P. *Equal Pay in the Public Sector: Fact or Fantasy.* Princeton, New Jersey: Princeton University, Industrial Relations Section, Department of Economics, 1977.

Snyder, Gary. *The Old Ways.* San Francisco, California: City Lights, 1977.

Stafford, Beer. *Designing Freedom.* New York: John Wiley and Sons, 1974.

Stanley, Manfred. *The Technological Conscience.* Chicago: University of Chicago Press, 1981.

Steinfels, Peter. *The Neo-Conservatives: The Man Who are Changing America's Politics.* New York: Simon and Schuster, 1979.

Stover, Carl F., ed. *The Technological Order.* Detroit: Wayne State University Press, 1963.

Teich, Albert H. *Technology and Man's Future.* 4th ed. New York: St. Martin, 1986.

Thomas, Norman. *Democratic Socialism: A New Appraisal.* New York: League for Industrial Democracy, 1953.

Thrall, Charles A., and Jerold M. Starr, eds. *Technology, Power and Social Change.* Carbondale: Southern Illinois University Press, 1974.

Toynbee, Arnold. *Mankind and Mother Earth.* New York: Oxford University Press, 1976.

Usher, D. *The Economic Prerequisite to Democracy.* Boston: Columbia University Press, 1981.

Van Den Berghe, Peirre L. *Human Family Systems: An Evolutionary View.* Westport, connecticut: Greenwood, n.d.

Van Den Doel, Hans. *Democracy and Welfare Economics.* Cambridge, Massachusetts: Cambridge University Press, 1979.

Veblen, Thorstein. *The Engineers and the Price System.* New York: Kelley, 1944.

Walters, V. *Class Inequality and Health Care.* London: Croom Helm, 1980.

Watkins, Bruce O. *Technology and Human Values.* Woburn, Massachusetts: Ann Arbor Science, 1979.

Weale, Albert. *Equality and Social Policy.* Boston: Rougledge and Kegan, 1978.

Welhoit, F. M. *The Quest for Equality in Freedom.* New Brunswick, New Jersey: Transaction Books, 1979.

Westley, William A. *The Emerging Worker: Equality and Conflict in a Mass Consumption Society.* Downsview, Ontario: McGill-Queens University Press, 1971.

Weston, A. F. *Privacy and Freedom.* Bodley Head, 1967.

White House Conference on Library and Information Services, Washington D.C., 1979. *Information for the 1980's.* Washingotn, D.C.: Government Printing Office, 1980.

Wilensky, Harold I. *The Welfare State and Equality: Structural and Ideological Roots of Public Expenditures.* Berkley: University of California Press, 1975.

Wilson, H. B. *Democracy and the Workplace.* Montreal: Black Rose Books, 1974.

Winner, Langdon. *Autonomous Technology: Technics-Out-of-Control as a Theme in Political Thought.* Cambridge, Massachusetts: MIT Press, 1977.

Witte, J. F. *Democracy, Authority and Alienation in Work.* Chicago: University of Chicago Press, 1980.

Wolf, Alan. *The Limits of Legitimacy.* New York: Free Press, 1977.

Wolgast, E. H. *Equality and the Rights of Women.* Ithaca: Cornell University Press, 1980.

Wood, Clive. *Human Health and Environmental Toxicants.* New York: Grune, n.d.

# Articles and Documents

Ackoff, R. K. "Management Information Systems." *Management Science 14* (1967), B147-B156.

Allen, William R. "Scarcity and Order: The Hobbesian Problem and the Human Resolution." *Social Science Quarterly 57* (1976), 263-275.

Anderson, Odin W. "Wisconsin: 2000 A.D." *On Wisconsin* (April 1987), 1.

Arato, A. C. Castoriadis. "From Marx to Aristotle, from Aristotle to Us." *Social Science Research 45* (Winter 1978), 667-738.

Archibald, W. P. "Face to Face: The Alienating Effects of Class, Status and Power Divisions." *American Sociological Review 41* (October 1976), 819-837.

Artandi, Susan. "Man, Information and Society: New Patterns of Interaction." *Journal of American Society for Information Science 30* (January 1979), 16.

Barry, B. "Political Accommodation and Consociational Democracy: Review Article."
*British Journal of Political Science 5* (October 1975), 477-505.

Basche, James. "Information Protectionism, Across the Border." *Conference Board 20* (September 1983), 38-44.

Bell, Daniel. "The Social Framework of the Information Society." in *The Computer Age: A Twenty-Year View,* eds. Michael L. Dertouzos and Joel Moses.
Cambridge, Massachusetts: MIT Press, 1979, 163-211.

Benn, A. W. "Democracy in the Age of Science." *Political Quarterly 50* (January 1979), 7-23.

Bentham, Jeremy. "Of the Principle of Utility." *In Communism, Fascism, and Democracy* ed. Carl Cohen. 2nd ed. (New York: Random House, 1972), 443-445.

Berkeley, Alfred R. "Millionaire Machine." *Datamation 24* (August 1981), 21-22.

Beum, Robert. "The Old Regimes and the Technological Society." *Journal of Politics 37* (November 1975), 937-954.

Bhatta, Charya D. "Development and Technology in the Third World." *Journal of Contemporary Asia 6*, no. 3 (1976), 314-322.

Bilson, J. F. D. "Civil Liberty—an Econometric Investigation.: *Kylos 1*, no. 35 (1982), 94-114.

Birch, A. H. "Some Reflections on American Democratic Theory." *Political Studies 23* (June/September 1975), 225-231.

Bollen, Kenneth A. "Issues in the Comparative Measurement of Political Democracy." *American Sociological Review 45* (June 1980), 370-399.

———. "Political Democracy and the Timing of Development." *American Sociological Review 44* (August 1979), 572-587.

Boulding, Kenneth E. "The Stability of Inequality." *Review of Social Economy 33*, no. 1 (April 1975), 1-14.

Bowles, Samuel, and Herbert Gintis. "The Crisis of Liberal Democratic Capitalism: The Case of the United States.: *Politics and Society 1* (1982), 51-93.

Brosnan, Peter. "Who Owns the Networks?" *Nation* (November 25, 1978), 561, 577-579.

Brown, Lynn E. "High Technology and Business Services." *New England Economic Review* (July-August 1983), 5-17.

Brown, S. R. "Foreign Technology and Economic Growth." *Problems of Communism 26* (July 1977), 30-40.

Budd, Edward C. "Postwar Changes in the Size of Distribution of Income in the

# 350 / Technodemocratic Economic Theory

United States." *American Economic Review* 60 (May 1970), 247-260.

Camiller, P., and H. Weber. "Euro-Communism, Socialism, and Democracy." *New Left Review*, no. 110 (July 1978), 3-14.

Campine, Benjamin. "The Evolution of the 'New Literacy.'" *National Forum*, no. 3 (Summer 1983), 10-12.

Chapman, John W., John C Harsanyi, Vernon Van Dyke, James Fishkin, Douglas Rae, Allan Bloom, and Benjamin R. Barker. "Justice: A Spectrum of Responses to John Rawls's Theory." *American Political Science Review* 69 (1975), 588-674.

Coleman, J. S. "Inequality, Sociology, and Moral Philosophy." *American Journal of Sociology* 80 (November 1974), 739-764.

Council of American Library Association, San Francisco, California. *Council Document No. 71.2*, (July 1, 1981).

Cummings, Martin M. "Medical Information Services: For Public Good or Private Profit?" *Information Society Journal* 1, no. 3 (1982), 249-260.

Cutright, Phillips. "Income Redistribution: A Cross-National Analysis." *Social Forces* 46 (December 1967), 180-190.

———. "Inequality: A Cross-National Analysis." *American Sociological Review* 32 (August 1967), 562-578.

Dahl, R. A. "On Removing Certain Impediments to Democracy in the United States." *Dissent* 25 (Summer 1978), 310-324. P. Green, "Reply with Rejoinder," 26 (Summer 1979), 351-368.

David, E. E., Jr. "On the Dimensions of the Technology controversy." *Daedalus* 109 (Winter 1980), 167-177.

Devall, William B. "Reformist Environmentalism." *Humboldt Journal of Social Science* 6 (1979), 129-158.

Devine, F. E., "Absolute Democracy or Indefeasible Right: Hobbes Versus Locke.: *Journal of Politics* 37 (August 1975), 736-768.

Dervin, Brenda. "Communication Gaps and Inequities." in Brenda Darvin and Mel Voigt, eds., *Progress in Communication Sciences*, vol. 2. Norwood, New Jersey: Ablex, 1980, 73-112.

———. "Mass Communicating: Changing Conceptions of the Audience." In William Paisley and Ronald Rice, eds., *Public Communications Campaigns*. Beverly Hills: Sage Publications, 1981, 71-88.

———. "More Will Be Less Unless: The Scientific Humanization of Information Systems: *National Forum* 63, no. 3 (1983), 25-26.

Dewey, John. "The Future of Liberalism." *Journal of Philosophy* 32, no. 9 (April 25, 1935).

Diamond, Martin. "The American Idea of Equality: The View from the Founding." *Review of Politics* 38 (July 1976), 313-331.

Dworkin, Ronald. "What is Equality? Part 1: Equality of Welfare." *Philosophy and Public Affairs* 10, no. 3 (Summer 1981), 185-246.

*Economist.* "How Much Technology?" *Economist* 261 (November 6, 1976), 102.

Egan, Jacques. "Publishing for the Future." *New York Times* (August 16, 1982), 10.

Ellul, Jacques. "The Technological Society." In Albert H. Teich, ed., *Technology and Man's Future*. 3rd ed. New York: St. Martin's Press, 1981, 40-62.

Encel, Sol, and Jarlath Ronayne, eds. "Conference on Science, Technology and Public Policy." *Science, Technology and Public Policy: An International Perspective.* Elmsford, New York Pergamon Books, 1979.

Enzenberger, Hans Magnus. "Constituents of a Theory of the Media." *New Left Review* 64 (November-December 190), 13-36.

Epstein, Nadine. "Et Viola! Le Minitel." *France Magazine*, nos. 4-5 (Summer 1986), 71 and 75.

Fave Della, L. R. "In the Structure of Egalitarianism." *Social Problems* 22 (December 1974), 199-213.

Ferkiss, Victor. "Christianity and the Fear of the Future." *Zygon* 10 (1975), 250-262.

——. "Man's Tools and Man's Choices: The Confrontation Between Political Science
and Technology." *American Political Science Review* 67 (1973), 973-980.

——. "The Pessimistic View of the Future." In Jib Fowles, Ed. *Handbook of Futures Research.* Westport, Connecticut: Greenwood Press, 1978.

——. "Post Industrial Society: Theory, Myth, Ideology." *Political Science Review*, 1981.

——. "Technology and Culture: Gnosticism, Naturalism, and Incarantional Integration." *Cross Currents* 30 (September 1980), 13-26.

——. "Technology Assessment and Appropriate Technology." *National Forum* 58 (1978), 3-7.

——. "Technology and American Political Thought: The Hidden Variable and the Coming Crisis." *Review of Politics* 42 (July 1980), 349-387.

Fliegle, F. C. "Comparative Analysis of the Impact of Industrialization on Traditional Values." Bibliography, *Rural Sociology* 41 (Winter 1976), 431-451.

*Fortune.* "A Cheap-Memory Chaser Pursues the 4,000 K Chip." *Fortune.* (May 16, 1983), 155.

Frisbie, W. P. "Measuring the Degree of Bureaucratization at the Societal Level." *Social Forces* 53 (June 1975), 536-573.

——. "Technology in Evolutionary and Ecological Perspective: Theory and Measurement at the Societal Level." *Social Forces* 58 (December 1979), 529-613.

Garrfield, Eugene. "Document-Delivery Systems in the Information Age." *National Forum* 63, no. 3 (Summer 1983), 8-10.

Gates, R. D., and A. St. Germain. "Interface '80—Humanities and Technology: Southern Technical Institute, Marietta, Georgia, October 23-24, 1980." *Technology and Culture* 22 (October 1981), 763-770.

Green, Philip, and Robert A. Dahl. "What is Political Equality?" *Dissent* 26 (Summer 1979), 352-368.

Grove, D. J. "Ethnic Socio-Economic Redistribution: A Cross-Cultural Study." *Comparative Politics* 12 (October 1979), 87-98.

Gruber, M. L. "Inequality in the Social Services." *Social Services Review* 54 (March 1980), 59-75.

Haas, E. B. "On Systems and International Regimes." *World Politics* 27 (January 1975), 147-179.

Hanes, D. "Democracy in the Service of Peace and Man." *World Marx Review* 19 (April 1976), 56-66.

Hanft, R. S., and J. Eechenholtz. "Regulating of Health Technology." *Academy of Political Science Proceddings* 4 (1980), 148-157.

Heilbroner, Robert. "The Human Prospect: Second Thoughts." *Futures* 7 (1975), 31-40.

Heise, D. G., G. Lenski, and J. Wardell. "Further Notes on Technology and the Moral Order." *Social Forces* 55 (December 1976), 326-337.

Heise, D. R., and G. W. Bohrnstedt. Validity, Invalidity, and Reliability." In Edgar F. Borgatta and George W. Bohrnstedt, eds., *Sociological Methodology*. San Francisco, California: Jossey-Bass, 1970.

Heller, Agnes. "Past, Present, and Future of Democracy." *Social Research* 45 (Winter 1978), 866-886.

Herz, J. H. "Technology, Ethics, and International Relations." *Social Research* 43 (Spring 1976), 98-113.

Hewitt, C. "Effect of Political Democracy on Equality in Industrial Societies: A Cross-national Comparison." *American Social Review* 42 (June 1977), 450-464. "Discussion," 44, 168-172; 45, 344-349 (February 1979, April 1980).

Hoivik, Tord. "Social Inequality—the Main Issues." *Journal of Peace Research* 7, no. 2 (1971), 119-141.

Horowitz, Irving Louis. "Printed Words, Computers, and Democratic Societies." *Virginia Quarterly Review* (Autumn 1983), 620-636.

Howe, I. "Seasons for Democracy." *Dissent* 21 (Fall 1974), 460-470.

Huskey, Harry D. "Computer Technology." *Annual Review of Information Science and Technology*, no. 5 (1970).

Hutchins, R. M. "Is Democracy Possible?" *Center Magazine* 9 (January 1976), 2-6.

Hyneman, Charles S. "Equality: Elusive Ideal or Beguiling Delusion?" *Modern Age* 24, no. 3 (Summer 1980), 226-237.

Inose, Hiroshi. "Social Benefits of Information Technology." *Economic Eye* (March 1985).

Iueller, D. C. "Constitutional Democracy and Social Welfare." *Quarterly Journal of Economics* 87 (February 1973), 60-80.

Jackman, R. W. "Political Democracy and Social Equality: A Comparative Analysis.: *American Sociological Review* 39 (February 1974), 29-45.

Jacobs, D. "Dimensions of Inequality and Public Policy in the States." *Journal of Politics* 42 (February 1980), 291-306.

Jacqz, Jane W. *Report on a Workshop on Technology Choices, Work, and Society's Future.* New York: Aspen Institute for Humanistic Studies, 1979.

Joannidis, Marie, and Jan Kristiansen. "Telecommunications: Its Irreversible Impact." *France Magazine*, nos. 4-5 (Summer 1986), 69-72.

Kellner, M. M. "Democracy and Civil Disobedience." *Journal of Politics* 37 (November 1975), 899-916.

Kelly, J., and H. S. Klein. "Revolution and the Rebirth or Inequality: A Theory of Stratification in Post-Revolutionary Society." *American Journal of Sociology* 83 (July 1977), 78-98.

Kent, A. K. "Scientific and Technical Publishing in the 1980s." In Phillip Hills, ed., *The Future of the Printed Word: The Impact and the Implications of the New Communications Technology.* Westport, Connecticut: Greenwood Press, 1980, 163-169.

Kishida, Junnosuke. "Civilized Society: In Search of New Forms." *Impact of Science on Society* 30, no. 2 (1980), 101-109.

Korek, Michael, and Ray Olszewski. "Telecom: The Winds of Change." *Datamation* 27 (May 1981).

Krolikouski, W. "Socialism and the Technological Revolution." *World Marx Review* 18 (September 1975), 44-51.

Laird, R. "Post-Industrial Society: East and West." *Survey* 21 (Autumn 1975), 1-17.

Lancaster, F. Wilfrid. "Electronic Publishing: Its Impact on the Distribution of Information." *National Forum* 63, no. 3 (Summer 1983), 3-5.

Lemos, R. M. "Moral Argument for Democracy." *Social Theory and Practice* 4 (Fall 1976), 57-74.

Levin, M. F. "Equality of Opportunity." *Philosophical Quarterly* 31 (April 1981), 110-125, 25-26.

Livingston, David, and Richard Masson. "Ecological Crisis and the Autonomy of Science in Capitalist Society: The Canadian Case Study." *Alternatives* 8 (1977) 3-19.

Lovins, Amory. "Energy Strategy: The Road Not Taken." *Foreign Affairs* 55 (1976), 65-96.

Lowenthal, R. "Social Transformation and Democratic Legitimacy." *Social Research* 43 (Summer 1976), 241-275.

Luhmann, N. "Future Cannot Begin: Temporal Structures in Modern Society." *Social Research* 43 (Spring 1976), 130-152.

Lukes, S. "Socialism and Equality." *Dissent* 22 (Spring 1975), 154-168.

Lustick, I. "Stability in Deeply Divided Societies: Consociationism Versus Control." *World Politics* 31 (April 1979), 325-344.

Maaranen, S. A. "Leo Strauss: Classical Political Philosophy and Modern Democracy." *Modern Age* 22 (Winter 1978), 47-53.

McBride, W. L. "Concept of Justice in Marx, Engels, and Others." *Ethics* 85 (April 1975), 204-218.

McDermott, John. "Technology: The Opiate of the Intellectuals." In Albert H. Teich, ed., *Technology and Man's Future.* 4th ed., New York: St Martin's Press, 1981, 95-121.

Madsen, D. "Structural Approach to the Explanation of Political Efficacy Levels Under Democratic Regimes." Bibliography, *American Journal of Political Science* 22 (November 1978), 867-883.

Malita, M. "Learning Processes in Man, Machine, and Society." *Impact of Science on Society* 27 (January 1977), 93-103.

Mankoff, Milton. "Toward Socialism: Reassessing Inequality." *Social Policy* 4 (March 1974), 20-31.

Margolis, J. "Political Equality and Political Justice." *Social Research* (Summer 1977), 308-329.

Meadows, Donald H., et al. "Technology and the Limits to Growth." In Donald H. Meadows and Others, *The Limits to Growth: A Report for the Club of Rome's Project on the Predicament of Mankind*, New York: Universe Books, 1972.

Mellors, Colin, and David Pollitt. "Legislation for Privacy: Data Protection in Western Europe." *Parliamentary Affairs* 37 (Spring 1984), 199-215.

Menninger, D. C. "Political Dislocation in a Technical Universe." *Review of Politics* 42 (January 1980), 73-91.

Miller, D. "Democracy and Social Justice." *British Journal of Sociology* 8 (January 1978), 1-19.

Miller, Herman P. "Inequality, Poverty, and Taxes." *Dissent* 22 (Winter 1975), 40-49.

Misra, Ramesh. "Welfare and Industrial Man: A Study of Welfare in Western Industrial Societies in Relation to a Hypothesis of Convergence." *Sociological Review* 21 (1973), 535-560.

Morison, Robert S. "Visions." In Albert H. Teich, ed. *Technology and Man's Future.* New York: St. Martin's Press, 1981, 7-22.

Mushra, R. "Technology and Social Structure in Marx's Theory: An Explanatory Analysis." *Science and Society* 43 (Summer 1979), 132-157.

Namus, Burt. "Restructuring the Information Ecology." *National Forum* 63, no. 3. (Summer 1983), 11-17.

National Commission on Libraries and Information Science. *Public Sector—Private Sector Interaction in Providing Information Services.* Washington, D.C.: Government Printing Office, 1982.

Neubauer, Deane E. "Some Conditions of Democracy." *American Political Science Review* 61 (December 1967), 1007-1009.

Nielson, K. "Impediments to Radical Egalitarianism." *American Philosophical Quarterly* 18 (April 1980), 121-129.

Nilles, J. M. "Opportunities and Threats from the Personal Computer." *Futures* 11 (April 1979), 172-176.

Nixon, C. R. "Equity, Identity, and Social Cleavage: Cross-cultural Perspectives.: *American Behavioral Scientists* 18 (Summer 1984), 4-14.

Noel, Mathilde. "The Phenomenon of Technology: Liberation or Alienation of Man." In E. Fromm, ed., *Socialist Humanism,* Garden City, New York: Doubleday, 1966, 334-346.

North, J. "Landscape of Equality." *Times Literary Supplement* 4088 (August 7, 1981), 903-904.

Owen, D. "Communism, Socialism and Democracy." *Atlantic Community Quarterly* 16 (Summer 1978), 154-166.

Painter, John H. "Approaching computer Based Education: How Will the University Respond?" *National Forum* no. 3 (Summer 1983), 20-22.

Pauly, David, and Carolyn Friday. "Computers Make the Sale." *Newsweek* (September 23, 1985), 46-47.

Peters, B. G. (and others). "Types of Democratic Systems and Types of Public Policy: an Empirical Examination." *Comparative Politics* 9 (April 1977), 327-355.

Pion, G. M., and M. W. Lipseg. "Public Attitudes Toward Science and Technology: What have the Surveys Told Us?" *Public Opinion Quarterly* 45 (Fall 1981), 303-316.

Piskinov, A. I. "The Soviet School and Soviet Pedagogy in the Period of the Competition of Socialist construction and Gradual Transition to Communism." *Soviet Education* (February-March 1978), 106-194.

Pyatt, G. "On International Comparisons of Inequality." *American Economic Review: Papers and Proceedings* 67 (February 1977), 71-75.

Raman, N. P. "Devising and Introducing Technology to Aid the Poorest." *Internal Development Review* 18, no. 3 (1976), 8-11.

Ramawamy, G. S. "Transfer of Technology Among Developing Countries." *International Development Review* 18, no. 3 (1976), 7-10.

Ranetz, J. R. "Science and Technology as Promise and Threat: The Scale and Complexity of the Problem." *Ecumenical Review* 31 (October 1979), 364-371.

Rickson, R. E. "Knowledge Management in Industrial Society and Environmental Quality." *Human Organization* 35 (Fall 1976), 239-251.

Robertson, Lawrence S. and Robert F. Aldrich. "Dissemination of Information." In Helen A Shaw, ed. *Issues in Information Policy*, Special Publication, National Telecommunication and Information Administration, U.S. Department of Commerce, 1981, 5-18.

Robinson, R. V., and W. Bell. "Equality, Success, and Social Justice in England and the United States." *American Sociological Review* 43 (April 1978), 328-329. A. C. Kerckhoff and R. N. Parker, "Reply with Rejoinder" 44 (April 1979), 328-339.

Rubinson, R., and D. Quinlan. "Democracy and Social Inequality: A Reanalysis." *American Sociological Review* 42 (August 1977), 611-623.

Rodman, John. "The Liberation of Nature?" *Inquiry* 20 (1977), 83-131.

Rohman, A. "Interaction Between Science, Technology, and Society: Historical and Comparative Perspectives." *Social Science Journal* 3, no. 33 (1981), 508-521.

Rosen, Saul. "Electronic Computers: A Historical Survey." *Computing Surveys* no. 1 (March 1969), 7-36.

Routley, Richard and Val. "Nuclear Energy and Obligations to the Future.: *Inquiry* 21 (Summer 1978), 133-179.

Rubinson, R., and D. Quinlan. "Democracy and Social Inequality: A Reanalysis." *American Sociological Review* 42 (1977), 611-623.

Sartori, G. "Will Democracy Kill Democracy: Decision-Making by Majorities and Committees." *Government and Opposition* 10 (Spring 1975), 131-158.

Schonfield, W. R. "Meaning of Democratic Participation." *World Politics* 28 (October 1975), 134-158.

Simpson, E. "Socialist Justice." *Ethics* 87 (October 1976), 1-17.

Sinal, I. R. "What Ails Us and Why?" *Encounter* 52 (April 1979), 8-17. "Discussion," 54 (February 1980), 87-93.

Smith, Kent A. "Information as a Commodity or Public Good." *National Forum* (Summer 1983), 27-29.

Spitz, P. "Silent Violence: Famine and Inequality." *International Social Science*

*Journal* 4, no. 30 (1978), 867-92.

Stack, S. "Political Economy of Income Inequality: A Comparative Analysis." *Canadian Journal of Political Science* 13 (June 1980), 273-286.

Stillman, Peter J. "The Limits of Behaviorism: A Review Essay on B. F. Skinner's Social and Political Thought.: *American Political Science Review* 69 (1975), 212-213.

Strassman, W. P. "Can Technology Save the Cities of Developing Countries?" *Journal of Economic Issues* 12 (June 1978), 457-465, 497-500.

Thompson, K. W. "American Democracy and the Third World: Convergence and Contradictions." *Review of Politics* 41 (April 1979), 256-272.

Thurow, L. "Pursuit of Equity." *Dissent* 23 (Summer 1976), 253-259.

Tonsor, S. J. "Liberty and Equality as Absolutes." *Modern Age* 23 (Winter 1979), 2-9.

———. "New Natural Law and the Problem of Equality." *Modern Age* 24 (Summer 1980), 238-247.

Tyree, A. "Gapo and Glissandos: Inequality, Economic Development, and Social Mobility in 24 Countries." *American Sociological Review* 44 (June 1979), 410-424.

UNESCO. "Information and Society." *UNESCO Journal of Information Science, Librarianship and Archive Administration*, no. 2 (January-February 1980).

U.S. News and World Report. "Quantum Leaps: The Video Revolution." *U.S. News and World Report* ( June 17, 1985), 63.

Van Es, J. D., and D. J. Koening. "Social Participation, Social Status and Extremist Political Attitudes." *Sociological Quarterly* 17 (Winter 1976), 16-26.

Wagner, J. "Defining Technology: Political Implications of Hardware, Software, Power, and Information." *Human Relations* 32 (August 1979), 719-736.

Watts, Meredith W. "B.F. Skinner and the Technological Control of Social Behavior." *American Political Science Review* 69 (1975), 214-227.

Wetlanfer, Suzanne, "Thinking Computers No Longer Science Fiction." *Wisconsin State Journal* (January 19, 1986), sec. 5, 1.

Wiarda, H. J. "Democracy and Human Rights in Latin America: Toward a New Conceptualization." *Orbis* 22 (Spring 1978), 137-160.

Wicklein, John. "How to Guarantee Diversity in the New Communications." *National Forum* 63, no. 3 (Summer 1983), 14-16.

Winner, Langdon. "The Political Philosophy of Alternative Technology." *Technology in Society* 1, no. 1 (1979), 75-86.

Wright, W. D. "Du Bois Theory of Political Democracy." *Crisis* 85 (March 1978), 85-89.

Wrong, D. H. "Development and Democracy." *Dissent* 21 (Spring 1974), 277-289.

———. "Rhythm of Democratic Politics." *Dissent* 21 (Winter 1974), 46-55.

Zetterbaum, M. "Equality and Human Need." *American Political Science Review* 71 (September 1977), 983-998.

# Index

Giant corporations, 3
Giant opportunity,
Government subsidies, 21
Graduation, 217

Health care, 227, 246, 293, 325
Historical materialism, 26, 29, 30, 33
Housing, 21

Individualism, 9, 313
Industrialization, 35
Information downflow, 269-270
Information technology, 224, 258, 290
Information upflow, 265-269
Inheritance, 181
Initial opportunity, 203, 205

Job market, 277

Kiosque, 253

Labor, 184, 198
Laissez-faire,
Laissez-innover,
Landsat, 255, 293
Legal services, 274
Less developed countries, 335
Library services, 278
Limited government, 248
Live programs, 288
Lost opportunity, 205

Magic mirror, 251
Managerial control, 61, 62, 67
Market economies of scale, 37
Market information, 274
Marketing, 275
Marx and Marxism, 25, 26, 29, 30,
    32, 33, 34, 35, 36, 109, 128, 129,
    130, 131, 132, 133, 134, 135,
    136, 137, 138-154, 162, 173
Mass media, 11
Means of production, 32, 235
Medical services, 273
Merger, 41, 42, 43, 45

Middle class, 2, 35
Militarism, 117, 120, 121
Military-Industrial Complex, 6
Minimum way, 219
Minitel, 253
Mobility, 218
Mode of production, 28, 91
Mode of production, 202
Monopolistic market, 44, 51, 52
Monopoly capitalism, 60, 105, 171,
    198
Music, 287

Old age benefits, 189, 214
Oligopoly, 43
Opportunity classes, 203

Pay system, 209, 284
Placement services, 277
Political parties, 108
Popular sovereignty, 178
Position classification, 185, 208, 324
Poverty, 7
Private organizations, 10
Private ownership, 235
Procedural democracy, 178, 180
Process of ownership,
Production, 295
Production process, 204, 278
Profits, 183, 198
Public institutions, 12
Purchasing, 275

Racism, 7
Recreation, 294
Religion, 314-315
Retirement, 220, 232, 244
Right to education, 245
Ruling class, 107, 122

Salary range, 218
Self-management, 224
Shared opportunity, 187, 188, 206,
    236
Social classes, 28